How Computers Work
Tenth Edition

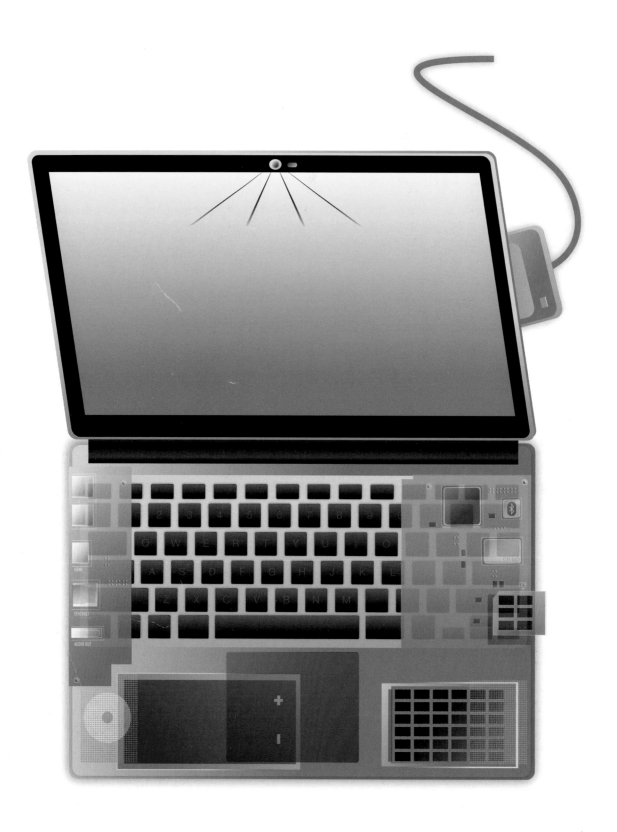

How Computers Work

The Evolution of Technology

Tenth Edition

Ron White

Illustrated by Timothy Edward Downs

800 East 96th Street
Indianapolis, IN 46240

How Computers Work, Tenth Edition

ISBN-13: 978-0-7897-4984-0

ISBN-10: 0-7897-4984-X

Library of Congress Control Number: 2014951587

Printed in the United States of America

First Printing: December 2014

Trademarks

All terms mentioned in this book that are known to be trademarks or service marks have been appropriately capitalized. Que Publishing cannot attest to the accuracy of this information. Use of a term in this book should not be regarded as affecting the validity of any trademark or service mark.

Warning and Disclaimer

Every effort has been made to make this book as complete and as accurate as possible, but no warranty or fitness is implied. The information provided is on an "as is" basis. The author and the publisher shall have neither liability nor responsibility to any person or entity with respect to any loss or damages arising from the information contained in this book.

Special Sales

For information about buying this title in bulk quantities, or for special sales opportunities (which may include electronic versions; custom cover designs; and content particular to your business, training goals, marketing focus, or branding interests), please contact our corporate sales department at corpsales@pearsoned.com or (800) 382-3419.

For government sales inquiries, please contact governmentsales@pearsoned.com.

For questions about sales outside the U.S., please contact international@pearsoned.com

Editor-in-Chief	Greg Wiegand
Executive Editor	Rick Kughen
Development Editor	Todd Brakke
Managing Editor	Sandra Schroeder
Project Editor	Mandie Frank
Copy Editor	Charlotte Kughen
Indexer	Lisa Stumpf
Proofreader	The Wordsmithery LLC
Editorial Assistant	Kristen Watterson
Designer	Mark Shirar
Compositor	Mary Sudul
Graphics	Timothy Edward Downs

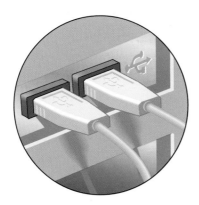

For Shannon and Michael, who always asked, "Why?"
And Sue, who asked "Why Not?"
—Ron

For my mother, Lillian, whose tireless work ethic and
uncompromising dedication to quality has inspired me all
of my life. I owe so much of who I am to you.
—Tim

Table of Contents

Part 3: How Computers Evolve   126

Part 4: How Computers Expand Our Senses   200

Part 5: The Little Net That Grew   248

Part 6: How Printers Put Data in Our Hands   312

Part 7: So, What's Next?   338

About the Author

RON WHITE has been writing *How Computers Work* for 20 years, during which time he's also been executive editor at *PC Computing* magazine, BYTE.com, and groovyPost.com. He's been a computer columnist for Windows Sources and 80 Micro. *How Computers Work* was named best nonfiction computer book, and his writing has been honored by the Maggie Awards, the Robert F. Kennedy Journalism Awards, and The National Endowment for the Humanities. He and his wife, Sue, have bounced back and forth between Boston and San Francisco before finally ending up in San Antonio.

About the Illustrator

TIMOTHY EDWARD DOWNS is the national award-winning illustrator of *How Computers Work* and *How Digital Photography Works*. Tim has been involved in all facets of graphic design in his illustrious career. From illustrator to creative director, Tim has led teams of artists and designers in advertising agencies, marketing communications firms, and consumer magazines to better tell their stories through illustration, photography, typography, and design. "Our job doesn't start when the writer hits Save. In order to effectively communicate the tone or the concept of the piece, we need to know and understand the story from the original brainstorm all the way through final execution," reminds Tim.

Examples of Tim's design, illustration, and photographic work can be seen at http://timothyedwarddowns.com.

Acknowledgments

YOU CAN'T WRITE 10 versions of the same book over a span of 20 years without a lot of help from a lot of people. This book certainly couldn't have been done without Tim Downs. His illustrations have set a new standard for technical art. And *art* is the word. Not only is he always careful to make sure his illustrations are correct technically, he has imbued them with his talent to make them works of art that could stand alone outside of this book's technical explanations. We've worked together for 20 years, and I'm happy that unlike some other partnerships I've entered into, I continue to think of Tim as not just an illustrator, but a dear friend.

This particular edition could not have been done without the aid of some others. My wife, Sue, has served as editor, critic, coach, and personal trainer. I know that the time I've spent in front of a keyboard was not always pleasant for either of us. But when I felt like chucking it all, Sue was there, helping me in the ways I needed most. Our son, Michael White, also spent hours helping with tedious research and checking for errors, despite running his own business and returning to the classroom. Thank you, both.

It's not fashionable among many writers to heap praise on their editors and publishers. But I can't heap enough on my editor, Todd Brakke, and Que Publisher Greg Wiegand. In this and other editions, Todd has been the editor all writers want, ever ready with unerringly good suggestions, encouragement, and lending a hand with the words when time was pressing. Greg has always seemed more like a friend than someone who hired me to write still another edition. When I was ill during the course of writing this, his concern was for my health, not the deadlines I missed. Thank you, guys.

I'm indebted to other editors who gave me the foundations to write. Roddy Stinson taught me the importance of listening to my own voice. Jim Dolan showed me how every detail matters. The late Jim Seymour, who was the editor-in-chief of *PC Computing* when it was launched in 1988, and his wife Nora, who was editor, gave me the opportunity to jump from newspaper to magazines, and were exceptional, warm friends. Preston Gralla guided me in setting up a How It Works section when I joined *PCC*. This book wouldn't be here without him, and I can never thank him enough for a friendship and too many acts of kindness to list.

I owe a huge debt to Mike Edelhart, who was editor-in-chief and publisher of *PC Computing* and who convinced a then dubious book publisher to take a chance on a kind of computer book that had never been done before. Deep thanks go to Randy Ross, Margaret Ficklen, Herb Brody, Brett L. Glass, Marty Jerome, Raymond Jones, Matthew Lake, Jack Nimersheim, Stephen Sagman, Jan Smith, Dylan Tweney, Doug van Kirk, Mark L. Van Name, Bill Catchings, Christine Grech Wendin, and Kenan Woods, all of whom helped in earlier editions.

Thanks to editors now and over the course of nine editions: Rick Kughen, Stephanie McComb, Tonya Simpson, Nick Goetz, Angelina Ward, Sarah Robbins, Cindy Hudson, Melinda Levine, Lysa Lewallen,

Renee Wilmeth, and Leah Kirkpatrick for pulling everything together. Juliet Langley pushed the first edition to book sellers with such fervor I doubt it could ever have been a success without her.

I'm also grateful to the dozens of people in the PC industry who've shared their knowledge, schematics, and white papers to infuse *How Computers Work* with detail and accuracy. I'm particularly grateful to Ray Soneira, author of Sonera Technologies' DisplayMate and the person who knows more about display technology than anyone else in the world; Griffin Lemaster of Creative Electron; Chris Thornton of ClipMate; Karen Thomas at Olympus; Joe Vanderwater, Bryan Langerdoff, Dan Francisco, Tami Casey, John Hyde, Bill Kircos, Susan Shaw, and Seth Walker at Intel; Russell Sanchez and Adam Kahn of Microsoft; Jim Bartlett, Ellen Reid Smith, Tim Kearns, and Desire Russell at IBM; Barrett Anderson and Todd Hollinshead at id Software; Marcie Pedrazzi of Adaptec; Eileen Algaze at Rockwell; A.J. Rodgers, Jennifer Jones, and Susan Bierma at Tektronix; Ben Yoder and Lisa Santa Anna at Epson; Dewey Hou at TechSmithCorporation; Kathryn Brandberry and Doyle Nicholas at Thrustmaster; Dani Johnston at Microtek Lab; Lisa Tillman of The Benjamin Group; Dvorah Samansky at Iomega; Brandon Talaich at SanDisk; Chris Walker with Pioneer USA; Carrie Royce at the Cirque Corporation; Andy Marken at Marken Communications; and Tracy Laidlaw at BeyondWords. If there are any mistakes in this book, I can't lay the blame on them.

As this *may* be the last edition of the book I work on, I want to thank all the readers for their kind comments, spotting errors, and, of course, shelling out money to buy it. This odyssey would not be possible without you.

We Want to Hear From You!

AS the reader of this book, *you* are our most important critic and commentator. We value your opinion and want to know what we're doing right, what we could do better, what areas you'd like to see us publish in, and any other words of wisdom you're willing to pass our way.

We welcome your comments. You can email or write to let us know what you did or didn't like about this book—as well as what we can do to make our books better.

Please note that we cannot help you with technical problems related to the topic of this book.

When you write, please be sure to include this book's title and author as well as your name and email address. We will carefully review your comments and share them with the author and editors who worked on the book.

Email: feedback@quepublishing.com

Mail: Que Publishing
         ATTN: Reader Feedback
         800 East 96th Street
         Indianapolis, IN 46240 USA

Reader Services

Visit our website and register this book at quepublishing.com/register for convenient access to any updates, downloads, or errata that might be available for this book.

About This Book

"Any sufficiently advanced technology is indistinguishable from magic."

—Arthur C. Clarke

SORCERERS have their magic wands—powerful, potentially dangerous tools with lives of their own. Witches have their familiars—creatures disguised as household beasts that could, if they choose, wreak the witches' havoc. Mystics have their golems—beings built of wood and tin brought to life to do their masters' bidding.

We have our personal computers.

PCs, too, are powerful creations that often seem to have a life of their own. Usually, they respond to a wave of a mouse or a spoken incantation by performing tasks we couldn't imagine doing ourselves without some sort of preternatural help. But even as computers successfully carry out our commands, it's often difficult to quell the feeling that there's some wizardry at work here.

And then there are the times when our PCs, like malevolent spirits, rebel and open the gates of chaos onto our neatly ordered columns of numbers, our carefully wrought sentences, and our beautifully crafted graphics. When that happens, we're often convinced that we are, indeed, playing with power not entirely under our control. We become sorcerers' apprentices, whose every attempt to right things leads to deeper trouble.

Whether our personal computers are faithful servants or imps, most of us soon realize there's much more going on inside those silent boxes than we really understand. PCs are secretive. Open their tightly sealed cases and you're confronted with poker-faced components. Few give any clues as to what they're about. Most of them consist of sphinx-like microchips that offer no more information about themselves than some obscure code printed on their impenetrable surfaces. The maze of circuit tracings etched on the boards is fascinating, but meaningless, hieroglyphics. Some crucial parts, such as the hard drive and power supply, are sealed with printed omens about the dangers of peeking inside—omens that put to shame the warnings on a pharaoh's tomb.

This book is based on two ideas. One is that the magic we understand is safer and more powerful than the magic we don't. This is not a hands-on how-to book. Don't look for any instructions for taking a screwdriver to this part or the other. But perhaps your knowing more about what's going on inside all those stoic components makes them a little less formidable when something does go awry. The second idea behind this book is that knowledge, in itself, is a worthwhile and enjoyable goal. This book is written to respond to your random musings about the goings-on inside that box you sit in front of several hours a day. If this book puts your questions to rest—or raises new ones—it will have done its job.

At the same time, however, I'm trusting that knowing the secrets behind the magician's legerdemain won't spoil the show. This is a real danger. Mystery is often as compelling as knowledge. I'd hate to think that anything you read in this book takes away that sense of wonder you have when you manage to make your PC do some grand, new trick. I hope that, instead, this book makes you a more confident sorcerer.

Introduction to the Tenth Edition

"If automobiles had followed the same development cycle as the computer, a Rolls-Royce would today cost $100, get a million miles per gallon, and explode once a year, killing everyone inside."

—Robert Cringely

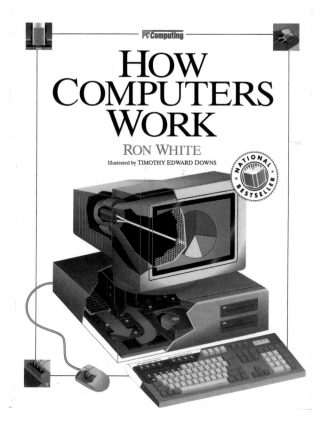

THIS BOOK was so much easier to write 20 years ago. Computers were relatively new, and they were all pretty much the same. There were only two important differences—whether a computer was an Apple or a Wintel, that is, running Windows on an Intel processor. There were some variations in size, portability, and the customization enthusiasts could do by installing different drives and expansion boards inside PCs. Stuffing the newest-fangled components into my computer at *PC Computing*, the magazine where I worked, was a wonderful pastime and the source of many stories in the magazine. If I made a mistake and the computer groaned its last breath, that often made for an even better story.

One reason PC disasters made for good reading is that every computer user had a similar story of computer disaster. We were all in the same boat because even the editors of computer magazines—if the truth be told—didn't know what they were doing a lot of the time. Back then if you took a class on computers in college, you waited your turn to run a program on some monster of a computer that would return a solution in the form of punch cards. There was no formal place to go to learn about personal computers. Manuals were useless beyond finding out how to plug a PC into the wall and where the switch was located. Programs that worked one way had no resemblance to how other programs worked. You learned about computers by trial and error, by going to user groups made up of equally befuddled PC owners, and by reading magazines.

Before I went to work for *PC Computing* in 1989, my teachers were *PC Magazine*, *PC World*, *Byte*, *Popular Computing*, and other magazines covering this new technical phenomenon. You found a morsel of information in one magazine, a nugget in another, and eventually you pieced together what was going on inside that steel box on your desktop.

But I was going to tell why it was easier to write this book 20 years ago. Back then, you could say all someone needed to know about a floppy disk in a couple of two-page spreads. Something as mind-busting and intricate as a monitor you could do with one illustration. The technology was, in retrospect, elementary. How computers and their components worked was actually simple when you sketched it all out and added some callouts and arrows. No wonder I figured I could, with the help of a great illustrator like Timothy Edward Downs, write a book that laid out for all to see the mysteries of what really is a fascinating technology.

But today? Lord love a duck! Today there's not even a simple explanation of what a computer is. Simply having a microchip doesn't cut it. Microchips are everywhere, in watches, cars, thermostats, ovens, refrigerators, flashlights, dog collars, coffee pots—just about anything that uses electricity. But these aren't computers. They're just electronic doo-dads that use the abilities of microprocessors to perform routine chores.

To be a computer, something must be programmable. It must be capable of doing different things based on the instructions you give it. Your yard's sprinkler system is a computer. True, it doesn't do a lot of different things, but you can program it to water different parts of your yard for different lengths of time, and on different days, or not at all if it's raining. Microwave ovens are computers you use by programming it on the fly by setting how long it will cook at different temperatures, or you can push a Popcorn button to tell the oven to use a preprogrammed sequence.

These are all computers, but the truth is they're not very interesting. How deeply do you care how your sprinkler works? But a computer that can be programed to do so... many... different... things—now, that is a computer worthy of the name, and we see them everywhere today. Phones, cameras, tablets, music players, and TVs have all become computers that are indispensable parts of everyday life. Our lives are richer for the knowledge, problem solving, communication, entertainment, health, and income they provide.

They certainly deserve to be included in a book that calls itself *How Computers Work*. The problem—my problem anyway—is that they make organizing a book like this an exercise in controlled chaos. In previous editions, I simply had a section on storage, another section on displays, one on networking.... I admit that in this edition I've fallen back on that system in some chapters out of pure convenience. But generally the workings of today's computers are not so compartmentalized. The more I looked at computing over the last 20 years, the more it struck me that the real story of how computers work is how they are like living creatures, organisms that have evolved and continue to evolve. These metal and silicon and plastic and glass animals have followed the same patterns of mutation, natural selection and survival of the fittest that Darwin found in plants and animals.

I've tried to explain how technological developments follow the same rise and fall that carry organic species to new shores. Today's achievements in computing are possible only because they rise out of the fossil beds of earlier technology. There is no way for today's technology to have been invented from scratch. I recall that some 30 years ago, I was working for a computing service company that relied on mainframes, an obsolete term to describe computers the size of a couple of high-end refrigerators slammed together. They used two kinds of storage: hard drives and magnetic tape. The 5 megabyte hard drives were the size of large garbage cans, and the platters where information was stored could have doubled as hub caps. You had to have seen the magnetic tape at work to understand one of computer's most common terms: RAM—random access memory. It sounds as if data is retrieved willy-nilly from all different parts of memory chips with no order system to it. Memory chips got their RAM moniker because retrieving tape memory was not random. If you wanted data stored on a reel at the innermost 10 inches of tape, the computer had to wind through the first 3,590 feet to get to that data.

Sure, it would have been better to skip tape altogether and go straight to hard disks. But to paraphrase a certain infamous quote, sometimes you don't build computers with the technology you wish you had; you build them with the technology you have.

Life in the primordial seas had to get the hang of existence as one-celled organisms before the cells could master hooking together and dividing up the jobs needed for mutual survival. Some of those bigger organisms learned to move by wiggling. They developed a way to filter oxygen from water, and later that system developed into lungs that could suck oxygen out of water. It took millions of years for these changes to evolve. You couldn't create magnetic disks until you'd learned how to record data to magnetic tape. Then it took years of engineers trying first this and then that to make the disks smaller and at the same time more capacious. Current solid state drives come from the fossils of technological forays, such as bubble memory, that didn't survive.

The most amazing aspect of this whirlwind of technical progress is that it's only taken 20 years to go from floppy to solid state, from displays that amounted to stick figures to animated graphics that are almost indistinguishable from film images. That smartphone in your pocket has more computing power than those refrigerator-sized mainframes. The wires that have been needed for communications for a century are likely to disappear completely in the next 10 years, along with the need for local data storage. It's possible the keyboard and mouse will become extinct. In fact much of the hardware we're used to today, as its gets smaller and more efficient, may migrate from our desks and our pockets to become parts of our eyes, ears, and brain.

And that's just in the next 20 years. Beyond that we can't imagine what will become of technology any more than one-celled organisms could have imaged a dinosaur. Let's check back with each other after a couple of decades and then see what may be possible.

Ron White
San Antonio, TX

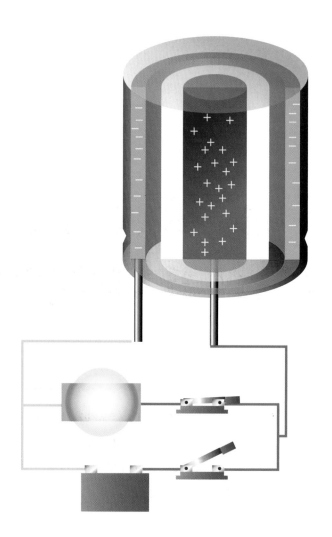

1

What Makes a Computer a Computer

If you want to find the secrets of the universe, think in terms of energy, frequency and vibration.

—Nikola Tesla

THOSE OF US who studied physics in high school half a century ago had to learn about the six **simple machines**. They were the wheel and axle, level, pulley, inclined plane, wedge, and screw—all centuries-old tools that made physical work easier. The explanations of how they saved us labor were invariably accompanied by illustrations of people who looked like they were working awfully hard.

Just as invariably, someone would quote Archimedes saying, "Give me a long enough lever and a place to stand, and I will move the earth." Note that Archimedes gave somebody else the really hard job—finding a lever that would have to stretch from Earth to Jupiter.

Still, in the days before any form of power other than the muscles of man and horse, the simple machines were ingenious. Those six machines were combined in various ways to create wagons, catapults, irrigation systems, roads, bridges, and, need I mention, the pyramids. Put some teeth on a wheel and you get a gear. Combine gears with levers and pulleys, and you have a clock.

The ingenuity with which clever people combined simple machines into complex and powerful machines grew every century, abetted by engines running on water, steam, compressed air, and chemical fuels that magnified the power of these simple machines turned complex to a point that even Archimedes didn't imagine.

Then came **electricity**. Here was a mysterious force that would run through the right kind of metal wires. Those wires could be bent and wrapped around other wires and pieces of metal to produce an engine that, unlike water mills, was portable; one that, unlike steam and chemically fueled engines, didn't threaten to blow up. If electricity had produced no more than a safer, more efficient motor to run all those simple/complex machines, that in itself would have been a boon to civilization. But scientists and engineers discovered new properties in this new force despite the fact they didn't know what it was and couldn't even see it.

You know the results: Everything from the electric light bulb to the computer, smartphone, or tablet on which you might be reading this very book. Electricity really began to pay off when engineers looked beyond its ability to make a filament glow or a motor turn. They began to discover more possibilities in electricity's partnership with magnetism, in the electromagnetic fields produced by electricity that could interact with other matter, even over great distances. They found that electricity and light were two facets of the same thing—an **electromagnetic spectrum** with mostly invisible fields made of waves vibrating at different frequencies and the sizes of which range from the microscopic to the Earth-encompassing.

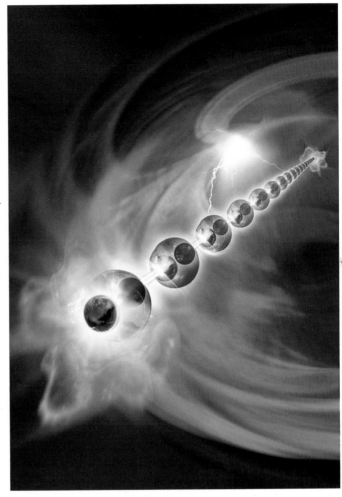

Like the simple machines of medieval ages, these new elementary principles could be combined in endless ways to create new tools to accomplish jobs that were previously unimaginable. The real power of electromagnetism, engineers found, was less in its ability to move trains, see inside a patient's body, and turn night into day than it was to store, manipulate, and distribute information.

Behind all these uses are some very fundamental principles of physics that have led us to the brink of discovering the true nature of everything in the universe. It's these simple principles of a new age that you're going to look at in the first part of this book. I can already hear some of you saying, "Hey, when do we get to the stuff about computers?"

You're there. The subjects of these first chapters *are* the stuff of computers. And it doesn't matter what type of computer you're talking about—mainframe, desktop, laptop, table, digital music player, camera, GPS, smartphone, smartwatch, or Glass. All are computers, and all work using some version of the principles and technology you'll find here.

CHAPTER

1

The Ghostly LEGOs of Computing

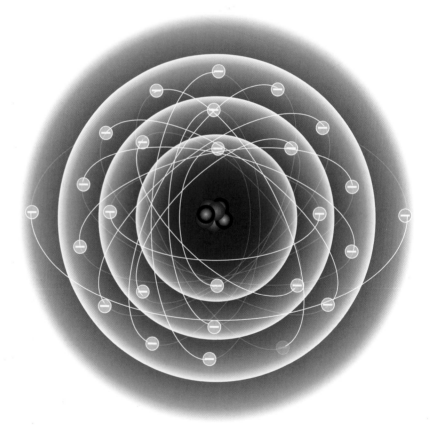

The entire world right now is run by information. Our entire world is being controlled and operated by tiny invisible 1s and 0s that are flashing through the air and flashing through the wires around us.

—Chris Doyen, computer activist hiding out in Canada

LOUIS C. K. has a routine where his daughter asks a simple question that leads to the metaphysical issue people have pondered for ages. It begins with a question about why she can't go outside in the rain, and why it's raining, and why there are clouds, and it becomes a dissertation on why Louis doesn't know more, and why he didn't listen in school, etc. The string of answers finally leads father and daughter to an ultimate question.

"Because some things are and some things are not."

"Why?"

"Because things that are not *can't be."*

"Why?"

"Because nothing wouldn't be...." *

Understanding how a computer works is a lot like that. You say a hard drive uses a magnet to write files, but then you're obligated to explain why. And then you have to say why magnets attract certain metals. And then explain why magnets have these invisible force fields.

And don't expect your computer to explain itself. It maintains a Sphinx-like silence. Shouldn't there be doodads and thingamajigs that are pumping or swinging, flashing or beeping, vibrating or rotating, at least ticking or tocking? For all you can tell about how your computer works from opening it up and looking inside, your computer might as well be carved out of soap.

In your computer, the things that *really* make it all work are ghosts. You never see them. You see only what they do—like a lamp thrown to the floor by a poltergeist. And computers, from PCs to a Galaxy S phone, tightly tuck away their secrets. You have to keep asking "Why?" And if you ask long enough, you get into physical states filled with objects so small you can't see them, or that exist only in ghostly states, such as the vast parts of the electromagnetic spectrum or some screwy spinning quantum string, all of which are invisible to mere humans.

The only way to even get a hint about what these little ghosts are like is to fling them around in giant, mile-wide magnets like the Large Hadron Collider, until they smash into each other and create even smaller, rarer ghosts that vanish as soon as they appear. We're just left with only the contrails they leave behind, and from those we try to figure out what just happened.

These little, invisible ghosts are the ultimate things—the "tiny invisible 1s and 0s," as Doyen says. The ghostly little digital LEGOs that unite in different combinations to create everything in your computer, tablet, or smartphone. To understand—really understand—how a microprocessor or monitor or printer works, you have to understand the ghostly workings of electricity, waves, magnetism, binary math, and data packets.

So let's examine them all. Don't be frightened. They're friendly ghosts...I think.

* You can watch the complete comedy bit on YouTube at www.youtube.com/watch?v=Tf17rFDjMZw.

How Waves Take The Universe on a Joy Ride

WAVES DO FAR MORE than carry surfers on a wet thrill ride. Waves are essential to the working of computers. They move data from one place to another and provide the beat that every PC component marches to. Without waves, we'd never be able to see the solutions, images, or words that result from the machine's computations. Without waves, we'd be beached. Or we might not exist at all.

According to some theories of physics, waves are the ultimate stuff of the universe. Space, Earth, you, and I are no more than the interference patterns created by the crisscrossing of waves, which are created by tiny, tiny, *tiny* vibrating strings. Indeed, at times it seems as if the thing we think of as solid Earth is just an illusion. Under the right circumstances waves pass through our buildings, rocks, water, other waves, and even our own bodies. It's as if Earth itself is no more than a wad of soppy tissue. Here's how this humming master of the universe reaches down to play its tunes on a computer.

1 If you've ever played with toys, you're familiar with the two most common **mechanical waves** in the universe: **transverse waves** and **longitudinal waves**. When you and a friend move the ends of a jump rope up and down, the graceful humps traveling the rope are a transverse wave.

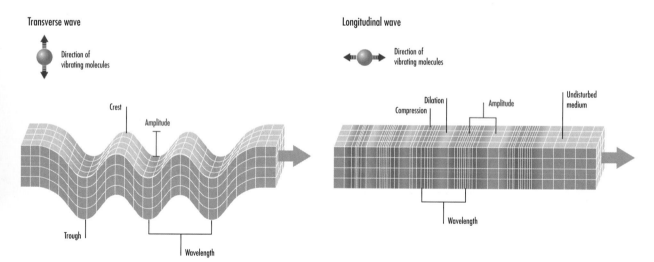

Transverse wave

Direction of vibrating molecules

Crest

Amplitude

Trough

Wavelength

Longitudinal wave

Direction of vibrating molecules

Dilation

Compression

Amplitude

Undisturbed medium

Wavelength

2 Examples of transverse waves include light, surface earthquake waves, surface water waves, magnetic waves, and the wave people in a football stadium create. Longitudinal waves are found in the depths of water and earth. A tsunami or earthquake moves tremendous energy through those media, until they reach Earth's surface or the shallows of the sea, where they convert to transverse waves. Freeway traffic jams, with their alternative congestion and fleeting moments of faster driving are also longitudinal waves.

3 Both types of waves can carry energy, information, and destruction. They can be measures of time and distance. Both types are created when some force—vocal cords, a rock thrown in water, a meteor smashing into Earth—is exerted against their mediums. Transverse waves can travel through solids and liquids, but they do not travel through gases because air doesn't have the elasticity needed to push the wave's vibrating molecules back into place. Only longitudinal waves may use gases as a medium. Despite that difference, longitudinal waves can morph into transverse waves, and vice versa, when they confront a different kind of medium. Both waves have similar components.

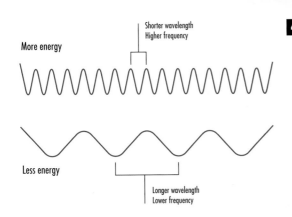

Shorter wavelength
Higher frequency

More energy

Less energy

Longer wavelength
Lower frequency

4 In both types of waves, two fundamental measurements are the **wavelength** and **frequency.** Wavelength is the distance between one crest, or compressed area, to the next. Frequency is the number of waves, measured by wavelength, that pass a stationary point in one second. The longer the wavelength is, the lower the frequency. Frequency is measured in **hertz (Hz).** Generally, the higher the hertz, the more energy a wave contains. In audio, higher hertz means higher pitched sound.

5 Transverse waves in the water and longitudinal sound waves in the air are both called **mechanical** because they depend on the mechanical mechanism of their media to propagate. That, however, is an illusion. The energy that goes into creating and maintaining waves is transferred by molecules knocking against each other, similar to how runners in a relay race hand off the baton. The next time you're at a lake or beach, observe how a boat or bird floating on the surface of the water only bobs up and down in place when a wave passes under it. Its horizontal position doesn't change.

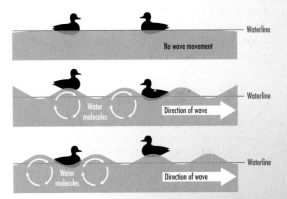

6 Another type of wave, **electromagnetic**, is not mechanical. Electromagnetic waves encompass light, infrared light, radio, X-rays, gamma rays, and neutrinos. They are all part of the **electromagnetic spectrum**, in which waves range from a wavelength smaller than an atom to wavelengths bigger than the earth.

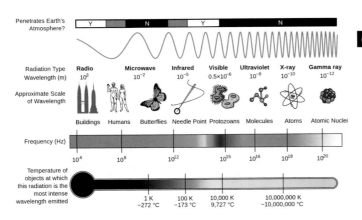

Source: Wikimedia Commons

7 Electromagnetic waves do not require any type of media and are the only waves that can travel through the vacuum of space. Although not mechanical, electromagnetic waves are transverse—doubly transverse. They consist of electric and magnetic fields that, like other transverse waves, vibrate perpendicular to the direction in which the wave is moving. But the two fields vibrate at right angles to each other, and each expansion and collapse of a field creates an opposite field. The vibrations of electrical fields generate magnetic fields. Vibrations of magnetic fields generate electric fields. The result is a never-ending boot strap that pushes the wave forward at the speed of light.

How Information Rides the Waves

WHAT DO SURFING, LASERS, computer circuits, television, rock concerts and the ever-popular death ray have in common? They all depend on waves. Without all the types of waves that surround us—and that penetrate us—at all times, and without the ability of waves to carry information nearly instantly to all parts of the globe, chances are civilization as we bask in it today would never have happened.

 It takes no great technology to use waves to send information. You simply turn a wave on and off. It's the basis for jungle drums, Morse code, and the earliest modems, and it's called **encoding**. Regardless of the form of encoding, the sound or electrical waves are not changed. Information is encoded in how often a wave is created and how long the wave exists. Morse code and the first 300 **baud** modems use short and long pulses of electricity to create a simple binary code, a forerunner of how data is stored and transmitted in computers. The short *dits* and the long *dahs* in different combinations represent letters of the alphabet.

A total of nine pulses of electricity are enough code to represent three letters "S O S," the Morse code distress cry. Note that the frequency and amplitude of the electrical signal does not change–only how long the same electromagnetic signal is broadcast.

High noise level when key is pressed.

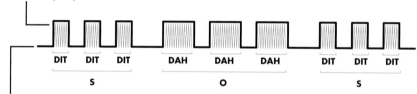

Little or no signal when key is not pressed.

2 Long and short drum beats are not possible with jungle drums. They depend on recognizable patterns in which the volume of individual beats and the length of silences between beats create a pattern that can convey information. Because we're not fluent in jungle drums, here is a visualization of a 22-second drum solo by Gene Krupa from "Sing, Sing, Sing." The breaks in the waveform depict bass drum beats. At the right end of the segment, you can see how intervals between each of the bass beats grow shorter, creating the type of pattern we could, if we didn't all have phones coming out our ears, use for communications.

Frequency modulation makes changes to the frequency of a wave.

Amplitude modulation makes changes to the amplitude of a wave.

3 Jungle drums and Morse code have obvious limitations. Both are slow and depend on a skilled person doing a hands-on job. What is needed are entirely different modulation methods. Three methods do the job: **Frequency modulation (FM)**, **amplitude modulation (AM)**, and **pulse modulation.**

4 Pulse modulation is the newest way to add information to waves—and get information out of them. It was developed because modems had reached a limit as to how quickly and accurately they could turn a signal on and off. The solution was to use different frequencies or amplitudes to stand for combinations of letters. This scheme is an enormous improvement over early modems, but it is limited to text and digital information. Transmitting analog signals without first converting them to digital signals requires AM or FM.

5 Either AM or FM can be used to convey information over radio waves or electrical circuits, using frequencies from 100,000Hz (radio) through microwave to 10,000 billion Hz (infrared).   The higher the frequency, the smaller the wavelength. Radio waves are about as long as your average skyscraper is tall. Microwaves are the length of an adult person, and infrared waves are the size of a computer mouse. Various factors govern a wavelength's usefulness for carrying data. Some radio waves penetrate brick and steel buildings. Others bounce off them. Generally the higher the frequency, the more data it can carry, because the more often a wave moves between peaks and valleys, the more opportunities there are for modulating it to carry information.

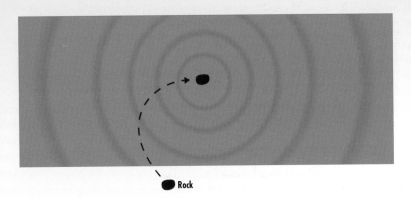

Rock

6 To understand modulation, go to a pond or lake and throw rocks into the water. If you throw only a single rock, it creates waves that expand in concentric circles, smoothly and evenly from the point of impact. We'll call this our **carrier wave**, and measure its wavelength, how quickly it expands, and how tall and deep are its crest and trough.

7 As the carrier wave spreads, toss a few pebbles across the width of the carrier. The pebbles make waves of their own. The pebbles' waves change—as in modulate—the carrier wave wherever they meet. If we measured all the directions the combined waves moved, their speed, and where they eventually meet the shore, and then—using some sort of math I don't even want to think about—we subtracted the influence of the carrier wave, we'd be left with the information we need to know: where each of the pebbles struck the water and the force behind each.

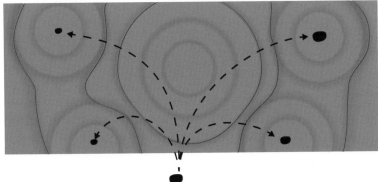

8 A radio carrier signal, like the watery carrier wave, is a simple, steady wave at a specific, known wavelength. We mix the carrier wave with a wave known as an **input signal** created by the sound—or sights—from another source. The two waves combine into a modulated signal that is then broadcast over air waves or through wires. When a radio, TV, or other device receives the modulated signal, it removes the influence of the original carrier wave. What remains is a replica of the input signal that created the modulation.

How Electromagnetism Is the Ghost in the Machine

THIS BOOK BEGINS with a quote from Arthur C. Clarke: "Any sufficiently advanced technology is indistinguishable from magic." Well, we're still not past the first chapter and it's already time to start the magic show. Like good magicians, electricity and magnetism—the twin powers of **electromagnetism**—hide what they are doing. They mostly show the results—the rabbit coming out of the hat, not how it got into the hat.

We can see the effects of magnetism on iron filings, refrigerator doors, and the giant generators that supply much of our energy, but we cannot see magnetism itself. It's the silent partner in the electromagnetic spectrum.

We can see electricity in the form of lightning and sparks from a shorting wall plug, and we can certainly feel electricity when static electricity (a build-up of surplus electrons) jumps from our fingers on a cold day.

Combined, magnetism and electricity form the electromagnetic spectrum—the full frequency range of the mysterious waves that permeate the universe. This partnership continues into other areas, where these conjoined energy ghosts form the basis for most of modern technology.

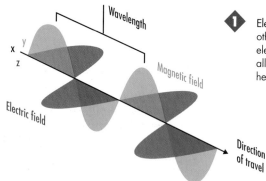

1 Electricity and magnetism cannot survive without each other. The previous illustration shows how magnetic and electric fields cooperate in a boot-strapping operation that allows electromagnetic waves, such as light, radio, and heat, to travel through a vacuum.

2 Let's start with the *electro* half of electromagnetism. In some atoms, such as copper and silver, the attraction is weak between the atoms' core—a **nucleus** made of positively charged protons—and the negatively charged **electron clouds** in the atoms' outer layers. In such **conductive** materials it's possible for electrons to jump freely from one atom to another. This movement of electrons, which occurs only under the right circumstances, is **electricity**, and it travels at the same speed as light (another form of electromagnetism)—186,000 miles each second.

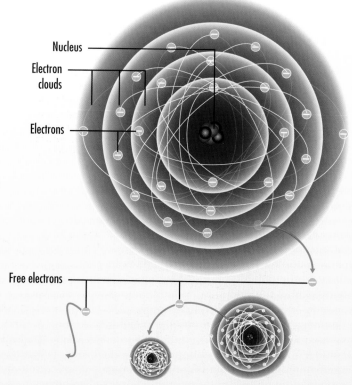

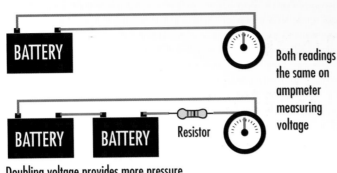

Both readings the same on ampmeter measuring voltage

Doubling voltage provides more pressure

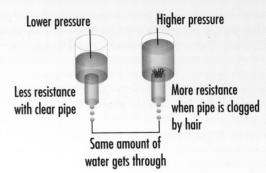

Lower pressure Higher pressure

Less resistance with clear pipe More resistance when pipe is clogged by hair

Same amount of water gets through

3 We apply three measurements when working with electricity: voltage, amperage, and resistance. It's convenient to think of **voltage,** or **charge,** as being like water pressure—how much power is behind electricity. **Amperage,** or **amps,** is the measure of how much electricity is flowing through wires, similar to how we measure the gallons of water that pass through pipes. **Resistance** is how the material through which the electricity is flowing. In the examples here, higher water pressure overcomes a clogged pipe, and doubling the voltage pushes through the same amount of current despite the addition of a resistor.

4 In some materials, such as rubber and glass, electrons are more closely bound to their nuclei and do not easily move from one atom to another. These **nonconductive** materials are **insulators**. Still other materials, such as **silicon**, can act as either conductors or insulators under different conditions. These are **semiconductors**, an important component of microchips and transistors.

5 When electricity moves through a wire, it creates a magnetic field that surrounds the wire. The magnetic field in a straight piece of wire is too weak to pick up even the smallest iron filings.

6 Conversely, when a wire moves through a magnetic field, the interaction creates an electrical current in the wire. Note that in order for either of these phenomena to work, the wire must be moving through the magnetic field, or the magnetic field needs to be collapsing or expanding across the wire.

Electricity flow

7 Both the magnetic fields caused by electricity moving through a wire and electricity created from magnetism can be made more powerful if the wires are wrapped around iron cores. Almost all electricity we use comes from **generators,** in which massive magnets surround equally massive coils of wire. Water from a dam, or steam created by a nuclear plant or fuel-burning plant, spins the wire coil rapidly, creating a high-voltage **alternating current** that is transmitted via thick, low-resistance cables to electrical substations throughout urban areas.

How We Control Electricity

STRAIGHT FROM THE GENERATORS, electricity measures in the thousands of **volts**, much more powerful than we need for everyday uses. Even in the home, the voltage of current from a wall plug is many times more than most household electronics need or can tolerate. Within those same electronics, different components require still smaller and varying voltages and amperages—higher or lower than the current flowing through most of the circuitry. How, then, can we control all this?

1 At a power station, steam generated from burning coal or heat from a nuclear plant turns a shaft within an **electric dynamo**. The shaft is attached to a **rotor** covered with thousands of wires called **bushings**. The rotor turns inside two permanent **stator magnets** whose fields generate high-voltage electricity in the bushings that is transmitted as **alternating current** on the public **power grid** to homes and businesses.

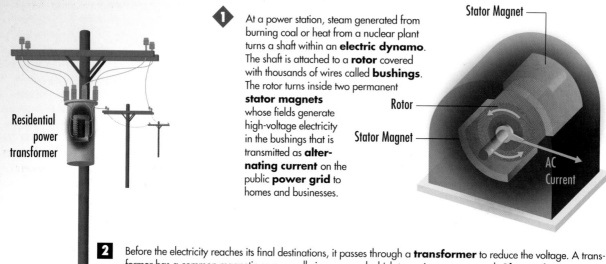

Stator Magnet

Rotor

Stator Magnet

AC Current

Residential power transformer

2 Before the electricity reaches its final destinations, it passes through a **transformer** to reduce the voltage. A transformer has a common magnetic core, usually iron, around which two wires are wrapped. **Alternating current (AC)**—electricity that flows first in one direction and then the other—moves through the **primary coil,** the wire that has more **wrappings** around the core. The transformer cannot use **direct current**, which flows in only one direction, because a magnetic field cannot create electricity in wires unless either the wires or the field are moving.

3 Each time the current switches directions, its magnetic field expands or collapses—which is the same as the field moving—and induces an electrical current in the coil. The current passes through the part of the core around which is wrapped the **secondary coil.** There the AC produces another magnetic field that envelops the wire wrapped around the core. The field creates a current in the secondary coil, but because the secondary has fewer wrappings, the current created in the second coil has a smaller voltage, making this a **step-down** transformer. A step-down transformer, which is most likely mounted on a utility pole near your home, cuts the voltage on the raw generator current from thousands of volts to 120 volts (V) before it's allowed inside.

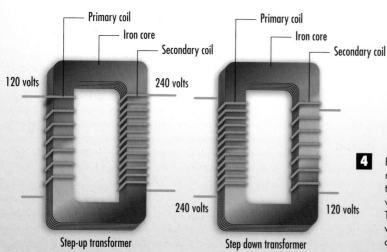

Primary coil

Iron core

Secondary coil

120 volts   240 volts

240 volts   120 volts

Step-up transformer   Step down transformer

4 Before a computer can use the household current, the current passes through a second step-down transformer, this time in the PC's **power supply,** the box festooned with warnings not to open it that's at the back of the computer. This transformer reduces the 120V current into two different voltages that separate wires carry to five-volt and three-volt components. Other electronic devices, such as amplifiers, use a **step-up** transformer to raise the same 120 volts to a level powerful enough to drive speakers.

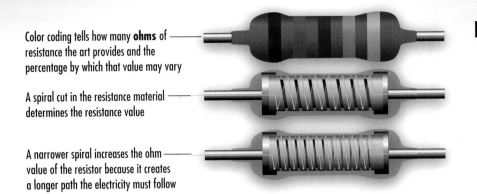

Color coding tells how many **ohms** of resistance the art provides and the percentage by which that value may vary

A spiral cut in the resistance material determines the resistance value

A narrower spiral increases the ohm value of the resistor because it creates a longer path the electricity must follow

5 We use **resistors** to decrease the flow of electricity, much like we use a valve to limit how much water flows through a pipe. Resistors are commonly made of carbon, plastic **doped** with metals, and metals such as nickel-chrome that do not conduct electricity well. Varying the materials and their size and shape changes how much resistance the component has, measured in **ohms**.

6 **Variable resistors**, such as the **rheostat** shown here, are used in situations that call for the resistance to be changed manually, on the fly. The best example is the traditional dial controlling volume on a radio. The outer ring, or **toroid coil**, consists of a resistive wire wrapped in a spiral about a ring of insulating material. Electricity must travel along a sliding **wiper** and through the coil before it leaves the resistor. When the knob is turned clockwise, the electricity has less wire to travel through so that the resulting current is stronger and the volume is louder.

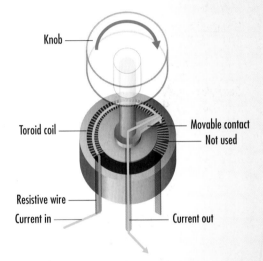

Knob

Toroid coil

Movable contact

Not used

Resistive wire

Current in

Current out

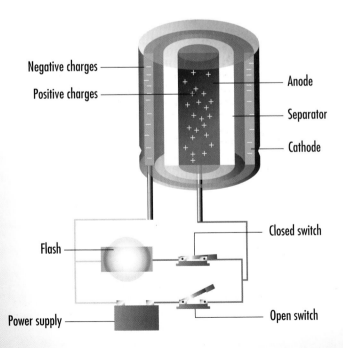

Negative charges

Positive charges

Anode

Separator

Cathode

Flash

Closed switch

Power supply

Open switch

7 **Capacitors** are made of two conductive materials that sandwich a material with limited conductivity, such as plastic, ceramic, or even paper. When current is applied to the two conductive **terminals**, the electricity does not flow through the capacitor. Instead, electrons from the power source pile up at one of the terminals, called the **anode**, like logs swept onto a dam. They leave a dearth of electrons at the second terminal—the **cathode**—so that it is charged positively by the protons that have been deserted by the electrons. The charges remain in the capacitor for a few seconds or several minutes, depending on the design. When a circuit connecting the two terminals closes, the capacitor **discharges** (the electrons jump the insulator) to send a bigger than usual burst of current needed for, say, a photo flash. Larger capacitors, such as those found in cathode ray tube (CRT) monitors and some power supplies, can be dangerous or fatal if handled improperly.

How Computers Create Our World Using Numbers

WAVES, electromagnetic fields, particles, electrons, light waves, and quarks. These are the elements by which computers compute—measuring, comparing, adding, and subtracting. All that computing brilliance has to be communicated to us less-brilliant organic units in some way. Unfortunately, the native tongue of computers is numbers, which most of us stopped thinking about within days of completing Algebra II. Because we are not fluent enough in numbers to enter the world of computers, computers have devised ways of using numbers to re-create our world as we understand it. Their numerical constructs are so smooth we are rarely aware that they are made of only 0s and 1s.

1 There are two ways to take stock of the world around us: analog and digital. An **analog** instrument expresses measurements in a manner that is analogous to whatever it is measuring. An old-fashioned thermometer—an analog device—has a glass tube filled with red-dyed alcohol. As the thermometer gets warmer, the heat causes the alcohol to expand and rise within the tube. We can look at the markings along the tube and say that a person's temperature is "about 99.5." We say "about" because our reading of the temperature depends on the precision used in making the thermometer and the acuity of our vision.

2 A **digital** thermometer has an electrical component called a thermistor. Rising temperatures make the thermistor less resistant to electrical current, allowing an increased electrical flow to a miniprocessor that converts the amount of electricity to numbers that represent the temperature. The numbers are displayed on a screen, but unlike the alcohol in the analog thermometer, the numbers don't swell or shrink in proportion to temperature variations.

Most of today's computers are digital because the transistors that jumble data are digital, either on or off and not some state in between. (Analog computers are used in situations involving constantly changing measurements, such as an automatic transmission or a bombardier's sight.) Digital computers, however, often start out with analog measurements that must be converted to digital.

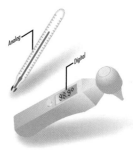

3 The computer-based digital camera replaces film with an **image sensor**, a microchip studded with **photodiodes**, transistors melded with substances that convert photo energy into electrical energy. Each of the photodiodes collects photons of light, building up electrical charges as long as the shutter is open. The brighter a part of a scene is, the more photons are focused on the pixels capturing that part of the scene. When the shutter loses, all the pixels have electrical charges that are proportional to the number of photons that hit each photodiode. If you picture photons piling up in mounds of glowing pebbles in buckets—some smaller, some larger—you've got the idea.

4 The camera's circuitry moves the charges collected by the image sensor into a single row that passes through an amplifier. The amp converts what are little more than faint static charges into an electrical current with varying voltages in proportion to the parade of changing charges.

Single-bit sampling

ON
OFF

Resolution threshold

0 1 1 1 1 0 0 0 0 0 0 1 1 0 0 0 0 0 1 1 0

5 The current passes into an **analog-to-digital convertor (ADC)**. Every few milliseconds, the ADC measures the voltage of the current as it passes through. If the voltage is above a certain level, the ADC produces a 1 bit, which it adds to a stream of digital values that it passes on to other components. If the voltage is beneath that same level, the ADC adds a 0 bit.

6 Data that has only two values, 0 and 1, doesn't have the versatility to represent in analog format the real world of images and sounds that, ironically, have become the most popular use of computers. With only two values, such as black and white—no grays—an image looks like this two-bit Mona Lisa.

One can obtain more precise digital representations of analog signals through **multi-bit sampling**. The current being measured, whether generated by the energy of light, sound, or chemical reactions, passes through a series of resistors. Each resistor depletes some of the current until it is no longer measurable. How many resistors it passes through determines a value, depending on the design, that is represented by 2, 4, or 8 bits—the bit rate. In Diagram A on the near right, with a bit rate of 4, there are four values the voltage could reach for each sample. Diagram B on the far right shows an ADC capable of registering eight values per reading.

Multi-bit sampling

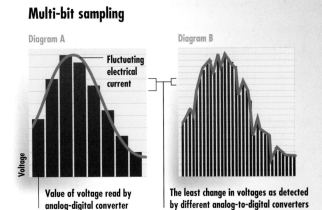

Diagram A — Fluctuating electrical current

Diagram B

Voltage

Value of voltage read by analog-digital converter

The least change in voltages as detected by different analog-to-digital converters

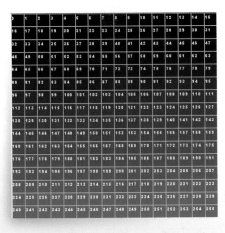

7 Diagram B also demonstrates how the conversion's **resolution** is made more accurate by increasing the **sampling rate**, the frequency at which samples of passing current are measured. In Diagram A, eight samples are taken for the period shown. Diagram B shows a sampling rate four times greater. If Diagram A were representing the digitizing of a music recording, its sampling, or frequency rate, might be appropriate for a smooth slide on a trombone. Diagram B has the same general shape as the red line in A. But the higher sampling rate provides opportunities to capture variations in sound that the first example can't handle, such as a rapid trill on a clarinet.

8 Having 16 bits for each sample might not sound particularly useful. But 16 bits in a binary number yields 256 different combinations. In creating video color, that means 16 bits can produce any of 256 shades of a color, as shown here with red. A bit value of 0000000000000000 binary or 0 in decimal is assigned to total black. All 1s—1111111111111111—binary or 256 decimal represents as pure and intense a red as a monitor can produce. Take any two adjacent red squares shown here and the difference between them is less than the human eye can distinguish. Combine 256 shades of red with 256 shades of each of the other two colors that go into a video image, green and blue, and the result is an amazing 16,777,216 possible colors.

9 An ADC has a functional mirror image in a **DAC**, or **digital-to-analog converter**. Some monitors and most sound speakers require analog currents. A DAC changes a string of digital values into rapidly changing voltages in an electrical current by routing a feeder current through a matrix of **resistors** that partially block the current. The resistors are weighted to represent different degrees of resistance. Sending current through resistors on different pathways turns out a final stream of current that corresponds to the digital data.

CHAPTER

2

How Computers Remember

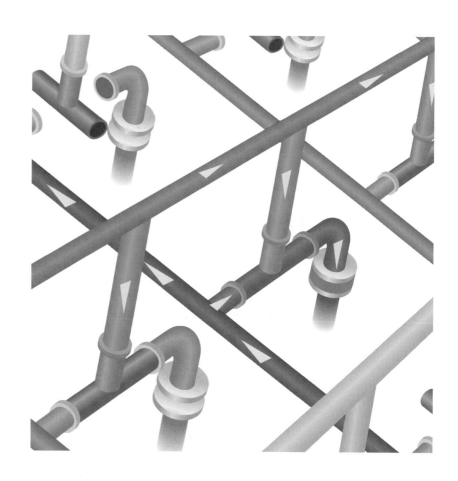

There are 10 kinds of people in the world. Those who understand binary, and those who don't.

—Programmer's joke

IT DOESN'T MAKE ANY DIFFERENCE if your electronic device of choice is a desktop computer, laptop, camera, smartphone, tablet, or glasses. Even if their functions wildly differ, all devices work using the same fundamental foundation of computing, the **transistor**.

The transistor—the basic building block from which all microchips are built—has an unsubtle way of handling information: binary. It has two choices; nothing in between. If current passes through a transistor, the transistor stands for a 1, or if current doesn't pass through it, it becomes a 0. From these 1s and 0s, called **bits**, a computer can create any number as long as it has enough transistors grouped together to hold them all.

Binary notation starts off simply enough:

Decimal Number	Binary Number	Decimal Number	Binary Number
0	0	6	110
1	1	7	111
2	10	8	1000
3	11	9	1001
4	100	10	1010
5	101		

The processors in the first personal computers could work with 16 bits at a time, which limits them to numbers no bigger than the decimal number 65,535. Why, that's not big enough to count all the people in Murfreesboro, Tennessee! Luckily processor upgrades gave PCs the ability to work with 32 bits at a time, taking them up to the decimal notation of 4,294,967,295. Not bad, but the processors in common use in 2014 and (spoiler alert!) for a long time into the future can juggle 64 bits with the ease of The Flying Karamazov Brothers throwing swords back and forth—and a lot more easily than the boys juggling 281,474,976,710,655 swords, the decimal equivalent of 64 bits.

A processor being able to tackle more bits simultaneously doesn't result only in bigger numbers. Higher bit counts mean more data and instructions can be moved from memory into the processor in a single trip. That means faster computing.

It's a mistake to think of transistors in terms of number alone, however. The same on/off bits can stand for true and false, enabling devices to work with **Boolean logic**. ("Select this AND this but NOT this.") Combinations of transistors in various configurations are called **logic gates**, which are combined into arrays called **half adders**, which in turn are combined into **full adders**, allowing the processor to calculate with numbers instead of merely counting. Transistors make it possible for a small amount of electrical current to control a second, much stronger current—just as the small amount or energy needed to throw a wall switch controls the more powerful energy surging through the wires to give life to a spotlight.

How a Little Transistor Does Big Jobs

THE MOST IMPORTANT INVENTION of the 20th century and the thing that will most influence technical and social progress in the 21st century is simply a switch. Well, not *simply* a switch. It's a **transistor** switch, a cousin of the wall switch that closes to let electricity flow through it or opens to block the current. The difference between the kin is that the transistor can be made exceedingly small. Its size gives it the ability turn off and on so rapidly that the number of times it closes or opens is measured in millionths of a second. And its size lets us join transistors into mighty armies that we call **microprocessors**, capable of conquering the prickly, unexplored wildernesses of science, music, and thought.

1 A small, positive electrical charge is sent down one aluminum lead that runs into the transistor. The positive charge spreads to a layer of electrically conductive polysilicon buried in the middle of nonconductive silicon dioxide. Silicon dioxide is the main component of sand and the material that gave Silicon Valley its name.

2 The positive charge attracts negatively charged electrons from the base made of P-type (positive) silicon that separates two layers of N-type (negative) silicon.

3 The rush of electrons out of the P-type silicon creates an electronic vacuum that is filled by electrons rushing from another conductive lead called the *source*. In addition to filling the vacuum in the P-type silicon, the electrons from the source also flow to a similar conductive lead called the *drain*. The rush of electrons completes the circuit, turning on the transistor so that it represents 1 bit. If a negative charge is applied to the polysilicon, electrons from the source are repelled and the transistor is turned off.

The Birth of a Microchip

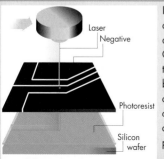

The first silicon transistor, shown in the photo, was invented at Bell Labs in 1947. The device, made of two gold electrical contacts and a germanium crystal, was built on a human scale, which make its workings easily visible. But to be really useful, a transistor needs other transistors—so many that creating them on Bell Labs' human scale would guarantee only gargantuan gadgets.

Scientists quickly developed ways that reduced the size and increased the efficiency of transistors. Today, a microchip is conceived on a computer that converts the engineers' logical concepts into physical designs used to fabricate the soul of a chip. The body of the chip is born of a thin, highly polished slice of silicon crystal grown in the lab. Although silicon is the second-most plentiful element on earth, it does not appear naturally in its pure form.

Building a Microprocessor

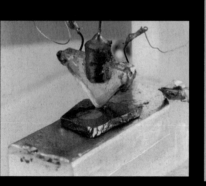

In a **photoetching** process, a chemical called **photoresist** covers the silicon wafer's surface. Intense thin beams of light are shown through a negative produced from the engineer's CAD designs. Or, the computer might guide a beam of electrons to trace the chip design. Photoresist that has been touched by beams of light or electrons is washed away, and where the silicon is no longer protected by photoresist, an acid bath etches channels into the silicon's surface. These channels are filled with conductive materials to create the circuits along which the computer's digital signals travel.

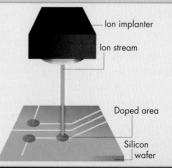

Laser
Negative
Photoresist
Silicon wafer

Ion implanter
Ion stream
Doped area
Silicon wafer

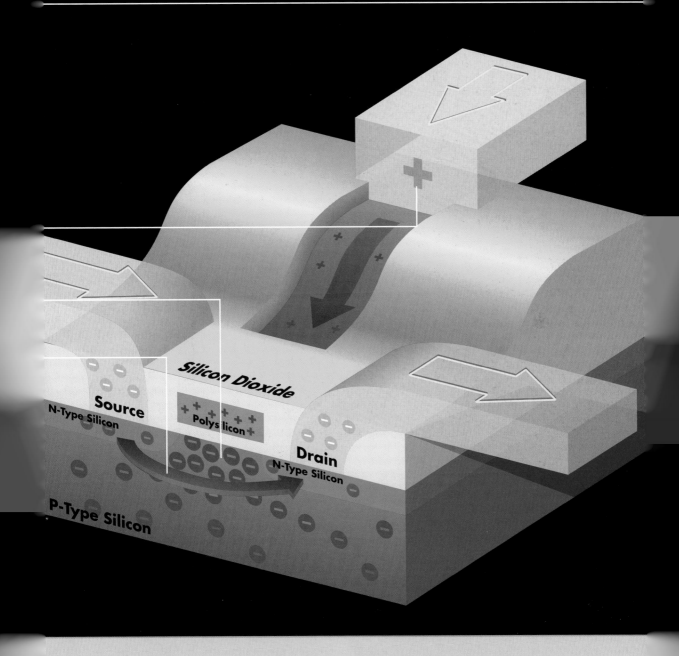

Silicon Dioxide

Source
N-Type Silicon

Poly silicon

Drain
N-Type Silicon

P-Type Silicon

on implanters next **dope** the silicon with impurities by
oting molecules into the silicon. By itself, silicon doesn't
duct electricity, but when doped, it becomes a semicon-
tor. The process is repeated for as many as 8 to 12 other
ers of a microchip, joining the layers on the fly. The use
ayers makes it possible for more than one circuit to cross
h other in the microchip's overall design without actually
shing on the same layer. The process can take weeks to
mplete but still manages to produce microprocessors in the
antities hungered for by new machines and their creators.

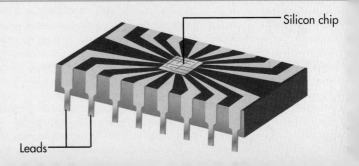

Silicon chip

Leads

Writing Data to RAM

1 Software, in combination with the operating system, sends a burst of electricity along an **address line**, which is a microscopic strand of electrically conductive material etched onto a RAM chip. Each address line identifies the location of a spot in the chip where data can be stored. The burst of electricity identifies where to record data among the many address lines in a RAM chip.

2 The electrical pulse turns on (closes) a transistor that's connected to a **data line** at each memory location in a RAM chip where data can be stored. A transistor is essentially a microscopic electronic switch.

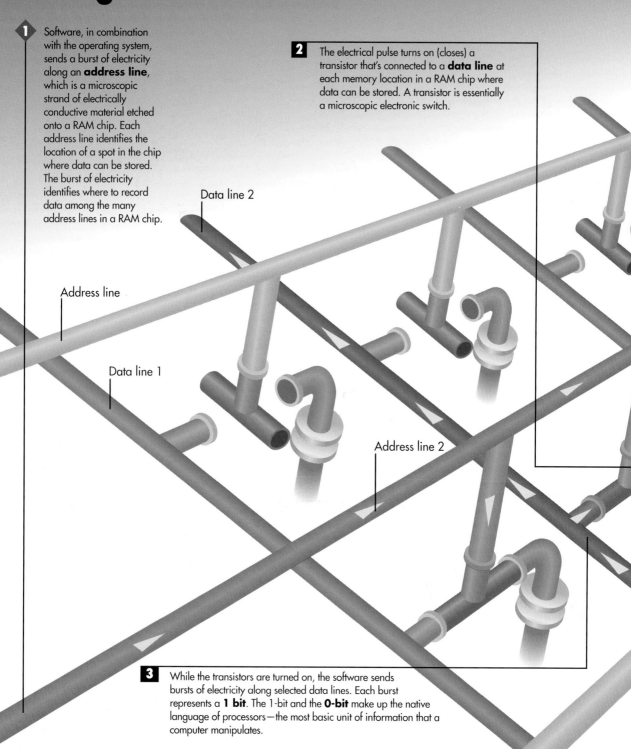

Data line 2

Address line

Data line 1

Address line 2

3 While the transistors are turned on, the software sends bursts of electricity along selected data lines. Each burst represents a **1 bit**. The 1-bit and the **0-bit** make up the native language of processors—the most basic unit of information that a computer manipulates.

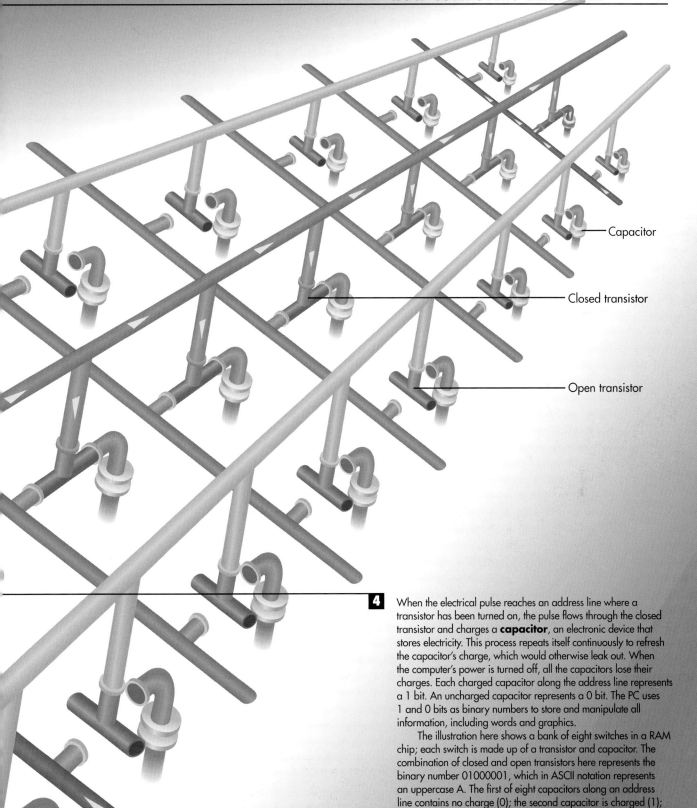

Capacitor

Closed transistor

Open transistor

4 When the electrical pulse reaches an address line where a transistor has been turned on, the pulse flows through the closed transistor and charges a **capacitor**, an electronic device that stores electricity. This process repeats itself continuously to refresh the capacitor's charge, which would otherwise leak out. When the computer's power is turned off, all the capacitors lose their charges. Each charged capacitor along the address line represents a 1 bit. An uncharged capacitor represents a 0 bit. The PC uses 1 and 0 bits as binary numbers to store and manipulate all information, including words and graphics.

The illustration here shows a bank of eight switches in a RAM chip; each switch is made up of a transistor and capacitor. The combination of closed and open transistors here represents the binary number 01000001, which in ASCII notation represents an uppercase A. The first of eight capacitors along an address line contains no charge (0); the second capacitor is charged (1); the next five capacitors have no charge (00000); and the eighth capacitor is charged (1).

Reading Data from RAM

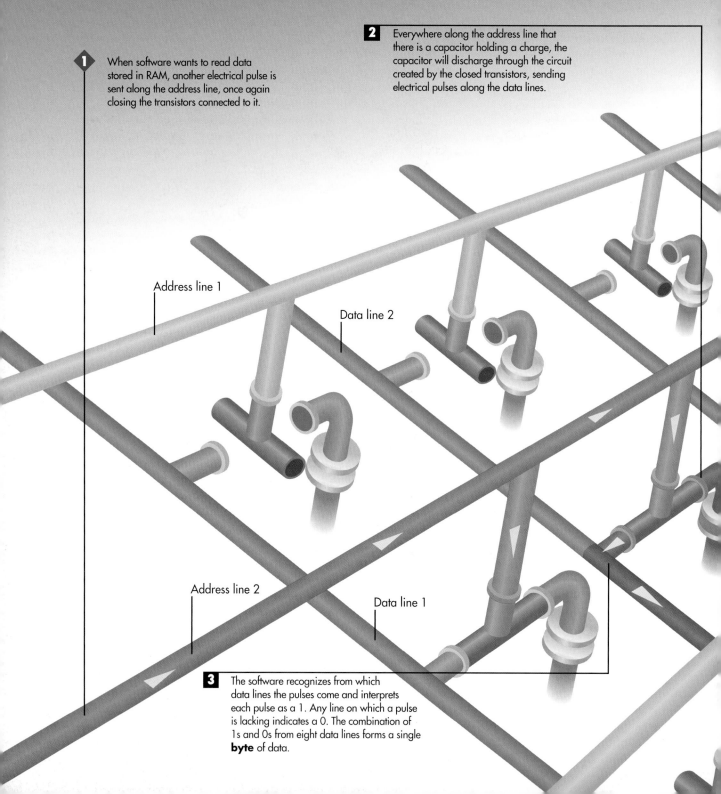

1 When software wants to read data stored in RAM, another electrical pulse is sent along the address line, once again closing the transistors connected to it.

2 Everywhere along the address line that there is a capacitor holding a charge, the capacitor will discharge through the circuit created by the closed transistors, sending electrical pulses along the data lines.

Address line 1

Data line 2

Address line 2

Data line 1

3 The software recognizes from which data lines the pulses come and interprets each pulse as a 1. Any line on which a pulse is lacking indicates a 0. The combination of 1s and 0s from eight data lines forms a single **byte** of data.

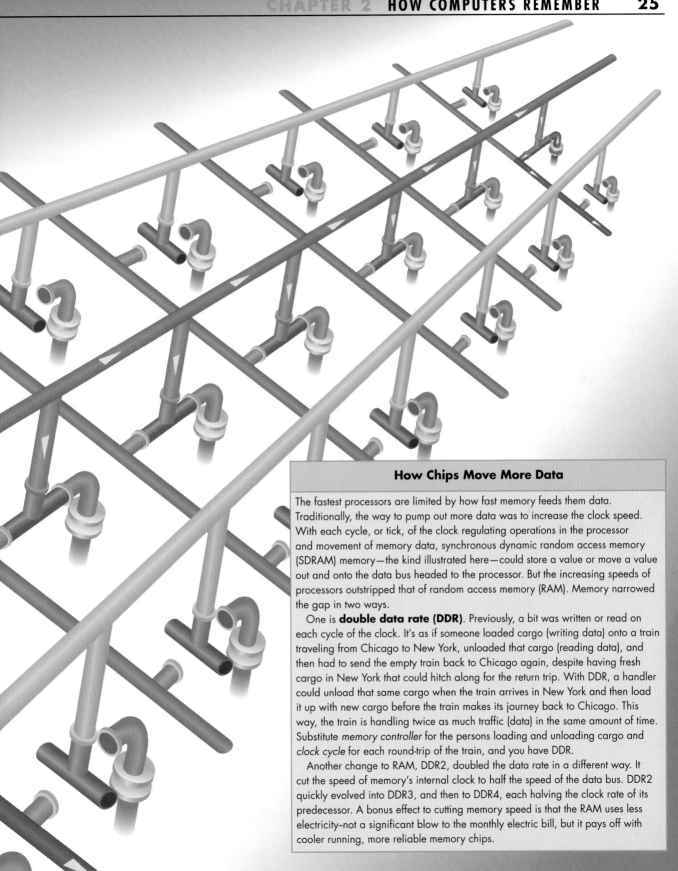

How Chips Move More Data

The fastest processors are limited by how fast memory feeds them data. Traditionally, the way to pump out more data was to increase the clock speed. With each cycle, or tick, of the clock regulating operations in the processor and movement of memory data, synchronous dynamic random access memory (SDRAM) memory—the kind illustrated here—could store a value or move a value out and onto the data bus headed to the processor. But the increasing speeds of processors outstripped that of random access memory (RAM). Memory narrowed the gap in two ways.

One is **double data rate (DDR)**. Previously, a bit was written or read on each cycle of the clock. It's as if someone loaded cargo (writing data) onto a train traveling from Chicago to New York, unloaded that cargo (reading data), and then had to send the empty train back to Chicago again, despite having fresh cargo in New York that could hitch along for the return trip. With DDR, a handler could unload that same cargo when the train arrives in New York and then load it up with new cargo before the train makes its journey back to Chicago. This way, the train is handling twice as much traffic (data) in the same amount of time. Substitute *memory controller* for the persons loading and unloading cargo and *clock cycle* for each round-trip of the train, and you have DDR.

Another change to RAM, DDR2, doubled the data rate in a different way. It cut the speed of memory's internal clock to half the speed of the data bus. DDR2 quickly evolved into DDR3, and then to DDR4, each halving the clock rate of its predecessor. A bonus effect to cutting memory speed is that the RAM uses less electricity–not a significant blow to the monthly electric bill, but it pays off with cooler running, more reliable memory chips.

ow Flash Memory Remembers
hen the Switch Is Off

A DESKTOP or laptop computer, data in RAM that's not saved to disk disappears when the computer is turned off. But computers ave evolved into smartphones, tablets, cameras, and other handhelds don't have disk drives for storage. They all use memory chips. et when you turn off your smartphone, your contacts, music, pictures, and apps are still there when you turn it back on. That's because e devices don't use ordinary RAM. They use **flash memory** that freezes data in place.

Flash memory is laid out along a grid of printed circuits running at right angles to each other. In one direction, he circuit traces are **word addresses**; circuits at a ight angle to them represent he **bit addresses**. The two addresses combine to create a unique number address called a **cell**.

The cell contains two transistors that together determine if an intersection represents a 0 or a 1. One ransistor—the **control gate**—is linked to one of he passing circuits called he **word line**, which determines the word address.

A thin layer of **metal oxide** separates the control gate from a second transistor, called the **floating gate**. When an electrical charge runs from he **source** to the **drain**, the charge extends through the loating gate, on through the metal oxide, and through the control gate to the word line.

A **bit sensor** on the word line compares the strength of the charge in the control gate to the strength of the charge on the loating gate. If the control voltage s at least half of the floating gate charge, the gate is said to be **open**, and the cell represents a 1. Flash memory is sold with all cells open. Recording to it consists of changing the appropriate cells to eros.

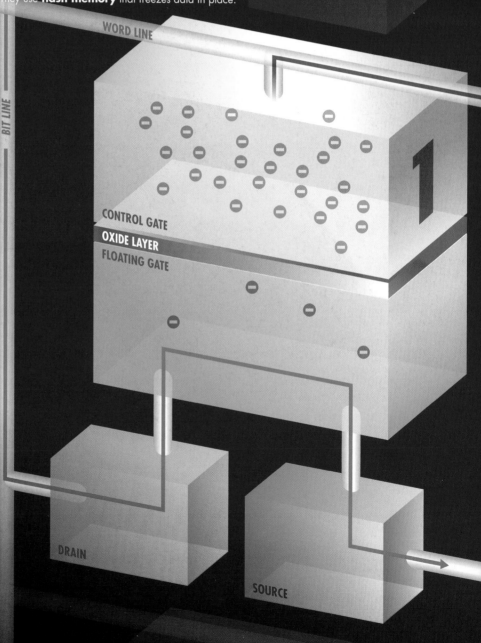

WORD LINE

BIT LINE

CONTROL GATE
OXIDE LAYER
FLOATING GATE

DRAIN

SOURCE

1

5 Flash memory uses **Fowler-Nordheim tunneling** to change the value of the cell to a zero. In tunneling, a current from the bit line travels through the floating gate transistor, exiting through the source to a **ground**.

6 Energy from the current causes electrons to boil off the floating gate and through the metal oxide, where the electrons lose too much energy to make it back through the oxide. They are trapped in the control gate, even when the current is turned off.

7 The electrons have become a wall that repels any charge coming from the floating gate. The bit sensor detects the difference in charges on the two transistors, and because the charge on the control gate is below 50 percent of the floating gate charge, it is considered to stand for a zero.

8 When it comes time to reuse the flash memory, a current is sent through **in-circuit wiring** to apply a strong electrical field to the entire chip, or to predetermined sections of the chip called **blocks**. The field energizes the electrons so they are once again evenly dispersed.

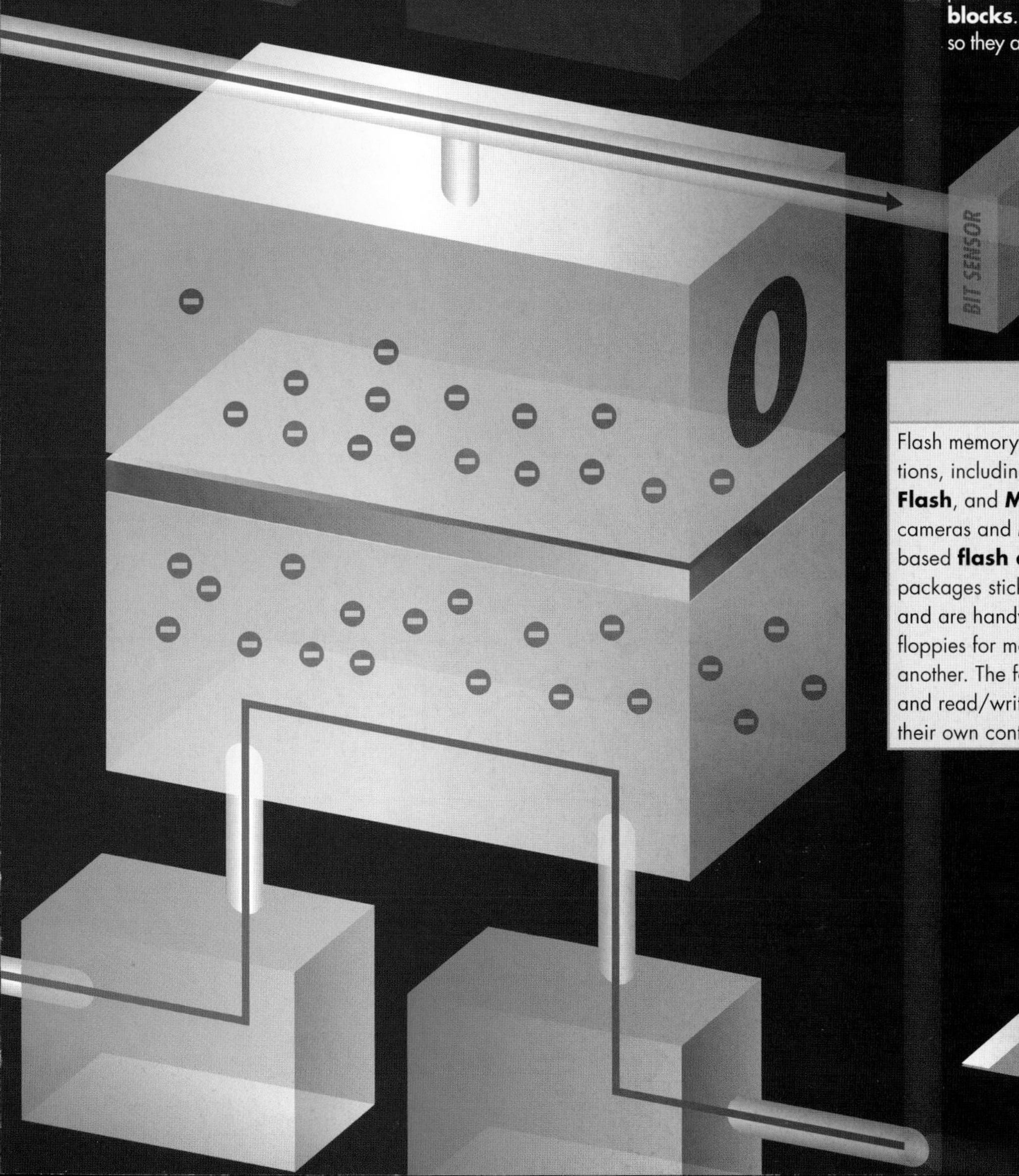

BIT SENSOR

Forms of Flash

Flash memory is sold in a variety of configurations, including **SmartMedia**, **Compact Flash**, and **Memory Sticks**, used mainly in cameras and MP3 players. There's also USB-based **flash drives**, which look like gum packages sticking out of the sides of computers, and are handy in a way once reserved for floppies for moving files from one computer to another. The form factors, storage capacities, and read/write speeds vary. Some include their own controllers for faster reads and writes.

256MB COMPACT FLASH

64MB SMART MEDIA

128MB MEMORY STICK

CHAPTER

3

How a Little Microprocessor Does Big Things

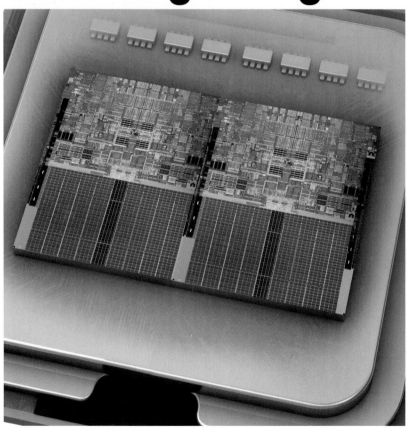

IF YOU WANT to feel what it's like to be a microprocessor, go to a toy store for tots and get one of those baby toys that has a bunch of different-sized rings the kid is supposed to put on a stick to make a kind of round pyramid thing. If you don't feel like blowing money on a kid's toy, pull some change out of your pocket. A dime, penny, nickel, quarter, half-dollar (if you can find one), and a dollar bill have a couple of things in common with the toy rings: None is the same size as any other, and they can be stacked. That's all you need for this passage into the brain-numbing world of the microprocessor.

This is called the Towers of Hanoi Puzzle. It's simple but tedious. All you have to do is move the complete stack of objects—rings, coins, plates, whatever—from their initial position, which I'll call "A," to one of two other spots, "B" and "C." There are two rules:

1) You can move only one object at a time.

2) You cannot place one object on an object smaller than the object you're moving. For example, you can't put a quarter on top of a dime.

In the original, legendary version of the game, you must move 64 rings while following those rules. It doesn't sound that complicated. And it's not, really. Mathematicians have pointed out the similarities between the Towers of Hanoi and binary computations, geometry, and the exact duplication of a function called the binary carry sequence.

But never mind all that. Let's play the game using only three rings, or disks, as we've drawn them here:

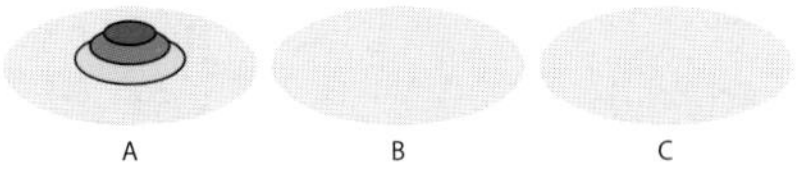

1. Take the top, purple disk and place in the empty B spot.

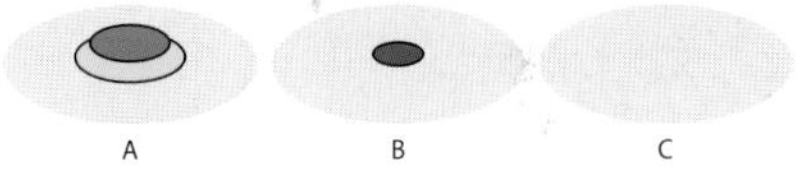

2. Place the green disk on C.

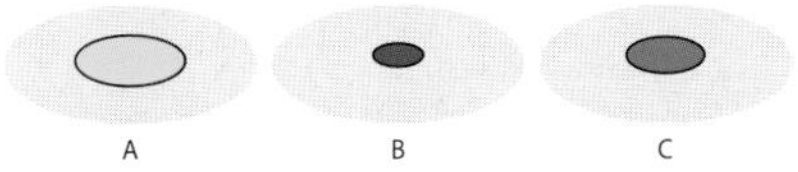

3. Put the purple disk from position B and put it on top of the green disk.

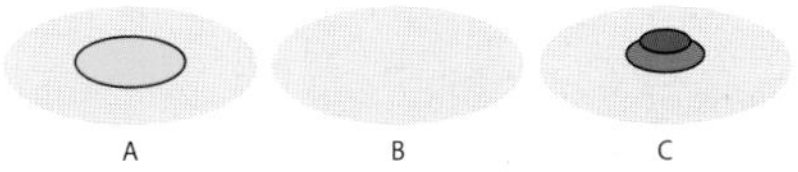

4. Move the yellow disk from A to the B position.

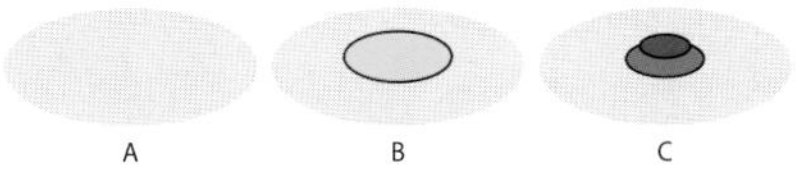

5. Put the purple disk on the now empty position A.

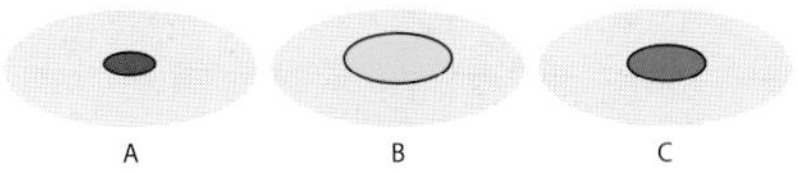

6. Move the green disk on top of the yellow disk at B.

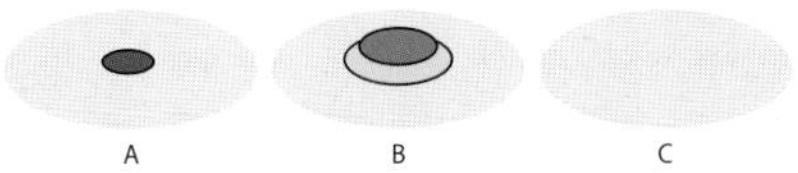

7. Move the purple disk to sit on the green disk.

There. In seven moves you've relocated three disks to a different spot. As you might have guessed, it gets more intricate as you move down through the stack—not more difficult, just more, and more, of the same. Add one more disk, and it takes 15 moves. Ten disks add 1,023 moves.

The Towers of Hanoi Puzzle was discovered by French mathematician Edouard Lucas in 1883. A legend, possibly created by Lucas, has it that there is a temple with a room that contains three poles and 64 gold disks with holes in the centers. The priests at the temple are on a mission from God to move all the discs from one pole to another, Towers-of-Hanoi style. When they complete the task, the world will come to an end. Not to worry. The number of moves to complete the puzzle increases exponentially as the number of discs increases. If the priests could move one disc each second, it would take them 2^{64}[ms]−1 seconds, or roughly 585 billion years, which is 127 times the age of the sun, to complete all the 18,446,744,073,709,551,615 moves required to finish the mission.

This sort of mind-numbing task was made for computing. The **CPU**, or **central processing unit**, whether in a computer, a watch, a smartphone, hearing aid, smart TV, or even a toaster oven plays its own version of the Towers of Hanoi. Like the moves in the puzzle, the methods used by processors work by doing the same thing many times. Multiplying 100 by 3,000 is accomplishing by adding 3,000 a hundred times. Division consists of subtracting one number from another continuously until the result is 0 or the final number is not large enough to subtract the divisor from it.

In the most powerful processors for PCs, the CPU can work with 64 bits at a time, but this doesn't mean that in the monks' full 65 ring game, a 64-bit computer could grab the first 64 disks and move them all at once. It still has to move only one tower ring with each tick of its internal clock, but the computer could simultaneously move one ring on 63 other towers. (A processor such as the Intel Core i7-965 Extreme Edition, with a clock speed of 3.20 gigahertz—3,200,000,000 ticks of the clock every second—could complete the monks' original tower exercise in 13 day and four hours.)

A processor is limited in the number of places it can put the binary numbers representing the bits while still carrying out its software's instructions. After adding two numbers, the CPU might need to put the result in a part of the chip that acts as a temporary holding pen. After adding two more numbers, it retrieves the stored number to add it to the sum of the second addition. It's kind of like how we humans scribble the result of some math operation on a slip of paper, so we can use it a minute later when we solve a related problem.

Much is made of all the amazing things computing can do, but what it can't do, so far, requires intuition, the ability to find a link among seemingly dissimilar ideas. When, in 1997, IBM's Big Blue computer was the first machine to win a tournament with a reigning chess champion—Garry Kasparov—it did so by playing "what if." What if it moved this piece, and then Kasparov moved that piece, and so on through six to eight moves starting from 20 or more contingencies. Big Blue was capable of 200 million positions a second. It's much like doing the Towers of Hanoi—very fast. Human chess champions, on the other hand, say they uniformly avoid the what-if approach in favor of patterns. They will look at the board, and the years of experience buried in their brains see patterns of pieces that reveal a strategy to a win. Or, in Kasparov's case, a loss.

Humans are very good at insight and hunches. Computing is very good at doing the same thing over and over again. Remember that when your computer seems to be taking too long to do something. It's just plodding along in its own manner. It doesn't have your skills.

How a Processor Tracks Numbers

FEW OF US can do complex math in our heads. Even for something as simple as adding several rows of numbers, we need a pencil and paper to keep track of which numbers go where. Microprocessors are not all that different in this regard. Although they are capable of performing intricate math involving thousands of numbers, they, too, need notepads to keep track of their calculations. Their notepads are called **registers**, and their pencils are pulses of electricity.

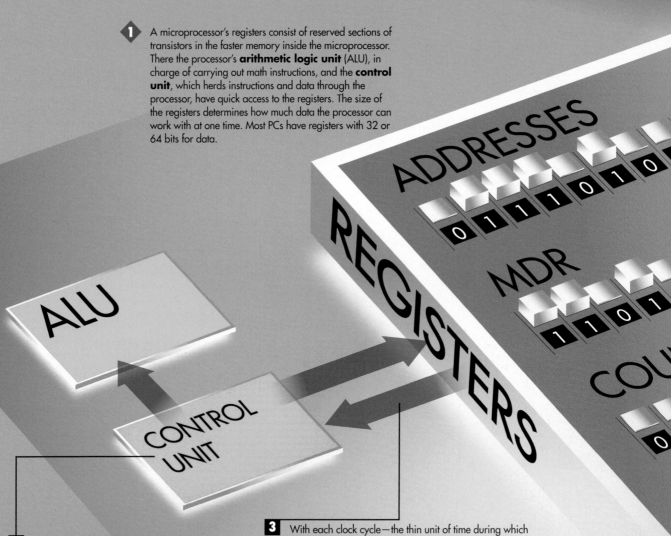

1 A microprocessor's registers consist of reserved sections of transistors in the faster memory inside the microprocessor. There the processor's **arithmetic logic unit** (ALU), in charge of carrying out math instructions, and the **control unit**, which herds instructions and data through the processor, have quick access to the registers. The size of the registers determines how much data the processor can work with at one time. Most PCs have registers with 32 or 64 bits for data.

2 The processor's **control unit** directs the fetching and execution of program instructions. (See "How a Microprocessor Moves Data", on pages 36-37.) It uses an electrical signal to fetch each instruction, decodes it, and sends another control signal to the arithmetic logic unit telling the ALU what operation to carry out.

3 With each clock cycle—the thin unit of time during which the different components of a computer can do one thing—the processor writes or reads the values of the bits by sending or withholding a pulse of electricity to each. Each chunk of binary numbers is only that. They have no labels to identify them as instructions, data, values going into a computation, or the product of executing instructions. What the values represent depends on which registers the control unit uses to store them.

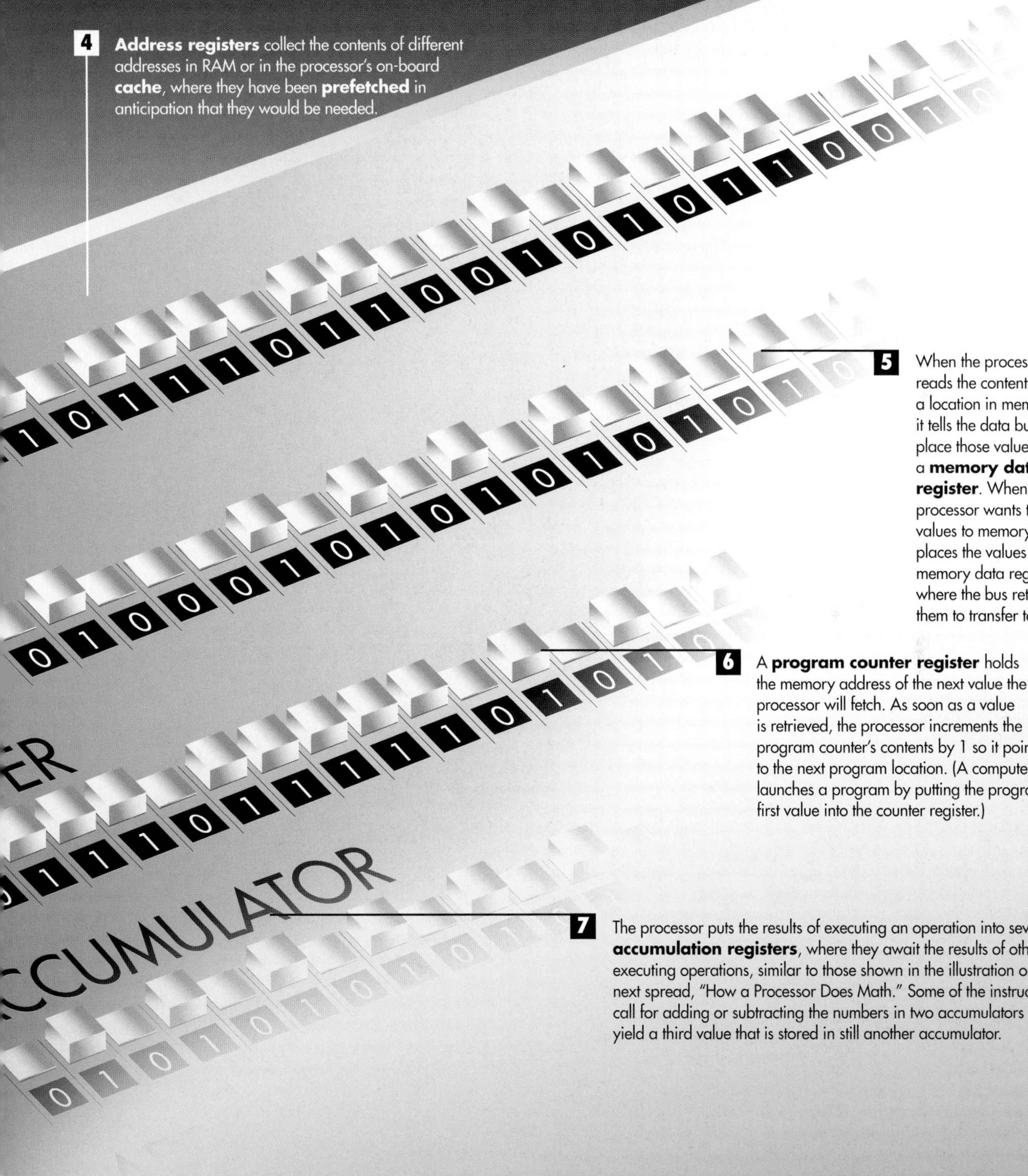

4 **Address registers** collect the contents of different addresses in RAM or in the processor's on-board **cache**, where they have been **prefetched** in anticipation that they would be needed.

5 When the processor reads the contents of a location in memory, it tells the data bus to place those values into a **memory data register**. When the processor wants to write values to memory, it places the values in the memory data register, where the bus retrieves them to transfer to RAM.

6 A **program counter register** holds the memory address of the next value the processor will fetch. As soon as a value is retrieved, the processor increments the program counter's contents by 1 so it points to the next program location. (A computer launches a program by putting the program's first value into the counter register.)

7 The processor puts the results of executing an operation into several **accumulation registers**, where they await the results of other executing operations, similar to those shown in the illustration on the next spread, "How a Processor Does Math." Some of the instructions call for adding or subtracting the numbers in two accumulators to yield a third value that is stored in still another accumulator.

How a Processor Does Math

1 All information—words and graphics as well as numbers—is stored in and manipulated by a PC in the form of binary numbers. In the binary numerical system, there are only two digits—0 and 1. All numbers, words, and graphics are formed from different combinations of those digits.

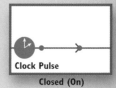

Decimal	Binary
0	0
1	1
2	10
3	11
4	100
5	101
6	110
7	111
8	1000
9	1001
10	1010

2 Transistor switches are used to manipulate binary numbers because there are two possible states of a switch, open (off) or closed (on), which nicely matches the two binary digits. An open transistor, through which no current is flowing, represents a 0. A closed transistor, which allows a pulse of electricity regulated by the PC's clock to pass through, represents a 1. (The computer's clock regulates how fast the computer works. The faster a clock ticks, causing pulses of electricity, the faster the computer works. Clock speeds are measured in **megahertz**, or millions of ticks per second.) Current passing through one transistor can be used to control another transistor, in effect turning the switch on and off to change what the second transistor represents. Such an arrangement is called a **gate** because, like a fence gate, the transistor can be open or closed, allowing or stopping current flowing through it.

3 The simplest operation that can be performed with a transistor is called a **NOT logic gate**, made up of only a single transistor. This NOT gate is designed to take one *input* from the clock and one from another transistor. The NOT gate produces a single *output*—one that's always the opposite of the input from the transistor. When current from another transistor representing a 1 is sent to a NOT gate, the gate's own transistor switches open so that a pulse, or current, from the clock can't flow through it, which makes the NOT gate's output 0. A 0 input closes the NOT gate's transistor so that the clock pulse passes through it to produce an output of 1.

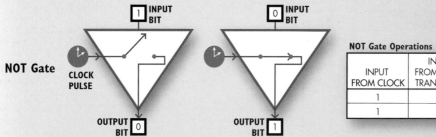

NOT Gate

NOT Gate Operations

INPUT FROM CLOCK	INPUT FROM OTHER TRANSISTOR	OUTPUT
1	1	0
1	0	1

4 NOT gates strung together in different combinations create other logic gates, all of which have a line to receive pulses from the clock and two other input lines for pulses from other logic gates. The **OR gates** create a 1 if either the first or second input is a 1, and put out a 0 only if both inputs are 0.

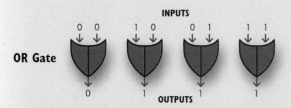

OR Gate

OR Gate Operations

1ST INPUT	2ND INPUT	OUTPUT
0	0	0
1	0	1
0	1	1
1	1	1

5 An AND gate outputs a 1 only if *both* the first and the second inputs are 1s.

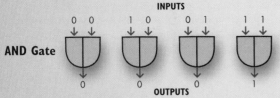

INPUTS

0 0   1 0   0 1   1 1

AND Gate

0   0   0   1

OUTPUTS

AND Gate Operations		
1ST INPUT	2ND INPUT	OUTPUT
0	0	0
1	0	0
0	1	0
1	1	1

6 An **XOR gate** puts out a 0 if *both* the inputs are 0 or if *both* are 1. It generates a 1 only if *one* of the inputs is 1 and the *other* is 0.

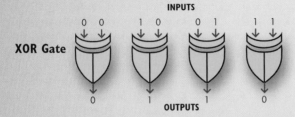

INPUTS

0 0   1 0   0 1   1 1

XOR Gate

0   1   1   0

OUTPUTS

XOR Gate Operations		
1ST INPUT	2ND INPUT	OUTPUT
0	0	0
1	0	1
0	1	1
1	1	0

7 With different combinations of logic gates, a computer performs the math that is the foundation of all its operations. This is accomplished with gate designs called **half-adders** and **full-adders**. A half-adder consists of an XOR gate and an AND gate, both of which receive the same input representing a one-digit binary number. A full-adder consists of half-adders and other switches.

1 + 1 DECIMAL

INPUT BITS 1 + 1 BINARY

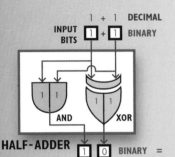

AND   XOR

HALF-ADDER 1 0 BINARY = 2 DECIMAL

8 A combination of a half-adder and a full-adder handles larger binary numbers and can generate results that involve carrying over numbers. To add the decimal numbers 2 and 3 (10 and 11 in the binary system), first the half-adder processes the digits on the right side through both XOR and AND gates.

9 The result of the XOR operation (1) becomes the rightmost digit of the result.

2 + 3 DECIMAL

1 0 + 1 1 BINARY

FULL-ADDER   **HALF-ADDER**

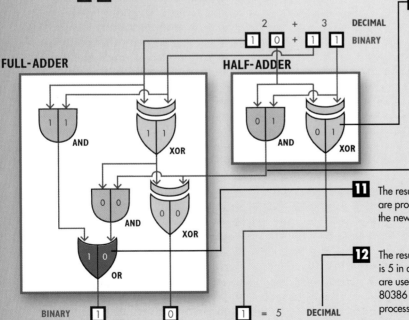

AND   XOR   AND   XOR

AND   XOR

OR

BINARY 1   0   1 = 5 DECIMAL

10 The result of the half-adder's AND operation (0) is sent to XOR and AND gates in the full-adder. The full-adder also processes the left-hand digits from 11 and 10, sending the results of both of the operations to another XOR gate and another AND gate.

11 The results from XORing and ANDing the left-hand digits are processed with the results from the half-adder. One of the new results is passed through an OR gate.

12 The result of all the calculations is 101 in binary, which is 5 in decimal. For larger numbers, more full-adders are used—one for each digit in the binary numbers. An 80386 or later processor, including today's Pentium class processors, uses 32 full-adders.

How a Processor Moves Data

TODAY'S MICROPROCESSORS have more than 100 billion transistors. Taking a walk through one of them could get a person hopelessly lost. Old or new, however, how a processor performs its most basic functions hasn't changed. They may have as many as eight execution cores and multiple caches—you can look at those on pages **XXX–xxx**—but, like the old single-core Pentium III processor illustrated here, they all face the same problem of how to move data quickly and with nary a hitch.

1 Meanwhile, the retirement unit is also inspecting the circular buffer. It first checks to see whether the μop at the head of the buffer has been executed. If it hasn't, the retirement unit keeps checking it until it has been processed. Then, the retirement unit checks the second and third μops. If they're already executed, the unit sends all three results—its maximum—to the store buffer. There, the prediction unit checks them out one last time before they're sent to their proper place in system RAM.

0 When a μop that had been delayed is finally processed, the execute unit compares the results with those predicted by the BTB. Where the prediction fails, a component called the **jump execution unit (JEU)** moves the end marker from the last μop in line to the μop that was predicted incorrectly. This signals that all μops behind the end marker should be ignored and can be overwritten by new μops. The BTB is told that its prediction was incorrect, and that information becomes part of its future predictions.

If an operation involves floating-point numbers, such as 3.14 or .33333, the ALUs hand off the job to the floating-point math unit, which contains processing tools designed to manipulate floating-point numbers quickly.

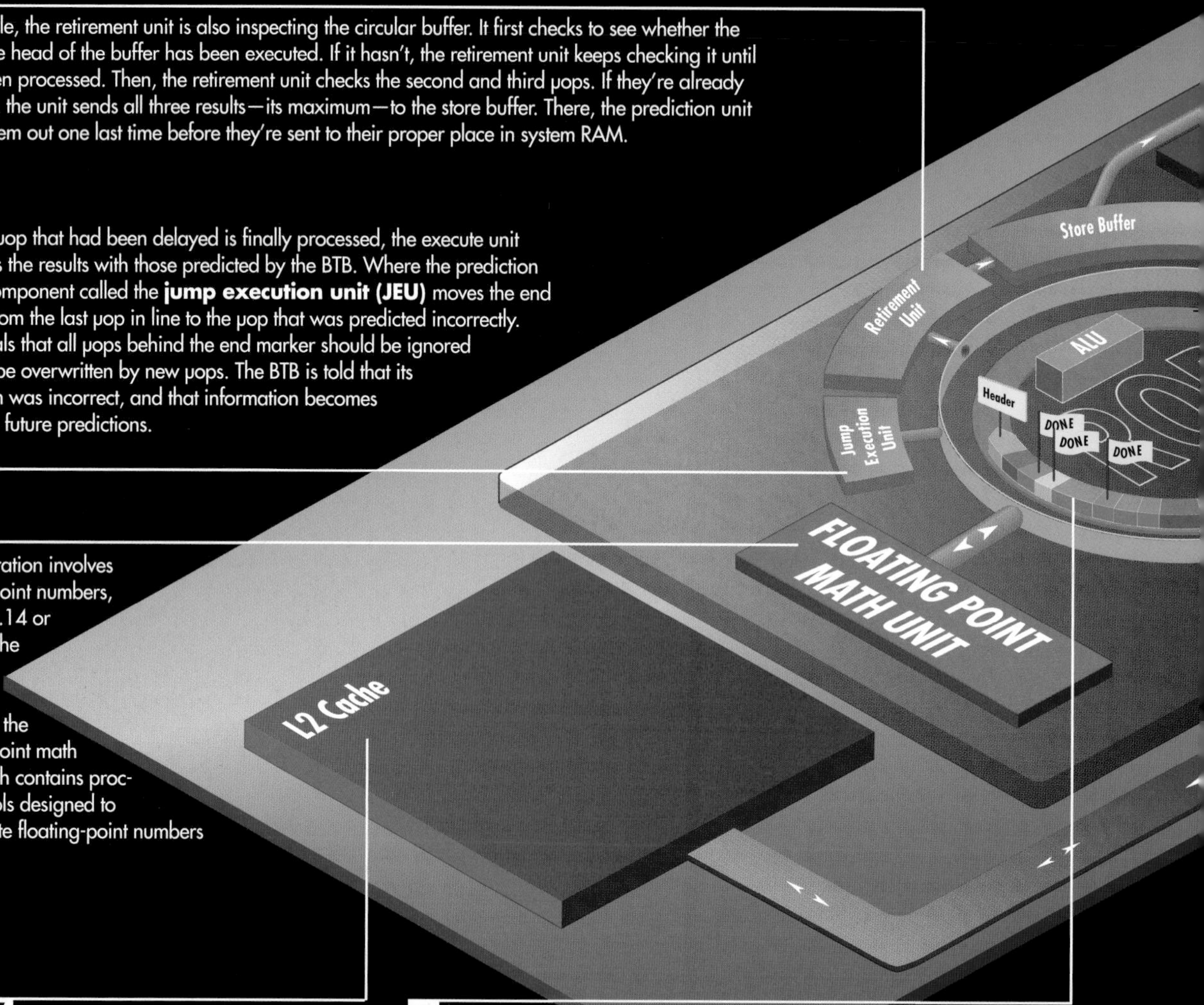

Store Buffer

Retirement Unit

ALU

Header

DONE
DONE
DONE

Jump Execution Unit

FLOATING POINT MATH UNIT

L2 Cache

7 If a μop needs data from memory, the execute unit skips it, and the processor looks for the information first in the nearby L1 cache. If the data isn't there, the processor checks the next cache level, L2 in this case. Cache size and organization vary based on the specific processor design, but each level of cache increases in both capacity and time

8 Instead of sitting idle while that information is fetched, the execute unit continues inspecting each μop in the buffer for those it can execute. This is called **speculative execution** because the order of μops in the circular buffer is based on the BTB's branch predictions. The unit executes up to five μops simultaneously. When the execution unit reaches the end of the buffer, it starts at the head again, rechecking all the μops to see whether any have finally received the data they need to be executed.

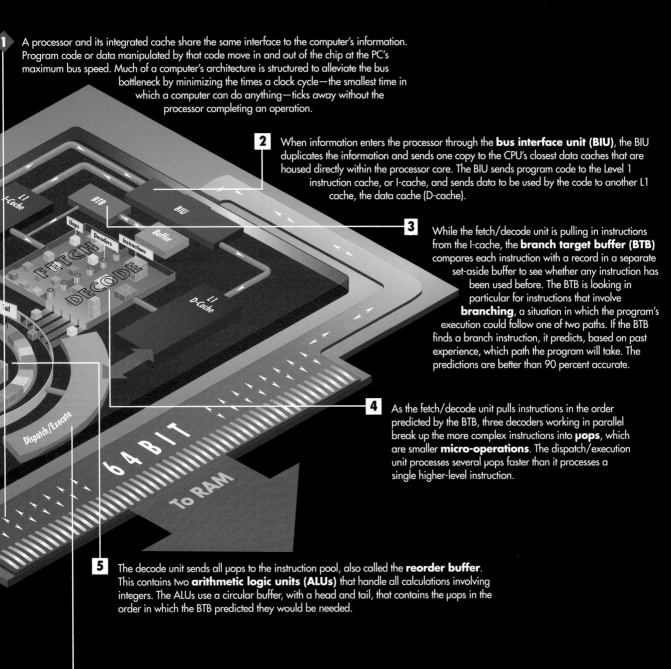

1 A processor and its integrated cache share the same interface to the computer's information. Program code or data manipulated by that code move in and out of the chip at the PC's maximum bus speed. Much of a computer's architecture is structured to alleviate the bus bottleneck by minimizing the times a clock cycle—the smallest time in which a computer can do anything—ticks away without the processor completing an operation.

2 When information enters the processor through the **bus interface unit (BIU)**, the BIU duplicates the information and sends one copy to the CPU's closest data caches that are housed directly within the processor core. The BIU sends program code to the Level 1 instruction cache, or I-cache, and sends data to be used by the code to another L1 cache, the data cache (D-cache).

3 While the fetch/decode unit is pulling in instructions from the I-cache, the **branch target buffer (BTB)** compares each instruction with a record in a separate set-aside buffer to see whether any instruction has been used before. The BTB is looking in particular for instructions that involve **branching**, a situation in which the program's execution could follow one of two paths. If the BTB finds a branch instruction, it predicts, based on past experience, which path the program will take. The predictions are better than 90 percent accurate.

4 As the fetch/decode unit pulls instructions in the order predicted by the BTB, three decoders working in parallel break up the more complex instructions into **μops**, which are smaller **micro-operations**. The dispatch/execution unit processes several μops faster than it processes a single higher-level instruction.

5 The decode unit sends all μops to the instruction pool, also called the **reorder buffer**. This contains two **arithmetic logic units (ALUs)** that handle all calculations involving integers. The ALUs use a circular buffer, with a head and tail, that contains the μops in the order in which the BTB predicted they would be needed.

6 The dispatch/execute unit checks each μop in the buffer to see whether it has all the information needed to process it, and when it finds a μop ready to process, the unit executes it, stores the result in the micro-op itself, and marks it as done.

How Multi-Core Processors Work

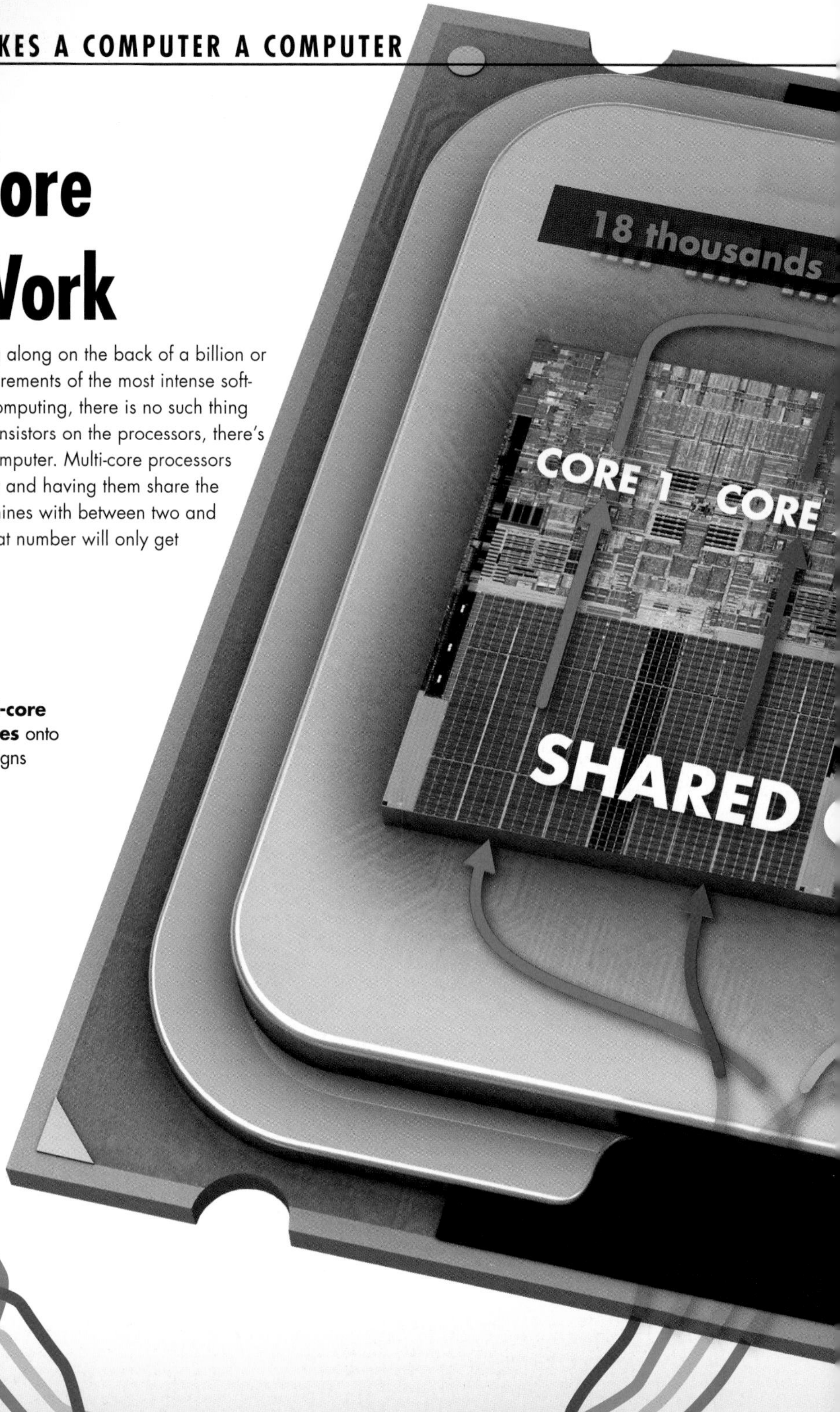

YOU'D THINK the microprocessors humming along on the back of a billion or so transistors would more than satisfy the requirements of the most intense software you can push through the chips. But in computing, there is no such thing as "enough." So if it's too hard to put more transistors on the processors, there's another solution: Put more processors in the computer. Multi-core processors are like bolting a couple of computers together and having them share the same memory, power, and input/output. Machines with between two and ten processor cores are standard issue, and that number will only get bigger.

Specific designs vary, but a typical **quad-core** processor combines four **execution cores** onto a single **die**, or **silicon chip.** Other designs spread their cores across two dies. Regardless, these identical cores are the heart of any microprocessor and the part that does the heavy work of executing instructions from software. The wildly colored areas above the cores in the photo are supporting the circuitry.

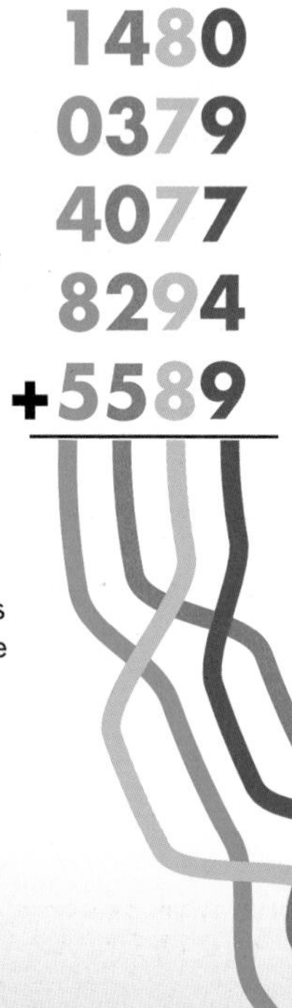

$$
\begin{array}{r}
1480 \\
0379 \\
4077 \\
8294 \\
+\,5589 \\
\hline
\end{array}
$$

18 thousands

CORE 1   CORE

SHARED

2 To gain the speed and other advantages possible with a multiprocessor computer, the **operating system (OS)** running on it must be designed to recognize that a PC has multi-core processors, be able to distinguish them, and know how to handle operations such as **hyper-threading**. Similarly, software applications, games, and utilities need to be rewritten to use the multiple cores. Such software is referred to as **threaded**, or **multi-threaded**. The software adding, say, a column of four-place numbers could divide the job into four threads: Adding the 1s-place numbers, the 10s-place numbers, the 100s-place numbers, and the 1000s-place numbers. Each of those subtasks is directed to a different core.

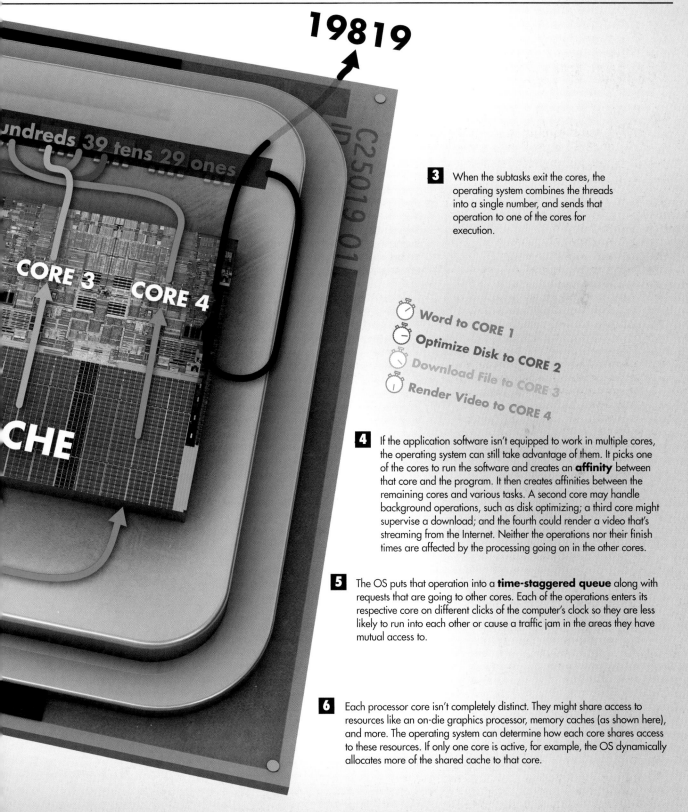

19819

ndreds 39 tens 29 ones

C25019 01

CORE 3 CORE 4

CHE

3 When the subtasks exit the cores, the operating system combines the threads into a single number, and sends that operation to one of the cores for execution.

Word to CORE 1
Optimize Disk to CORE 2
Download File to CORE 3
Render Video to CORE 4

4 If the application software isn't equipped to work in multiple cores, the operating system can still take advantage of them. It picks one of the cores to run the software and creates an **affinity** between that core and the program. It then creates affinities between the remaining cores and various tasks. A second core may handle background operations, such as disk optimizing; a third core might supervise a download; and the fourth could render a video that's streaming from the Internet. Neither the operations nor their finish times are affected by the processing going on in the other cores.

5 The OS puts that operation into a **time-staggered queue** along with requests that are going to other cores. Each of the operations enters its respective core on different clicks of the computer's clock so they are less likely to run into each other or cause a traffic jam in the areas they have mutual access to.

6 Each processor core isn't completely distinct. They might share access to resources like an on-die graphics processor, memory caches (as shown here), and more. The operating system can determine how each core shares access to these resources. If only one core is active, for example, the OS dynamically allocates more of the shared cache to that core.

How Desktop CPUs Keep It Complex

THE CHORES that desktop computers face—putting out a company payroll, rendering blueprints for a new factory—require solving a lot of complex computations. That's why the everyday desktop processors, modeled after Intel's **x86** line, use **complex instruction set computing (CISC)**. It uses complicated, intertwined instructions to bite off manageable problems that it solves and returns to a still-churning solution.

1 Built into a CISC microprocessor's read-only memory is a large set of commands containing several subcommands that must be carried out to complete a single operation, such as multiplying two numbers or moving text. When software makes a demand, the program sends the processor the name of the command along with any other information it needs, such as the locations in RAM of two numbers to be multiplied.

2 Because the CISC commands are not all the same size, the microprocessor checks how many bytes of processing room the command needs and then sets aside that much internal memory. There are also several different ways the commands can be loaded and stored, and the processor must determine the correct way to load and store each of the commands. Both these preliminary tasks add to execution time.

3 The processor sends the command requested by the software to a **decode unit**, which translates the complex command into **microcode**, a series of smaller instructions that are executed by the **nanoprocessor**, which is like a processor within the processor.

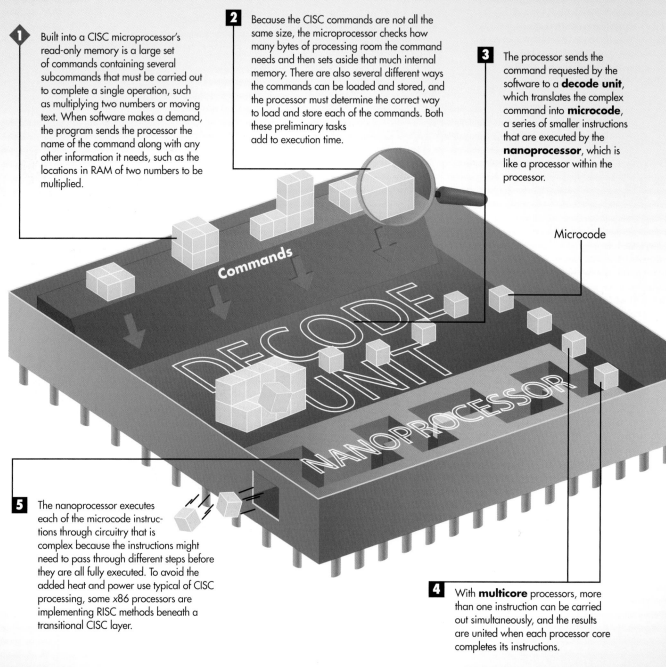

Microcode

Commands

DECODE UNIT

NANOPROCESSOR

5 The nanoprocessor executes each of the microcode instructions through circuitry that is complex because the instructions might need to pass through different steps before they are all fully executed. To avoid the added heat and power use typical of CISC processing, some x86 processors are implementing RISC methods beneath a transitional CISC layer.

4 With **multicore** processors, more than one instruction can be carried out simultaneously, and the results are united when each processor core completes its instructions.

How Mobile CPUs Keep It Simple

THE JOBS that mobile devices take on—dialing a phone number, displaying web pages, playing Angry Birds—are simple as far as computing goes. So they use a simpler system to execute code: **reduced instruction set computing (RISC)**. It deals with instructions that are already broken into chewable pieces, which it quickly gnashes before it spits out the result, using less power and generating less heat in the process. RISC is the basis for the many variants of **ARM architecture** prevalent in 75 percent of mobile products, including everything from tablets to smartphones to digital cameras.

2 All RISC commands are the same size, and there is only one way they can be loaded and stored. Because each command is already a form of microcode, RISC processors don't require the extra step of passing instructions through a decode unit to translate them into simpler microcode. This lets the processor load commands for execution faster than in a CISC processor.

1 Command functions built into an RISC processor consist of several small, discrete instructions that perform only a single job. Apps tell the processor which combination of its smaller commands to execute in order to complete a larger operation.

3 During the compilation of RISC apps, the compiler determines which commands will not depend on the results of other commands. Because these commands don't have to wait on other commands, the processor can simultaneously execute several commands in parallel.

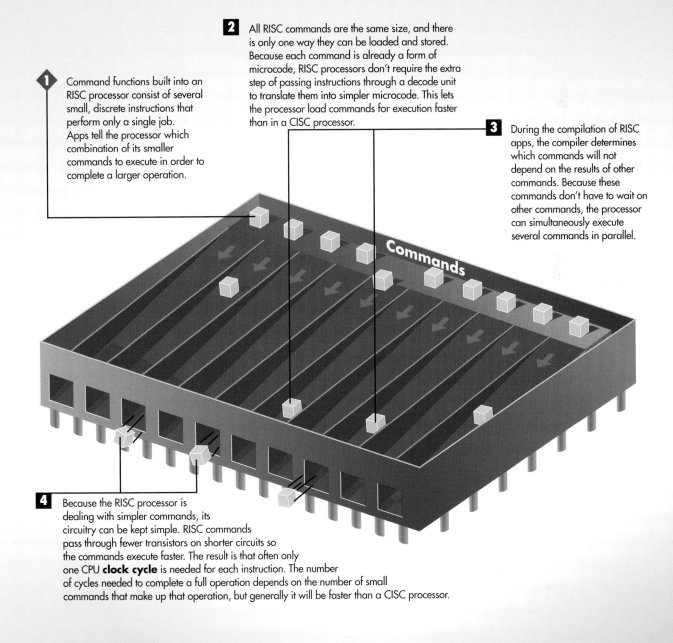

Commands

4 Because the RISC processor is dealing with simpler commands, its circuitry can be kept simple. RISC commands pass through fewer transistors on shorter circuits so the commands execute faster. The result is that often only one CPU **clock cycle** is needed for each instruction. The number of cycles needed to complete a full operation depends on the number of small commands that make up that operation, but generally it will be faster than a CISC processor.

CHAPTER

4

How Motherboards Conduct a Symphony of Data

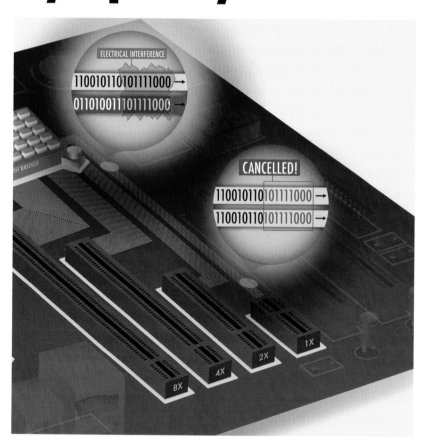

UNDER the big top of your computer—or the little top of your smartphone or tablet—the microprocessor (the central processing unit or CPU) is always the headliner. You don't see ads or reviews raving that a new PC has "revolutionary 100-ohm resistors!" Flash drives and incredibly realistic displays have the top supporting roles, but when it comes to the components on the motherboard—the mother of all boards—the CPU steals the spotlight.

There are many good reasons for the CPU's fame, but like all stars, it owes a lot to the little components—the circuit board supporting parts without which the central microprocessor would be only a cold slab of silicon. And conversely, without the CPU and other specialized processors to keep all the parts running in harmony, the motherboard would be an orchestra without a conductor. Its components wouldn't be able to hear what other members are playing. Electronic messages meant for the CPU would crash into the chips and each other, moving so fast there would be no time to read their license plates. Other messages would arrive like dying murder victims at the ER, so weak they can only whisper their crucial clues in pulses so faint the microprocessor can't understand them. Computing would become a cacophony.

The role of the motherboard was much smaller in the early days of PCs because it was basically a platform for the microprocessor. It was a transportation grid for conveying signals back and forth between the CPU and the parts the CPU controlled—disc controller cards, video cards, sound cards, input/output cards. Back then, nearly everything that made a PC a PC was handled by expansion cards, which was handy because you could easily update a single component as innovation and budget allowed. Today, almost any computer comes with sound, video, disk controllers, and an assortment of input/output options all on the motherboard. Increasingly, some of these functions are now built into the CPU as well, but even then your computer's character is largely determined by the motherboard's capability, and those capabilities are largely defined by the parts that populate it.

Once again, we're in LEGO land. The components that support the motherboard are made up of similar smaller parts divided among themselves in various strengths and concentrations. So here, ladies and gentlemen, are the little parts that make it all possible.

■ Tiny canisters house the circuit board's strong men—the **resistors**! Clad in metal and ceramics, wrapped with colored stripes, they clamp down on the wild, untamed electricity before it has the chance to burn up the rest of the components. They literally take the heat for the rest of the motherboard.

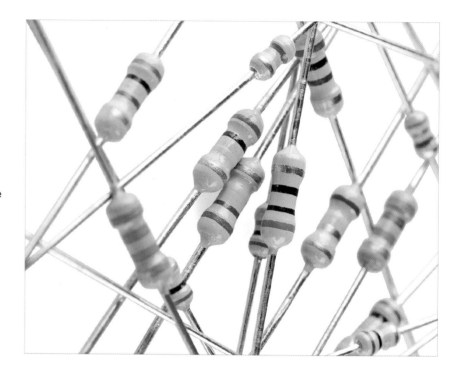

■ Wrapped in ceramic casing and coats of plastic are the voracious, singing **capacitors**! They hum as they consume great quantities of electrical charge, holding it in so other components can have a steady supply or a sudden surge of electricity when they need it.

■ Scattered everywhere on the motherboard are those mysterious, miniature monoliths, the **microchips**! What the millions of transistors do inside them is known to only a few.

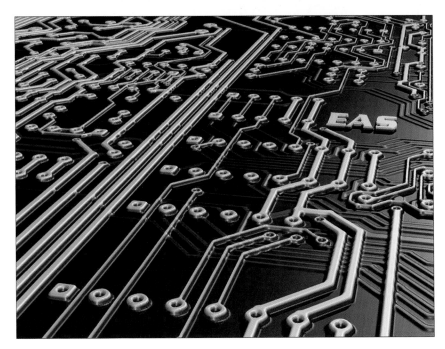

■ And connecting them all are stripes of copper and aluminum, **circuit traces,** that tie it all together so the individual players are a coordinated whole.

How a Motherboard Brings It All Together

Memory Slots: Memory slots usually come two or four to a board and are often color-coded to tell you where to place matching memory cards (called dual-channel). Modern motherboards use memory based on the DDR (double-data rate) technology—DD3 is the current standard and DDR4 is on the horizon.

Power Supply Connections: Your computer's power supply provides power to the motherboard via this connector, and then the motherboard distributes that power as needed to the rest of the system. This basic ATX-style power connector is a mainstay of motherboard design, although it has evolved over time from a 20-pin connector to one using 24 pins.

CPU Socket: This determines what kind of **microprocessor**, or **CPU**, the motherboard uses. The vast majority of boards are designed to work with processors from either **Intel** or **AMD**. Motherboards do not work with all CPUs from the same company. The socket and board are designed for specific lines of microprocessors, with a specific size, shape, and number of pins.

Bus: To send data to any of the other motherboard components—a **write** operation—the microprocessor, or another component, raises the voltages of a combination of 24 of the traces that make up the **address bus**. This combination of traces, or **lines**, is the unique address of something on the **internal bus**, such as a location in memory; one of the components located on the motherboard itself, such as expansion cards inserted in the board's add-in slots; or a device, such as a disk drive on the **external bus**, also called the **expansion bus**.

The processor puts the data it wants to write on a bank of electrical traces, the **data bus**, by raising the voltages on some to represent ones and leaving voltages unchanged on others to represent zeros. Other lines are used to pass **control signals** for common specific commands, such as read and write commands for memory and each input/output device.

The Motherboard: As its name implies, the motherboard is the uniting element among all the chips and circuitry that make up a computer. Devices communicate with each other through the motherboard's circuits, from which they also draw their power. Motherboards come in different **form factors** that align the board with different sizes and styles of computer cases. They also come with different sockets, slots, and connectors that determine what types of gizmos you can use with your computer.

Ports: An **input/output panel** holds the miscellaneous ports on the back and front of the PC that are used for communicating with external devices. Here you find USB connectors, video connectors like DVI and HDMI, eSATA connectors, and a host of audio input/output ports.

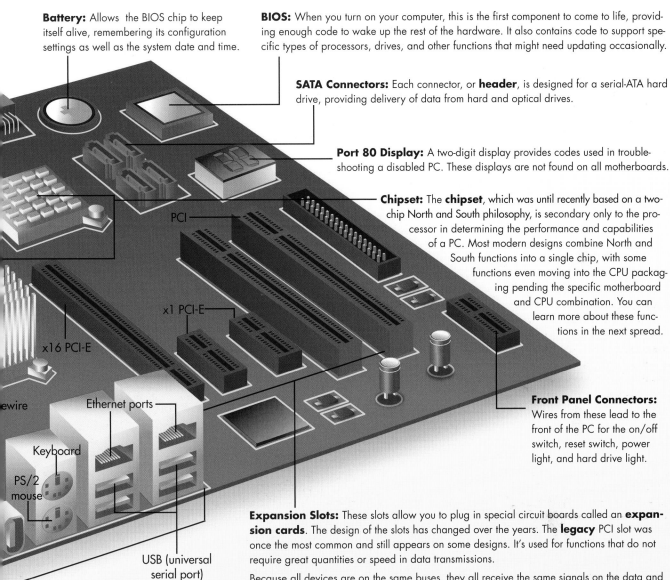

Battery: Allows the BIOS chip to keep itself alive, remembering its configuration settings as well as the system date and time.

BIOS: When you turn on your computer, this is the first component to come to life, providing enough code to wake up the rest of the hardware. It also contains code to support specific types of processors, drives, and other functions that might need updating occasionally.

SATA Connectors: Each connector, or **header**, is designed for a serial-ATA hard drive, providing delivery of data from hard and optical drives.

Port 80 Display: A two-digit display provides codes used in troubleshooting a disabled PC. These displays are not found on all motherboards.

Chipset: The **chipset**, which was until recently based on a two-chip North and South philosophy, is secondary only to the processor in determining the performance and capabilities of a PC. Most modern designs combine North and South functions into a single chip, with some functions even moving into the CPU packaging pending the specific motherboard and CPU combination. You can learn more about these functions in the next spread.

Front Panel Connectors: Wires from these lead to the front of the PC for the on/off switch, reset switch, power light, and hard drive light.

PCI

x1 PCI-E

x16 PCI-E

ewire

Ethernet ports

Keyboard

PS/2 mouse

USB (universal serial port)

Expansion Slots: These slots allow you to plug in special circuit boards called an **expansion cards**. The design of the slots has changed over the years. The **legacy** PCI slot was once the most common and still appears on some designs. It's used for functions that do not require great quantities or speed in data transmissions.

Because all devices are on the same buses, they all receive the same signals on the data and control buses. The memory controller, expansion cards, and other input/output devices along the bus constantly monitor the command lines. When a signal appears on the write command line, for example, all the input/output devices recognize the command. The devices, alerted by the write command, turn their attention to the address lines. If the address specified on those lines is not the address used by a device, it ignores the signals sent on the data lines.

If the signals on the address lines match the address used by the adapter, the adapter accepts the data sent on the address lines and uses that data to complete the write command.

PCI-Express slots are best known for being paired with powerful graphics cards that push video, games, and so on to your computer's display. They come in multiple sizes and are the do-all, fit-all slot for a variety of expansion board types, not just graphics. The shorter ones here are **x1 PCI-E** slots and are common to all PCI Express slots. To handle graphics and sound data faster, the PCI-E slot can be expanded to **x4**, **x8**, or, shown here, **x16** slots, where the numbers represent multiples of the speed of an x1 PCI-E slot. Their ability to move data is indicated by the multiplier factor in their designations.

How the Chipset Directs Traffic

THE PERSONAL COMPUTER has become so complex that even the most recent, powerful processors can't do the entire job of managing the flow of data by themselves. The CPU has been given help in the form of the **chipset**, located nearby on the motherboard. Until recently, the chip traditionally consisted of two microchips, often referred to as the **North Bridge** and the **South Bridge**, that act as the administrators to the CPU, or chief executive. The chipset bridges logical and physical gaps between the CPU and other chips, all the time watching and controlling the input and output of specific components. The exact function of the chipset is constantly changing. The bridges have been put into one chip in most modern designs, and even the CPU packaging now reclaims some functions. But in all cases, the bridges determine what kinds of memory, processors, and other components can work with that particular motherboard. Here, we stick with the conventional North-South distribution because it makes it easier to illustrate all these functions.

1 You can distinguish the North Bridge because it resides as close as possible to three other components that get special attention from the chip: the CPU, the memory, and the graphics port. You wouldn't think that a difference of a couple of inches could matter, but when you're counting in nanoseconds—billionths of a second—even small differences make themselves felt.

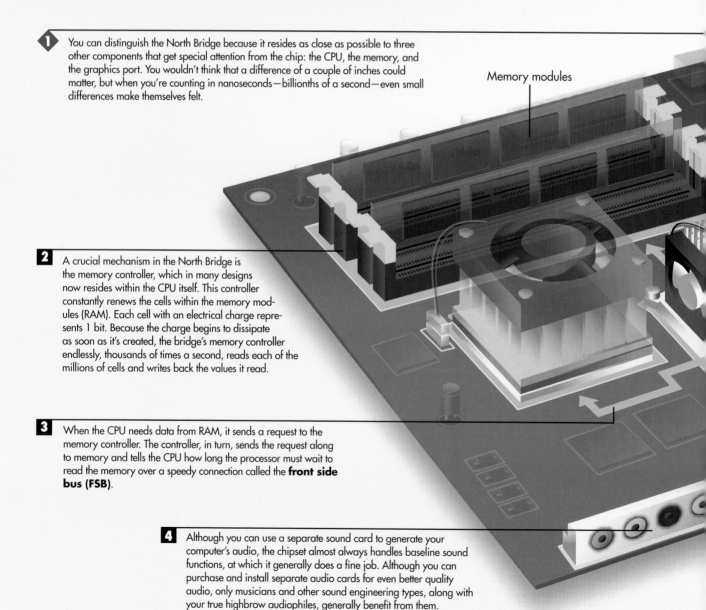

Memory modules

2 A crucial mechanism in the North Bridge is the memory controller, which in many designs now resides within the CPU itself. This controller constantly renews the cells within the memory modules (RAM). Each cell with an electrical charge represents 1 bit. Because the charge begins to dissipate as soon as it's created, the bridge's memory controller endlessly, thousands of times a second, reads each of the millions of cells and writes back the values it read.

3 When the CPU needs data from RAM, it sends a request to the memory controller. The controller, in turn, sends the request along to memory and tells the CPU how long the processor must wait to read the memory over a speedy connection called the **front side bus (FSB)**.

4 Although you can use a separate sound card to generate your computer's audio, the chipset almost always handles baseline sound functions, at which it generally does a fine job. Although you can purchase and install separate audio cards for even better quality audio, only musicians and other sound engineering types, along with your true highbrow audiophiles, generally benefit from them.

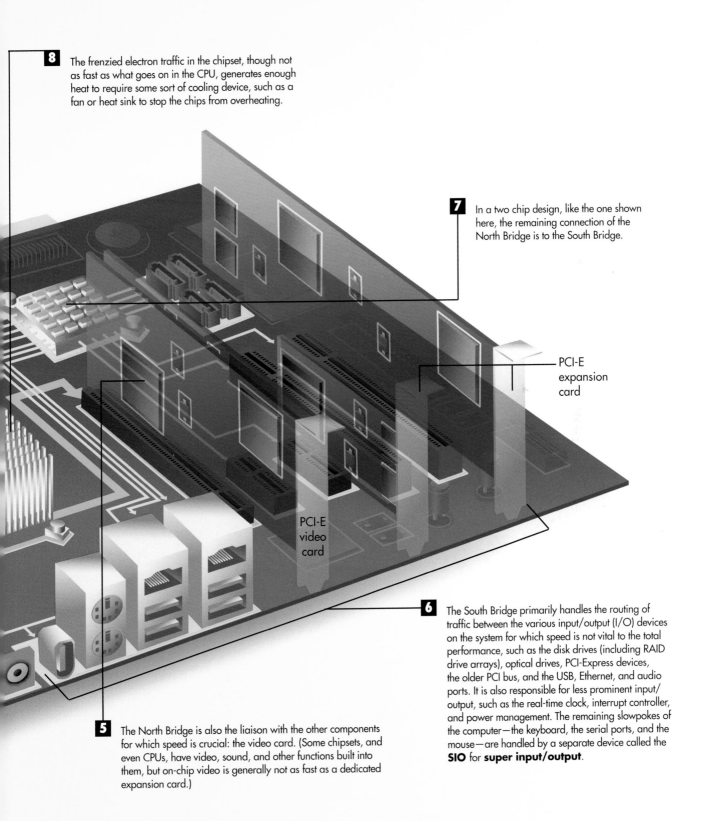

8 The frenzied electron traffic in the chipset, though not as fast as what goes on in the CPU, generates enough heat to require some sort of cooling device, such as a fan or heat sink to stop the chips from overheating.

7 In a two chip design, like the one shown here, the remaining connection of the North Bridge is to the South Bridge.

PCI-E expansion card

PCI-E video card

6 The South Bridge primarily handles the routing of traffic between the various input/output (I/O) devices on the system for which speed is not vital to the total performance, such as the disk drives (including RAID drive arrays), optical drives, PCI-Express devices, the older PCI bus, and the USB, Ethernet, and audio ports. It is also responsible for less prominent input/output, such as the real-time clock, interrupt controller, and power management. The remaining slowpokes of the computer—the keyboard, the serial ports, and the mouse—are handled by a separate device called the **SIO** for **super input/output**.

5 The North Bridge is also the liaison with the other components for which speed is crucial: the video card. (Some chipsets, and even CPUs, have video, sound, and other functions built into them, but on-chip video is generally not as fast as a dedicated expansion card.)

How PCI-Express Breaks the Bus Barrier

APPLICATIONS, such as streaming video and photo editing, put heavy demands on PCs to move vast amounts of data ever quicker. Until recently, our PCs were bogged down as data was trundled among components by outdated **buses**—the **peripheral components interconnect (PCI)** and the **accelerated graphics port (AGP)**. Even the fastest of them, AGP, which spewed out 2.134 gigabytes a second, couldn't keep up with the demands of real-time—photorealistic animation that needs values for the colors of millions of pixels pushed through the circuits 60 times or more each second. The solution is a bus architecture that uses both parallel and serial transfers. It's called **PCI-Express**, or **PCI-E**.

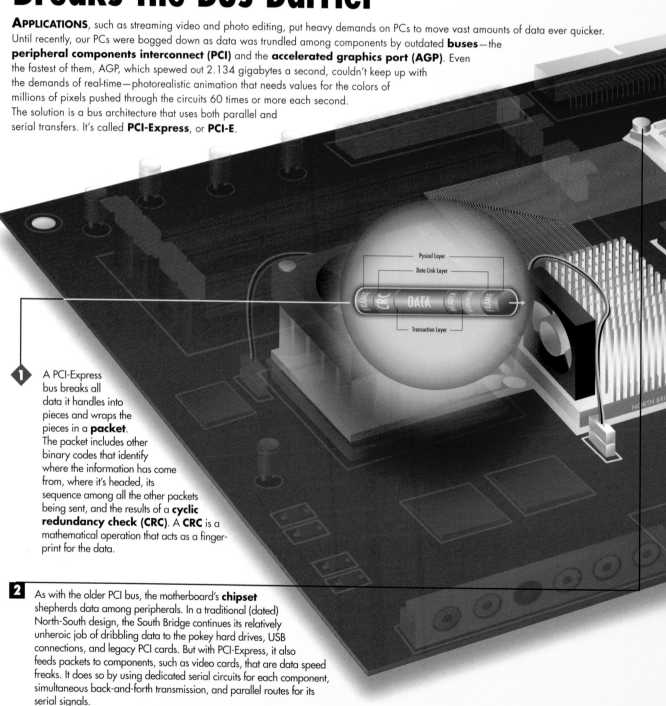

Pysical Layer

Data Link Layer

FRAME CRC DATA HEADER SEQUENCE FRAME

Transaction Layer

NORTH BRIDGE

1 A PCI-Express bus breaks all data it handles into pieces and wraps the pieces in a **packet**. The packet includes other binary codes that identify where the information has come from, where it's headed, its sequence among all the other packets being sent, and the results of a **cyclic redundancy check (CRC)**. A **CRC** is a mathematical operation that acts as a fingerprint for the data.

2 As with the older PCI bus, the motherboard's **chipset** shepherds data among peripherals. In a traditional (dated) North-South design, the South Bridge continues its relatively unheroic job of dribbling data to the pokey hard drives, USB connections, and legacy PCI cards. But with PCI-Express, it also feeds packets to components, such as video cards, that are data speed freaks. It does so by using dedicated serial circuits for each component, simultaneous back-and-forth transmission, and parallel routes for its serial signals.

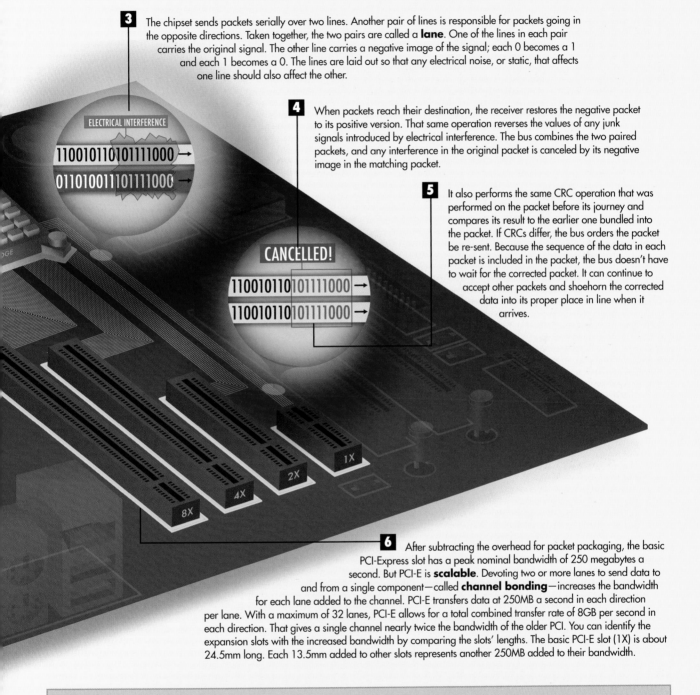

3 The chipset sends packets serially over two lines. Another pair of lines is responsible for packets going in the opposite directions. Taken together, the two pairs are called a **lane**. One of the lines in each pair carries the original signal. The other line carries a negative image of the signal; each 0 becomes a 1 and each 1 becomes a 0. The lines are laid out so that any electrical noise, or static, that affects one line should also affect the other.

ELECTRICAL INTERFERENCE

11001011010101111000 →

01101000111101111000 →

4 When packets reach their destination, the receiver restores the negative packet to its positive version. That same operation reverses the values of any junk signals introduced by electrical interference. The bus combines the two paired packets, and any interference in the original packet is canceled by its negative image in the matching packet.

5 It also performs the same CRC operation that was performed on the packet before its journey and compares its result to the earlier one bundled into the packet. If CRCs differ, the bus orders the packet be re-sent. Because the sequence of the data in each packet is included in the packet, the bus doesn't have to wait for the corrected packet. It can continue to accept other packets and shoehorn the corrected data into its proper place in line when it arrives.

CANCELLED!

11001011010101111000 →

11001011010101111000 →

8X   4X   2X   1X

6 After subtracting the overhead for packet packaging, the basic PCI-Express slot has a peak nominal bandwidth of 250 megabytes a second. But PCI-E is **scalable**. Devoting two or more lanes to send data to and from a single component—called **channel bonding**—increases the bandwidth for each lane added to the channel. PCI-E transfers data at 250MB a second in each direction per lane. With a maximum of 32 lanes, PCI-E allows for a total combined transfer rate of 8GB per second in each direction. That gives a single channel nearly twice the bandwidth of the older PCI. You can identify the expansion slots with the increased bandwidth by comparing the slots' lengths. The basic PCI-E slot (1X) is about 24.5mm long. Each 13.5mm added to other slots represents another 250MB added to their bandwidth.

Goodbye to the Party Line

In the older PCI bus, all the devices share the same parallel circuits and receive the same data. The data includes an identifier that says which device the signals are destined for. All other devices simply ignore them. But like telephone users on a party line, the components can't receive data while some other device monopolizes the connection. The links in PCI-E are **point-to-point**. The chipset uses a **crossbar switch** to route incoming signals from one point to another down circuit lines dedicated to specific components. Data goes to several components at the same time. It's like talking on a private, single-line phone.

29 pixels

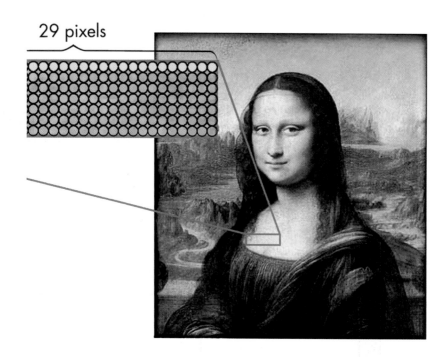

2

Software—The Computer's Own Poetry

Sa-la-ga-doo-la Men-chic-ka Boo-la Bibbidi-Bobbidi-Boo. Put them together and what have you got? Bibbidi-Bobbidi-Boo.

—Walt Disney's Cinderella

CODE IS POETRY

—Tattoo on a programmer's arm

The Language programmers use to create software sounds a lot like the fairy godmother's incantation: *grep, mov, endif, cur_x,* and *selField.* And software really is magical. You invoke your computer—maybe with a touch, at the command of your voice, with the wink of an eye, or by pointing at a little picture with a mouse and clicking—and suddenly all these things begin to happen that could only be witchery. Beautiful color images and voices and sounds emanate from your PC. The software looks at a few numbers and predicts banana futures in three months. Ask your smartphone for information on a person, a country, or a date, and the phone responds like a crystal ball. You ask the software in a tablet to take you high in the clouds over someone's home on the other side of the world, and you're there in seconds—*seconds!* Magic carpets just can't compete.

Software's abracadabra needn't be a mystery to those of us who don't speak VB, Java, C, C++, C#, PHP, and other curiously named software languages. It's its own form of poetry. Within the words are hidden meanings, plots and subplots, forms more rigid than an iambic pentameter. And like a lot of ordinary poetry, it's difficult for the layman to understand it all. We have to turn to the experts—the machines that read software.

You've done just that. Before you bought your desktop PC, your iPad, or your Galaxy 5S, you had used software. Software doesn't include only things like Word, Photoshop, and Angry Birds. Software is also music recordings and Blu-ray discs. Blueprints for building a dog house, a dress pattern, and a telephone number are **programs**. A program is simply any set of instructions for an ordered series of actions. A program can exist as a printout of computer code or as a recipe in a cookbook. And you're already a programmer, even if you've never touched a computer.

Have you created a playlist of the best of Green Day? Have you set your DVR to record every episode of *The Daily Show,* excepting the reruns? Have you entered the phone numbers of your contacts into your phone? Each time, you were programming. A program is simply a recipe, whether for Aunt Hattie's chocolate pie or for how to calculate the paychecks for a thousand employees.

There are, inevitably, layers of nuance. Think of what you do when you use a microwave. You press buttons in a certain order to make the microwave work at a specific power level for a certain length of time, then change to a different power level, and so on until your program produces a steaming hot beef stew. That's programming—a set of instructions in a particular order—created on the fly. But if you press a button that's preset for microwave popcorn, you're using software—a preconfigured set of programming instructions that, in this case, are recorded permanently in a microchip inside the microwave.

Hardware is capable of doing a variety of tasks, but without programming and software to control it, hardware can't do much of anything. By itself, for example, a claw hammer is useful only as a paperweight, but used by a carpenter, it can drive nails, pull out old nails, and even crack walnuts. The carpenter swinging the hammer is programming it on the fly. A home entertainment center is a complex system of hardware capable of generating a variety of sights and sounds, but it can't whisper a peep on its own. It needs software in the form of a disc, or a Roku video streamer, or at least a basic cable connection. The signals from the disc, the network connection, and cable tell the hardware what electrical pulses to use to re-create the sounds of Mahler's Tenth Symphony or the sights of *The Avengers*.

Software of the Second Millennium

If you think of software as a recorded set of instructions that control the actions of a machine, then software's really been around for quite some time. Music notation is written instructions for programming a piano on the fly. But if you have a player piano, the rolls of punched paper are its software. In the 18th century, weaving was done by someone manually slipping a bobbin wrapped with thread over and under other threads on a loom. The process was slow and rife with opportunities for slip-ups. But in 1804, Joseph-Marie Jacquard programmed a weaving loom using a series of **punched cards** that controlled what patterns were woven into a fabric. Different cards resulted in different patterns. Jacquard's invention is considered the birth of modern computer programming, and punch cards were used with computers well into the 20th century. The invention was also the occasion for the first wave of being scared by technology. In 1811, Ned Ludd, a Nottingham weaver who feared the new looms would replace people, led his co-workers in a frenzied attack on the machinery. **Luddite** has come to mean any person who resists technology advancements.

The Jacquard Loom

In 1804, Joseph-Marie Jacquard programmed a weaving loom using a series of punched cards to form patterns in the fabric. Punch cards to enter data and instructions into computers were used well into the 20th century.

Software made little progress for the next century. In 1889, Thomas A. Edison invented the kinetoscope, a hardware device that let people view moving pictures on film. Film, sound recordings, and radio broadcasts—things we don't normally think of as software—are, in fact, just that, and the most prevalent form of software in the first half of the 20th century.

The first computers had neither a keyboard nor a monitor, and they had no software. Their creators programmed instructions by tediously flipping a series of switches in a precise arrangement. This set up a pattern of on and off electrical currents, and the computer in turn activated more electrical switches in the form of vacuum tubes. Finally, the result was displayed in the form of a panel of lights turned off or on to represent the zeroes and ones in the binary number system.

John von Neumann in 1945 first proposed the idea of a general-purpose electronic **digital computer** with a stored program. But the computer, the ENIAC, was not built until 1952. Meanwhile, scientists in England in 1948 created the Manchester Mark I, the first computer that could store a program electronically instead of making programmers set switches manually.

During the next two decades, computers gained such accouterments as keyboards and displays. They used software in the form of punched cards, punched paper tape, and magnetic tape. All those forms of software were awkward and slow to use compared to modern software, but they made life much easier for early programmers.

Not that there were many programmers back then to have easier lives. Some of the earliest writers of software sprang from a model railroad club at MIT. The railroaders used telephone switches to control their complex system of tracks, crossings, and rail switches. In the railroad, they had created a simple and very specialized form of computer. They already thought in terms of switches, the perfect training for writing software.

Most of the software writing then was going on in the universities, military, and businesses that were big enough to afford the then room-filling computers, called **mainframes**. But regardless of where different programs originated, in the 1960s they had one thing in common: They would work only on a specific computer for a specialized purpose. A program that was written, for example, to handle Gizmo Corp.'s payroll was customized specifically to match that company's accounting practices and record keeping, and it would run only on a computer configured like the one at Gizmo Corp. If another company wanted a payroll program, it was written from the ground up again. And if a manager at Gizmo wanted to look at payroll information from a different angle, the entire program had to be altered.

Programs back then had one other thing in common: They were either very expensive or free. Computer companies, such as IBM, saw software as a tool to sell hardware—"**big iron**." Because each program was a custom job—in a discipline that was still finding itself—companies expected to spend thousands of dollars. And compared to a computer that cost millions, a few thousand for software didn't seem so bad.

On the other hand, computer companies didn't charge for an **operating system**—the crucial software that lets a computer run a program that performs specific applications. Think of an operating system as the producer of a movie. The producer doesn't appear on screen. But that person works behind the scenes, hiring writers, directors and actors, finding and paying the hundreds of people responsible for building sets, lighting the scenes, driving stars to locations, and serving lunch—all so that the actors can do their best without having to worry about the hundreds of details that are essential to creating a blockbuster—or a flop.

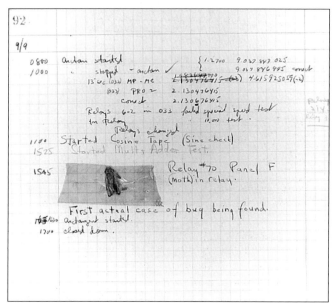

Although a computer bug has come to be associated with faulty software, the bug from which the term derives its name was found in a computer's mechanical relay, causing it to malfunction. It was taped into a logbook by Dr. Grace Hopper.

Early on, programmers routinely swapped their software code with other programmers. Many saw computers as more than business tools. Computers, somehow, were going to be the great equalizer. Information was going to be the next industrial revolution, and computers were going to give Joe Blow access to the same information available to the board of GM. Such idealism, joined with the fact that all programmers were really just in the learning stage, led to a philosophy that all software should be distributed for free. That ideal is still alive today in the open source movement, where powerful operating systems such as Linux are free and users are encouraged to make improvements for all to share.

Gradually, the nature of software changed. Computer companies began unbundling software from hardware. A new working class—the "cowboy," programmer for hire—traveled from company to company customizing programs and then moving on. In the mid-'60s, it occurred to some of these cowboys that they could write one program and sell it to several companies. A new industry was born.

Killer Software

When the personal computer came along, software followed a similar route. The users of the first personal computers—the Altair and the Commodore Pet—were pioneers who expected to do their own programming. They happily shared the coding tricks they learned and the programs they created. A revolution was in the making, although few realized it at the time. All the revolution needed as a spark was the "killer app."

A **killer app** is an application program so useful and popular that it can create a demand for hardware. The first killer application for the personal computer was VisiCalc. An MIT graduate, Dan Bricklen, made one of those connections that changes society. He saw that millions of accountants, business managers, executives, bankers, and stock brokers were wasting their time doing something a computer can do easier and faster: number crunching. Using mechanical adding machines, people were feeding in enormous strings of numbers and crunching them into other numbers. The possibilities for error were great. And the certainty of monotonous labor was greater.

The result of Bricklen's inspiration is the **electronic spreadsheet**, a killer application by definition because it was easily understood—at least by people who work

The first computer program, written in 1948 by Tom Kilburn for the Mark 1, was designed to find the highest proper factor of any number. The necessary divisions were done not by long division but by repeated subtractions. It took 52 minutes to solve the problem for the number 218.

with numbers—and in the time saved, it quickly paid for itself and a computer to run it on. On the monitor of the first truly mass-market computer, an Apple II, VisiCalc looked substantially like a paper ledger sheet. The hapless accountant still had to enter the numbers to be crunched by the computer, but he didn't have to add, subtract, divide, multiply them or do it a second time to check his work. VisiCalc did that according to **formulas**—another type of program—which the computer user types into "cells," those little rectangles created by the grid of a ledger's lines. The formulas, of course, were created by humans, and there was always the possibility of human error. But after you got the formula right, you didn't have to think about it again, and you didn't have to worry about math mistakes. Just as importantly, you had to enter each relevant number only once. If a five percent sales tax was added to each purchase, the spreadsheet user had only to enter it once for VisiCalc to add the correct sales tax for each purchase.

But it wasn't only accuracy, speed, and ease that made VisiCalc so popular. It was also a matter of power, something business people understood even if they had only the vaguest idea of how these new electronic spreadsheets worked. Until VisiCalc, when a business manager wanted information about customers, sales, inventory, or budget, the manager had to send a request to the IS department, which would get around in the next few days to loading a program and data from huge spools of magnetic tape, letting it all churn for a while and then spitting out the information in the form of cards with holes in them or long streams of green-and-white striped paper. Wars have been fought in less time than it took most managers to get a budget projection.

The personal computer changed all that. Within a few minutes, any business person with a passable knowledge of algebra and some fortitude could crunch his own numbers. Knowledge was literally at his fingertips. And in modern commerce, knowledge was valuable. It was power. That power has increased exponentially as people find new and more varied ways to parse huge volumes of data. Facebook, for example, is built on that power.

There was another lesson in VisiCalc. The software market was to become something so volatile, so innovative, and so important that no application remained top killer for long. When the IBM PC debuted in 1981, it could not run the software then available for the Apple. Bricklen's company was slow in creating a version that would run on a PC. Before anyone knew it, the software scene was dominated by a new killer app—one that would run on a PC. The program was Lotus 1-2-3.

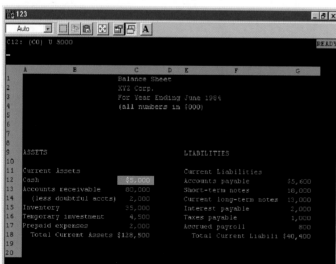

Lotus 1-2-3

Lotus 1-2-3 was the first big business hit on the IBM PC because it combined the functions of an electronic spreadsheet, a database, and graphing. Courtesy of Lotus Corp.

Introduced in 1982, Lotus was, like VisiCalc, an electronic spreadsheet. But it expanded the definition of spreadsheets by adding capabilities for graphing the data in the spreadsheet and manipulating its information the way a database manager does. The use of graphics was particularly impressive for the IBM PC, which was designed basically to display only text. Lotus 1-2-3 justified the buying of IBM PCs and compatibles in many offices. It also revealed the perils at that time of buying IBM clones. 1-2-3 took advantage of some quirks in the IBM PC to speed up performance. But the same quirks weren't duplicated in imitation IBM PCs, with the result that 1-2-3 wouldn't work on some systems. Computer builders were forced to reproduce what they considered flaws in the IBM machine to be sure they could run any software the IBM PC could run.

The 1980s were a decade of explosive growth—and often rapid death—of computer makers and software publishers. Software with eccentric names such as Electric Pencil and Volkswriter, both word processors, quickly expanded the capabilities of PCs. The early success of dBASE II, a database manager, inspired countless other programs with "base" in their names. Inevitably, someone created 4-5-6, which added more features to 1-2-3. Many programs filled in functions PCs were lacking. Peter Norton launched a series of products with Norton Unerase, capitalizing on the fact that the PC's operating system neglected to provide a way to retrieve a file that had been deleted accidentally.

At the same time commercial software was burgeoning into every possible niche, another software movement grew alongside the programs from big corporations. In 1982, Andrew Fluegleman created PC-Talk, a program allowing computer users to communicate over phone lines. Despite the name, you did not use PC-Talk by talking. Conversations were typed, but you could also transfer entire programs from one computer to another. The decisive feature of PC-Talk, however, was the fact you could get it for free, and it established an important category of software: **freeware**.

The first word processing program to make it to stardom was WordStar, a DOS-based text program notorious for shortcut keys, visible codes, hidden tricks, and the fact it could easily be modified.

In the years preceding the Internet, freeware programs were distributed without charge over electronic bulletin boards accessed with a modem and at the meetings of computer clubs called user groups. Often, freeware was totally free. Other **shareware** gave you a chance to try the program risk free, but if you liked the software and continued to use it, you were expected to send some money to its author. At $5 to $40, the suggested prices were still cheap compared to software sold in boxes at stores. Some programmers humbly suggested users send whatever they thought the program was worth. Not unsurprisingly, a lot of people used the programs without paying. But enough people were honorable enough and enough shareware was good enough that at least a few programmers made respectable livings.

The shareware tradition continues today on the World Wide Web, although now programs you download from the Internet are likely to have some features disabled or stop working after a month to encourage users to pay registration fees. Others, usually on mobile platforms like tablets and smartphones, give you free access to core features but force you to pay small **microtransactions** to enable extended functions.

The abundance of software in the early years also meant confusion. Many programmers had idiosyncratic concepts of what software should do and how it should do it. And they found equally idiosyncratic users. WordStar, for example, quickly dominated the word processor market despite a system for formatting documents based on starting lines with a period—hardly an intuitive approach. But WordStar could be modified by anyone with scant programming knowledge, a bit of daring, and a different idea of how a word processor should work.

Power to the Software

The dominating factor in the early software leaders was not that it came out of the box as an ideal product. Instead, programs like WordStar, 1-2-3, dBASE, and WordPerfect could be manipulated by non-programmers. This was the opposite extreme from the days of big iron, when a bright idea for a way to handle information had to be submitted to the computer pros, who would get around to it Real Soon Now. The factor distinguishing software from all the helpful tools invented before it was that software was malleable. You weren't limited to using it as intended. One Lotus 1-2-3 user devised a way to use the number cruncher as a word processor. Users of WordPerfect routinely pressed the word processor's mail merge functions into duty as a database manager.

What really accounted for the popularity of the best software was the empowerment it gave people over computers. The best software came with macro or scripting capabilities that gave a layman user enormous control over this new machine. Macros let you record a series of keystrokes or write a list of simple commands for the software to follow. You made the software work the way you thought it should. You could create your own menus, fill in rows of information with a couple of keystrokes, or make your computer connect to a bulletin board service to download the latest games as you slept. There is a physical, Frankensteinian thrill to creating a macro or writing a script in and watching your computer obey your instructions like a faithful genie.

There was, of course, despair as well as thrill. The truly insane greatness of the '80s was as confusing as it was empowering. There was no master plan, no one person in charge of creating software. This often led to brilliant breakthroughs born of an individual spark of genius. But it also led to a new round of learning with each new program. In some programs, you might display a help screen by pressing Alt+H. Or Ctrl+H, or F7, or F1. It was an industry in desperate need of standards. (1-2-3's F1 came to be accepted by other programs as the standard help key because of 1-2-3's dominance and the universal need for help.)

It wasn't until Microsoft's domination of the operating system—first with MS-DOS and then Windows—did some semblance of order contain the wild garden that software was throughout the 20th century.

Operating Systems And Other Software

There are basically two types of software: **operating systems** and **applications**, regardless of whether your computer is a PC, Mac, iPad, Android tablet, or smartphone (applications are called "apps" in the mobile computing market, but that's just shorthand.)

An operating system is fundamentally different from all other types of software in that an operating system is the one program you *must* have to do anything with your computer. No computers need a word processing program or a spreadsheet or the game *World of Warcraft* just to work. But each computer must have an operating system.

On its own, a computer can do little more when you turn it on than wake up and, like an infant, search for something to feed it. The food of computers is software, and the appetizer is always the operating system. When a computer boots, it only has enough code built into it to look on a disk or in chip memory for a few crucial operating system files. It pulls those into memory, and they in turn load the rest of the operating system. The loaded operating system establishes rules by which the computer can then load other programs and work with hardware that the computer isn't smart enough to handle on its own.

The name for Microsoft's DOS, for example, comes from disk operating system. Originally, DOS was designed as a software tool to create disk files, copy files, delete them, and organize them. All this was done by typing text commands on a black screen. More significantly, DOS let you run other software simply by typing the name of a program. Today Windows, Macs, tablets, and smartphones do the same thing with a click or tap on a tiny cartoon.

If you look at the operating system as an office's mid-level manager then applications are an office's top executives. Like most executives, the applications have a lot of bright ideas but not the slightest clue about how to carry them out. But applications, like executives, have someone to do the real work. Applications give the OS some general, vague instructions—such as "Save this file with the name mybudget." The operating system, in turn, passes more detailed instructions on to the office's clerks, who are the ones who really get their hands dirty. In our little metaphor, the clerks are the computer codes contained in the BIOS, dynamic link libraries, and drivers. These are the people/code who know how the office actually runs—how to record a file or add two numbers.

OS/2

Operating System 2 (OS/2) began in 1983 as a joint project between Microsoft and IBM for high-end computers. Windows would be the operating system for entry-level PCs. Ten years later, the two companies let the joint development agreement expire. Windows and OS/2 competed for the same market, but OS/2 lost the numbers game. For the first time, a computer company other than IBM carried the standard to which other developers conformed.

The Devolution of the OS

If you've been using a PC long enough to know what a DOS prompt is, then you know that MS-DOS wasn't designed to be easy to use. Actually, DOS was only one of two operating systems for the PC. Initially, IBM sold the PC with both Microsoft's DOS and CP/M-86, an upgrade for the 8086 processor of CP/M (Control Program for Microcomputers). CP/M was a down-and-dirty operating system found on several brands of microcomputers at the time. Both DOS and CPM-86 were more concerned with providing a learning path that would be familiar to people who already knew CP/M, the original computer geeks.

Microsoft and other companies realized early on that this shortcoming was a roadblock to more widespread user acceptance, and there were continual attempts on several fronts to improve or replace DOS with an operating system that extends the computer's capabilities and makes it easier to use. Some operating systems, such as GEOS and DR DOS, gained cult followings but never had the market commitment needed to overtake Microsoft's own evolving operating system.

What an operating system needed more than bells and whistles — what it had to have — was the capability to run the thousands of programs that had already been developed under DOS. Software developers were loath to jump on any bandwagon unless they were sure the public would follow. Microsoft had the only working bandwagon in town. Almost.

There was also Apple, which ran on its own proprietary operating system and had a strong, loyal market of students, graphic designers, and iconoclasts. And it had all the pretty little bells and whistles that seemed to make Macs so much easier to use than a computer that required users to memorize command words, along with **switches** — letters or words typed in after the command word to control how a DOS function or an application carries out the command.

Although there was a strong, loyal market for Mac computers the key factor in Apple's success, apart from the charisma of Steve Jobs, was its **graphic user interface (GUI)**, which let users make choices with their mouse by clicking small pictures called **icons**.

Windows 1

In 1985, Microsoft introduced Windows, a graphic interface that let you make selections with a mouse from menus and run more than one program at a time. It was slow, required major memory, and received a universal yawn.

When Microsoft's own attempt at a graphic interface, Windows, first appeared in November 1985, it was slow, crash-prone, and demanded processing and memory resources that were then prohibitively expensive. It used graphics and a mouse pointer to do the jobs that required obscure typed commands in DOS. It was an unimaginative copycat of the Macintosh operating system. Still, Microsoft, better than any competitor, could guarantee that billions of dollars of software and business data already created under DOS would still be usable.

Technically, Windows was at first an "operating environment," window-dressing that hid the fact that DOS continued to do the dirty work behind the curtains. And the dirtiest of them all was running program code that was originally designed for the PC's first processor, which could at best manipulate only 16 bits of data at a time. Many programs written for DOS depended on that 16-bit mechanism even after Intel introduced the 80386, which could process 32 bits of data at once. DOS, and even more recent Windows variants like Windows 95, 98, and Me, had to maintain parts of its own code that handled 16-bit operations. Microsoft did develop a variant of Windows — Windows NT, which became

Windows 2000—that ran only 32-bit instructions. NT was a more stable variation of Windows, and it's steadily evolved into the most common versions of Windows we use today, but at the time it couldn't run older applications designed for older processors.

Despite the deservedly cold reception Windows first received, Microsoft kept revising Windows until, with version 3.1 in June 1992, it had an operating system that, although still far from ideal and still tied down by 16-bit code, was fast enough and stable enough to convince the public and software publishers to hop on.

In 2001, Windows finally made the big step. Microsoft updated its consumer-oriented OS to a fully 32-bit operating system, giving it speed, features, and security equal to that of Windows 2000. Some software creators still had to rewrite their programs to take advantage of the 32-operations, but for programs that clung to their 16-bit ways, Microsoft gave XP a "compatibility mode" that could still run the older programs. By the close of the decade, most of us had migrated to 64-bit versions of Microsoft's operating systems, in Windows 7 and 8, that still maintain all of this backward compatibility while also attempting to bridge the gap to an ever-more-mobile world.

There have been other operating systems, such as Linux, and non-Microsoft programming languages, such as Java, that were not a serious challenge to Windows—more like annoying gnats circling your head. Linux is a version of Unix, a geeky operating system for high-powered computers. Linux has gained popularity as an example of kumbaya software. It is free, and the underlying code is available to anyone. Other programmers are encouraged to make improvements to the code and share them with fellow Linux users. Linux has the idealism found in the earliest programmers who considered selling software for profit the equivalent of crossing over to the Dark Side. Programmers use Java, developed by Sun Microsystems to create nondenominational software. That is, a program written in Java runs on an IBM PC as well as a Mac or a Linux desktop. All those computers have to have is an **interpreter** that looks at each line of code in a program and translates the command in each line into something that computer's OS understands.

Even with such competition, it looked for years as if Microsoft and Windows would continue to rule the marketplace. Other operating systems might have their fiefdoms, but Windows was king.

And then the Internet became emperor.

The Internet created a new space for programs to run, **clouds** to store information, and ways for computers to communicate with each other and tap into vast storehouses of knowledge. Although Microsoft was looking to the big systems as the most likely threat to grind Windows under their heel, it has actually been little guys of computing that have taken over and changed how we use computers.

The little guys actually are little—the **tablet** computers, **smartphones**, which are really just portable computers that you can also use to make phone calls, and wearable computers such as smartwatches, Fitbits, and Google's **Glass**. Apple and Microsoft both have dogs in this fight, but the mutt that has exploded from the pack is an **Android** and it comes from Google.

In this part of the book, you first look at the programming languages that software developers use to create other software. You might never use programming languages, but understanding how a program is created can help explain some of the inexplicable eccentricities of your computer. Then you look at applications and how they do the heavy lifting that lets you run an ever-more-complex life just a little bit more simply.

CHAPTER
5

How Words Are Stitched into Programs

BASIC SOFTWARE

IF EXISTS FILENAME.EX
GOTO BRANCH
FORMAT F:
ECHO ANOTHER
:BRANCH
ECHO THE...

INTERPRETER

VALID COMMANDS

APPEND	GRAFTABL
ASSIGN	GRAPHICS
ATTRIB	HELP
BACKUP	IF
BREAK	JOIN
CALL	KEYB
FORMAT	LABEL
GOTO	LH

OUR most fundamental tool as intelligent beings is language. It is through language that you learn new information and share your knowledge, feelings, and experiences with others. Through language, you can express any thought anyone has ever had and describe any event, real or fictional. The world is controlled through language. Presidents to petty functionaries, generals to GIs, CEOs to clerks—all rely on language to give instructions to others and to gather information.

Language is a necessity for a computer, too. Software is created using special languages that provide instructions for telling the computer what to do. And language defines the data with which the instructions will work. Computer language is similar to human language in many ways. The nouns, verbs, prepositions, and objects found in English, for example, have their counterparts in programming code—or the source code, the actual lines of text that get translated into functioning programs. But software sentences have their own syntax, and the words that make up the languages have their own precise meanings.

Computer language is more exacting and more limited than English. An often-repeated story tells how, in an early attempt to use a computer to translate English into Russian, the phrase "The spirit is willing, but the flesh is weak" was interpreted as "The vodka is ready, but the meat is rotten." The story might be mythical, but it illustrates a reality—that computers and their languages do not do a good job of managing the ambiguities and shades of meaning in human language that any four-year-old understands (although advances in voice recognition have computers understanding what we say, if not what we mean).

If programming languages lack the subtleties of human language, human language cannot match the precision of computer-speak. Try, for example, to describe a simple spiral without using your hands. It's impossible in English. But because math is an integral part of computer languages, those languages cannot only describe a spiral but also can provide the instructions to create an image of that spiral on a display or printer.

Different Programming Languages

Just as there is more than one language for humans, so is there more than one computer language, even for the same type of computer. Generally, the various languages are described as low-level or high-level. The more a computer language resembles ordinary English, the higher its level. Lower-level languages are more difficult to work with, but they usually produce programs that are smaller and faster.

On the lowest level is **machine language**. This is a series of codes, represented by numbers (ones and zeros), used to communicate directly with the internal instructions of the PC's microprocessor. Deciphering machine language code or writing it is as complex a task as one can tackle in computing. Luckily, we don't have to do it. Programs called **interpreters** and **compilers** translate commands written in higher-level languages into machine language. This chapter covers both interpreters and compilers.

On a slightly higher level than machine language is **assembly language**, or simply **assembly**, which uses simple command words to supply step-by-step instructions for the processor to carry out. Assembly language directly manipulates the values contained in those memory scratch pads in the microprocessor called **registers**. In machine language, the hexadecimal code 40 increases by one the value contained in the register named AX; assembly language uses the command INC AX to perform the same function. Although assembly language is more intelligible to humans than machine language codes, assembly is still more difficult to use than higher-level languages. Assembly remains popular among programmers, however, because it creates compact, fast code.

On the high end, languages such as C++ and Java allow programmers to write in words and terms that more closely parallel English. And the programmer using these languages need not be concerned with such minutiae as registers. The C language is powerful and yet reasonably simple to write and understand. Currently, Java is the rising star among languages because a program written in Java runs on any computer no matter what the operating system. This is a distinct advantage when you're writing programs people will use over the Internet, using anything from PCs to Macs and Android portables. Software written in C, in contrast, must be modified to allow a program written for one type of computer to be used on another.

At the highest level are languages such as BASIC (Beginners All-purpose Symbolic Instruction Code), Visual Basic, the DOS batch language, and the macro languages used to automate applications such as Microsoft Office and Corel WordPerfect Office.

Software Construction

A program can be a single file—a record of data or program code saved to a disk drive. But generally, complex software consists of one file that contains a master program—the **kernel**—surrounded by a collection of files that contain subprograms, or **routines**. The kernel **calls** the routines it needs to perform some task, such as display a dialog box or open a file. A routine can also call other routines in the same file, in another file that's part of the program, or in files provided by Windows for common functions. Together, the kernel and subprograms give programs a way to receive, or **input**, information from the keyboard, memory, ports, and files, rules for handling that input data, and a way to send, or **output**, information to the screen, memory, ports, and files.

Typically, when a user types information into a program, it is stored as a **variable**. As the term suggests, the information a variable stores varies from one instance to another. Programs on their own are also capable of storing in variables the information based on the results of a calculation or manipulation of data. For example, to assign the value 3 to a variable X, BASIC uses the command X = 3. Assembly language accomplishes the same thing by assigning the value to the AX register with the command MOV AX,3. Some languages require several commands to achieve the same effect another language accomplishes with a single command.

After a program has information in a variable, it can manipulate it with commands that perform mathematical operations on numbers or parse text strings. **Parsing** is the joining, deletion, or extraction of some of the text characters to use them elsewhere in the program. When a variable is text, it is often called a **string**. You can have math strings, but most often, the term *string* refers to an uninterrupted series of alphanumeric and punctuation characters. Through parsing, a program can locate, for example, the spaces in the name "Phineas T. Fogg"; determine which parts of the string make up the first name, the middle initial, and the last name; and assign each segment to a separate variable. A typical math manipulation would be X = 2 + 2, which results in the variable X having the value 4. If that command is then followed by X = X + 1, the new value of X would be 5. The command X = "New" + " " + "York" assigns the string "New York" to variable X.

Programs can rely on the BIOS (see Chapter 3, "How a Microprocessor Juggles Data") to perform many of the input and output functions—such as recognizing keystrokes, displaying keystrokes onscreen, sending data through the parallel and serial ports, reading and writing to RAM, and reading and writing disk files. The programming language still must have commands to trigger the BIOS services. Consider the following series of BASIC commands:

```
OPEN "FOO" FOR OUTPUT AS #1
    WRITE #1, "This is some text."
    CLOSE #1
```

These commands create a file named FOO that contains the text in quotes: This is some text. It then closes the file. The language Pascal does the same with these commands:

```
Assign (TextVariable, "FOO");
    WriteLn (TextVariable, "This is some text.");
    Close (TextVariable);
```

So far, I've described a fairly straightforward scheme: in, process, out. The reality is more complex. A program must be capable of performing different tasks under different circumstances—a feature that accounts for programming languages' power and versatility. And because a program hardly ever proceeds in a straight line from start to finish, there are commands that tell the computer to **branch** to different parts of the program to execute other commands. In BASIC, the command GOTO causes the execution to move to another part of the program. Assembly language does the same with the command JMP (short for jump).

Branching is used in combination with the **Boolean logic** functions of the programming languages. For example, when a program needs to change what it's doing because a particular condition exists, it can use an "**if... then...**" statement. The program checks to see whether a certain condition is true, and if it is, the program then performs a certain command. For example, if the variable State is the string "Texas," the program uses the abbreviation TX to address a letter.

So you get an idea of how programs are written, this chapter shows you a **flowchart**—a kind of map sometimes used by programmers to lay out the logical connections among different sections of the program code. The example uses a type of game that was popular in the days when text-only adventures like *Zork* were plentiful. In such games, the user types in elementary commands, such as "Go east," "Go north," "Take knife," and "Hit monster." And the game displays a sentence describing the consequences of the player's action. The example is oversimplified and takes into account only one small portion of such a game. As such, it gives you an idea of how many commands and how much programming logic go into even the simplest code. In the example adventure, the player is already on the balcony of a castle turret surrounded by Fire Demons....

How a Program is a Roadmap

Start here. "While" command sets up way to quit game by pressing Esc key.

While key not = Esc, continue game

Variables are set to initial values.

Set variables:
Location = Balcony
Match = False
Cannon = Present
Struck = False
Object = false
Chances Left = 4

Display text on screen:
"You are standing on the balcony of a castle turret. There is a cannon and a match. To the north you see a hoard of Fire Demons approaching. The rail on the east side of the balcony is broken."

Get input from player

First of series of decisions. Command word is compared to list of valid commands: "Go," "Take," "Strike Match," and "Fire Cannon."

Is command word legal?

If command is legal, the program compares it to three of four possibilities: "Go," "Take," "Strike Match." If a possibility matches, flow continues along the "yes" arrow; if not, flow follows the "no" direction to another decision point.

Display text on screen:
"I don't recognize that command. Please try again."

Game loops back if command is not recognized.

Display:
"You took too long. The Fire Demons overpower you and tear you to shreds. Game over."

Is Chances Left = 0?

If Chances Left = 0, game is over.

Is command "Go"?

North?

Display:
"You look over the edge. The Fire Demons are closer."

Is command "Take"?

Is object "match"?

Variable "match" is set to true.

Match = True

Display:
"You have the match."

Test whether player has match.

Is command "Strike match"?

Is match = true?

Variable "Struck" is set to true. Timer routine simulates time it takes match to burn out.

Struck = True start timer

Display:
"The match is burning."

Command = "Fire Cannon"

Because three commands have been eliminated, command must be the only possibility left. "Fire Cannon."

Is match = true?

Display:
"You can't light the cannon without a match."

Chances Left = Chances Left − 1

Subtract 1 from chances left.

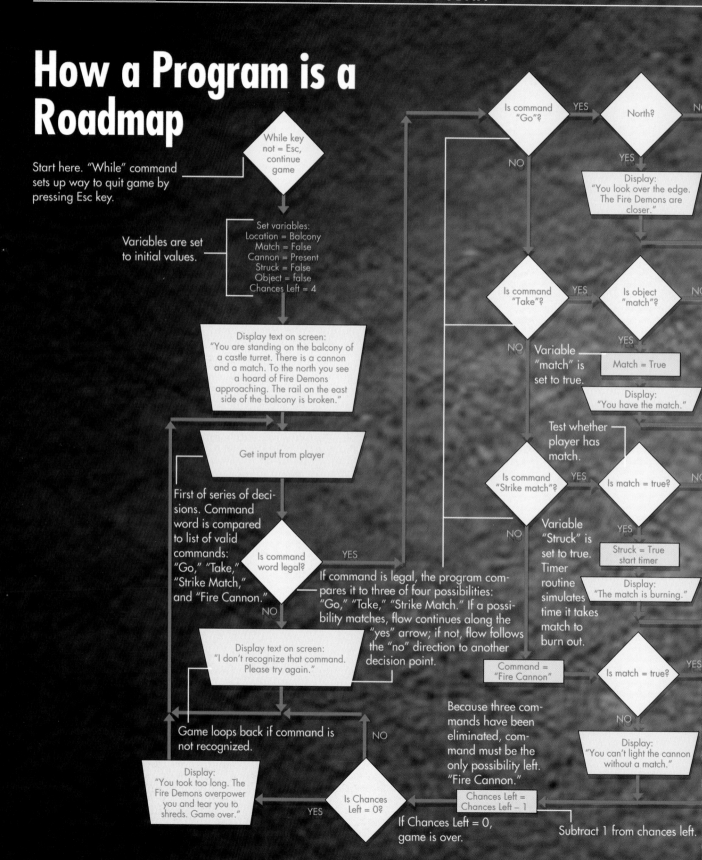

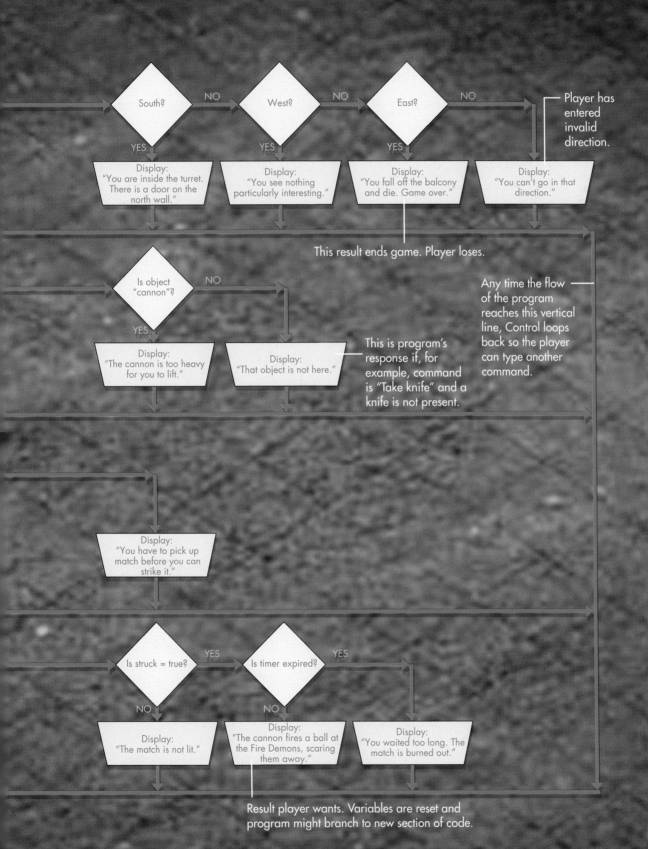

South? — NO → West? — NO → East? — NO → Player has entered invalid direction.

South? YES → Display: "You are inside the turret. There is a door on the north wall."

West? YES → Display: "You see nothing particularly interesting."

East? YES → Display: "You fall off the balcony and die. Game over."

Display: "You can't go in that direction."

This result ends game. Player loses.

Is object "cannon"? — NO →

Any time the flow of the program reaches this vertical line, Control loops back so the player can type another command.

Is object "cannon"? YES → Display: "The cannon is too heavy for you to lift."

Display: "That object is not here."

This is program's response if, for example, command is "Take knife" and a knife is not present.

Display: "You have to pick up match before you can strike it."

Is struck = true? — YES → Is timer expired? — YES →

Is struck = true? NO → Display: "The match is not lit."

Is timer expired? NO → Display: "The cannon fires a ball at the Fire Demons, scaring them away."

Display: "You waited too long. The match is burned out."

Result player wants. Variables are reset and program might branch to new section of code.

How Software Interpreters Generate Action

SOME SOFTWARE LANGUAGES are like world leaders at a global conference. After one of them speaks a sentence or two, everyone must wait while different interpreters translate the leaders' words into the languages each of the listeners understand. If the listeners have a point to raise, those too must go through the interpreters.

Software languages that operate like this are called, not unsurprisingly, **interpreted software**. They require help to get the commands, which are written in **high-level language** that humans can be fluent in, translated into the **low-level machine language** that only a processor can read. **Java**, **Python**, **Ruby**, **HTML**, the venerable **BASIC,** and **scripting** or **batch** languages are interpreted languages. Although interpreted programs do not operate as fast as the **compiled** programs on the next spread, they are more adept at handling data that might not have been available until the program is run. The primary advantage of these programs is that the program's code, written only once, can be used on different types of computers with the aid of an intervening interpreter that converts the code into the machine language needed ultimately for specific hardware, whether it be a desktop, tablet, or smartphone.

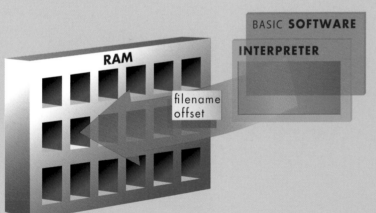

1 When you launch a purely interpreted program, its interpreter, designed particularly for the device it's running on, establishes a small area in memory where it places the name of the program and the current **offset**, a bookmark the interpreter uses to keep track of its place in the code.

2 As the interpreter reads each line of the program, it compares the first word in the line to a list of valid **commands**. It may also store a **variable**, a word, or numbers used to store some temporary data, such as a piece of data or part number that will be referenced later in the program.

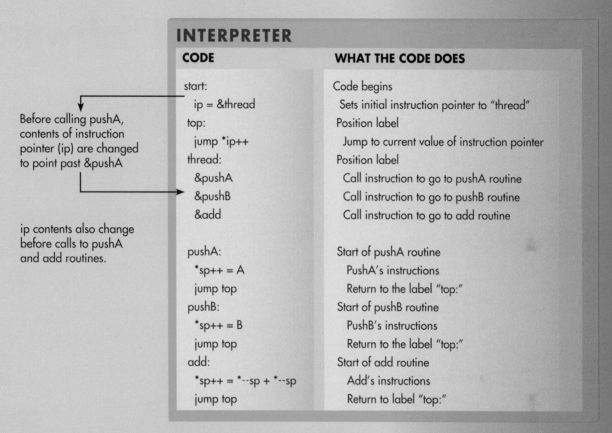

INTERPRETER

CODE	WHAT THE CODE DOES
start:	Code begins
ip = &thread	Sets initial instruction pointer to "thread"
top:	Position label
jump *ip++	Jump to current value of instruction pointer
thread:	Position label
&pushA	Call instruction to go to pushA routine
&pushB	Call instruction to go to pushB routine
&add	Call instruction to go to add routine
pushA:	Start of pushA routine
*sp++ = A	PushA's instructions
jump top	Return to the label "top:"
pushB:	Start of pushB routine
*sp++ = B	PushB's instructions
jump top	Return to the label "top:"
add:	Start of add routine
*sp++ = *--sp + *--sp	Add's instructions
jump top	Return to label "top:"

Before calling pushA, contents of instruction pointer (ip) are changed to point past &pushA

ip contents also change before calls to pushA and add routines.

3 To use less memory in early RAM-strapped computers, programmers devised ways to avoid repeating the same frequently used instructions. Each time an instruction is needed, the interpreter saves an **instruction pointer** that identifies the location in memory where the instruction is stored in the form of a **subroutine call**. The same subroutine may be called at several different points in the code, but the routine itself only needs to be included once.

4 The interpreter uses a **register** to note its current place in the program, and then reads and executes the instruction at the memory location the subroutine call is pointing to. When the instruction is completed, the interpreter returns to executing code at the point where it left off.

5 Some versions of interpreters compile some of the code before sending it to the microprocessor for execution. **Ahead of time compilation (AOT)** translates the original code into **bytecode** for common operations. Then, as its name implies, a **just-in-time compiler** converts the bytecode into the proper machine language for whatever device—PC, smartphone, tablet—that the program is running on.

6 Interpreters use various shortcuts to make the code shorter or faster to execute. A common method creates **tokens** only a single byte long that refer to a **jump or index table** that lists the memory locations to find the data or code the token represents. To make index tables more efficient, some programs use a scheme called **Huffman threading**, which uses tokens of various lengths. The more frequent calls are given the shortened tokens. The method allows conversion of a lot of data into tokens without increasing the size of the code. Token-threaded code is usually half to three-fourths the length of code that doesn't use tokens, which are a quarter to an eighth the size of compiled programs.

How a Compiler Churns out Software

1 The **interpreter** in the previous illustration and a **compiler** are both software programs that translate program source code that humans understand, such as BASIC or C+, into machine language, which computers understand. The difference between a compiler and an interpreter is this: An interpreter translates the source code, line by line, each time the source program is run; a compiler translates the entire source code into an **executable** file that a specific type of computer, such as a PC or Mac, runs without need of an interpreter. Most commercially sold or downloaded programs are compiled.

4 When the lexer finds a string of characters that don't form a reserved word, the lexer assumes that those characters stand for a **variable**. It assigns the variable a place in an **identifier table** that tracks the name and contents of every variable in the program. Then the lexer generates a **variable token** that points to the variable's position in the identifier table. When the lexer finds a string of numeric characters, the lexer converts the string into an integer and produces an **integer token** to stand for it.

5 The result of the lexical analysis is a stream of tokens that represents everything of significance in the program— commands, variables, and numbers.

2 The compiling process begins with a part of the compiler program called a **lexer**. It reads the entire source code one character at a time, and performs a process called **lexical analysis**. As it reads characters, the lexer tries to assemble them into **reserved words**—computer commands—or punctuation characters that it understands. The lexer discards spaces, carriage returns, and remarks included by the programmer to explain what sections of the code are supposed to do.

3 When the lexer comes across a reserved word or punctuation mark, it generates a **code token**. A token is like an abbreviation, representing more information succinctly.

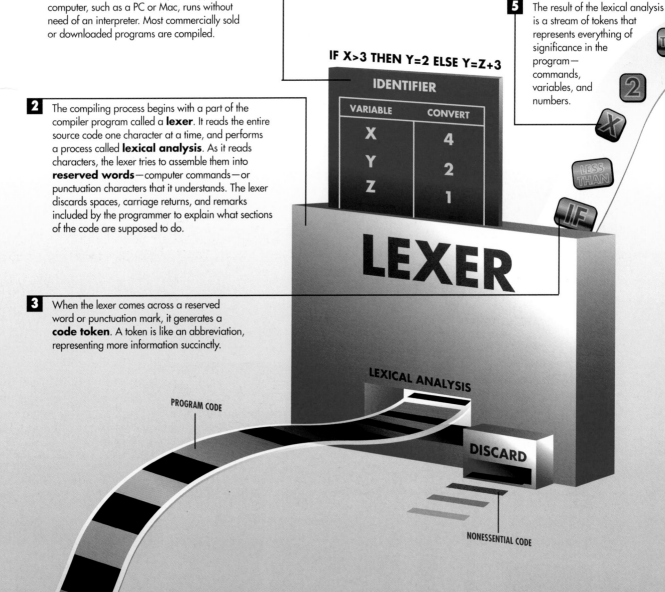

IF X>3 THEN Y=2 ELSE Y=Z+3

IDENTIFIER	
VARIABLE	CONVERT
X	4
Y	2
Z	1

LEXER

LEXICAL ANALYSIS

PROGRAM CODE

DISCARD

NONESSENTIAL CODE

THE

2

X

LESS THAN

IF

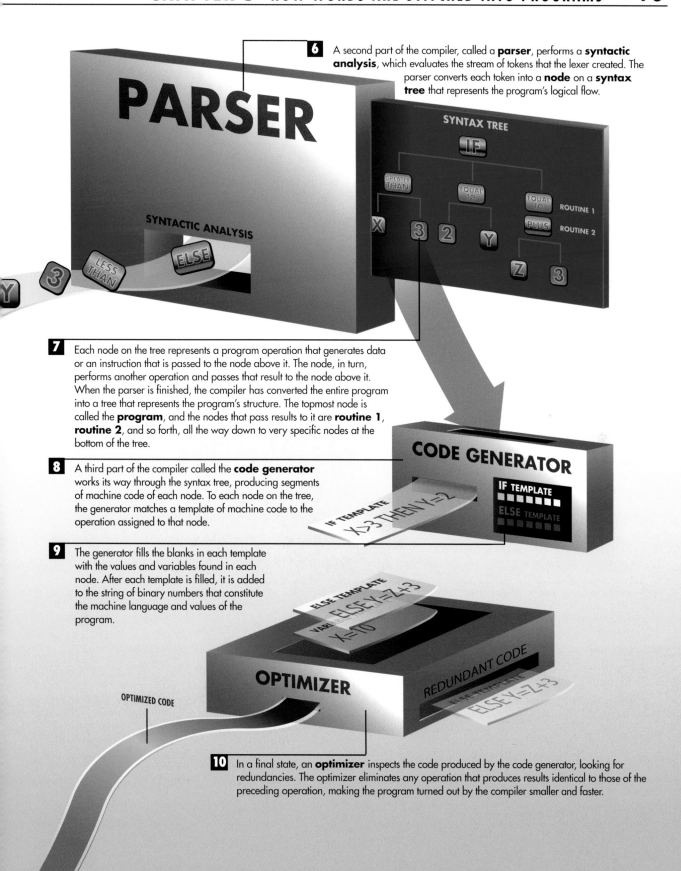

6 A second part of the compiler, called a **parser**, performs a **syntactic analysis**, which evaluates the stream of tokens that the lexer created. The parser converts each token into a **node** on a **syntax tree** that represents the program's logical flow.

SYNTAX TREE

IF

GREATER THAN

EQUAL TO

EQUAL TO   ROUTINE 1

PLUS   ROUTINE 2

X   3   2   Y

Z   3

PARSER

SYNTACTIC ANALYSIS

ELSE

LESS THAN

3

Y

7 Each node on the tree represents a program operation that generates data or an instruction that is passed to the node above it. The node, in turn, performs another operation and passes that result to the node above it. When the parser is finished, the compiler has converted the entire program into a tree that represents the program's structure. The topmost node is called the **program**, and the nodes that pass results to it are **routine 1**, **routine 2**, and so forth, all the way down to very specific nodes at the bottom of the tree.

8 A third part of the compiler called the **code generator** works its way through the syntax tree, producing segments of machine code of each node. To each node on the tree, the generator matches a template of machine code to the operation assigned to that node.

CODE GENERATOR

IF TEMPLATE

ELSE TEMPLATE

IF TEMPLATE
X>3 THEN Y=2

9 The generator fills the blanks in each template with the values and variables found in each node. After each template is filled, it is added to the string of binary numbers that constitute the machine language and values of the program.

ELSE TEMPLATE
ELSE Y=Z+3

VARI
X=10

OPTIMIZER

REDUNDANT CODE

ELSE TEMPLATE
ELSE Y=Z+3

OPTIMIZED CODE

10 In a final state, an **optimizer** inspects the code produced by the code generator, looking for redundancies. The optimizer eliminates any operation that produces results identical to those of the preceding operation, making the program turned out by the compiler smaller and faster.

CHAPTER

6

How Applications Work So You Can Play

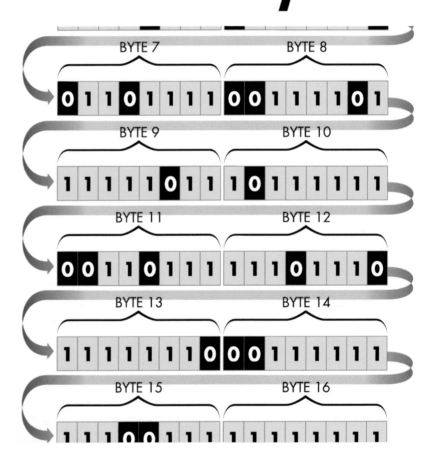

WHETHER you use a desktop, a laptop, a tablet, or even a smartwatch, the quick definition of an application—or **app**, if you prefer—is this: It's everything except the operating system. Windows, OS X, UNIX, iOS, Android, and other operating systems exist only so you can run applications. The long definition of apps encompasses everything from first-person shooter games such as *Bioshock: Infinite,* to the most strait-laced accounting program, to that app on your phone that tells you how many steps you've taken today.

The lines between the operating system and apps have grown increasingly blurry in recent years, but there are still applications whose power and scope exceed anything that could be packed into an operating system. In fact, if a job involves information, there's a program out there that will handle it.

What all software has in common is **data**. Data can appear in the form of stock prices, addresses, money, dates, statistics, phone numbers, recipes, probabilities, dots of color, pages of text, notes of music, the number of lives left in a game, positions in a virtual world, or your longitude and latitude on Earth. Data are raw facts. Names are data, and so are the letters that make up the word "names." Even computer code is considered data (which means data is manipulating data, a line of thought that is perilous to pursue). And all data are numbers, even if they're words or colors.

Computerdom has, by mutual consent, agreed on a standard called **ANSI (American National Standards Institute)**. In ANSI, each letter of the alphabet, punctuation, numbers, and even an empty space is assigned an 8-bit binary number. Eight bits is enough to represent all the decimal numbers between 0 and 255. A capital "A" is 65. A capital "B" is 66. A lowercase "b" is 98. An @ symbol is 64. $ is 36. ? is 63. 1 is 49, and 49 is 52 followed by 57. (Another path better left untrampled.)

All sounds can be expressed in numbers in the form of frequencies, amplitudes, and decibels. Your PC displays the colors on your screen by resorting to some combination of red, blue, and green—the only pure colors a display can create. With only 256 values representing 256 shades each of red, blue, and green, your monitor can produce more colors than most eyes can distinguish.

No matter what kind of data you feed into a computer, the PC ultimately sees it only as numbers, strings of zeroes and ones written with transistors in the microchips of your motherboard. The decimal numbers of ANSI are converted to binary. A capital "A" becomes 01000001. A lowercase "b" is 01100010. After you master the concept that virtually anything can be represented as some collection of numbers—especially binary numbers—you have a good concept of what computing is made of.

Data, alone, though, is not really helpful. For example, 2.439, King Arthur, green tells you nothing. It is not yet information. What software does is make data useful; it processes the data into information. No one program can process all kinds of data. Different raw data must be processed differently. Generally, software falls into one of these categories: database management, word processing, number crunching, graphics, multimedia, communications, or utilities.

How Text SHOUTS and *Whispers*

IN A MULTIMEDIA WORLD of music and video bathing us from when we wake up to an iPod until we nod off watching 70-inch HDTV screens, what could possibly be more boring than Courier? `This is Courier, the typeface that was the only choice on a century of typewriters.` It's serviceable, to be sure. But we're past serviceable. These days we want our words to zing, ring, and sing. And they can by using the typographical formatting available on any form of computing. Here are the three ways most of it is done.

In-line Formatting

The oldest form of formatting, still used in WordPerfect and web pages, places invisible formatting **tokens** in the middle of words or sentences to change font, attributes such as bold and lightface, type size, or even to hide it from view. WordPerfect has a function to reveal those codes, and the first paragraph on this page as originally written looks like this:

Styles

A shortcut used by in-line formatting and programs such as Microsoft Word, on the facing page, is **styles**. A style is a collection of formatting attributes that a writer uses all together. By including font, size, attributes, line spacing, and other formatting in a collection, which is given a name, all that formatting can be applied at once by selecting that style from a menu. Styles also make it easy to change a look throughout a document by editing the contents of the style, which is then applied wherever the style is used.

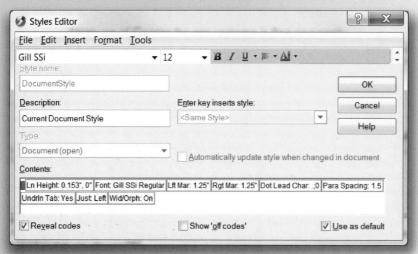

Text Mapping

With a computer you can delete, insert, move, and rewrite words right up until a deadline. But when, for example, you move a paragraph to a different page, it's really not moved. Computing files are made up of one continuous string of bits. Taking out bits one place to insert somewhere else would require rewriting the entire file. Instead, text editors make a record of the places in the file affected by the changes and write any new, moved, or inserted text to the end of the file along with a **marker** that says where each belongs. When it's time to print, the software follows this map to put all the text in the right order.

Word's Way with Words

1 Microsoft Word uses a collection of tables to track all formatting information. One table tracks section properties, such as headers that appear at the top of each page, tab settings, and whether the page orientation is *portrait* (vertical) or *landscape* (horizontal).

2 A second table tracks the formatting properties applied to paragraphs, such as the margin settings, first-line indentations, and line spacing.

3 A third table tracks formatting properties applied to individual characters, such as typeface and size, boldfacing, italicizing, and underlining.

4 Pointers in the section, paragraph, and character tables lead to the sections of text where one or more of the attributes should be used.

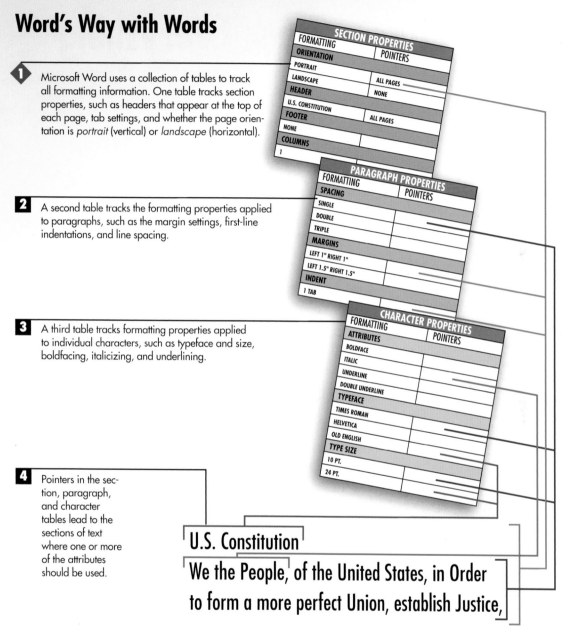

SECTION PROPERTIES

FORMATTING	
ORIENTATION	**POINTERS**
PORTRAIT	
LANDSCAPE	ALL PAGES
HEADER	NONE
U.S. CONSTITUTION	
FOOTER	ALL PAGES
NONE	
COLUMNS	
1	

PARAGRAPH PROPERTIES

FORMATTING	
SPACING	**POINTERS**
SINGLE	
DOUBLE	
TRIPLE	
MARGINS	
LEFT 1" RIGHT 1"	
LEFT 1.5" RIGHT 1.5"	
INDENT	
1 TAB	

CHARACTER PROPERTIES

FORMATTING	
ATTRIBUTES	**POINTERS**
BOLDFACE	
ITALIC	
UNDERLINE	
DOUBLE UNDERLINE	
TYPEFACE	
TIMES ROMAN	
HELVETICA	
OLD ENGLISH	
TYPE SIZE	
10 PT.	
24 PT.	

U.S. Constitution

We the People, of the United States, in Order to form a more perfect Union, establish Justice,

𝔘.𝔖. Constituti...

We the People, of the United States, in O... to form a more perfect Union, establi...

U.S. Constitution

We the People, of the United States, in Order to form a more perfect Union, establish Justice,

5 As you type or scroll through a document, the word processor reads more text and formatting codes from RAM and sends its own commands to Windows, which passes them to the **display driver**, a collection of codes for controlling your specific display adapter card. Finally, the card sends to the monitor the electrical signals that turn on and off pixels as needed to display text, graphics, or any other part of the document. When the word processor sends text to be printed, a printer driver performs a similar function to translate text and formatting into the patterns of dots created by all printers, whether dot matrix, ink-jet, or laser.

How Databases Track Everything

NO MATTER whether your device of choice is a PC, tablet, smartphone, or smart glasses, you use database software many times a day. Spelling checkers store the correct spellings in a database. It takes a database to keep track of the number of hits you've sustained in your favorite shooter. Even Twitter and Facebook records of your friends and followers are databases. Databases work silently, mostly behind the scenes, but without them, we might as well use our computers to print out sticky notes. Here's how a database manages more information than you'll acquire in a lifetime.

Fixed-Length Field Records

1 Most database information is stored in **fixed-length fields**, so called because the number of characters—spaces—that can be used for each field is determined when the database is created. The beginning of a fixed-length field file contains information that defines the file's **record structure**—each field's name, **data type** (usually numeric or alphanumeric), and length. In addition, the structure might include information on the format of the data held in the field; for example, a field used to record dates might require the MM-DD-YY (month-day-year) format.

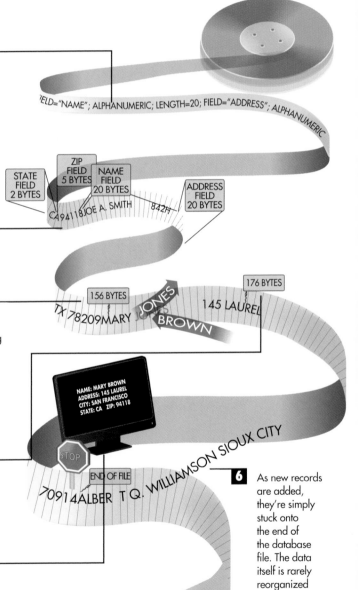

2 The rest of the file is data, laid down in one continuous stream. The locations at which specific pieces of data are recorded are determined by the lengths allotted to each field.

3 To find any given record, the database software calculates the location's **offset** through a simple formula: The number of a particular record multiplied by the total length of each record equals the starting point of that record. With the starting point calculated, the program reads the bytes beginning at that point in the file.

4 To locate fields *within* each record, the program follows a similar process of calculating the number of bytes in the fields preceding the field it wants to find, and then reads bytes at the field's starting point.

5 To **modify** an existing record, the database software reads the record into variables it creates in the computer's RAM and lets you modify the information in these variables through an onscreen form. The software then writes the new contents of these variables to the database file.

6 As new records are added, they're simply stuck onto the end of the database file. The data itself is rarely reorganized or sorted in the file in any way. For that, the software uses **indexes**.

Variable-Length Field Records

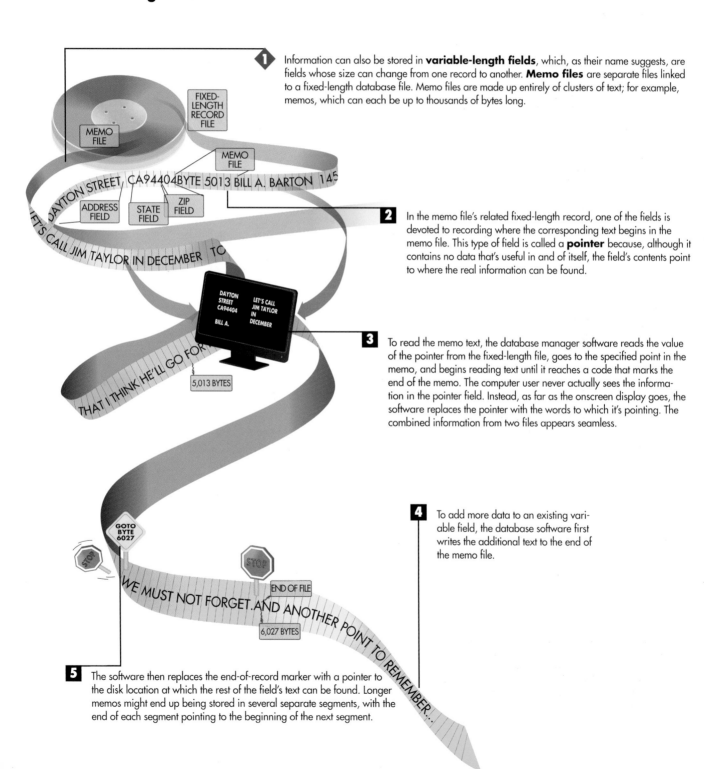

1 Information can also be stored in **variable-length fields**, which, as their name suggests, are fields whose size can change from one record to another. **Memo files** are separate files linked to a fixed-length database file. Memo files are made up entirely of clusters of text; for example, memos, which can each be up to thousands of bytes long.

2 In the memo file's related fixed-length record, one of the fields is devoted to recording where the corresponding text begins in the memo file. This type of field is called a **pointer** because, although it contains no data that's useful in and of itself, the field's contents point to where the real information can be found.

3 To read the memo text, the database manager software reads the value of the pointer from the fixed-length file, goes to the specified point in the memo, and begins reading text until it reaches a code that marks the end of the memo. The computer user never actually sees the information in the pointer field. Instead, as far as the onscreen display goes, the software replaces the pointer with the words to which it's pointing. The combined information from two files appears seamless.

4 To add more data to an existing variable field, the database software first writes the additional text to the end of the memo file.

5 The software then replaces the end-of-record marker with a pointer to the disk location at which the rest of the field's text can be found. Longer memos might end up being stored in several separate segments, with the end of each segment pointing to the beginning of the next segment.

How Databases Pack it In

1 To index records, the database manager first requires you to tell it on which of the fields the index is to be based. This field is called the **key field**. Some databases can have more than one index and more than one key field.

BOOKS TABLE			
NO.	TITLE	AUTHOR KEY FIELD	PRICE
1	A FAREWELL TO ARMS	HEMINGWAY	10.95
2	THE GREAT GATSBY	FITZGERALD	12.88
3	HOW COMPUTERS WORK	WHITE	29.95
4	THE OLD MAN & THE SEA	HEMINGWAY	9.99
5	WORLD ACCORDING TO GARP	IRVING	20.95
6			

2 The database manager reads each record and constructs a temporary file consisting of the values contained in each record's key field and corresponding pointers that give the location of each record in the database file. If duplicate values are found, each duplicate entry is recorded in the index file.

TEMPORARY FILE	RECORD NOS.
AUTHOR	1, 4, 8, 12, 15
HEMINGWAY	2, 6, 20, 94
FITZGERALD	3
WHITE	5, 10, 33, 61
IRVING	

3 After the database program has read all the values and their pointers, or record numbers, into the temporary file, it arranges the copied values in alphanumeric order, creating an *index*.

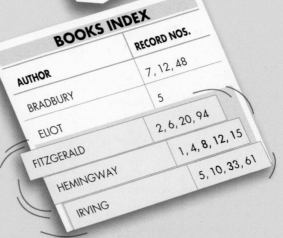

BOOKS INDEX	RECORD NOS.
AUTHOR	7, 12, 48
BRADBURY	5
ELIOT	2, 6, 20, 94
FITZGERALD	1, 4, 8, 12, 15
HEMINGWAY	5, 10, 33, 61
IRVING	

4 The database writes the ordered information to an index file that is structured as a binary tree. The binary tree, or b-tree, is designed to speed up the process of finding information in the index file. It's an upside-down tree in which each node has two branches. These branches break logical divisions of the index file into increasingly smaller halves. For example, A–M represents one of the first two branches of the tree and N–Z represents the other main branch. A b-tree search lets a database search a million-entry index by checking only 20 sets of nodes rather than each of the one million nodes.

5 When the database manager needs to find records based on the key field, it checks successive branches of the b-tree. If the manager is looking for records whose key fields begin with an I, for example, the manager starts by looking down the main trunk of the tree, where it finds key-field values beginning with A–M.

6 Because I comes before M in the alphabet, the manager next looks at the key-field values halfway between A and M. There, it finds values beginning with G. I comes after G, so the manager looks halfway between G and M, and so on, until it finds values beginning with I.

7 Eventually, the manager arrives at an end node—the leaf, so to speak—which contains a short, fixed number of entries (eight or so, depending on the program) and their pointers. It finds the entry it has been looking for and uses the pointer to locate the actual record in the database table.

8 To re-index the database after new records have been added to the database, the program puts each new index entry into a blank space under the proper "leaf" in the index's b-tree.

9 If there's no room under the leaf, the software creates two new nodes under what had been the last node. For example, an L node would be divided into an LA–LK node and an LL–LZ node, each of which would receive roughly half of the parent node's information.

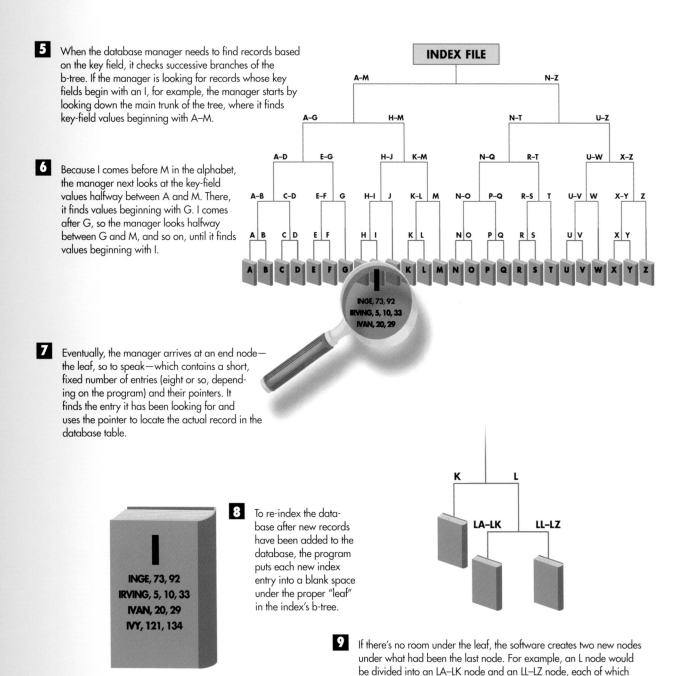

INDEX FILE

INGE, 73, 92
IRVING, 5, 10, 33
IVAN, 20, 29

INGE, 73, 92
IRVING, 5, 10, 33
IVAN, 20, 29
IVY, 121, 134

K   L

LA–LK   LL–LZ

How Databases Make Connections

1 Imagine moving to a new city and filling out a single form that automatically updates information about your new address and phone number on your driver's license, in the phone book, all your subscriptions, your bank records—everyone you deal with. That's the concept behind a **relational database**. It separates information into **tables** that share each other's data. A change of information in any one of the tables is picked up by any other table that needs it. A relational database is designed so that most information must be entered only once, and yet it can be used by more than one table of data.

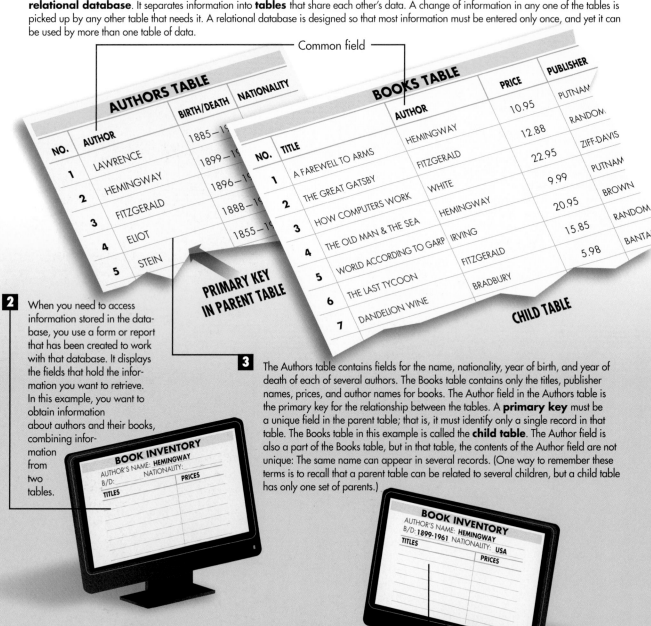

2 When you need to access information stored in the database, you use a form or report that has been created to work with that database. It displays the fields that hold the information you want to retrieve. In this example, you want to obtain information about authors and their books, combining information from two tables.

3 The Authors table contains fields for the name, nationality, year of birth, and year of death of each of several authors. The Books table contains only the titles, publisher names, prices, and author names for books. The Author field in the Authors table is the primary key for the relationship between the tables. A **primary key** must be a unique field in the parent table; that is, it must identify only a single record in that table. The Books table in this example is called the **child table**. The Author field is also a part of the Books table, but in that table, the contents of the Author field are not unique: The same name can appear in several records. (One way to remember these terms is to recall that a parent table can be related to several children, but a child table has only one set of parents.)

4 The **form** for this example specifies several fields from the Authors table, so the software finds that table, pulls out the contents of those fields for the current record, and displays them onscreen.

5 The database manager then goes to the index of the Books table to find all the records with "Hemingway" in the Author field. It uses the pointers of those index entries to locate the right records in the Books table, and then it pulls out the requested fields and displays those onscreen. When you switch to a new record in the Author table (for example, Fitzgerald), the software displays that information from the Author table, and then goes back to find all the records in the Books table that have Author fields matching the new record.

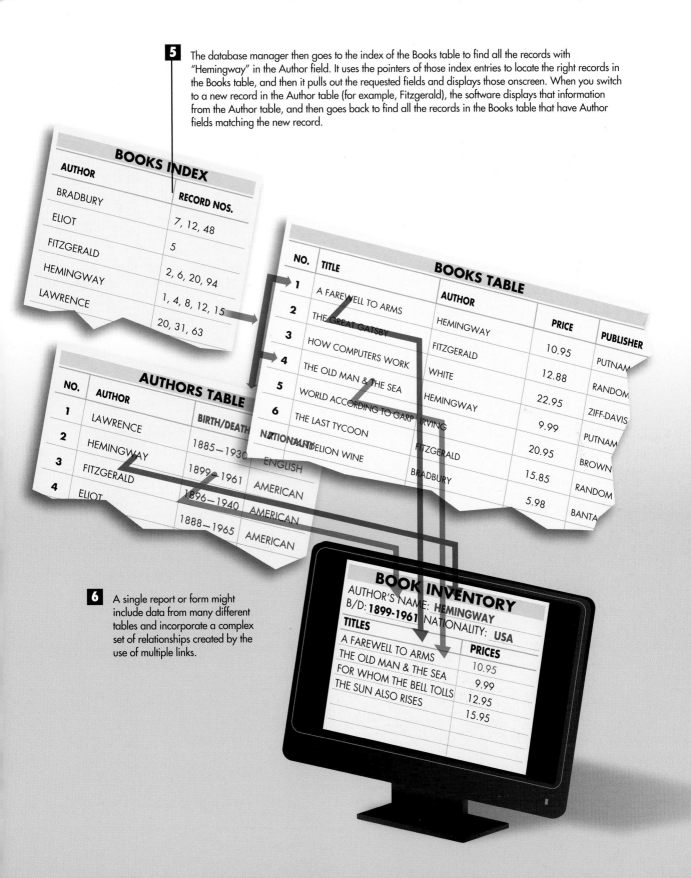

BOOKS INDEX

AUTHOR	RECORD NOS.
BRADBURY	
ELIOT	7, 12, 48
FITZGERALD	5
HEMINGWAY	2, 6, 20, 94
LAWRENCE	1, 4, 8, 12, 15
	20, 31, 63

AUTHORS TABLE

NO.	AUTHOR	BIRTH/DEATH	NATIONALITY
1	LAWRENCE		ENGLISH
2	HEMINGWAY	1885–1930	AMERICAN
3	FITZGERALD	1899–1961	AMERICAN
4	ELIOT	1896–1940	AMERICAN
		1888–1965	AMERICAN

BOOKS TABLE

NO.	TITLE	AUTHOR	PRICE	PUBLISHER
1	A FAREWELL TO ARMS	HEMINGWAY		PUTNAM
2	THE GREAT GATSBY	FITZGERALD	10.95	RANDOM
3	HOW COMPUTERS WORK	WHITE	12.88	ZIFF-DAVIS
4	THE OLD MAN & THE SEA	HEMINGWAY	22.95	PUTNAM
5	WORLD ACCORDING TO GARP	IRVING	9.99	BROWN
6	THE LAST TYCOON	FITZGERALD	20.95	RANDOM
	DANDELION WINE	BRADBURY	15.85	BANTA
			5.98	

6 A single report or form might include data from many different tables and incorporate a complex set of relationships created by the use of multiple links.

BOOK INVENTORY

AUTHOR'S NAME: **HEMINGWAY**
B/D: **1899-1961** NATIONALITY: USA

TITLES	PRICES
A FAREWELL TO ARMS	
THE OLD MAN & THE SEA	10.95
FOR WHOM THE BELL TOLLS	9.99
THE SUN ALSO RISES	12.95
	15.95

How Spreadsheets Solve Formulas

1 When you type a formula into a cell, the spreadsheet processes the formula through a **minicompiler** that converts the function names into a more efficient, tokenized format, in which functions are represented by specific numbers. For example, functions such as SIN and COS are converted into specific byte values the spreadsheet recognizes as meaning sine or cosine. The compiler also stores the formulas in **reverse Polish notation**, so that, for example, (3 + 2) * 10 becomes 3 2 + 10 *. This type of notation is more efficient in terms of both space and speed.

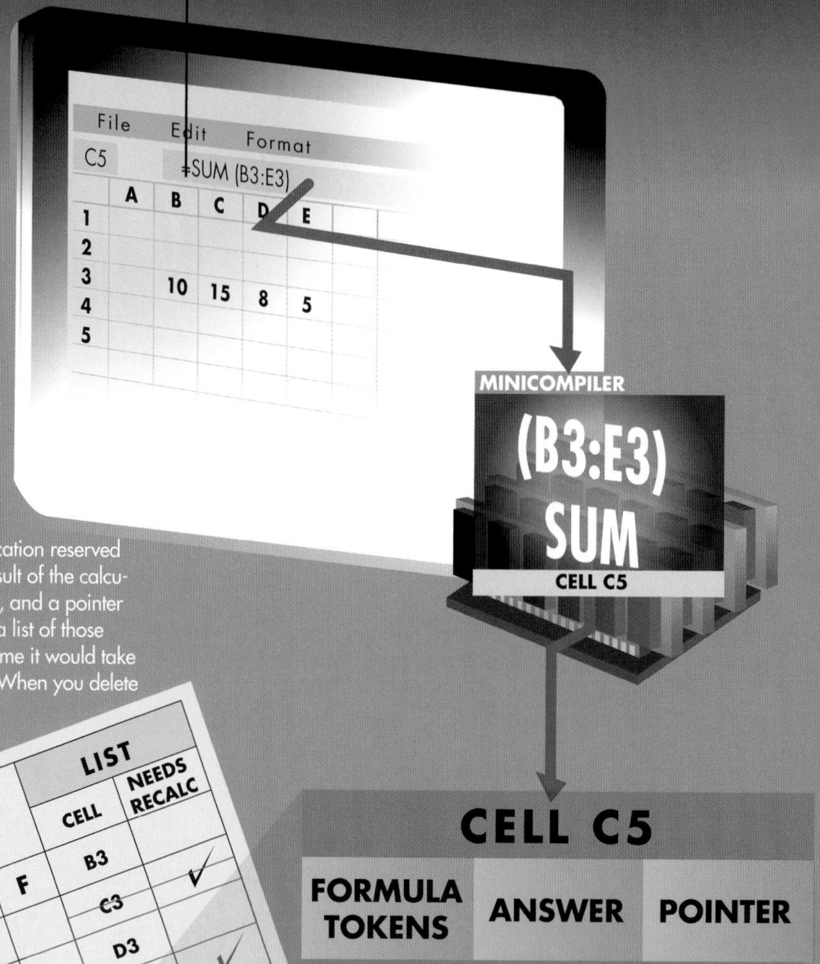

File	Edit	Format

| C5 | =SUM (B3:E3) |

	A	B	C	D	E	
1						
2						
3		10	15	8	5	
4						
5						

MINICOMPILER

(B3:E3)
SUM
CELL C5

2 The result of the compilation is written to a memory location reserved for that cell. The location also includes room for the result of the calculation, a pointer to the next formula in the spreadsheet, and a pointer to the previous formula. The pointers create, in effect, a list of those cells that contain formulas and save the program the time it would take to search every cell for formulas during recalculation. When you delete one formula, its pointer to a previous formula is used to reconnect the formula chain.

LIST

CELL	NEEDS RECALC
B3	✓
C3	
D3	✓
E3	✓
C5	
C6	
D6	✓
E6	

CELL C5

FORMULA TOKENS	ANSWER	POINTER

3 When the spreadsheet is recalculated, the program saves work and time by making a first pass through the list created by the pointers of cells that contain formulas. It finds those formulas that depend on data that has changed, and marks each one that needs to be recalculated.

4 The program then makes a second pass through the list, this time paying attention to only the formulas marked for recalculation. For each, the spreadsheet determines whether that formula depends on another formula that hasn't been recalculated yet. If so, it adjusts the cell's pointers and the pointers of connected cells so that the dependent formula moves to the end of the list. (This process pays off the next time the spreadsheet is recalculated—the program won't have to change the pointers again.) If the formula doesn't depend on any other formulas or if the formulas on which it depends have already been recalculated, the software recalculates the cell immediately.

	A	B	C	D	E	F	LIST	
							CELL	NEEDS RECALC
1							B3	
2							C3	
3							D3	✔
4							E3	
5							C5	✔
6							C6	✔
7							D6	
							E6	✔

CALCULATION ENGINE

E3

D3 3

C3 B3

SUM

ANSWER: 38

5 To calculate a formula, the spreadsheet software feeds the data the formula and the formula codes requested into a **calculation engine** that generates the answer and writes it to the part of memory allocated to hold information for that cell.

6 The spreadsheet then moves to the next formula and repeats the process until it ends by finally calculating those formulas (earlier placed at the end of the list) that are dependent on other formulas.

ANSWER: 38

7 In some spreadsheet programs, such as Excel, the software updates each cell onscreen as soon as it has been calculated. Other spreadsheets wait until the whole spreadsheet has been recalculated before updating the display.

Auto Recalc

Unless you specifically disabled it, a spreadsheet's automatic recalc feature automatically updates every time you make a change that affects any formula. How does it do this? When you create a formula, the spreadsheet software marks all the cells on which that formula depends by changing a notation in each of their records. In addition, it leaves itself hints in those cells about how to find the formulas that depend on them, a more efficient method than using pointers. When you make a change to any cell that's been marked in this way, the software finds the formula or formulas that are affected and recalculates them.

	A	B	C	D	E
File	Edit	Format			
C5		=SUM (B3:E3)			
1					
2					
3		10	15	8	5
4					
5			38		

How Numbers Become Pictures

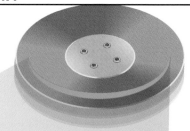

1 When your PC, smartphone, or tablet displays an image, it must first look at information contained in the file's *header*, which is several bytes at the beginning of the file that contain information the program needs to interpret the data in the rest of the file. The header begins with a **signature** that identifies the file as a bitmap. You don't see this signature, but you can tell that a file is a bitmap if it has an extension such as .BMP, .PNG, .TIF, or .JPG. Following the signature, the header tells the width and height of the image in **pixels**, which are distinct points of light, and then defines the *palette* (how many and which colors are used in the image).

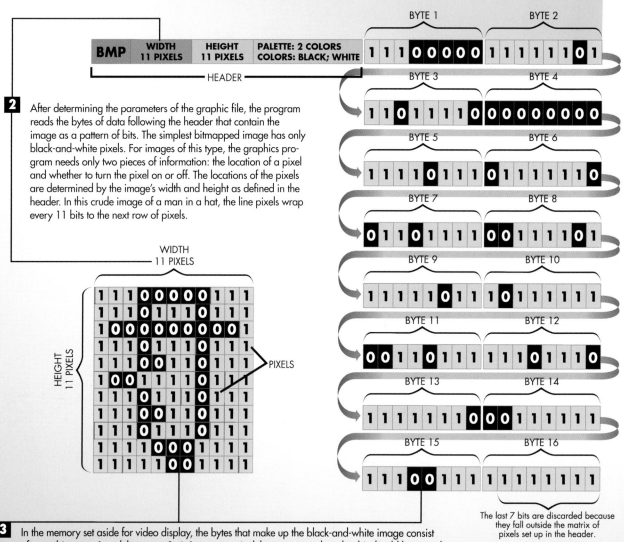

2 After determining the parameters of the graphic file, the program reads the bytes of data following the header that contain the image as a pattern of bits. The simplest bitmapped image has only black-and-white pixels. For images of this type, the graphics program needs only two pieces of information: the location of a pixel and whether to turn the pixel on or off. The locations of the pixels are determined by the image's width and height as defined in the header. In this crude image of a man in a hat, the line pixels wrap every 11 bits to the next row of pixels.

The last 7 bits are discarded because they fall outside the matrix of pixels set up in the header.

3 In the memory set aside for video display, the bytes that make up the black-and-white image consist of some bits set to 1 and the rest to 0. A 1 means a pixel that corresponds to that bit should be turned on. A 0 bit indicates a pixel should be turned off. The man in the hat consists of 121 pixels, which in a black-and-white image can be stored in 16 bytes.

4 A color bitmap requires more than 1 bit of information for each pixel. Eight bits (or 1 byte) per pixel are enough data to define a palette of 256 colors because 8 bits of binary information has a total of 28 possible values, or 256. (The values shown here are in *hexadecimal*, a BASE-16 number system that uses A–F as well as 0–9.) Each possible 8-bit value is matched in the palette to a specific combination of red, blue, and green dots that make up a single pixel. Although the dots of color are separate, they're close enough to each other that the eye sees them as a single point of blended color, called a **virtual pixel**.

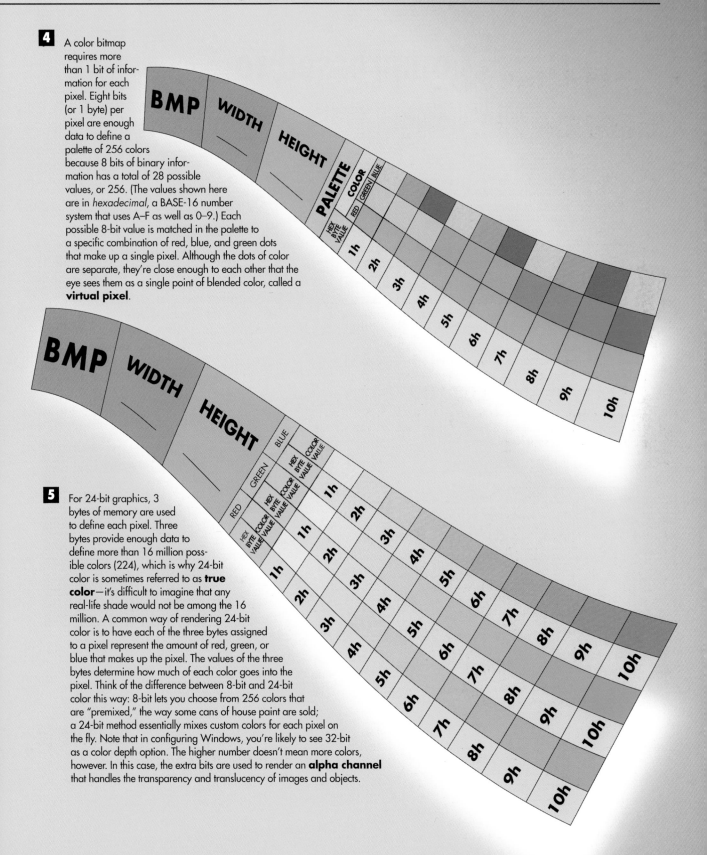

5 For 24-bit graphics, 3 bytes of memory are used to define each pixel. Three bytes provide enough data to define more than 16 million possible colors (224), which is why 24-bit color is sometimes referred to as **true color**—it's difficult to imagine that any real-life shade would not be among the 16 million. A common way of rendering 24-bit color is to have each of the three bytes assigned to a pixel represent the amount of red, green, or blue that makes up the pixel. The values of the three bytes determine how much of each color goes into the pixel. Think of the difference between 8-bit and 24-bit color this way: 8-bit lets you choose from 256 colors that are "premixed," the way some cans of house paint are sold; a 24-bit method essentially mixes custom colors for each pixel on the fly. Note that in configuring Windows, you're likely to see 32-bit as a color depth option. The higher number doesn't mean more colors, however. In this case, the extra bits are used to render an **alpha channel** that handles the transparency and translucency of images and objects.

How Art Is Compressed to Save Space

1 Because bitmap files can get extremely big, some image file formats have built-in compression, called **run-length encoding (RLE)**, that shrinks the data in the files to take up less room on disk. RLE takes advantage of the fact that, in many images, large stretches of pixels are exactly the same. RLE works by using something called a **key byte**, which tells the software whether the next byte represents several pixels or only one. The software checks the first bit of the key byte. If it's a 1, the software reads the value of the remaining 7 bits in the byte—we'll call the value *N*—and interprets the values of the next N bytes as color combinations for individual, consecutive pixels. At the end of the N bytes, there is another key byte.

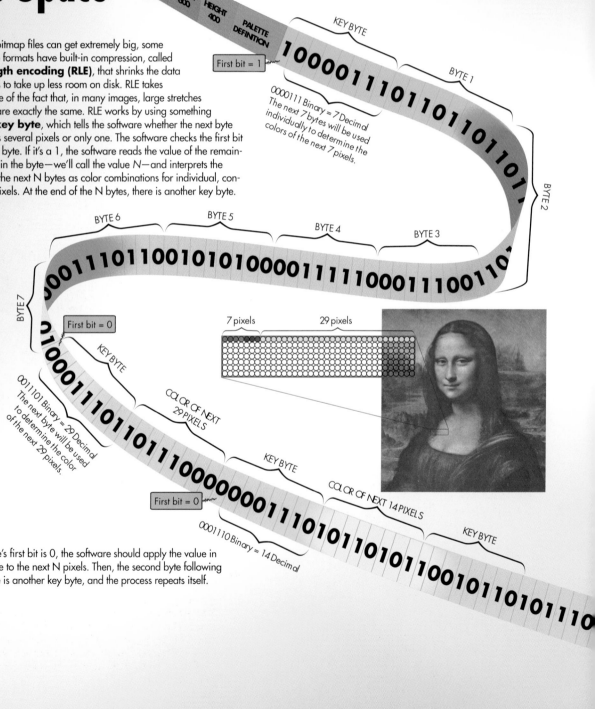

BMP WIDTH 600 HEIGHT 400 PALETTE DEFINITION

First bit = 1

KEY BYTE

BYTE 1

BYTE 2

1000011101101101011

0000111 Binary = 7 Decimal
The next 7 bytes will be used individually to determine the colors of the next 7 pixels.

BYTE 6 BYTE 5 BYTE 4 BYTE 3

00011101100101010000111110001110011

BYTE 7

First bit = 0

KEY BYTE

010001110110110111100000000111010

0011101 Binary = 29 Decimal
The next byte will be used to determine the color of the next 29 pixels.

7 pixels   29 pixels

COLOR OF NEXT 29 PIXELS

KEY BYTE

First bit = 0

COLOR OF NEXT 14 PIXELS

0001110 Binary = 14 Decimal

KEY BYTE

1101011001011010110

2 If a key byte's first bit is 0, the software should apply the value in the next byte to the next N pixels. Then, the second byte following the key byte is another key byte, and the process repeats itself.

BEFORE JPEG COMPRESSION

AFTER JPEG COMPRESSION

3 Software, in a camera or computer, that compresses a file in the JPEG format examines the file for pixels whose absence is unlikely to be noticed by the uncritical human eye. More accurately, it's not their absence that's overlooked; it's the fact that they've been disguised to look like neighboring pixels. If half of the area of a landscape photograph is devoted to a cloudless sky, saving the color values of each of the pixels making up the sky is an extravagance when many of the pixels are exactly the same shade and intensity of blue.

4 Rather than recording the 24 bits needed to describe each pixel, the compression software records the bits for only one—the **reference pixel**—and then writes a list of the locations of every pixel that is the same color.

5 For more drastic compression, another trick is to divide an image into 8-by-8 pixel blocks and calculate the average color among the 64 pixels in that block. If none of the pixels are too different from the average, the compression changes the colors of all the pixels to the average; your eye is none the wiser.

Banding

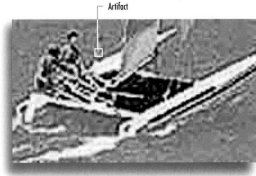

Artifact

6 A problem with JPEG compression has been that a photo is recompressed—with more original pixels thrown away—each time it is resaved to the JPEG format. If it's saved too many times, you increase the appearance of unnatural **banding**—obvious strips of color instead of smooth gradations as you see, for example, in the sky. It also causes **artifacts**—shapes and colors that weren't in the original photo and are solely the product of mathematics. Eventually the photo may come to look **posterized**, so named after posters that have been simplified by using only a few colors.

7 A more recent form of JPEG, called **JPEG 2000**—using a **.jp2** or **.j2k** file extension—compresses photos by using **wavelet** technology, a type of mathematical calculation that transforms pixel values into strings of numerical **tokens** for frequently recurring combinations of pixels, such as combinations of red and blue pixels that might be used to create a brown tree trunk. The strings replace the cruder blocks of JPEG compression and result in smaller files without the same types of visual artifacts seen in standard JPEG photos.

How Imaging Software Paints by Numbers

The humongous advantage of using numbers to represent images is that you can lighten or darken an image, bring out contrast, sharpen or blur it, turn it upside down, or transform it into a psychedelic abstract, all by using simple arithmetic. It's not so simple that you can sit at a computer with the *Mona Lisa* on the screen and subtract numbers from the color values in Mona's portrait, turning her smile into a frown. It would be an excruciating job, the kind of job computers are made for. A PC can calculate a frown job on Mona in less than 10 seconds. It's all just a numbers game.

 Your digital camera records your digital photo as a set of tiny pixels. As you look closer at a photo, you begin to see the pixels as jagged edges and then squares. What you thought were distinct lines and boundaries turn out to be more gradual transitions between colors.

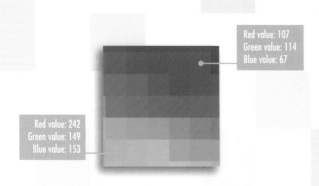

Red value: 107
Green value: 114
Blue value: 67

Red value: 242
Green value: 149
Blue value: 153

2 Zoom in far enough and you see that each pixel is actually a tiny square consisting of a single, solid color.

3 When you tell your image-editing software to make a change, such as to sharpen, brighten, or apply effects, the software looks at the differences in color between pixels. Often, it compares those values with pixels that are close but not touching the pixels under scrutiny.

SHARPEN FILTER

4 The software applies a mathematical formula to recalculate the color of each pixel. It starts with the formula for the type of editing or effect you are asking it to do. It also takes into account the differences in color between pixels, often those in or near transition areas.

5 Not all pixels are changed equally. Some pixels might retain the same general color but take on a slightly darker or lighter tone. Other pixels might be assigned a very different color. Pixels that are not near a border area might not be changed at all.

How Photo Editors Revive Old Memories

COLOR PHOTOS are subject to the same slings and arrows of outrageous shoe boxes that torment black-and-white pictures—the dirt, the creases, the spills, the humidity, and of course the fatal reactions that occur when the still-active chemicals of one photograph are crammed up against those of another picture for a decade or so. But the chemicals in color photos are still more volatile and more susceptible to turning the only picture of beloved Uncle Ernie into what looks like an extra-terrestrial blob of protoplasm. Luckily for all the myriad misfortunes that can affect photos, we have an arsenal of E.R. weaponry to bring them back from the brink. There are so many tools in the digital dark-room, there's no space to cover them all in detail, but here are some of the most common devices available in programs such as Photoshop, Elements, and Paint Shop Pro to bring color—the right color—back to the cheeks of fading ancestors.

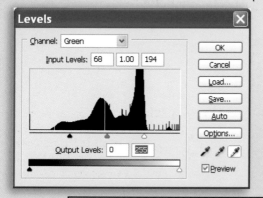

Levels (histograms) is the most versatile of several methods to isolate and tame discolorations that have taken over the photograph.

Levels dialog box:
- Channel: Green
- Input Levels: 68 1.00 194
- OK
- Cancel
- Load...
- Save...
- Auto
- Options...
- Output Levels: 0 255
- Preview

Burn and **Dodge** duplicate the techniques of the old chemical darkroom so the retoucher can darken and lighten specific portions of the photo.

Healing brush repairs numerous dust spots, scratches, and assorted and unexplained flaws by duplicating the pixels surrounding the damage so they cover the defects seamlessly.

Selection tool isolates the mother and baby so they can be worked on without affecting the background. The selection can also be reversed to work on the background without worrying that touch-ups will spill over onto the mother and child.

Layers provide a way of working on a duplicate of the photograph within the same file and then controlling how changes are blended into the original picture. Two duplicate layers of the washed-out image that emerged from color changes were *multiplied* to increase the contrast and color depth of the photo.

Gradient tool fills a sky that has lost all hint of color, permitting the blue to fade as it approaches the horizon.

Airbrush brings out clouds that have been submerged by the blue gradient. The airbrush also adds a hint of eyeballs that have been lost entirely in the shadows of the mother's eyes.

Cloning tool covers bigger and more complex flaws by copying, through a sort of artistic wormhole, good portions of the photo to replace flawed areas with the same control you have using a brush. Here, some of the dark trees on the right were replaced with light trees from the left of the photo.

Variations are used as a final touch so the retoucher is able to see and choose from a selection of thumbnail versions of the same photograph in which hues and brightness are slightly varied. This enables the retoucher to see, at a glance, which variation produces the most pleasing result.

Sharpen tool restores definition to edges that have become blurred through fading or by the retouching itself.

How Apps Fuel Mobile Devices

THE APPS that run on your mobile devices are the smaller off-spring of **applications**, which have had their heyday on the big desktop computers and laptops. But there are differences:

- **Apps are cheap.** You could spend hundreds of dollars for Windows or Mac applications, but mobile apps are at most a few bucks or, as often as not, free. Some are ad-driven, some make up the difference in micro transactions, and others are functionally more limited than their desktop counterparts.

- **There are a heck of a lot of them.** As I'm writing this, a study by New Fossil had found there are 1.5 million apps in the Apple App Store and Android's Google Play. On average, each of the more than two billion smartphones in the world run an average of 42 of these apps. Of course, with this many apps it should come as no surprise that one in four apps is abandoned after the first use and more than 60 percent of apps at the Apple Store are never even downloaded.

- **They're a heck of a lot of fun.** Apps are not made to manage all of L.A.'s traffic lights, detect cancers, or manage a space station. There are plenty of useful productivity apps out there, but they're generally for a single, dedicated purpose. Still more are, for the most part, intended for enjoyment—watching movies, listening to music, social networking, and game playing. When you consider that the processing power, storage capacity, and RAM in any mobile device is dwarfed by a cheap desktop PC from the last century, it's a wonder they perform as well as they do. Here's their secret: There's a big computer behind the curtain pulling the strings.

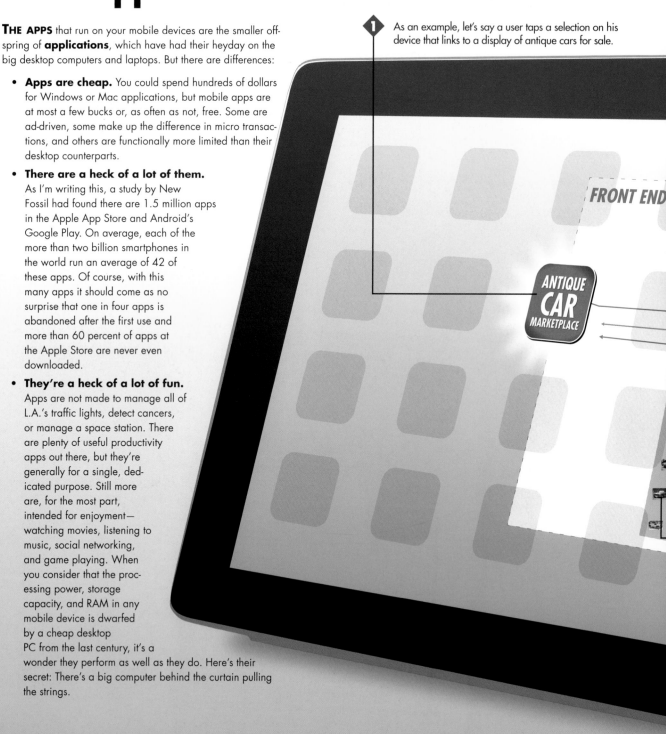

1 As an example, let's say a user taps a selection on his device that links to a display of antique cars for sale.

FRONT END

ANTIQUE CAR MARKETPLACE

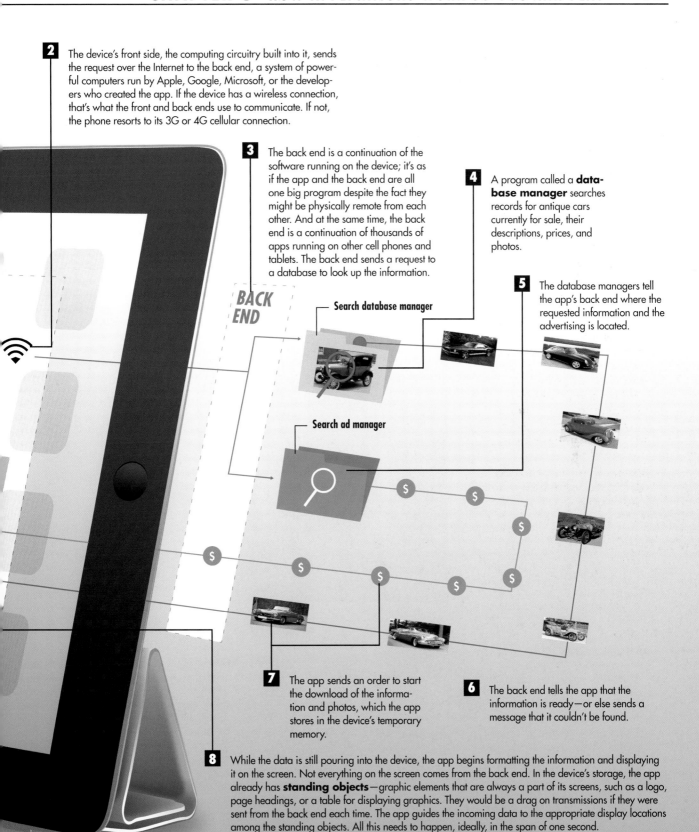

2 The device's front side, the computing circuitry built into it, sends the request over the Internet to the back end, a system of powerful computers run by Apple, Google, Microsoft, or the developers who created the app. If the device has a wireless connection, that's what the front and back ends use to communicate. If not, the phone resorts to its 3G or 4G cellular connection.

3 The back end is a continuation of the software running on the device; it's as if the app and the back end are all one big program despite the fact they might be physically remote from each other. And at the same time, the back end is a continuation of thousands of apps running on other cell phones and tablets. The back end sends a request to a database to look up the information.

4 A program called a **database manager** searches records for antique cars currently for sale, their descriptions, prices, and photos.

5 The database managers tell the app's back end where the requested information and the advertising is located.

BACK END

Search database manager

Search ad manager

7 The app sends an order to start the download of the information and photos, which the app stores in the device's temporary memory.

6 The back end tells the app that the information is ready—or else sends a message that it couldn't be found.

8 While the data is still pouring into the device, the app begins formatting the information and displaying it on the screen. Not everything on the screen comes from the back end. In the device's storage, the app already has **standing objects**—graphic elements that are always a part of its screens, such as a logo, page headings, or a table for displaying graphics. They would be a drag on transmissions if they were sent from the back end each time. The app guides the incoming data to the appropriate display locations among the standing objects. All this needs to happen, ideally, in the span of one second.

How Games Create New Worlds

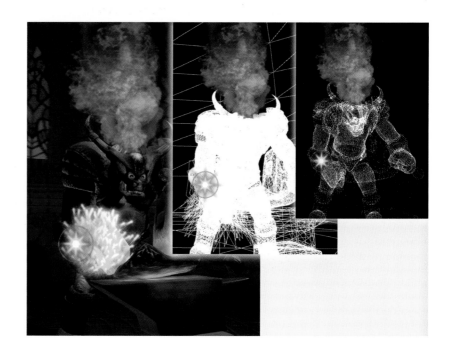

WHEN I BOUGHT my first computer waaaay back in 1980, I told my wife that I could use it to make money. And as it turned out that was true. Within a few months I had snagged an assignment to create a database that more than covered the $3,000 I had paid for my Eagle II.

But deep in my heart of hearts, I wanted a computer so I could play games. I had seen some games on a friend's Apple, and in computer stores watched open-mouthed as Flight Simulator created a flexible, organic world in real time. Forget about word processing and electronic spreadsheets. Games on a computer were miraculous! It was as if the PC brought to life all the imaginings we had as children having a tea party with dolls or when we ran with our arms held straight out from our sides, pretending we were piloting a Northrop Black Bullet.

I had to get me one of those computers.

But as it turned out, my Eagle didn't handle graphics, as advertised, unless you added a circuit board and used programs no one had heard of then, or since. I was stuck playing **adventure games**, such as *Zork*, which were all text. I played by typing commands such as "Go north" and "pick up sword." (See the pseudocode for an adventure game in the Chapter 5 spread, "How a Program is a Roadmap.") Actually the adventure games weren't that bad, but it wasn't what I had in mind when I bought a computer for...work.

Today's computer games have made me forget that initial disappointment. Now graphics are photorealistic to the point of showing each blade of grass in a meadow being blown by a breeze independently of how the other thousands of blades are moving. At the same time games have captured realism, they have also transcended reality to add new spatial dimensions and to create entire worlds on which millions of people can play and interact with each other in real time via the Internet.

And the wonder of wonders is that you no longer need a computer—at least not a computer by the old definition of a desktop box, monitor, and keyboard. You don't even need a dedicated game console, such as the X-Box or PlayStation. You can now play just as many computer games on the new definition of computers, which includes smartphones and tablets. Angry Birds, anyone?

How Computers Plot a 3D World

Finding Your Place in Three Dimensions

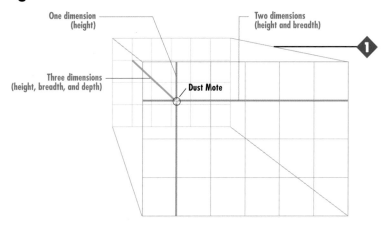

One dimension
(height)

Two dimensions
(height and breadth)

Three dimensions
(height, breadth, and depth)

Dust Mote

1 Imagine a speck of dust floating near your head. As long as it stays put, you have no problem telling someone exactly where the speck is: Six and a half feet off the floor, 29 inches from the north wall, and a foot from the west wall. You need only three numbers and some agreed-upon starting points—the floor, the walls—to precisely pinpoint anything in the universe. (For our purposes, we'll ignore that curved space thing Einstein came up with.) That's how 3D games got started, by using three numbers to determine the position of all the important points in the graphic rendition of the world they're creating. Of course, today's PC games are pinpointing 47 billion dots a second, but the principle's the same as you are putting numbers to the dust mote's location.

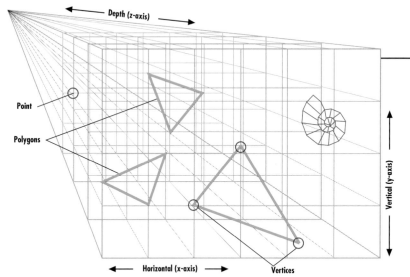

Depth (z-axis)

Point

Polygons

Vertical (y-axis)

Horizontal (x-axis)

Vertices

2 In 3D games, as in life, we locate points along three axes: horizontal, vertical, and distal—the x-axis, y-axis, and z-axis, respectively. In three-dimensional space as well as games, three points are all that's needed to define a two-dimensional plane. 3D graphics create entire worlds and their populations from 2D **polygons**, usually triangles, because they have the fewest angles, or **vertices**, making them the easiest and quickest polygon to calculate. Most times, even a square, rectangle, or curve consists of combinations of flat triangles. (The vertices, as you'll soon see, are mere anchor points for straight lines.)

3 Three-dimensional objects are created by connecting two-dimensional polygons. Even curved surfaces are made up of flat planes. The smaller the polygons, the more curved an object appears to be. The graphics processing unit on the video card (or cards) has a **geometry engine** that calculates the height, width, and depth information for each corner of every polygon in a 3D environment, a process called **tessellation**, or **triangulation**. The engine also figures out the current camera angle, or vantage point, which determines what part of a setting can be seen. For each frame, it rotates, resizes, or repositions the triangles as the viewpoint changes. Any lines outside the viewpoint are eliminated, or **clipped**. The engine also calculates the position of any **light sources** in relation to the polygons. Tessellation makes intense use of floating-point math. Without video cards with processors designed specifically for 3D graphics, the primary Pentium and Athlon CPUs in the computers would be woefully overtaxed. A changing scene must be redrawn at least 15 to 20 times a second for the eye to see smooth movement.

—— = Foreground
—— = Background

Polygon 3D object

Turning Geometry into Things

1 The results of the geometry engine's calculations—the three-dimensional location of each vertex in the camera's viewing range—are passed to the **rendering engine**, another part of the **graphics processing unit (GPU)**. The rendering engine has the job of rasterization—figuring out a color value, pixel by pixel, for the entire 2D representation of the 3D scene. It first creates a wireframe view in which lines, or wires, connect all the vertices to define the polygons. The result is like looking at a world made of glass with lines visible only where the panes of glass intersect.

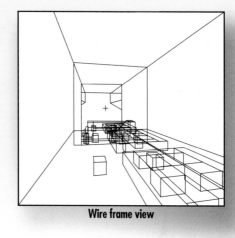

Wire frame view

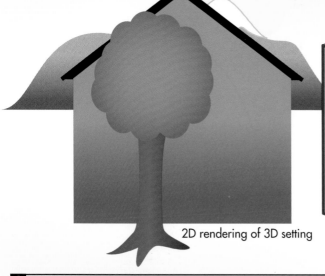

2D rendering of 3D setting

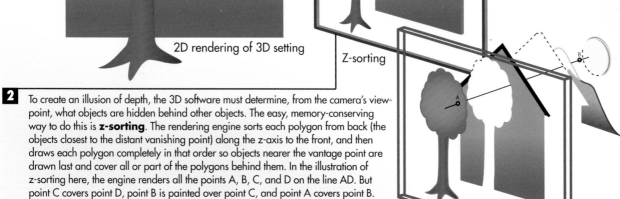

Z-sorting

Z-buffering

2 To create an illusion of depth, the 3D software must determine, from the camera's viewpoint, what objects are hidden behind other objects. The easy, memory-conserving way to do this is **z-sorting**. The rendering engine sorts each polygon from back (the objects closest to the distant vanishing point) along the z-axis to the front, and then draws each polygon completely in that order so objects nearer the vantage point are drawn last and cover all or part of the polygons behind them. In the illustration of z-sorting here, the engine renders all the points A, B, C, and D on the line AD. But point C covers point D, point B is painted over point C, and point A covers point B.

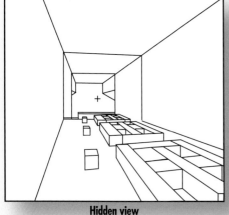

Hidden view

3 **Z-buffering** is faster than z-sorting but requires more memory on the video card to record a depth value for each pixel that makes up the surface of all the polygons. Those pixels that are nearer the vantage point are given smaller values. Before a new pixel is drawn, its depth value is compared to that of the pixels along the same AB line that passes through all the layers of the image. A pixel is drawn only if its value is lower than that of all the other pixels along line AB. In the illustration here of z-buffering, pixel A is the only one the engine bothers to draw because pixels in the house, mountain, and sun along line AB would be covered by pixel A. With either z-sorting or z-buffering, the result is called a **hidden view** because it hides surfaces that should not be seen.

How 3D Gets Dressed

DRAWING LINES among all the vertices on a screen produces a wire frame, or **mesh**. But it's a naked mesh that gives only rudimentary clues as to what it depicts. To turn these digital skeletons into digital objects is to clothe the mesh. The easiest technique to accomplish this is to run a flat layer of even color connecting all sides of each polygon, like a tent stretched taut over its poles. Needless to say, the effect is still more virtual cartoon than virtual reality. Few things are smooth and evenly colored. In the real world, objects have spots, streaks, grit, grain, bumps, lumps, and, in a word, texture. And so were born…

Texture Maps

Texture maps are **bitmaps** (unchanging graphics) that cover surfaces like an endless sheet of wallpaper. Texture maps are tiled to cover an entire surface, such as the stone and lava shown here. In simple 3D software, a distortion called **pixelation** occurs when the viewpoint moves close to a texture-mapped object: The details of the bitmap are enlarged and the surface looks as if it has large squares of color painted on it.

Distance fogged | Not fogged

Texture maps

MIP Mapping

MIP mapping corrects for pixelation. The 3D application uses variations of the same texture map—MIP stands for *multim in parvum*, or "many in few"—at different resolutions, or sizes. One texture map is used if an object is close up, but a bitmap saved at a different resolution is applied when the same object is distant.

Perspective Correction

Perspective correction makes tiles of texture maps at the far end of a wall narrower than tiles near the viewer and changes the shape of texture maps from rectangles to a wedge shape.

Alpha Blending

An effect such as the semi-transparency that occurs through smoke or under water. The rendering engine uses texture maps that represent the surface of an object and other texture maps representing such transient conditions as fog or blurriness. The rendering engine compares the color of each **texel**—a texture map's equivalent of a pixel—in a texture map with a texel in the same location on a second bitmap. Then, it takes a percentage of each color and produces an alpha value somewhere between the two colors. A less memory-intensive way to accomplish a similar effect is **Stippling**, which draws the background texture and then overlays it with every other texel of the transparency texture.

Fogging and Depth Cueing

Fogging and depth cueing are two sides of the same effect. **Fogging**, shown in the screen shot from *British Open Golf*—and not to be confused with the effect of wisps of fog that comes from **alpha blending**—combines distant areas of a scene with white to create a hazy horizon. **Depth cueing** adds black to colors by lowering the color value of distant objects so, for example, the end of a long hall is shrouded in darkness. The effect is not merely atmospheric. It relieves the rendering engine of the amount of detail it has to draw.

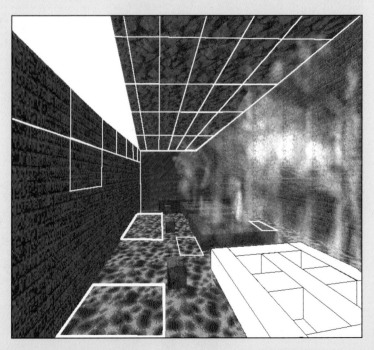

The Evolution of Lara Croft

When Eidos Interactive created *Tomb Raider* in 1996, its heroine, Lara Croft, was little more than some crude triangles thrown together to create a 3D character. Over the years, the triangles became so small and so numerous that the 3D illusion has become ever more convincing. Like Lara, most game characters start off as triangles. In the images below, Dawn, a fairy mascot of video chip maker nVidia, is constructed

Courtesy of xeno55, DeviantArt

entirely of polygons, but there are so many that you would never notice, even looking up close. That's because she has so many polygons that when you see her in **wireframe**, as in the middle shot, the polygons blend into a white silhouette. It's only when you remove the lines that connect the vertices that you see the construction of her body in the form of hundreds of thousands of points. High-end video cards are capable of rendering well more than a billion triangles a second.

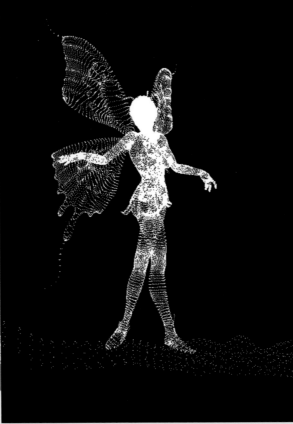

How Shaders Control the World

VISION INCLUDES shape, **color**, and, even more importantly, **value**, or **shading**. You don't have to have all of these to determine what you're looking at, but you do have to have shape and shading. Look at the depictions of the same object on the left. Color is not at all as helpful in identifying a shape as is the values—the intensities, or the lightness or darkness—of colors for different portions of an object. This is why 3D graphics gave birth to **shaders**. The first shaders did exactly what their name implies: They shaded certain polygons on specific sides of an object to give the illusion of depth and fullness. The technique began simply enough, using a single shade to each polygon, much as you might paint different walls of a room, but it became...

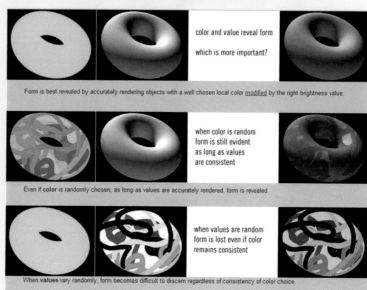

color and value reveal form

which is more important?

Form is best revealed by accurately rendering objects with a well chosen local color <u>modified</u> by the right brightness value.

when color is random form is still evident as long as values are consistent

Even if **color** is randomly chosen, as long as values are accurately rendered, form is revealed.

when values are random form is lost even if color remains consistent

When **values** vary randomly, form becomes difficult to discern regardless of consistency of color choice.

Joseph Francis, digitalartform.com

Bilinear Filtering

Bilinear filtering smoothes the edges of textures by measuring the color values of four surrounding **texture-map pixels**, or **texels**, and then making the color value of the center texel an average of the four values. **Trilinear filtering** smoothes the transition from one MIP map to a different size of the same texture.

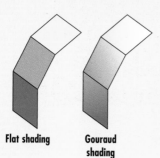

Flat shading

Gouraud shading

Shading

Using information from the geometry engine about the location of light sources, the rendering engine applies shading to surfaces of the polygons. The rudimentary flat shading applies a single amount of light to an entire surface. Lighting changes only between one surface and an adjacent surface. A more sophisticated and realistic method is **Gouraud shading**, which takes the color values at each vertex of a polygon and interpolates a graduated shading extending along the surface of the polygon from each vertex to each of the other vertices.

Ray Tracing

Before long, software and hardware developers realized they could have their shaders do more than apply different colors to polygons. They melded the abilities of shaders with other rendering techniques, such as **ray tracing**, which plots the path of rays of light as they are naturally reflected, absorbed, or refracted by the materials they shine on. The combination allowed shaders to create polygon chameleons who could take on qualities even real chameleons couldn't.

Vertex Shaders

The Gouraud shading technique has found new application in one of the most powerful rendering methods to date: **vertex shading**. Just as Gouraud shading creates a graduated shading stretching among the three vertices of a triangle, vertex shading does the same, only with any property animators want to assign an object, such as luminosity, temperature, and qualities that are not at all visual, such as weight and specific density.

From Pacific Fighters, Ubisoft

From Pacific Fighters, Ubisoft

One of the most useful vertex shaders is **displacement**. In these screenshots, the one on the left is an ordinary animation with a necessarily limited number of polygons creating the ocean surface. On the right displacement, shaders control not just the height of the polygons but also the height of individual pixels making up the polygons for a more complex, more realistic surface.

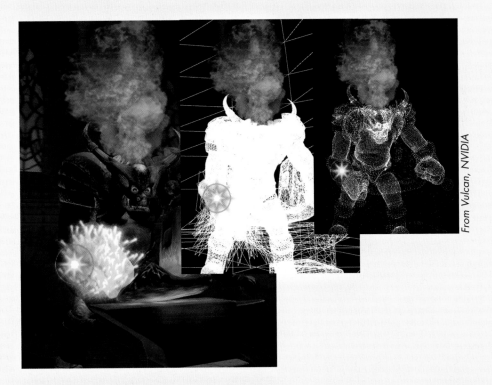

From Vulcan, NVIDIA

Particle Shaders

Vertex shaders are helpful in many areas where objects are so fluid or scattered that the traditional polygons handicap the realism of the animation. In these scenes from a short animation by NVIDIA featuring Vulcan, the god of fire, you can see how traditional polygons are used to construct Vulcan's body. But notice that the fire leaping from his body is not wireframed. That's because the animation uses **particle shaders**, which operate on each pixel independently of polygons to give a unified appearance to fluid objects that are nevertheless separate particles, or molecules.

How Games Populate New Worlds

Every day, all over the planet, thousands of people quietly disappear from our world and then materialize on worlds the rest of us have never seen. These worlds brim with monsters and wizardry, space aliens and people just trying to make a living. The escapees from our planet become fearless adventurers, plucky damsels, sorcerers' apprentices, or the bold leaders of hundreds of others who, too, had become bored with modern life, sat down at their computers, and transported themselves to alternate universes. They reappeared in a type of game called a **MMORPG (massively multiplayer online role playing game)** or just MMO for short. The key word is *massively*. A successful MMO has millions of paying users that are able to play the same game at the same time through their computers and the Internet.

1 You take the first step toward fleeing this world when you install **client** software, bought off the shelf or downloaded, on your computer or device. The client connects over the Internet to **server** programs that require scores of networked computers to hold all the information required to create a virtual world of the size you find in an MMO. One of the largest, *World of Warcraft*, covers more than 80 virtual square miles— four times the size of Manhattan. The servers must account for every square inch in the world and all that inhabit it—literally—every animal, the weather, changing seasons, and the characters not controlled by flesh-and-blood players.

2 The first time you enter an MMO, you begin by creating your avatar, also called a **PC**, for **player character**. This is what other players see when you're around them. You can change your hair color, body type, gender, or even species. A game usually gives you a choice of characters that come with specialized skills, designed to work in concert with other player character types. A warrior, naturally, does well in battle, a wizard can cast damaging spells from a distance, whereas a healer might enhance or "buff" other characters while keeping them alive.

Worlds Within Worlds

MMOs are a direct descendent of the non-computerized role-playing game *Dungeons and Dragons*. That partially explains why so many MMOs have medieval settings, mythological monsters, and more than a modicum of magic. But MMOs are not limited to the classic D'n'D genre. You can also choose sci-fi MMOs, including *Star Wars: The Old Republic* and *EVE Online*. As time marches inexorably forward, the variety and scope of MMOs continues to broaden.

3 If this is not your first time in the game, your client tells the server you want to join, and the server downloads to the client all the information about you that it needs to run the game on your end: your health, possessions, skills, and your appearance. The server and client do not keep in constant contact with each other. With thousands of players, reporting every little move would immediately clog the communication channels. The server generally maintains the overall status of the game, and the client is responsible for any local happenings, including the strenuous calculations necessary to present the 3D world on your PC's screen. At set intervals—called a **tick** in MMOs—the two exchange status updates and instructions.

4 When you step into the world, you encounter the avatars of other players. A computer server devoted solely to **chat** lets you communicate with other players. Some games have **player killers (PKs)** who prey on fellow playing characters, and some of the other PCs might look fearsome, but generally the games are designed so you gain more from cooperation than competition. Some games require the solving of puzzles, and if you're not a puzzle person, it's a good idea to travel with someone who is. And sometimes the only way to overcome some of the more dangerous creatures, such as dragons, is to have plenty of bodies to throw at them.

5 The final type of creature to inhabit an MMO is a **mob**, short for **mobile object**, controlled by the game's servers rather than by players. Mobs include harmless woodland creatures and **non-player characters (NPCs)**, who are the cast of necessary bit players, such as merchants whose computer consciousness is limited to how much to charge for a loaf of bread or a new sword. (MMOs' economic systems spill over into the real world, where players on eBay sell MMO gold for actual greenbacks. Economists are studying the games as microcosms of **RL (real life)** economies.) Although merchants are technically mobs, the term is more identified with creatures more dangerous than salesmen, including evil magicians, dragons, orcs, giant sewer spiders, and zombies. The MMO constantly loses some of these creatures to the inevitable clashes with players, and the mobs must be regenerated. Certain spots in the world are often designated **spawning points**, or **camps**, where new bog slugs, swamp seeps, and gruttooth brutes come into the world.

6 Although some MMOs let you develop a character who's a nonviolent artist or craftsman, fighting monster mobs is a large part of most multiplayer games. When you initiate a battle—by approaching a mob too closely or brandishing a weapon—the client reports the ensuing rumble to the server. The server notes what kind of mob it is, and looks up the creature's health and the attacks it can use. The server sends this information to the client, which executes the mob's attack using the mob's artificial intelligence.

7 As you fight, the client gives the server an update of successful blows on both sides, and it deducts health points from both sides. When the number of points for you or your opponent falls below a certain level, one of you is dead. If it's not you, you and any other PCs who helped slay the beast are entitled to take from the mob whatever loot you want. The client depicts your avatar moving the loot from the mob; the server makes it official by moving the loot from the mob's database record to yours. Killing mobs is also the only way you earn **experience**, the closest thing to a scoring system. With greater experience comes better abilities and skills. Kind of ghoulish, but better than 8-to-5 at the office.

CHAPTER

8

How Security Software Fights Off Invaders

WE should be grateful that most computer crackers are grossly egotistical. Breaking into a megacorporation's servers, leaving a virus, or substituting a screen of his own scatological design for the company's home page—that's done by someone who wants attention. They can't resist leaving a program or note that's a digital sign of Zorro, something to let you know that although you might own the computer, the cracker owns its soul.

I'm using the term **cracker** here instead of **hacker**, which most people think of when they hear about some teenager who broke into the high school's computer and gave himself a lot of As. Self-described hackers break into computer systems out of curiosity or to test their skills without stealing information and without trashing the hacked system. Hackers look down on crackers as immature, unsophisticated kiddies.

Crackers and hackers have one thing in common: Both must have endless patience and a dedication to their life's calling that you rarely find outside of a monastery. It means starting as a *script kiddie*, running program scripts written by others that sniff and nudge and try to bluff their way past a computer's defenses. The world of hacking is ultra-cool and ultra-exclusive. You will only be admitted—make that tolerated—when you show that you've mastered those scripts and even written some of your own. You might take on a monster crack to prove you're up to snuff.

The act of proving oneself is the undoing of many crackers. It's difficult to do a crack and leave no clues behind—if only because the up-and-coming cracker just has to let someone know he did it. The only payoff in this game is recognition. The only way you earn it is to have encyclopedic knowledge of network security, including all the holes and back entrances that not even the people running a network know about.

Although no system, from a home PC to an Internet-connected corporate supercomputer, is truly crack-proof—just ask Sony or Target—as a user there are tools at your disposal that help you keep control of your PC. These days those tools—firewalls and antivirus software—are almost always built right into the operating system you already have. These utilities help you keep control of your PC where it belongs—in your hands.

Still, the next time you tune in to the news and learn about a new virus, a denial-of-service attack that overwhelms an organization's incoming lines, or a crash that spreads like a California wildfire, remember this: These aren't the truly scary cyber-attacks. You can always replace your credit card or change your password. A really dangerous cracker, however, keeps his activities secret, and limits himself to, say, small transfers of money, none so large as to attract attention. When the real master cracker comes along, no one knows anything's going on. In fact, it could be going on right now, but you'll never really know if he's stopped.

How Computer Hackers Break In

Corporate partners

1 Unlike in movies, where hackers break into a computer in minutes with only a few keystrokes, hacking deep enough into a computer to take control of it might take days or weeks. The computer hacker methodically follows a set of procedures that pries open a crack wider and wider with each step.

2 The hacker performs a **footprint analysis** of the intended target using publicly available information, such as its size, subsidiaries, and vendors that might have access to the target's computers.

3 Using readily available hacking software, he scans the target computer's **ports** for potential break-in points. Ports are numbers used to identify different services the computer provides, such as network input/output and email.

4 Based on the analysis, the hacker creates a map of the ports and their relationships to each other. He uses this to try to identify the types of file transfer and email the system uses by sending random data to the ports. Many port services respond to data with a **banner** that identifies the software that's using the port. The hacker looks up the software in online databases that list the software's vulnerabilities. Some ports yield real pay dirt in the form of user names and dates that passwords change.

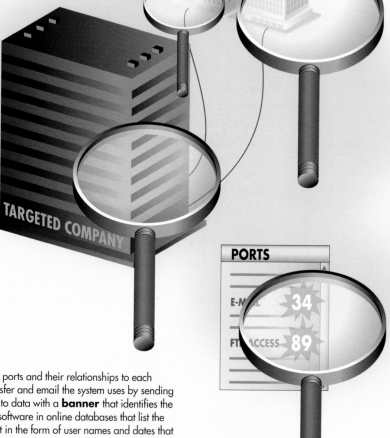

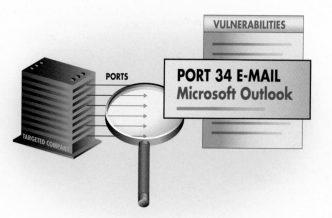

VULNERABILITIES

PORT 34 E-MAIL
Microsoft Outlook

5 To gain access to the target system, the hacker has two approaches. The low-tech method involves contacting employees to trick them into revealing their passwords. The hacker might call pretending to be part of the IT help staff, claiming that a security malfunction requires the employee to verify her password. A daring hacker might visit the offices in person to look for passwords employees have taped to their monitors.

PASSWORD

****

Password: tricky kitty

COMMON PASSWORDS

12345
funguy
opensesame
mypassword
thisoneworks
version4
newpassword
default
guestpassword
password1

6 The second method is a **brute force** attack. The hacker uses a hacking program to try to log onto the system with the usernames she's acquired. When the system asks for a password, the program responds with a word from a list of likely passwords, such as *opensesame* or *12345*. The program repeats the process until the list is exhausted, it chances upon the right password, or the host locks the user out for too many failed attempts.

REGISTRY KEYS

Black, Kevin
Brown, Mindy
Doe, Jane
Doe, John
Green, Lori
Jones, Ken
Smith, Lisa
Smythe, Tom
White, Jim

TARGETED COMPANY

7 After the hacker has entered the system with user-level privileges, he looks for passwords of higher-level users that grant greater access to the system. Good sources are registry keys and email.

8 Finally, with access to the most secret ranges of the network, the hacker uploads innocuous-seeming **trojan** programs to one or more of the computers on the network. These programs appear to the human eye or a virus scanner to be ordinary, harmless files. In actuality, they are programs that open a **backdoor** through which the hacker may now enter the network at will.

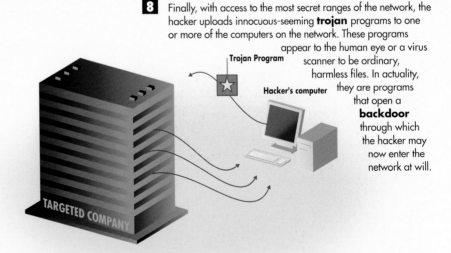

Trojan Program

Hacker's computer

TARGETED COMPANY

How Spyware Reports Everything You Do

1 **Spyware** is a program on your hard drive that sends information about you and how you use a PC to marketers and advertisers, usually without you being aware it's happening. **Malware** cousins of spyware use spyware information to display advertising for products it's betting will interest you based on your website browsing habits.

2 A web link might launch a spy program to your hard drive when you click the link. Normally, however, spyware enters your system when you download free software from less-than-reputable sources (and some reputable ones too, unfortunately). Installation of the program you wanted also installs the spyware. Antivirus software and firewalls do nothing to block spyware installed with a download you ask for.

3 A warning that you have installed a program that collects information from your computer usually appears in a **Privacy Policy** where you found the download or during installation. Such fine print is notoriously unread.

Downloading ...

Spyware

Desired download

LICENSING AGREEMENT

blah blah blah blah blah blah blah blah
blah blah blah blah blah blah blah
blah blah blah blah blah blah blah blah
blah blah blah blah blah blah blah blah
blah blah blah blah blah blah
blah blah blah blah blah blah blah blah
blah blah blah blah blah blah blah blah
blah blah blah blah blah blah blah
blah blah blah blah blah blah blah blah
blah blah blah blah blah blah blah blah
blah blah blah blah blah blah
blah blah blah blah blah blah blah blah
blah blah blah blah blah blah blah blah
blah blah blah

blah blah blah blah blah blah blah blah
blah blah blah blah blah blah blah
blah blah blah blah blah blah blah
blah blah blah blah blah blah blah blah

[X] I agree   [ ] I disagree

WINDOWS REGISTRY

```
100110100110101011010011010101101001101001010101101001011010101101011010101011010
010101010011000101001011010110110101111101001100100101101001100110010010011001010 1
011010101011011010100101001101011101010110101010101011010101010101010101010101101
```

Spyware

4 Most spyware is installed as just another program in the Program Files folder. Other spyware embeds itself in the operating system, where it is harder to find and more dangerous to extract.

5 The spyware program begins gathering information. Some programs limit themselves to generic information and don't collect any data that would identify you. But other types of spyware might record all your keystrokes (including any password you type), snoop through documents you create with a word processor or spreadsheet, track each page you visit on the Web, or scour your files for anything that looks like a credit card number. The information might be stored in a **cookie**, but cookies in themselves are not harmful and don't indicate the presence of spies.

6 Spy programs aren't limited to harvesting data. Spyware conceivably does anything your computer can do. It can insert websites in your browser's bookmarks and change your home page.

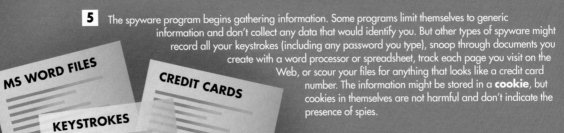

MS WORD FILES

CREDIT CARDS

KEYSTROKES

WEBSITES VISITED

SPYWARE COLLECTION

SPYWARE

CHANGE HOMEPAGE

ADD BOOKMARK

7 The spyware opens a **backchannel**—an Internet link hidden in the background of your computer's operations and leads to whoever created the spy. It uses the backchannel to send information found on your computer. If the program is adware, it uses the information it obtains to display advertising that matches your interests.

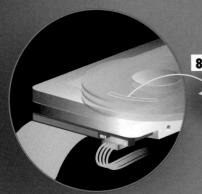

8 Attempts to remove spyware are often thwarted. Some spy programs include **tricklers**, which re-install the spy files as fast as you delete them. At the least, uninstalling usually causes the program you downloaded with the spy to stop working.

Counter Spies

Don't try to remove spyware on your own—it'll outsmart you every time. If your system doesn't have its own spyware management tool (Windows includes its own, for example), get a program such as Spybot Search and Destroy or Ad-Aware SE, both free. Just keep in mind that tracking down and eliminating spyware is an ever-moving project and even the best of these programs can't uncover everything 100% of the time.

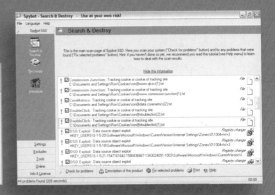

How Viruses Invade Your Computer

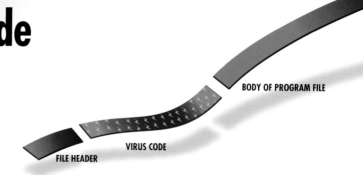

BODY OF PROGRAM FILE

VIRUS CODE

FILE HEADER

1 A **virus** is created when a programmer intentionally infects a program with computer code that has the capability to replicate itself, hide, watch for a specific event to occur, and deliver a destructive or prankish payload.

2 When the infected program runs, the virus code executes first. The code typically performs four actions:

Replication: The virus inserts copies of itself into other program files. Each descendant of a virus then replicates itself each time the computer accesses a potential host program.

Boot record viruses target the master boot record. The computer must read this record to find out how the disk is organized before it can get to any of the other files. By hiding here, the virus can run even before an operating system is loaded.

Program viruses look for executable .COM and .EXE program files. The virus often inserts its copy immediately behind the program's **header**, a small section of code at the beginning of the file that contains information about what kind of file it is. This ensures that the virus is always executed before the legitimate portion of the file.

Event watching: Every time the virus runs, it checks for a certain condition, usually a specific date. Whenever the triggering condition exists, the virus delivers its destructive payload. If the triggering event is not present, it does nothing but replicate itself.

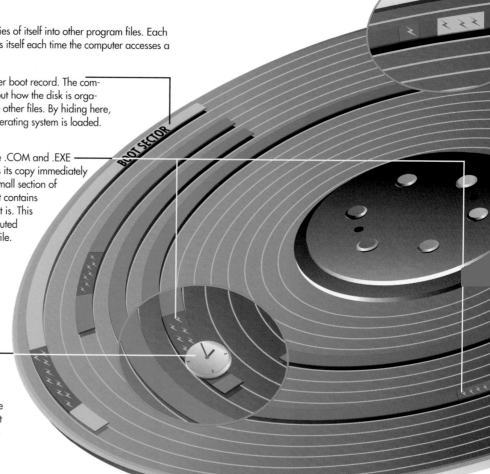

BOOT SECTOR

Camouflage: Stealth viruses disguise themselves to avoid detection by antivirus software. The disguises used by a morphing virus consist of nonfunctioning, changing sections of fake code interspersed among working sections of the virus. Each time the virus replicates, it creates different fake code to break up its identifying signature. The virus might also falsify information in the header about the file's length so the program file appears to be the correct size.

Delivery: When the triggering condition is met, the virus unleashes its payload—the operation that is its *raison d'être*. The payload might be harmless, such as displaying a "you've been had" message. Or, the payload can be destructive, erasing or scrambling files or information on the drive that tells the operating system how to find files on the disk. The most insidious viruses are those that do not announce their presence and make subtle changes to files. It could, for example, randomly change numbers in an accounting program, steal passwords, or introduce delays to make a computer run slower.

3 Some viruses copy themselves to memory. There, the virus can constantly check for a triggering action such as certain keystrokes. The **memory-resident virus** can also watch for attempts by antivirus software to find infected files and return phony information that hides the virus from detection.

How Viruses Hitch Rides in Your Email

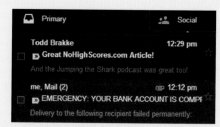

1 An unsuspecting victim receives an email that appears to have been sent by someone the victim knows, or perhaps an official entity like the bank the victim uses. The subject of the message is worded to entice the patsy to open the email, such as "Wild party pictures!!!" or "Your account has been compromised."

AccountSecurity.doc.vbs

An **attachment virus** is a program attached to an email message. It can take many forms, but most often it pretends to be a photo or movie the victim can view on his computer. The name of the attachment is disguised to hide its true nature. For example, the attachment could be vacation.jpg.vbs. Many users notice the "jpg" and assume it's a vacation photo without realizing the "vbs" identifies the attachment as a Visual Basic script, a type of program. Attachments are the most common type of virus. After you open such an attachment, you're infected.

3 What makes the virus launch its attack depends on what type of virus it is.

The **attachment virus** runs only when the victim double-clicks the attachment's filename.

2 Hidden within the email is one of three types of viruses.

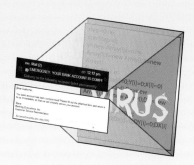

An **HTML virus** is **active content** code, essentially a small program written in **JavaScript** or **ActiveX** software languages. Active content is used on the Web whenever you buy something, fill in forms, vote in a poll, or take part in any other interactive pages on the Web. The HTML virus is not displayed when you open a message formatted in HTML.

The **HTML virus** jumps into action when the victim opens the message to read it. Merely displaying the message in the preview window also launches the virus.

A **MIME (Multi-Purpose Internet Mail Extensions) virus** takes advantage of a security hole in some browsers and email applications. The perpetrator fills in forms in the email's header with more information than the header can hold in its **buffer**—memory reserved for the form entries. When the buffer runs out of room to hold the entry, the **overflow**—the virus—spills into **stack** memory being used by the microprocessor to run programs, and the virus is executed instead of legitimate code.

The **MIME virus** can run even if it's not seen. Part of the code hidden in the header tells your email application that the message is a file it can execute without the victim doing anything. Fortunately, most modern email clients have protection from this sort of attack.

4 Viruses hidden in email do different kinds of mischief, but the first thing any of them does is propagate itself. It searches the victim's address book, old email, even documents created with Word or Excel. From these, it extracts names and email addresses.

5 The virus uses the addresses to send duplicates of itself to the victim's friends and business acquaintances, hidden in the same email it rode into the computer. To make itself harder to trace, the virus might pick a name at random from the address book and put that in the From: field. In minutes, the virus spreads itself to hundreds of other computers, sometimes accompanied by haphazard attachments of letters and spreadsheets the virus has found among the victim's files.

6 Eventually, thousands of copies of the original virus deliver their payloads, which are anything from taunting messages to erasing hard drives. They might dump their payloads right after they've finished replicating themselves, after so much time has passed, or they might all go off at the same time on the same day.

Tricky Viruses

Over time, virus creators have become increasingly clever in their attempts to trick you into infecting your own computer. The VBS.Hard.A@mm virus, for example, is an attachment that comes on an email message, warning against a nonexistent worm called VBS.AmericanHistoryX_II@mm. The subject of the message is "FW: Symantec Anti-Virus Warning;" the message promises more information in the attached memo.

When the attached file, www.symantec.com. vbs, is opened, it makes the Internet Explorer home page a phony website that warns about a fictitious worm. It also sends copies of the bogus virus warning to everyone in the address book. Each November 24, infected computers display the same message: "Don't look surprised! It is only a warning about your stupidity. Take care!"

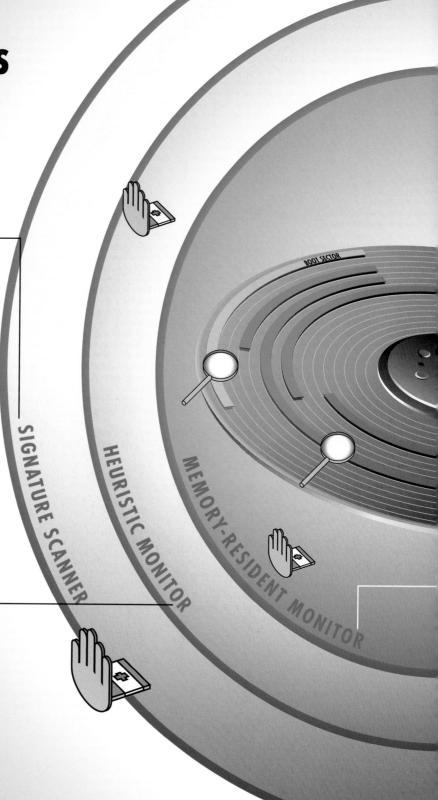

How Antivirus Software Fights Back

1 The first line of defense against viruses is **antivirus software** that inspects the master boot record, program files, and macro code for the presence of viruses. **Signature scanners** look at the contents of the boot record, programs, and macros for telltale sections of code that match viruses contained in a table of all currently known viruses. Such tables must be updated regularly to be effective against new viruses.

2 Because stealth viruses evade detection by signature scanners, **heuristic detectors** look for sections of code triggered by time or date events, routines to search for .EXE files, and disk writes that bypass the operating system.

BOOT SECTOR

SIGNATURE SCANNER

HEURISTIC MONITOR

MEMORY-RESIDENT MONITOR

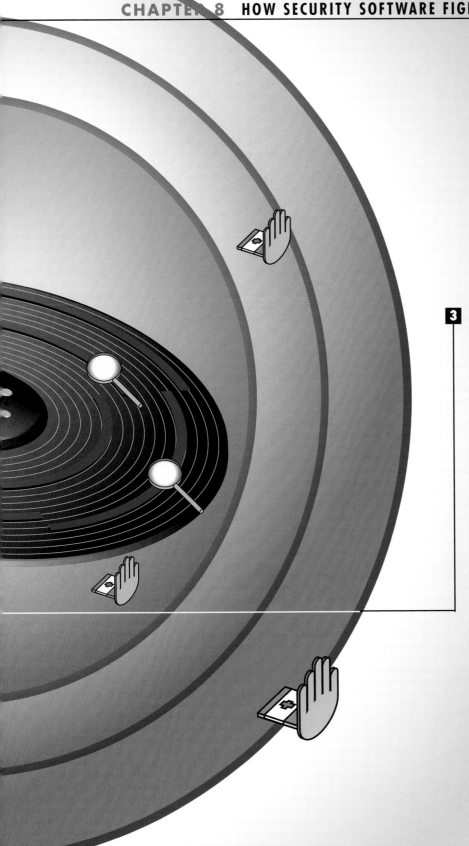

3 **Memory-resident** antivirus software installs programs in RAM that continue to operate in the background while other software applications are running. These programs monitor all the computer's operations for any action associated with viruses, such as downloading files, running programs directly from an Internet site, copying or unzipping files, attempting to modify program code, or programs that try to remain in memory after they're executed. When they detect suspicious operations, the memory-resident programs call a halt to operations, display a warning message, and wait for the user's OK before allowing the task to continue.

How Firewalls Keep Hackers Out

1 Computer owners or network managers place a **firewall** between their computers and the Internet by installing both firewall software and hardware. In the case of the latter, usually this functionality is built into the router. Both types are designed to block a hacker's attempts to break into a computer or network.

2 The firewall's manager sets up **rules** the firewall uses to filter out unwanted intrusions from the Internet. The wall shuts any nonessential **ports** a hacker might probe for openings. The manager might block all inbound traffic except for email or data that someone inside the firewall has requested.

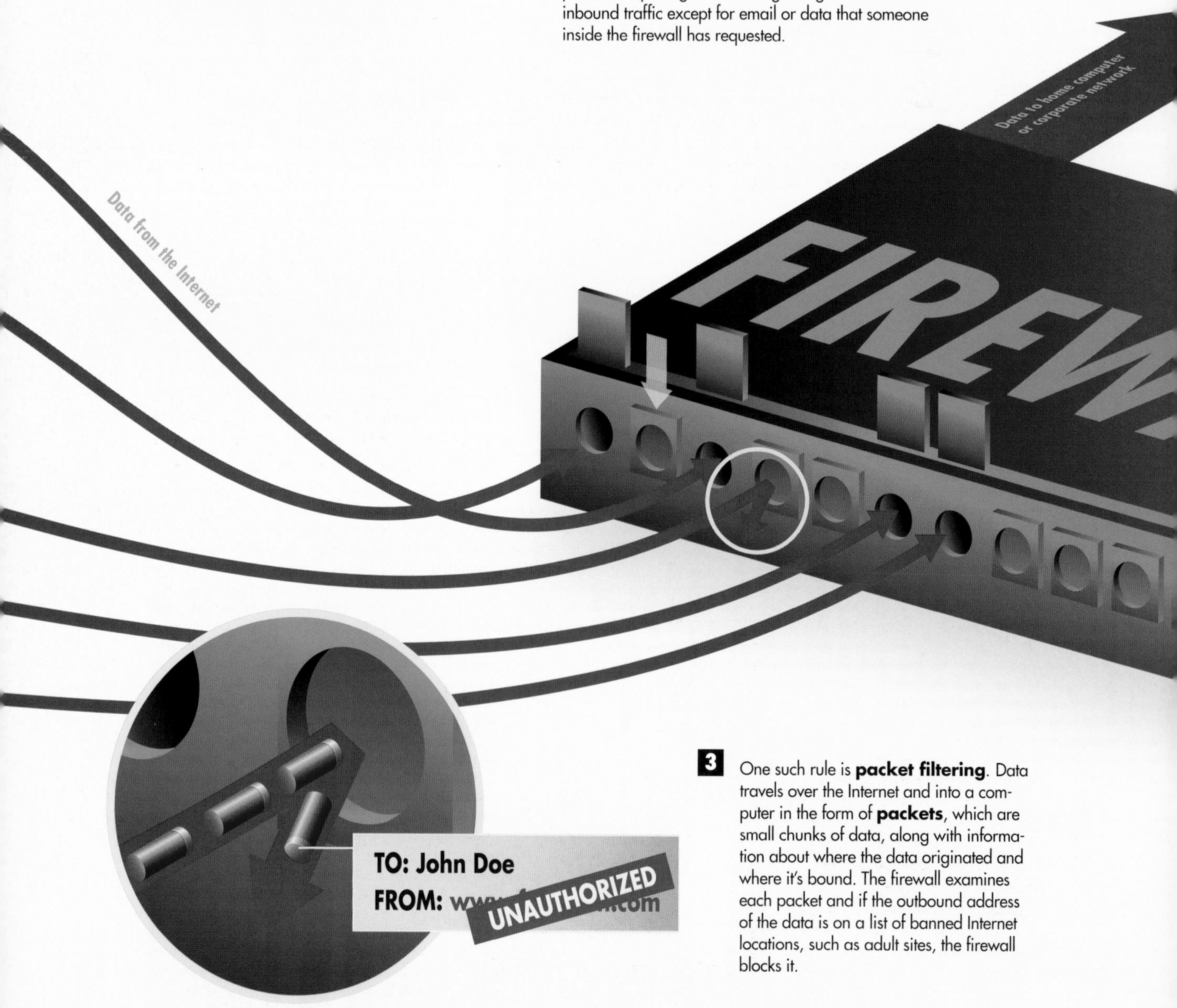

Data from the Internet

Data to home computer or corporate network

FIREW

TO: John Doe
FROM: www. UNAUTHORIZED .com

3 One such rule is **packet filtering**. Data travels over the Internet and into a computer in the form of **packets**, which are small chunks of data, along with information about where the data originated and where it's bound. The firewall examines each packet and if the outbound address of the data is on a list of banned Internet locations, such as adult sites, the firewall blocks it.

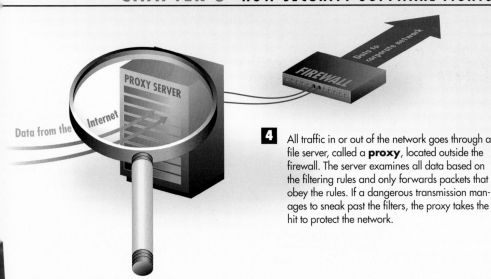

4 All traffic in or out of the network goes through a file server, called a **proxy**, located outside the firewall. The server examines all data based on the filtering rules and only forwards packets that obey the rules. If a dangerous transmission manages to sneak past the filters, the proxy takes the hit to protect the network.

5 The firewall compares key parts of each packet to a database of known safe data using a process called **stateful inspection**. The packet data must resemble data the firewall has seen before. The wall sends incoming data that passes muster to its final destination. Packets that fail the test are discarded by letting subsequent data packets write over them.

6 When a firewall detects suspicious activity, it sends an **alert** in the form of a pop-up window or email to notify the computer's user or the network manager that someone might have tried to break in.

7 The firewall also adds the intrusion to a **security log**, including information about the type of attack and the IP address of the computer sending the intrusive code. Typically, the firewall also saves records of packets that have gone in and out of a computer. This information can be reported to a user's Internet service provider (ISP) or to the computer help staff.

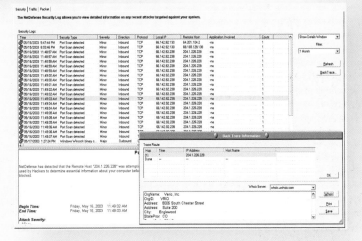

How Spammers Find You

Public Sources for Spammers

1 Not all spammers compile their own spam lists. Many buy lists from others, who use a variety of techniques to harvest email addresses or potential email addresses, and then sell those lists to the highest bidder.

2 Spammers send out automated spiders across the Internet that crawl across web pages looking for email addresses in mail:to links or posted on the page. The spiders send all the addresses back to the person compiling the spam list.

3 Spiders also look through Usenet newsgroups for email addresses, and when they find them, they send the addresses back to the spam list compiler.

4 Other kinds of spiders visit chat rooms and grab all the email addresses of those in the rooms.

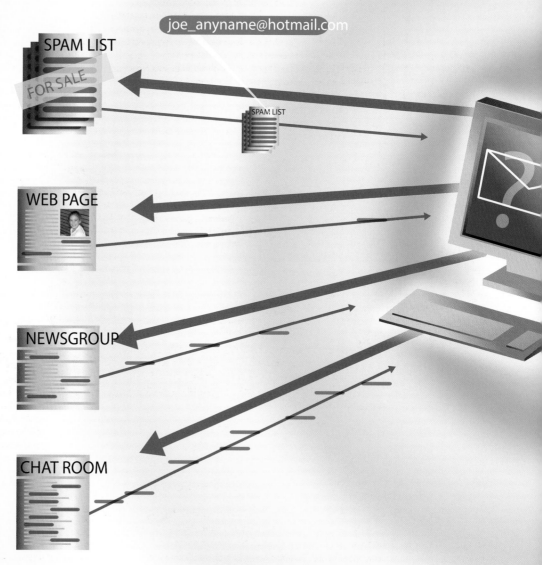

Harvesting from Email Directories

5 A **dictionary attack**, also called a **directory harvest attack**, is another common technique for harvesting email addresses. These attacks harvest email addresses from Internet Service Providers, mail services such as Gmail, and private corporations. In the attack, software opens up a connection to a mail server and sends millions of delivery attempt requests to email addresses on the server, such as timsmith@gmail.com, tim_smith@gmail.com, timsmith123@gmail.com, and so on.

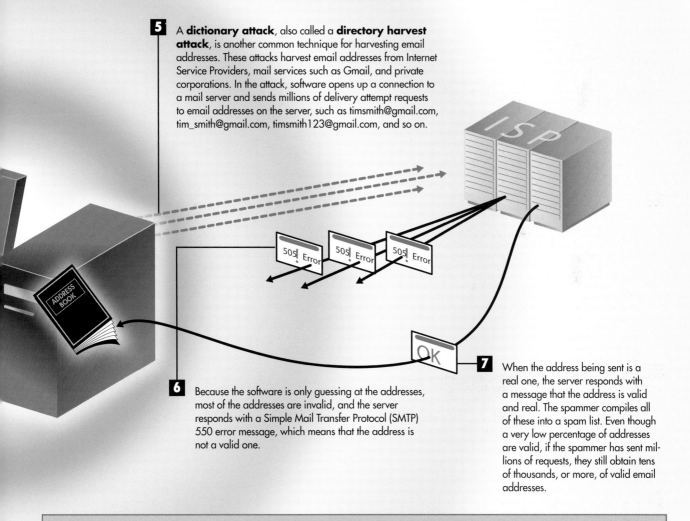

6 Because the software is only guessing at the addresses, most of the addresses are invalid, and the server responds with a Simple Mail Transfer Protocol (SMTP) 550 error message, which means that the address is not a valid one.

7 When the address being sent is a real one, the server responds with a message that the address is valid and real. The spammer compiles all of these into a spam list. Even though a very low percentage of addresses are valid, if the spammer has sent millions of requests, they still obtain tens of thousands, or more, of valid email addresses.

The Speed at Which Spam Spreads

How effective are spammers in harvesting email addresses from public locations? According to an investigation by the Federal Trade Commission and several law enforcement agencies, they are remarkably efficient. The commission and agencies posted 250 fresh, new email addresses in 175 locations on the Internet to see how much spam each received. The addresses were posted on web pages, dating services, chat rooms, message boards, Usenet newsgroups, and other locations. In the six weeks after posting, the addresses had received 3,349 pieces of spam. Eighty-six percent of addresses posted to web pages drew spam, and an equal percent of addresses posted on newsgroups drew spam. And chat rooms were possibly the biggest spam magnets of all: One address used in a chat room received spam a mere nine minutes after it was first posted.

How Antispam Software Sniffs out Phony Email

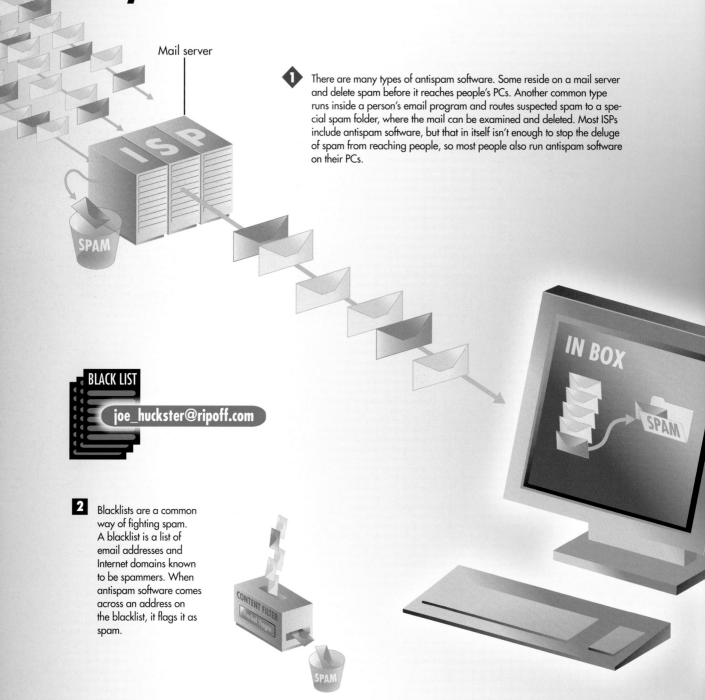

Mail server

1 There are many types of antispam software. Some reside on a mail server and delete spam before it reaches people's PCs. Another common type runs inside a person's email program and routes suspected spam to a special spam folder, where the mail can be examined and deleted. Most ISPs include antispam software, but that in itself isn't enough to stop the deluge of spam from reaching people, so most people also run antispam software on their PCs.

BLACK LIST
joe_huckster@ripoff.com

2 Blacklists are a common way of fighting spam. A blacklist is a list of email addresses and Internet domains known to be spammers. When antispam software comes across an address on the blacklist, it flags it as spam.

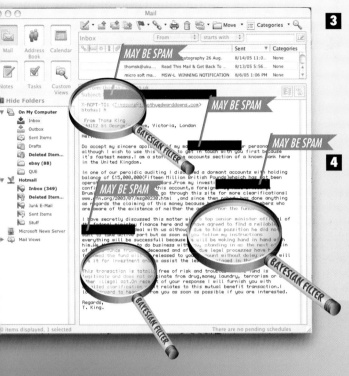

3 Antispam software also uses content filtering, in which the software examines the body and subject line of an email message and looks for specific words that indicate spam. The software contains a database of terms and phrases that spammers often use, such as *Big Money*. So if the software comes across a subject line such as *Earn Big Money from Home!*, it would consider the message spam.

4 A Bayesian filter might be the most powerful antispam technique of all. A Bayesian filter analyzes the actual content of a message, compares the content to a database of spam characteristics, and calculates the probability that the message is spam. All messages above a certain threshold are considered spam, and messages below that threshold are not considered spam. You can tune the filter to change the threshold level, depending on whether you want to be more aggressive or less aggressive in flagging spam. Being more aggressive means you'll get less spam, but also more **false positives**, messages that are not actually spam. Being less aggressive means that more spam will get through, but you'll get fewer false positives. When you use a Bayesian filter, as you get mail, you flag certain messages as spam and others as not being spam. So the more you use a Bayesian filter, the more effective it becomes because as you tell it what is spam and what isn't, it adds that information to its database. Bayesian filters are more effective than content filters that only block email with certain words or phrases because spammers can easily alter the spelling of words.

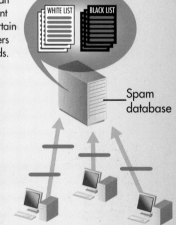

Spam database

5 Whitelists can be used to tell antispam software that certain addresses are valid, and so should always be let through by antispam software. For example, some antispam software examines a person's contact list and automatically adds all those addresses to a whitelist. Additionally, you can add addresses to a whitelist, telling the antispam software to let certain addresses through.

6 Some software uses peer-to-peer technology to fight spam. Everyone who uses the antispam software flags certain messages as spam. This information is sent to a central server, which compiles blacklists and whitelists. The software on every person's computers is then updated by the central server.

What Is Spammerwocky?

Some spam includes random words and lines of gibberish, such as "inexorable lie stone liver conclude grandma trickster." This technique, called spammerwocky, tries to fool spam filters into believing the message is not spam. The spammer hopes that the inclusion of random words will not be construed as spam by Bayesian filters. But spam-killing software has caught on and includes methods for detecting spammerwocky.

How Prime Numbers Protect Prime Secrets

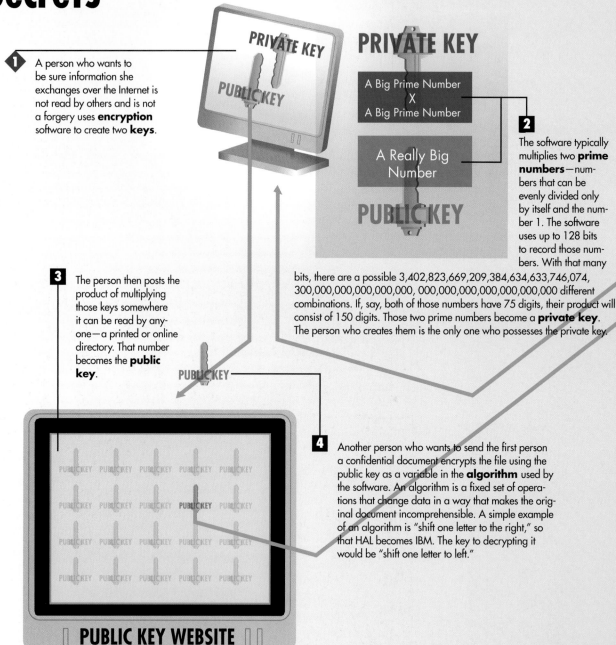

1 A person who wants to be sure information she exchanges over the Internet is not read by others and is not a forgery uses **encryption** software to create two **keys**.

PRIVATE KEY

A Big Prime Number
X
A Big Prime Number

A Really Big Number

PUBLIC KEY

2 The software typically multiplies two **prime numbers**—numbers that can be evenly divided only by itself and the number 1. The software uses up to 128 bits to record those numbers. With that many bits, there are a possible 3,402,823,669,209,384,634,633,746,074, 300,000,000,000,000,000, 000,000,000,000,000,000,000 different combinations. If, say, both of those numbers have 75 digits, their product will consist of 150 digits. Those two prime numbers become a **private key**. The person who creates them is the only one who possesses the private key.

3 The person then posts the product of multiplying those keys somewhere it can be read by anyone—a printed or online directory. That number becomes the **public key**.

4 Another person who wants to send the first person a confidential document encrypts the file using the public key as a variable in the **algorithm** used by the software. An algorithm is a fixed set of operations that change data in a way that makes the original document incomprehensible. A simple example of an algorithm is "shift one letter to the right," so that HAL becomes IBM. The key to decrypting it would be "shift one letter to left."

PUBLIC KEY WEBSITE

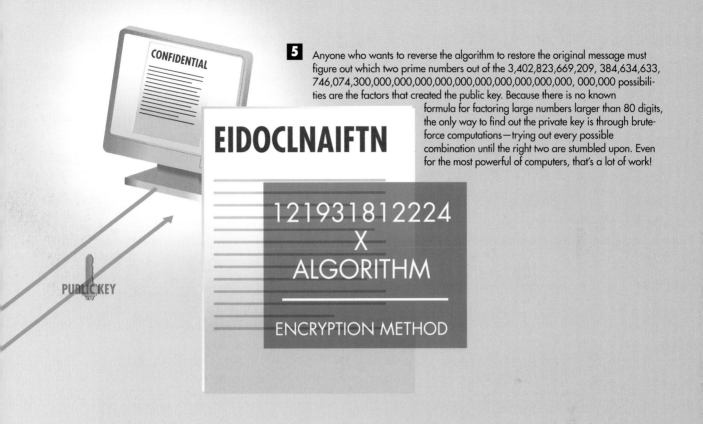

5 Anyone who wants to reverse the algorithm to restore the original message must figure out which two prime numbers out of the 3,402,823,669,209, 384,634,633, 746,074,300,000,000,000,000,000,000,000,000,000, 000,000 possibilities are the factors that created the public key. Because there is no known formula for factoring large numbers larger than 80 digits, the only way to find out the private key is through brute-force computations—trying out every possible combination until the right two are stumbled upon. Even for the most powerful of computers, that's a lot of work!

6 Public key encryption is also used to create **digital signatures**. A digital signature is typically created by computing a **message digest** or **hash value**. These are numbers created when the contents of the document are run through a hashing algorithm. The resulting value is a mathematical summary of the document. The hash value is then encrypted using the private key.

7 The recipient of the message uses the sender's public key to decrypt the hash values. The recipient runs the document through the same algorithm the sender did and, if the document is from whom it claims to be from, the two sets of hash values will match. If as little as a comma has been changed, or if the sender is impersonating someone else, the hash values won't match.

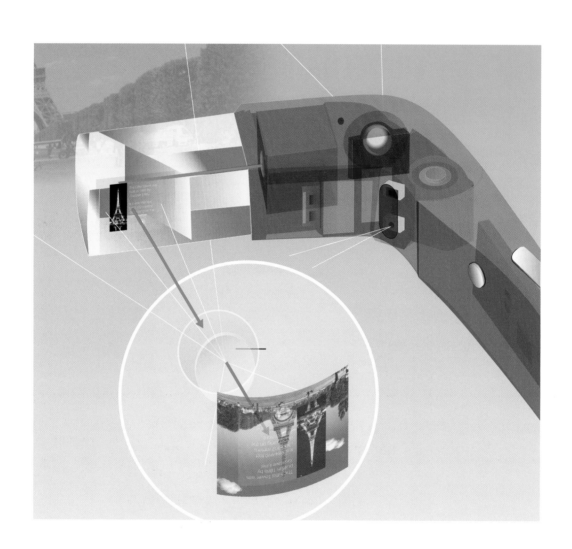

PART

3

How Computers Evolve

The theory of evolution by cumulative natural selection is the only theory we know of that is in principle capable of explaining the existence of organized complexity.

—Richard Dawkins

It sounds strange to think of an inanimate object evolving. When we think of evolution, we think of the eons it took fish to emerge from the waters and walk, or crawl, or slither, or whatever they did to become full-fledged land lubbers. Dinosaurs dominated Earth for millennia before a giant asteroid hit and created the Gulf of Mexico, along with enough dirt and debris to envelope the world for years, cutting off the sunlight plants needed—the same plants the dinosaurs needed. The dying strains of dinosaurs gave earth its first birds, which evolved into the 10,000 species of little feathered dinosaurs we have today. Also among the survivors were **synapsids**, creatures that, over 65 million years, evolved into the mammals we know today, including ourselves.

Evolution is not limited to plants and animals. Non-living systems such as languages and societies evolve. Even rocks evolve. What begins as a layer of shells and bone left behind by deceased sea creatures experiences a few million years of pressure created by its own weight to turn into limestone. A few more million years of pressure morphs the limestone into marble. Still more years pass, and it turns into a bathroom countertop.

The changes that rock undergoes might not qualify as true evolution because the concept of **survival of the fittest** does not come into play. However, survival of the fittest does rule in the evolution of computers, where survival sometimes comes with a cutthroat viciousness that rivals any terrors of the Jurassic age. Evolutional changes may dawdle about for eons in the biological world, technological evolution comes with a swiftness that often brings the Next Big Thing before we've paid off the Previous Big Thing.

The reason for the speed is that unlike the biological evolution, where changes in species, for better or worse, come from random, spontaneous mutations, evolutionary changes in technology come from conscious, deliberate decisions by inventors, engineers, software developers, and the wily, poison-spitting raptors of our age—marketeers. They are the trail bosses of guided evolution, making both minor and major changes on the fly, all to fight off attacks by rivals while still planning a safe and profitable route for their creations to follow a decade ahead.

Just because there's no directing intelligence in biological evolution, that doesn't mean a planned, deliberate change in hardware and software always works the way it was envisioned, or that even if it does work, that it will turn out to be a good idea. Embellishing mice by putting a scroll wheel and buttons to navigate through web pages was a splendid idea—a survivor trait. Replacing the mouse, as someone really did about 20 years ago, with two foot pedals, one to move the cursor up and down and the other to move it sideways, was a terrible idea, and it became extinct faster than you can say *Galapagos*.

That ridiculous mouse replacement was not alone. Extinction is the norm in technological development. When IBM launched its Personal Computer in 1987, it was an instant success because it had mutated small computers from toys for hobbyists into tools for business. Made from off-the-shelf components, it was affordable for those pining to have their own computers. But IBM's strategy that laid bare the machine's DNA led to a viral breakout of IBM clones. Within a few years, there were dozens of IBM imitations, some better, some cheaper, some both. The battle for survival was intense. The IBM PC was one of the non-survivors, although its ghost lives on at Lenovo, the Chinese company that bought rights to its laptop progeny. The chart on this page shows who today is at the top of the food chain.

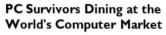

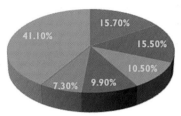

PC Survivors Dining at the World's Computer Market

Number of Quarterly PC Sales (Accurate as of 3Q, 2012)
■ Lenovo 13.8 million
■ Hewlett-Packard 13.6 million
■ Dell 9.2 million
■ Acer 8.6 million
■ AsusTek 6.4 million
■ Others 36.0 million

The initial eruption of PCs was followed by an aftershock of software. The first word processor to gain wide popularity was the cleverly named Electric Pencil, created for the Apple in 1976. Its fate should be a lesson to you that cleverness doesn't take you all that far. By 1979 Electric Pencil had fallen to WordStar, whose power and versatility kept it on top until WordPerfect beat WordStar and 55 other word processors in 1986. Arguably, by me anyway, still the best word processor to crawl out of the program primeval. WordPerfect lost its dominance to Microsoft Word and Microsoft's marketing muscle, proof that "fittest" can trump "best" in the battle for survival.

WordPerfect is still a survivor, but a good rule of thumb is that any technology rises to the top only so it has a good spot to take a fall. (The big exceptions are Intel's microprocessors, although **ARM processors** are gaining as Android grows in popularity.) The electronic spreadsheet Visicalc which alone justified the purchase of millions of personal computers, is extinct, killed off by Lotus 1-2-3, which fell in turn to Excel. The browser Internet Explorer pushed Netscape out of its cat-bird seat, but Explorer now has Firefox and Chrome gnawing at its heels. The small computer operating system CP/M was perfectly positioned to become the OS of choice on the new IBM PCs, but a simple twist of fate[1] gave that role to MS-DOS, which evolved into Windows, which is itself fast losing ground to Android in an increasingly mobile world.

Today, the Internet is the massive asteroid that is changing the technological ecosystem by choking old tech and opening up fresh ranges for new tech. Although Windows is hardly an endangered species (yet), Google's Android operating system thrives in the Web world, along with microprocessors designed for mobile computing. These are the beasts to watch. This part of *How Computers Work* is devoted to revealing the way that technology evolves, where it came from, and what it's evolved into, without going into the shock and awe of marketing. Said marketing is influential but beyond the scope of a book bound with technology and steeped in physics rather than the fiscal.

---

[1] *Interesting aside: CP/M was the creation of the late Gary Kildall, and had no serious rivals in the pre-IBM PC microcomputer market. Naturally, IBM wanted to talk to Kildall about modifying CP/M to run on its new computer. But when IBM executives went to see him, Kildall was out of the office flying his plane. The person in charge, Kildall's wife, Dorothy, didn't like the non-disclosure agreements the IBM suits insisted on, and so IBM approached this other guy, Bill Gates, who had had a modest success with a programming language, BASIC.*

IBM asked Gates if he had an operating system that could be made to run with the Intel 8086 processor that would be the heart of their new computer. Gates knew that the fittest don't survive by saying they can't do something. So he told them, "Yes," and quickly paid $50,000 to programmer Tim Patterson, who had developed an operating system adaptable to the 8086 with the name QDOS, for Quick and Dirty Operating System. (Really.) And the rest was not only history. It was survival.

CHAPTER

The Origins of Computer DNA

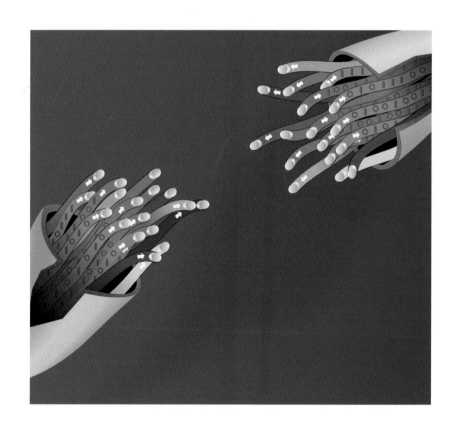

JUST AS we carbon-based units have an ancestry that began some hundreds of thousands of years ago, computing has an ancestry—not nearly as long, but just as important when it comes to understanding the workings of the digital machines we use today. Some of the nomenclature doesn't make sense without knowing a word's gene-alogy. Hard drives are so named because they evolved from something we rarely see today, a floppy drive. Why are CDs called "compact" discs? Because they are the offspring of video discs the size of LP-sized vinyl records.

Random access memory (RAM) seems like an unnecessary term. First of all, it seems like it is memory designed for someone with attention deficit syndrome—someone who keeps flitting from data in memory one place to a totally unrelated data at another location. But RAM is more understandable when you know that before memory chips and floppy and hard drives, programs and data were usually stored on magnetic tape a lot like the tape in video cas-settes (another fossil). Just as you couldn't hop from the start to the middle of a video tape, computer users from the ancient days, who wanted some bit of data stored only at the end of a gigantic roll of magnetic tape, had to fast forward through hundreds of inches of tape to get what they were after.

But DNA is not just nomenclature. Just like you don't get an elephant without there first having been a mastodon, without many of the fossils of the premobilian era we wouldn't have the kinds of computers, phones, TVs, tablets, printers, cars, medical devices— the list is endless—that we have today.

When you look at some fossils, they seem so primitive you're amazed anyone ever used them. The first modems sent text (only) over phone lines so slowly you could watch as e a c h   c h a r a c t e r   a p e a r e d. But to those who never previously had the ability to send written messages on a phone line, the creeping words were just terrific! And without them, we wouldn't have the Internet we have today.

There's another lesson to be learned by digging up digital bones: What inventions that today seem, well, kinda lame or too limited—such as 3D printers and 3D TV, voice recognition, artificial intelligence, and household robots—are most likely the future ancestors of technology about which our own carbon descendants will wonder how we ever got along without them. So show some respect.

Fossils of the Premobilian Era

THERE WAS A TIME in the office primeval that desktops were dominated by desktop PCs, which included Apple Macs. The hulking size of these giants denied the computers the mobility we take for granted in our age. Their bulk also made the desktop PCs a joy to expand, customize, and—in a Frankensteinian fever—hook up components from abandoned computers for the simple delight of creating a unique, powerful machine. In the modern era, mobile devices have changed the nature of the jungle and what survives. The bones strewn through these two are from an earlier edition of How Computers Work showing a PC loaded with the leading components of its day.

- Parts that are now extinct or well on their way to the fabled PC graveyard are in red.

- Survivors that have adapted to the changing computing ecosystem are indicated with green labels.

- Those still in the process of evolving are shown with blue labels.

A Power supply: Big computers need something to convert the raging flows of alternating current from the common wall plug into gentler streams of direct current. Mobile devices, from laptops on down the scale, eliminate much of the constant the power doctoring by using batteries.

B Optical drives: Until clouds become the all-pervasive method of storing and distributing files, a DVD drive will remain in desktops and bigger laptops if only to load new programs, rip CDs, and create backups of the family photos for people who don't trust clouds. For any device smaller than a laptop, optical storage is not simply extinct; it never qualified to be a contender.

C Tape drive: Slow and laborious for finding individual files, tape backups were used only because they were cheap compared to hard drives of the time. No one today mourns their extinction.

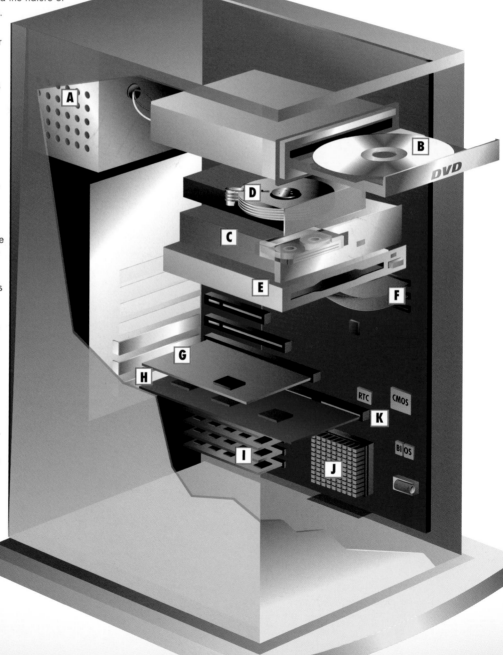

D Hard disk drive: It's still the cheapest way to store mass quantities of data, and it's been used in mobile devices as small as an iPod. But smartphones, which have more to do than simply store and play songs, are using RAM and clouds for storage. And in all devices, RAM-based solid-state drives are replacing the spinning disks for all but gargantuan mass storage.

E Floppy drives: They sleep with the fishes.

F Wide, flat drive cables: The old connections from the motherboard to the drives were stiff and a pain to maneuver through the usual tangle of wires. They're replaced by the slimmer, more manageable SATA cables.

G Video card: Unless you're a hell-bent-for-leather gamer, the video circuitry that comes on your motherboard will do nicely, thank you.

H Sound card: At one time if you wanted to hear more than a beep from your computer, you needed a sound card. Today built-in sound on desktops and laptops rivals home theater amps. An expansion card isn't needed unless you're a picky, picky audiophile.

I RAM: No matter whether you're a desktop, laptop, notebook, tablet, smartphone, MP3 player, smartwatch, or smartgoggles, you gotta have RAM. That's all there is to it. Of course that could mean some sort of **quantum memory**.

J Microprocessor: No matter what the device, no matter how large or how small, there will always be a microprocessor—the brain—which goes through its own sort of evolution to become faster and smarter.

K Required equipment on desktops and laptops has always included:
- A real-time clock to keep all components marching to the same drummer.
- The CMOS chip that retained basic, necessary information when the computer was turned off, along with the battery that kept the CMOS chip powered.
- And the BIOS (basic input/output system), a compendium of information about the components in a computer and how to get information in and out of them.

The information and functions this trio serves is moving, particularly in mobile devices, to flash memory that takes less space and is more easily updated.

L Fans/cooling: Work generates heat, and as chips and other computing parts work hard, they make devices hotter. Fans continue to cool down desktops, but smaller devices don't have room for fans. Unless something evolves that's small but does a big job of cooling, the limitation to how much and how fast smartphones, goggles, and tables can do may be how much heat human bodies can tolerate.

M USB ports: Universal serial ports are such an effective and fast way to move data among devices, from desktops to smartphones and smaller, that they will be around for a long time.

N Keyboard port and mouse port: Are you kidding? That's what USB ports
O and Bluetooth are for these days.

P Parallel port: Used to be you could connect a printer without one of these. Now your printer can use USB, networks, WiFi, or Bluetooth.

Q Serial ports: Non-universal, that is. These were versatile in their day. If you didn't mind reconnecting the pin-outs in different, sometimes mysterious ways, you could get them to connect to nearly anything. Today, the universal version does a far better job without the futzing.

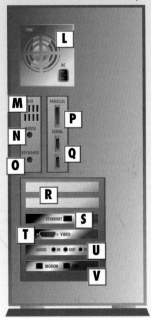

R Expansion slots: When computers came as basic devices that you could configure to make it do new and wonderful things, expansion slots were essential. Today, they're a luxury for supernerds who want to push their computers to the limits.

S Network ports: Hard wiring still exists in the local area network world, but so does WiFi, which makes an ethernet port unnecessary—and on mobile devices, impossible.

T Video ports: The standard VGA port has been joined on desktop PCs and laptops by digital video and HDMI ports. On tablets and smartphone devices, with their built-in screens, WiFi and near-field connectivity, there's not a lot of demand for wired video output, but they can still manage it with mini-HDMI and micro-HDMI ports and adapters.

U Audio ports: You'll still see a full-array of output ports on desktops to handle 5.1 and 7.1 audio, but mobile devices have it down to a single headphone port for stereo and an HDMI port if it needs to pump out heavy duty audio. And that's moving to Bluetooth.

V Modem: Already, using a modem to connect to the rest of the world seems as primitive as twirling a stick to make a fire.

Persistent Relics: The Mouse

TWO ARTIFACTS of prehistoric computing (pre-IBM PC) that have survived all sorts of changes in processors, storage, user interfaces, and fans are the mouse and the keyboard (see the next page). Although the transition to mobile computing, with the need for a computer to fit into a pocket, briefcase, or purse, has done much to sever both input methods, we still need them for some things. Anyone who has tried to type on the virtual keyboard of a smartphone will confess to hooking up a wireless keyboard when the typing gets serious. And although gesture interfaces are, indeed, handy on mobile devices, those who want to touch up a photo or play an action game on a tablet or phone will soon be longing for the feel of a mouse between their fingers.

1 As you move an **optical mouse**, a laser or an LED-light emitting diode lights up the surface the mouse is moving across. Dedicated gamers argue about the accuracy, precision, and tracking ability of laser versus LED mice. If you are playing fast-paced action games, the differences won't matter to you.

2 A digital camera, smaller than a dime, peers through a plastic lens at the surface lit up by the light. The camera takes hundreds of photos a second, looking for differences among the images that indicate the speed and direction of the mouse.

3 The camera sees the surface in only black and white. Here the surface's microscopic pattern has moved up and to the right from one frame to another, indicating that the mouse moved to the left and down.

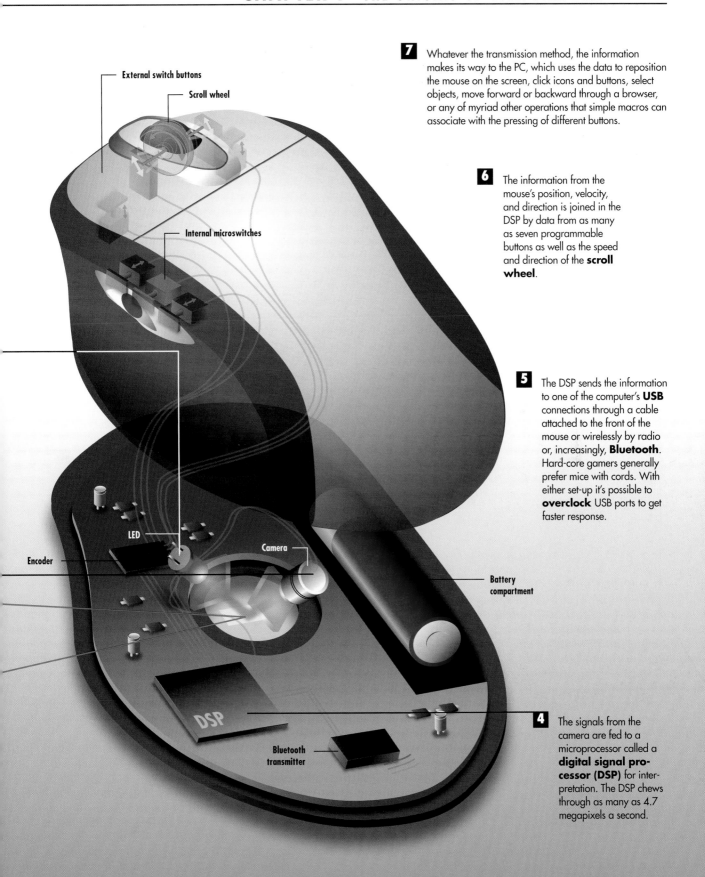

External switch buttons

Scroll wheel

Internal microswitches

LED

Encoder

Camera

Battery compartment

DSP

Bluetooth transmitter

7 Whatever the transmission method, the information makes its way to the PC, which uses the data to reposition the mouse on the screen, click icons and buttons, select objects, move forward or backward through a browser, or any of myriad other operations that simple macros can associate with the pressing of different buttons.

6 The information from the mouse's position, velocity, and direction is joined in the DSP by data from as many as seven programmable buttons as well as the speed and direction of the **scroll wheel**.

5 The DSP sends the information to one of the computer's **USB** connections through a cable attached to the front of the mouse or wirelessly by radio or, increasingly, **Bluetooth**. Hard-core gamers generally prefer mice with cords. With either set-up it's possible to **overclock** USB ports to get faster response.

4 The signals from the camera are fed to a microprocessor called a **digital signal processor (DSP)** for interpretation. The DSP chews through as many as 4.7 megapixels a second.

Persistent Relics: The Keyboard

SURE, THESE DAYS, whether you have a PC or Mac, you can write the script for the next boffo slasher movie by talking into it, scanning, hand-writing, and waving your hands in the air. But any computer veteran will tell you that when it comes to pushing text to screen at the speed of thought, nothing beats a keyboard.

 Pressing a key causes a change in the amount of current flowing through a circuit associated specifically with that key.

2 A microprocessor built into the keyboard constantly scans circuits leading to the keys. It detects the increase and decrease in current from the key that has been pressed or released. Each key has a unique set of codes, so the processor can, for example, distinguish between the left and right Shift keys. To distinguish between a real signal and an aberrant current fluctuation, the scan is repeated hundreds of times each second. The processor only acts upon signals detected for two or more scans.

3 Depending on which key's circuit carries a signal to the microprocessor, the processor generates a number, called a **scan code**. There are two scan codes for each key, one for when the key is depressed and the other for when it's released. The processor stores the number in the keyboard's own memory buffer, and it loads the number in a port connection where it can be read by the computer's **BIOS** (basic input/output system). The processor then sends an interrupt signal over the keyboard cable to tell the processor that a scan code is waiting for it. An interrupt tells the processor to drop whatever else it is doing and to divert its attention to the service requested by the interrupt.

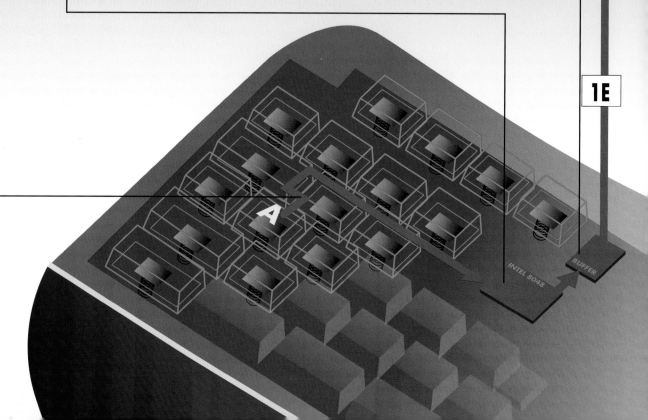

1E

SCAN CODE TABLE

1E	A
30	B
2E	C

1E

Keys to the PC

Two primary types of keys appear on keyboards. **Capacitive** keys are built around a spring that makes a clicking noise when the key is depressed. Pressing it causes a metal plunger to pass between two metal pads on the underlying circuit boards that act as a capacitor. The plunger causes a change in the electrical potential between the two pads, which signals that the key is pressed down. **Hard-contact** keys are mounted above a rubber dome. Pressing the key collapses the dome and presses two metal plates together so current flows through them. When the key is released, the dome pops the keycap back up.

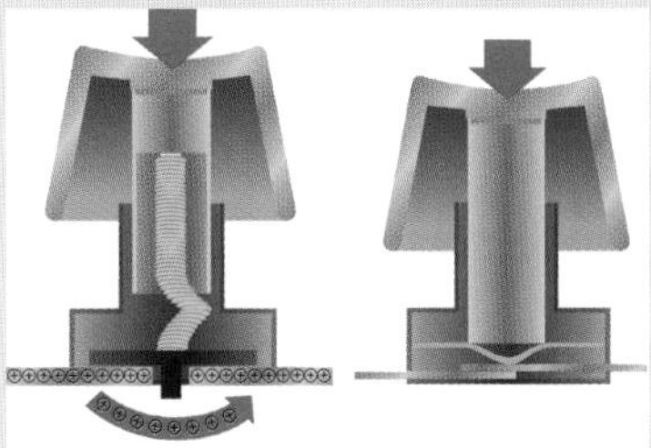

Capacitive key   **Hard-contact key**

4 The BIOS reads the scan code from the keyboard port and sends a signal to the keyboard that tells the keyboard it can delete the scan code from its buffer.

RAM

5 If the scan code is for one of the ordinary shift keys or for one of the special shift keys and toggle keys—Ctrl, Alt, Num Lock, Caps Lock, Scroll Lock, or Insert—the BIOS changes two bytes in a special area of memory to maintain a record of which of these keys has been pressed.

6 For all other keys, the BIOS checks those two bytes to determine the status of the shift and toggle keys. Depending on the status of those bytes, the BIOS translates the appropriate scan code into an ASCII code, used by the PC, that stands for a character, or into a special code for a function key or a cursor movement key. Uppercase and lowercase characters have different ASCII codes. Applications can choose to interpret any keystroke to display a character, or as a command. Windows applications, for example, universally use Ctrl+B to toggle the boldface attribute. In either case, the BIOS places the ASCII or special key code into its own memory buffer, where the operating system or application software retrieves it as soon as any current operation is finished.

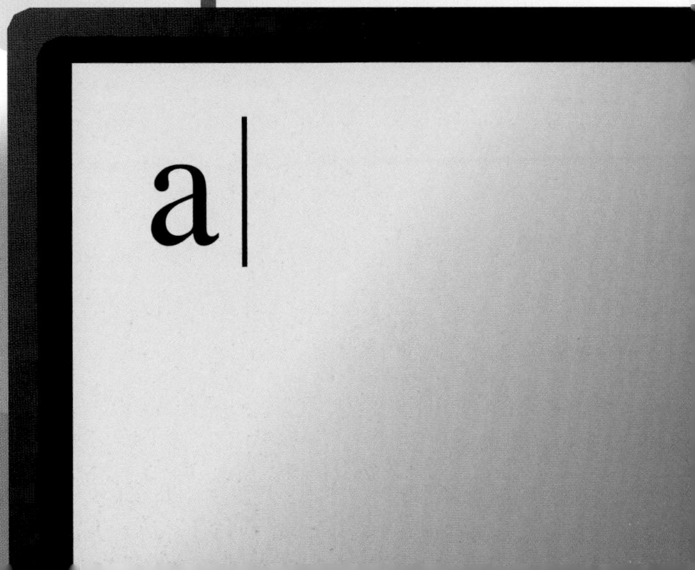

a

How the Workaday Floppy Drive Ruled

WE LOOK BACK today at the floppy as an agonizingly slow drive that didn't really hold diddily. But for all its deficiencies, the floppy drive was an underappreciated wonder of its time. Think of it: An entire book full of information could be contained on a cheap disk that you could slip into your pocket. Until the advent of the cloud and cheap USB flash drives, floppy drives were a sure and convenient way to get small amounts of data from one PC to another. No communication lines, protocol setups, networks, or gateways were needed; just pull the floppy out of one machine and slip it into another. It has a legacy that can't be matched, and its simplicity makes the floppy drive an ideal leap-off for learning how computing storage works.

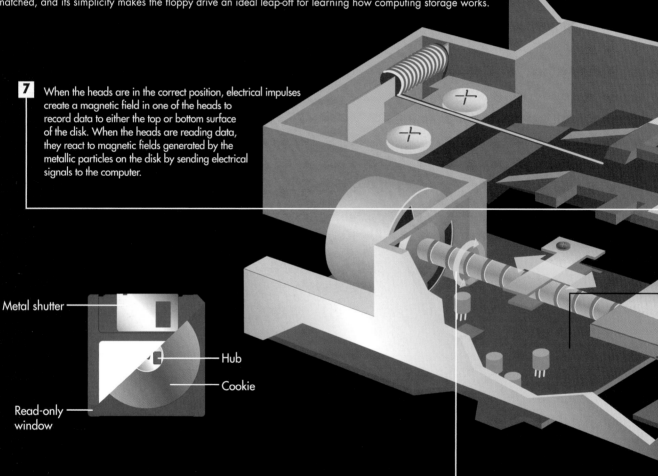

7 When the heads are in the correct position, electrical impulses create a magnetic field in one of the heads to record data to either the top or bottom surface of the disk. When the heads are reading data, they react to magnetic fields generated by the metallic particles on the disk by sending electrical signals to the computer.

Metal shutter

Hub

Cookie

Read-only window

6 A **stepper motor**—which can turn a specific distance in either direction according to signals from the circuit board—moves a second shaft that has a spiral groove cut into it. An arm attached to the read/write heads rests inside the shaft's groove. As the shaft turns, the arm moves back and forth, positioning the read/write heads over the disk.

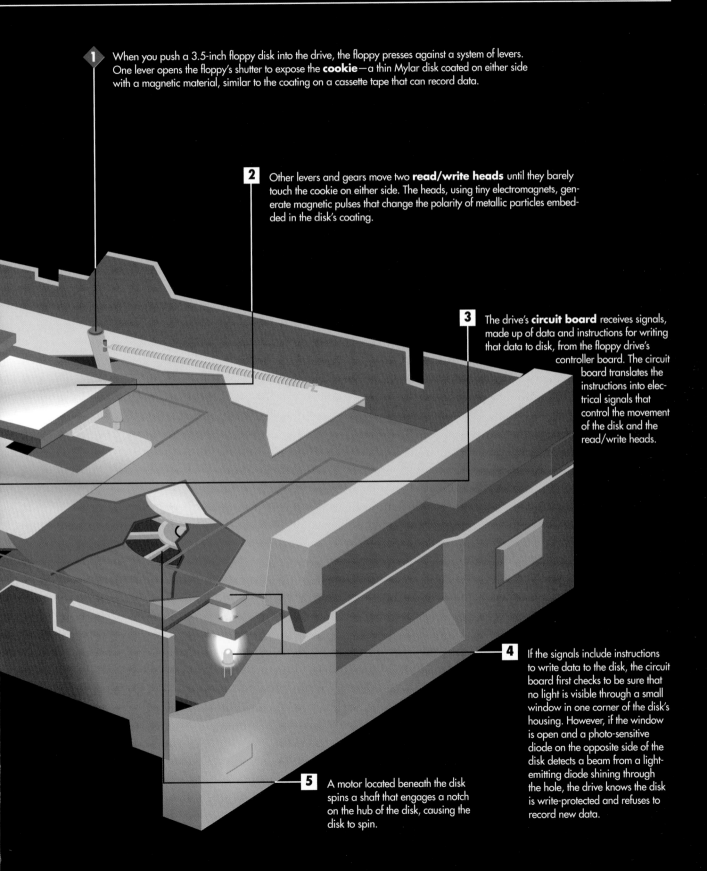

1 When you push a 3.5-inch floppy disk into the drive, the floppy presses against a system of levers. One lever opens the floppy's shutter to expose the **cookie**—a thin Mylar disk coated on either side with a magnetic material, similar to the coating on a cassette tape that can record data.

2 Other levers and gears move two **read/write heads** until they barely touch the cookie on either side. The heads, using tiny electromagnets, generate magnetic pulses that change the polarity of metallic particles embedded in the disk's coating.

3 The drive's **circuit board** receives signals, made up of data and instructions for writing that data to disk, from the floppy drive's controller board. The circuit board translates the instructions into electrical signals that control the movement of the disk and the read/write heads.

4 If the signals include instructions to write data to the disk, the circuit board first checks to be sure that no light is visible through a small window in one corner of the disk's housing. However, if the window is open and a photo-sensitive diode on the opposite side of the disk detects a beam from a light-emitting diode shining through the hole, the drive knows the disk is write-protected and refuses to record new data.

5 A motor located beneath the disk spins a shaft that engages a notch on the hub of the disk, causing the disk to spin.

How the CRT Was The Grande Dame of Displays

THE CRT is like a legendary soprano. It's been such a good computing display that for decades after the younger LCDs began stealing the spotlight, the CRT is still regarded by display aficionados as the standard by which all other performers must be judged. As is inevitable in a technology ruled by evolution, the CRT is rarely seen these days, but those who knew CRTs well are still in awe at how it used controlled lightning to paint computing's first color displays.

2 The DAC compares the digital values sent by the PC to a look-up table that contains the matching voltage levels for the three primary colors needed to create the color of a single pixel. In a normal VGA adapter, the table contains values for 262,144 possible colors, of which 256 values can be stored in the VGA adapter's memory at one time. Today's Super-VGA adapters have enough memory to store 16 bits of information for each pixel (65,536 colors, called **high color**) or 24 bits a pixel (16,777,216 shades—or **true color**).

3 The adapter sends signals to three electron guns located at the back of the monitor's cathode-ray tube (CRT). Through the vacuum inside the CRT, each electron gun shoots out a stream of electrons, one stream for each of the three primary colors. The intensity of each stream is controlled by the signals from the adapter.

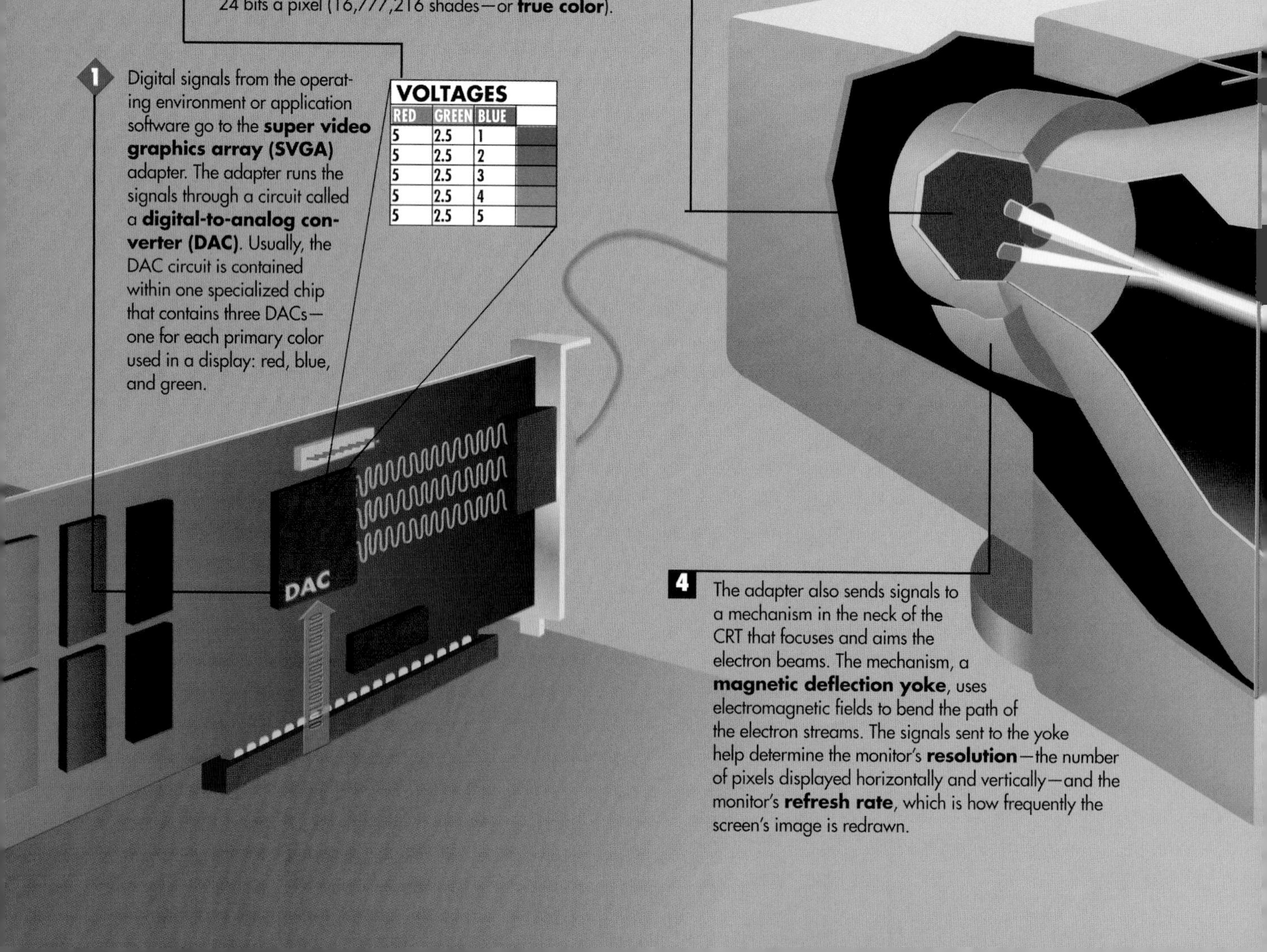

1 Digital signals from the operating environment or application software go to the **super video graphics array (SVGA)** adapter. The adapter runs the signals through a circuit called a **digital-to-analog converter (DAC)**. Usually, the DAC circuit is contained within one specialized chip that contains three DACs— one for each primary color used in a display: red, blue, and green.

VOLTAGES

RED	GREEN	BLUE
5	2.5	1
5	2.5	2
5	2.5	3
5	2.5	4
5	2.5	5

DAC

4 The adapter also sends signals to a mechanism in the neck of the CRT that focuses and aims the electron beams. The mechanism, a **magnetic deflection yoke**, uses electromagnetic fields to bend the path of the electron streams. The signals sent to the yoke help determine the monitor's **resolution**—the number of pixels displayed horizontally and vertically—and the monitor's **refresh rate**, which is how frequently the screen's image is redrawn.

5 The beams pass through holes in a metal plate called a **shadow mask**. The purpose of the mask is to keep the electron beams precisely aligned with their targets on the inside of the CRT's screen. The CRT's **dot pitch** is the measurement of how close the holes are to each other; the closer the holes, the smaller the dot pitch. This, in turn, creates a sharper image. The holes in most shadow masks are arranged in triangles, with the important exception of those of the Sony Trinitron CRT used by many monitor manufacturers. The Trinitron's holes are arranged as parallel slots.

6 The electrons strike the phosphors coating the inside of the screen. **Phosphors** are materials that glow when they are struck by electrons. Three different phosphor materials are used—one each for red, blue, and green. The stronger the electron beam that hits a phosphor, the more light the phosphor emits. If each red, green, and blue dot in an arrangement is struck by equally intense electron beams, the result is a dot of white light. To create different colors, the intensity of each of the three beams is varied. After a beam leaves a phosphor dot, the phosphor continues to glow briefly, a condition called **persistence**. For an image to remain stable, the phosphors must be reactivated by repeated scans of the electron beams before the persistence fades away.

7 After the beams make one horizontal sweep across the screen, the electron streams are turned off as the magnetic yoke refocuses the path of the beams back to the left edge of the screen at a point just below the previous scan line. This process is called **raster scanning**.

8 The magnetic deflection yoke continually changes the angles at which the electron beams are bent so that they sweep across the entire screen surface from the upper-left corner of the screen to the lower-right corner. A complete sweep of the screen is called a **field**. Upon completing a field, the beams return to the upper-left corner to begin a new field. The screen normally is redrawn, or **refreshed**, about 60 times a second (or more).

9 Some display adapters scan only every other line with each field, a process called **interlacing**. Interlacing allows the adapter to create higher resolutions—that is, to scan more lines—with less expensive components. But the fading of the phosphors between each pass can be noticeable, causing the screen to flicker.

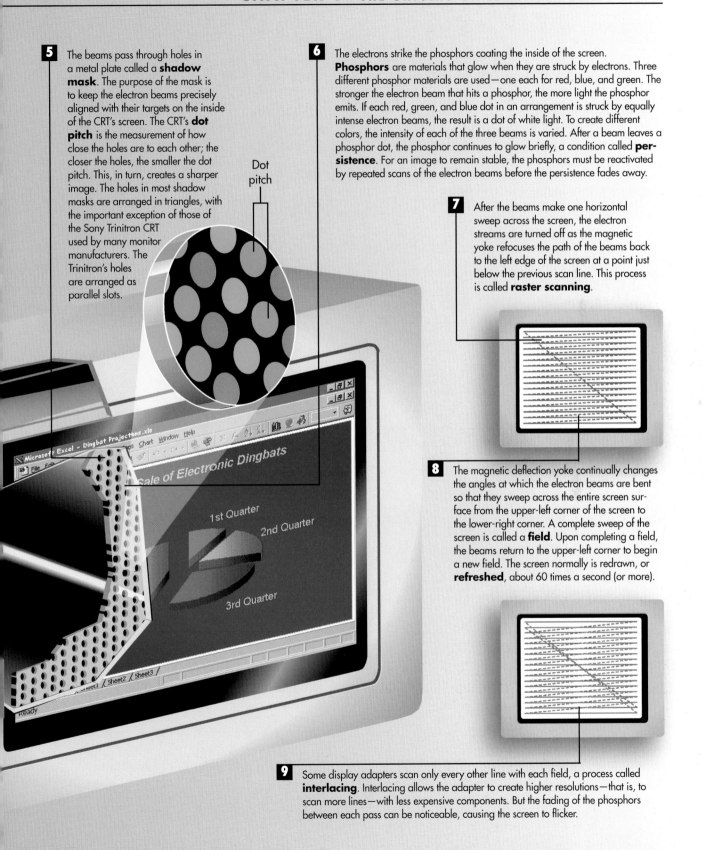

Dot pitch

How the Impact Printer Was Right on the Spot

THERE WAS SOMETHING viscerally satisfying about the first computing printers. They created text—and sometimes some rudimentary graphics—by pounding little metal rods onto a typewriter ribbon. They were noisy—somewhere between a clatter and a whine. Because it took them forever to print the simplest page, the racket could be interminable, but the sound was reassuring. It let you know you were printing; better still, you weren't typing something yourself.

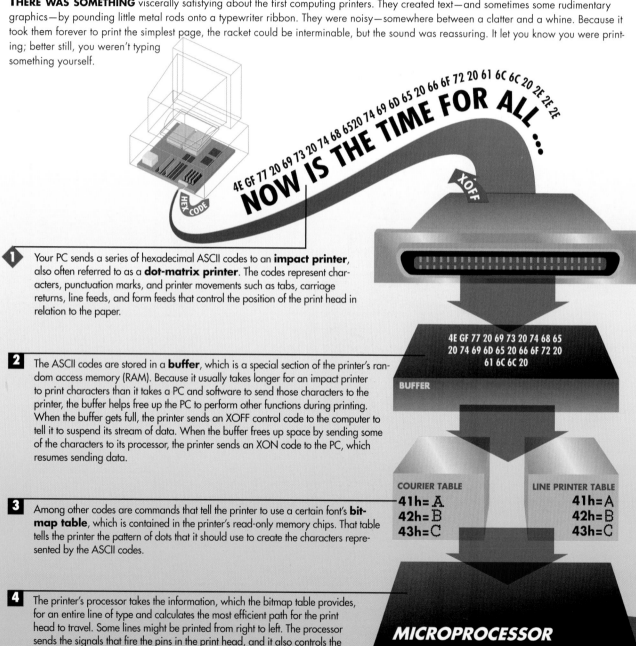

1 Your PC sends a series of hexadecimal ASCII codes to an **impact printer**, also often referred to as a **dot-matrix printer**. The codes represent characters, punctuation marks, and printer movements such as tabs, carriage returns, line feeds, and form feeds that control the position of the print head in relation to the paper.

2 The ASCII codes are stored in a **buffer**, which is a special section of the printer's random access memory (RAM). Because it usually takes longer for an impact printer to print characters than it takes a PC and software to send those characters to the printer, the buffer helps free up the PC to perform other functions during printing. When the buffer gets full, the printer sends an XOFF control code to the computer to tell it to suspend its stream of data. When the buffer frees up space by sending some of the characters to its processor, the printer sends an XON code to the PC, which resumes sending data.

3 Among other codes are commands that tell the printer to use a certain font's **bitmap table**, which is contained in the printer's read-only memory chips. That table tells the printer the pattern of dots that it should use to create the characters represented by the ASCII codes.

4 The printer's processor takes the information, which the bitmap table provides, for an entire line of type and calculates the most efficient path for the print head to travel. Some lines might be printed from right to left. The processor sends the signals that fire the pins in the print head, and it also controls the movements of the print head and platen.

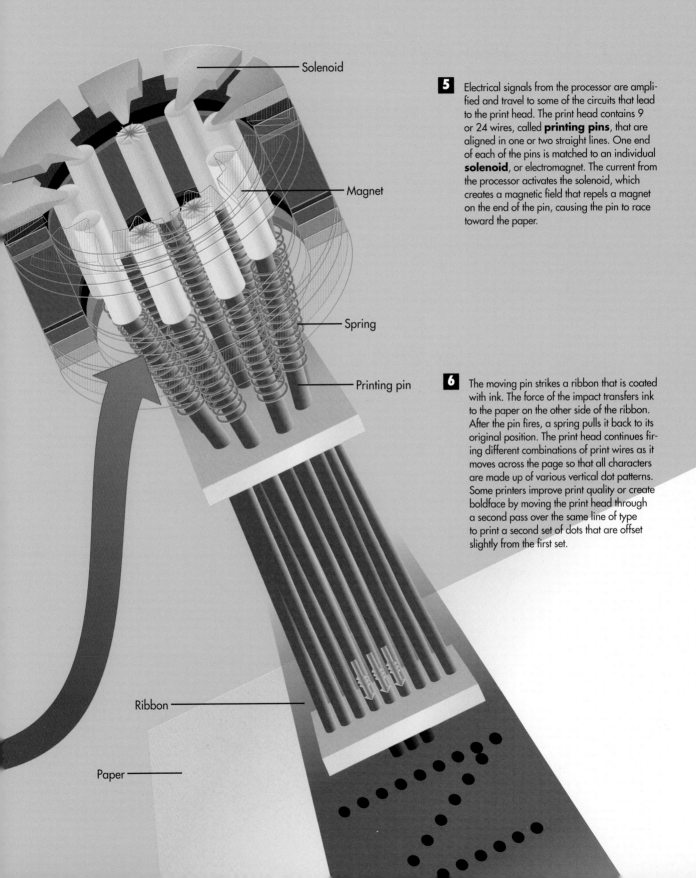

Solenoid

Magnet

Spring

Printing pin

Ribbon

Paper

5 Electrical signals from the processor are amplified and travel to some of the circuits that lead to the print head. The print head contains 9 or 24 wires, called **printing pins**, that are aligned in one or two straight lines. One end of each of the pins is matched to an individual **solenoid**, or electromagnet. The current from the processor activates the solenoid, which creates a magnetic field that repels a magnet on the end of the pin, causing the pin to race toward the paper.

6 The moving pin strikes a ribbon that is coated with ink. The force of the impact transfers ink to the paper on the other side of the ribbon. After the pin fires, a spring pulls it back to its original position. The print head continues firing different combinations of print wires as it moves across the page so that all characters are made up of various vertical dot patterns. Some printers improve print quality or create boldface by moving the print head through a second pass over the same line of type to print a second set of dots that are offset slightly from the first set.

The Unlikely Progenitor to the Internet: The Dialup Modem

NOTHING SAYS 1988 LIKE the hissing and growling of an old-fashioned dial-up modem. At first used to connect individual computers together across copper phone lines, these little boxes were many people's first gateway to the Internet. For those unfortunate enough to not have broadband access, these monumentally slow devices remain the only way to access the Web from a desktop computer.

33.6 K **56.6 K**

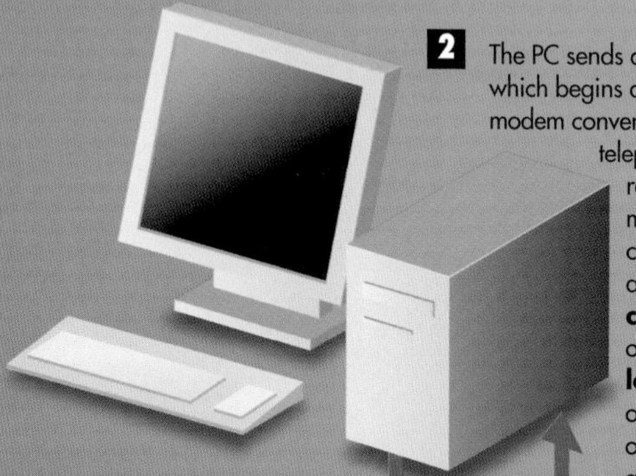

2 The PC sends a message or a request, which begins as digital data in the PC. The modem converts the bits to an ordinary telephone analog signal. The request travels from the PC's modem along two twisted copper wires that lead to a local telephone company's **central office**. This stretch of wire is called the **analog local loop** and the outgoing signals that travel on it, under ideal conditions and with data compression, are limited to 36,000bps.

1 The final standard in dial-up modem technology is called 56K, or V.92. It allows a person to send data at the normal analog modem rates of 33,600bps (bits per second), but get information back nearly twice as fast. When a PC uses a 56K modem to connect to a **host**, the modem probes the connection to determine whether the host modem supports the V.92 standard of transmitting 56,600bps. If it's not then the modems on either end of the connection default to normal transmissions. If it is, the PC and host modems synchronize their timing to help ensure the accuracy of the downloaded data.

10 In the client modem, a digital signal processor returns the voltages to their digital symbol values and translates those values, according to the symbol scheme that the V.92 protocol uses, into data in the form of bits sent to the computer.

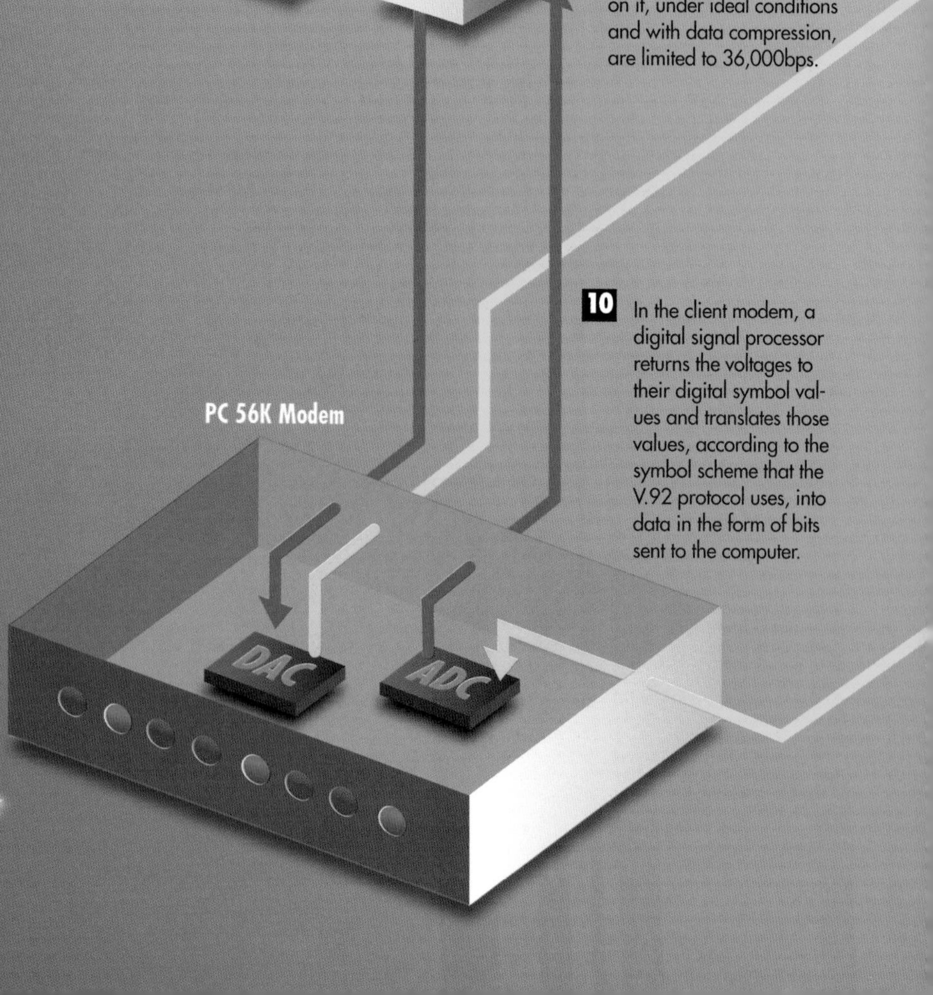

PC 56K Modem

μ-Law Stream
Analog Stream
Digital Stream

DAC   ADC

3 At the central office, the signal enters e **public switched telephone network (PSTN)**, what we generally think of as simply "the telephone system." There, the analog signal is transformed into a digital signal. Except for the local analog loops, virtually the entire U.S. phone system transmits data digitally, which theoretically allows data to move as fast as 64,000bps and makes V.92 technology possible.

4 At the telephone facility, an **analog-to-digital converter (ADC)** samples the incoming analog waveform 8,000 times a second, and each time the signal's approximate amplitude, or the strength of the current, is recorded as an 8-bit **pulse code modulation (PCM)**. Although there are an infinite number of values for the amplitude each time it's sampled, the ADC can detect only 256 discrete levels. That's because along the path the electronic signals travel, it encounters fleeting electromagnetic fields that can come from innumerable sources, including the phone wires themselves. These fields produce a current voltage that distorts the signal's value—makes it fuzzy. This **line noise** limits analog lines to 33.6Kbps.

5 The data travels through the phone system until it arrives at a host system, usually a local **Internet service provider (ISP)**. The provider's 56K modems recognize whether the signal is coming from a matching modem.

Host 56K Server Modem

6 In response to the request from the PC, the service returns some sort of information, which could be a web page filled with art and music, a shareware program, plain text, or simply a "Not Found" message. The service sends the information through, 8 bits at a time, to a device called a **μ-law codec** (μ-law coder/decoder). μ-law is named for a mathematical progression in which the difference between one value and the next larger value gets larger itself as the values increase.

7 The codec translates the data into values corresponding to the most recognizable of the 256 possible voltages that can be distinguished on an analog loop. These values are called **symbols**—information-bearing tokens.

8 If the modems could use all 256 possible symbols, they could send 64,000 bits of data each second. But the host and client modems use some of the symbols to keep tabs on each other. The symbols whose values approach zero are too closely spaced to each other to be distinguished accurately on a noisy phone line. The modems rely on the 128 most robust symbols, which only allow 56,600bps. (FCC regulations limit the power that can be used for phone signals, which limits real-world transmission rates to about 53Kbps.)

9 When the signals reach the analog local loop, a **digital-to-analog converter (DAC)** generates 8,000 electrical pulses each second. The voltage of each pulse corresponds to one of the 128 possible symbol values.

How Cabling Was Worse: Serial

SERIAL COMMUNICATIONS send data back and forth one bit at a time. This isn't as bad as it sounds. USB is an extremely high-speed serial interface and so is Serial-ATA. This progenitor, which adhered to a standard called **RS-232**, traveled in the slow lane. They were good for connecting dial-up modems, the occasional '90s-era scientific or troubleshooting gadget, and not much else.

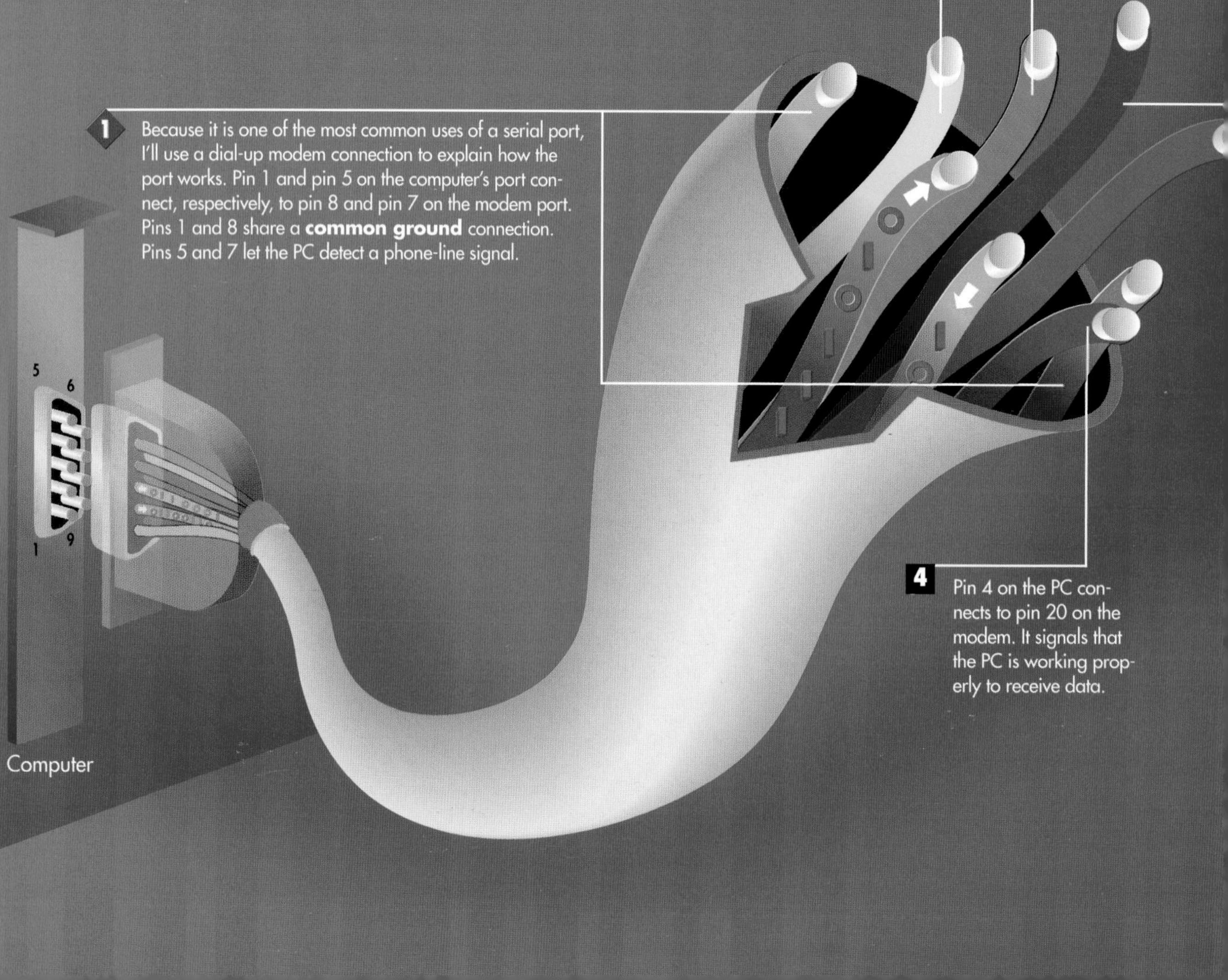

3 Pin 7 on the PC connects to pin 4 on the modem. The modem puts a voltage on this line to create a request, a signal to the PC that the modem is ready to receive data.

2 Pin 6—the same on both ends—sends a signal that data is ready to be sent (**data ready**).

1 Because it is one of the most common uses of a serial port, I'll use a dial-up modem connection to explain how the port works. Pin 1 and pin 5 on the computer's port connect, respectively, to pin 8 and pin 7 on the modem port. Pins 1 and 8 share a **common ground** connection. Pins 5 and 7 let the PC detect a phone-line signal.

4 Pin 4 on the PC connects to pin 20 on the modem. It signals that the PC is working properly to receive data.

5   6

1   9

Computer

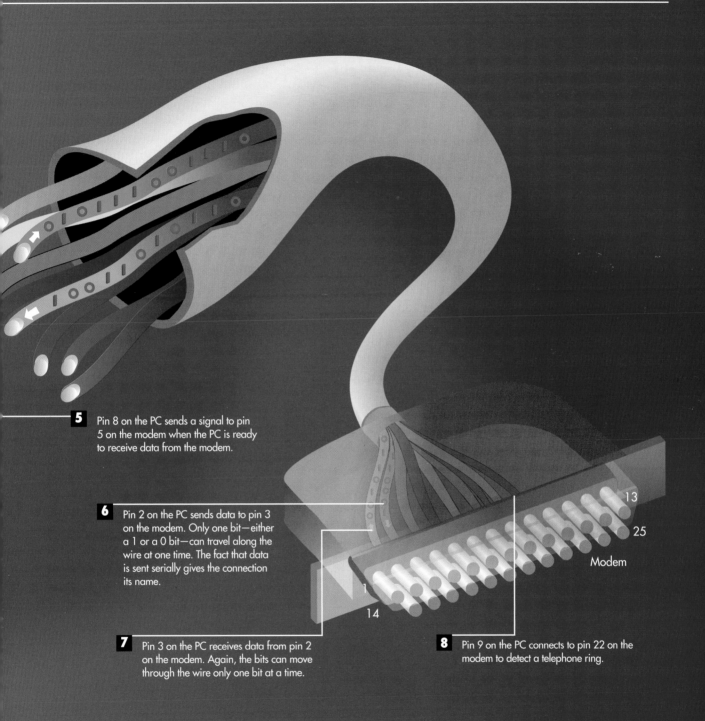

5 Pin 8 on the PC sends a signal to pin 5 on the modem when the PC is ready to receive data from the modem.

6 Pin 2 on the PC sends data to pin 3 on the modem. Only one bit—either a 1 or a 0 bit—can travel along the wire at one time. The fact that data is sent serially gives the connection its name.

13

25

Modem

1

14

7 Pin 3 on the PC receives data from pin 2 on the modem. Again, the bits can move through the wire only one bit at a time.

8 Pin 9 on the PC connects to pin 22 on the modem to detect a telephone ring.

Soldiers All in a Row

A serial connection is comparable to soldiers lined up in a single row. Only one of them at a time would be able to cross a line drawn on the ground. It would take more than a minute for all the soldiers in a battalion to cross the line serially.

How Cabling Was Worse: Parallel

BEFORE SERIAL LEARNED how to channel its inner hyperdrive, parallel communications became the solution to speeding up data transfers by transferring 8 bits of data at a time. These ports were primarily used for connecting printers, before USB went and made them obsolete.

1 A signal to the PC on line 13—called the **select line**—from the peripheral, usually a printer, tells the computer that the printer is online and ready to receive data.

2 Data is loaded on lines 2 through 9, shown here as green, in the form of a "high" voltage signal—actually about five volts—to signify a 1, or a low, nearly zero voltage signal to signify a 0.

3 After the voltages have been set on all the data lines, line 1 sends a **strobe signal** to the printer for one microsecond to let the printer know that it should read the voltages on the data lines.

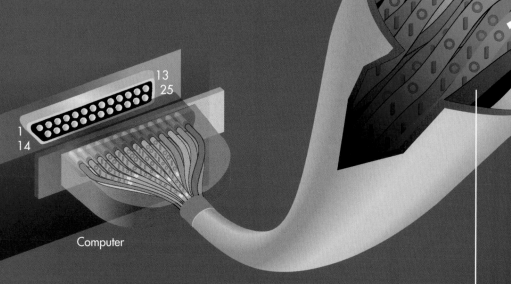

13
25

1
14

Computer

9 A low-voltage or zero-voltage signal from the PC on line 14 tells the printer to advance the paper one line when it receives a carriage return code. A high-voltage signal tells the printer to advance the paper one line only when it receives a line-advance code from the printer.

10 A signal from the PC on line 17 tells the printer not to accept data. This line is used only with some printers, which are designed to be switched on and off by the PC. Lines 18 through 25 are simply ground lines.

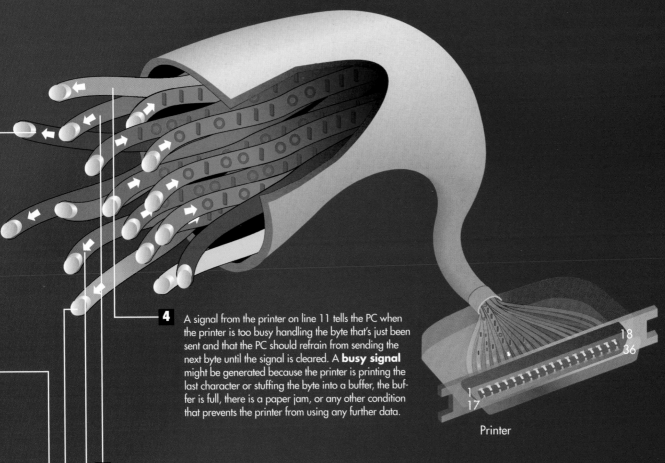

Printer

4 A signal from the printer on line 11 tells the PC when the printer is too busy handling the byte that's just been sent and that the PC should refrain from sending the next byte until the signal is cleared. A **busy signal** might be generated because the printer is printing the last character or stuffing the byte into a buffer, the buffer is full, there is a paper jam, or any other condition that prevents the printer from using any further data.

5 A signal from the printer on line 10 **acknowledges** receiving the data sent on lines 2 through 9 and tells the PC that the printer is ready to receive another character.

6 Line 12 sends a signal from the printer to the PC if the printer runs out of paper.

7 The printer uses line 15 to tell the PC some error condition exists, such as a jammed print head or an open panel. However, it doesn't specify the nature of the error.

8 A signal from the PC on line 16 causes the printer to **reset** itself to its original state—the same as if the printer were turned off and on.

Parallel Soldiers

Think of parallel communications as being like a platoon of soldiers marching eight abreast. Draw a line in the ground in front of the soldiers, and eight soldiers will cross it simultaneously, followed by the eight soldiers behind them. A battalion marching in this manner could cross the line in about 10 seconds.

How the Power Supply Hasn't Changed

Power cable

The **power supply unit (PSU)** is as fundamental and important component to a computer as even the processor or motherboard. A PC won't even start unless the supply can provide it with the proper amount and voltage of electricity. It then runs a series of internal tests to make sure it is working properly and supplying the right voltage and amount of power. If everything is working properly, it sends a Power Good signal to the PC's motherboard that alerts the motherboard to start up. It is constantly sending that signal. If the power supply stops working properly at any time, it stops sending the signal, and the PC shuts down.

 The power supply's power cord plugs into a normal electrical outlet that in the United States provides **alternating current (AC)** power at 110 volts and 60Hz. The 110 volt AC power coming into the power supply needs to be transformed into **direct current (DC)** power at much lower voltages than can be used by the sensitive electronic components inside a PC.

2 The incoming power is **dirty power**; that is, there are small fluctuations in its current and power. PC components could theoretically be damaged by these variations, so some power supplies (generally the more expensive ones) filter and condition the power before converting it to lower-voltage DC power. The power flows through an **electromagnetic interference (EMI)** filter to smooth out fluctuations and line-conditioning circuitry to maintain a consistent power level.

9 The power is sent to a series of cables that ultimately provide power to the PC's components. Each cable has several wires in it, and each of those wires carries different voltages. Twelve-volt power is for devices such as disk-drive motors, while 3.3-volt and 5-volt power is used by PCI/AGP cards, ISA cards, CPUs, DIMMs, and other components. The cable joins with the PC via cable connectors. Each connector is **keyed** so that it only attaches in a certain way, which ensures that the proper voltage is supplied in the proper place.

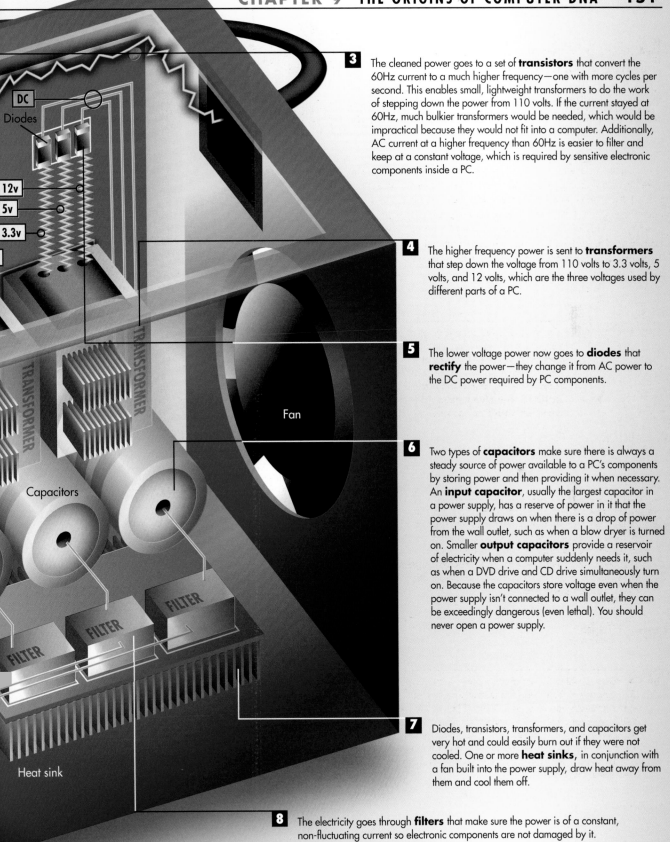

DC

Diodes

12v

5v

3.3v

TRANSFORMER

TRANSFORMER

Capacitors

Fan

FILTER

FILTER

FILTER

Heat sink

3 The cleaned power goes to a set of **transistors** that convert the 60Hz current to a much higher frequency—one with more cycles per second. This enables small, lightweight transformers to do the work of stepping down the power from 110 volts. If the current stayed at 60Hz, much bulkier transformers would be needed, which would be impractical because they would not fit into a computer. Additionally, AC current at a higher frequency than 60Hz is easier to filter and keep at a constant voltage, which is required by sensitive electronic components inside a PC.

4 The higher frequency power is sent to **transformers** that step down the voltage from 110 volts to 3.3 volts, 5 volts, and 12 volts, which are the three voltages used by different parts of a PC.

5 The lower voltage power now goes to **diodes** that **rectify** the power—they change it from AC power to the DC power required by PC components.

6 Two types of **capacitors** make sure there is always a steady source of power available to a PC's components by storing power and then providing it when necessary. An **input capacitor**, usually the largest capacitor in a power supply, has a reserve of power in it that the power supply draws on when there is a drop of power from the wall outlet, such as when a blow dryer is turned on. Smaller **output capacitors** provide a reservoir of electricity when a computer suddenly needs it, such as when a DVD drive and CD drive simultaneously turn on. Because the capacitors store voltage even when the power supply isn't connected to a wall outlet, they can be exceedingly dangerous (even lethal). You should never open a power supply.

7 Diodes, transistors, transformers, and capacitors get very hot and could easily burn out if they were not cooled. One or more **heat sinks**, in conjunction with a fan built into the power supply, draw heat away from them and cool them off.

8 The electricity goes through **filters** that make sure the power is of a constant, non-fluctuating current so electronic components are not damaged by it.

How the iPhone Made It Slick

YOU COULD ARGUE that everything in Apple's iPhone had been done before. Web surfing? Been there. Photo snapping? Done that. Playing MP3s? Heard that. Instant messaging? Wrote that. Making phone calls? Give me a break. They've all been done before. The thing about the iPhone is that it was the first technology to do them all, so slickly, and in a new form that let you carry all these digital tools in your pocket. The iPhone wasn't the first attempt at such a thing, but it was the first big success story, and that makes it the crucial link between computers and phones. (Except for the fact, of course, that it's not crucial. Apple has sold 500 million iPhones.)

Fans for Apple and Android will argue ceaselessly about what's the best smartphone. But the thing you can't argue is that the iPhone is responsible for computing's transition into a new era of technology, and like all evolution, there's no going back. Here's what made the iPhone the granddaddy of whatever smartphone you're packing today.

A flexible printed circuit connects the circuit board to the phone's Retina display, which packs in upward of a whopping 326 pixels per inch for HD-quality resolution.

The iPhone processor looks for **patterns** in what someone's typing and completes words automatically or enlarges the touch area on the screen that will respond to what the iPhone guesses the next letter will be.

The iPhone's complex touch mechanisms respond to pressure, shape, and movement of fingers. They allow the screen to respond to **gestures** made with one or more fingers. For example, the iPhone interprets a finger and thumb moving away from each other as a zoom command, and it responds by enlarging the screen image. This technology is called **multitouch**.

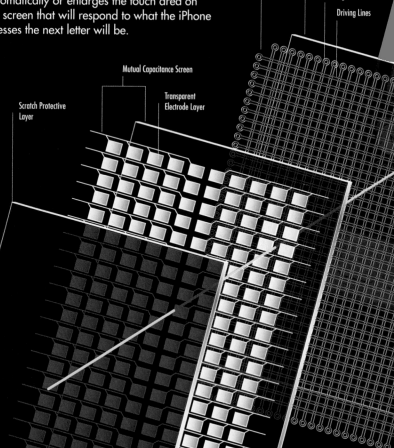

Self-capacitance Screen

Sensing Lines

Driving Lines

Mutual Capacitance Screen

Transparent Electrode Layer

Scratch Protective Layer

The iPhone **multitasks** just as a full-sized computer does. For example, while you browse the Web, the phone can update your contacts, email, calendar, etc.

Infrared LED and sensor detect when the phone is removed from the ear and hangs up

Jacks for earphones and power cord

Camera

SIM

Micro Processors

Infrared Sensor

SIM card for phone service activation

Circuit board with two microprocessors

BATTERY

Battery

9:42 AM

Tuesday

9

Calendar

Photos

Camera

Maps

73°

Weather

Notes

Settings

Safari

iPod

Antennas for cellular service, Bluetooth, and Wi-Fi

Anetnnas

Accelerometer

Accelerometer

An **accelerometer** detects whether the iPhone is being held vertically or horizontally and changes the screen display to match the phone's orientation.

The screen incorporates two types of touch sensors. Electrical lines set at right angles to each other are embedded in the **mutual capacitive screen**. One set, the **driving lines**, carry an electrical current that creates an electromagnetic field that is read by the **sensing lines.** In the **self-capacitive screen**, electrodes with capacitance-sensing circuits are buried throughout the screen. When a finger touches the iPhone's screen, it creates a change in the electromagnetic fields that is detected by both types of sensors. There, data is sent to the phone's processor, which interprets it in the context of what's on the screen and what application is running.

CHAPTER

10

How Small Mutations Pay Off Big

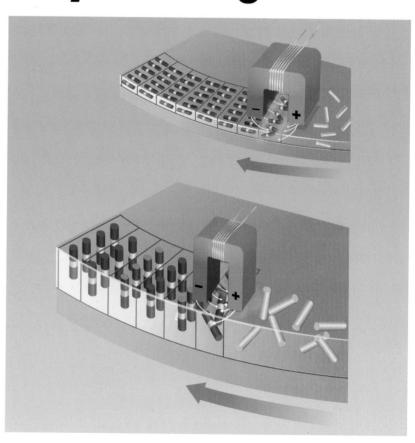

SMALL THINGS, like cellular mutations and the smallest pieces of machinery, can have a big impact.

The first clocks were *not* small things. These clocks, which first appeared in the 16th century B.C. in Babylon and Egypt, ranged from desk size to house size. In their simplest form, a bowl with a hole in the bottom was filled with water. The water slowly dripped through the hole, filling a container below it. As the water rose in the container, a float rose with it. A pointer on the float indicated the time using a series of markings on the inside of the container.

The water clock, called a **clepsydra,** wasn't very accurate. An indicator of how inaccurate a clepsydra was is the fact that a sundial was used to make corrections in the water clock's time-keeping. Attempts to improve its accuracy usually involved adding more leaking water bowls until it came to weigh several hundred pounds, which is much too heavy for most wrists.

It wasn't until 1250 A.D. that a mechanical mutation came along to change all that. It was a very small and very simple device that would revolutionize time-keeping, and it is still in use today. It's called the **escapement**. This is a picture of it.

A life-sized model of a 1434 A.D. Korean water clock known as Jagyeongnu, on display at The National Palace Museum of Korea. As the water rises in the large tank, a floating rod touches a lever, causing beads to trigger devices that strike a gong, bell, or drum, and lift up a time announcement board.

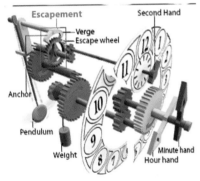

The **escape wheel** with all the points on it is turned by the constant force from a battery, spring, or weight. A shaft from the wheel connects to a system of gears to turn the hands of a clock. The piece just above the wheel—called the **anchor**—has two **catch hooks** on either end. The job of the anchor is to rock back and forth, stopping the wheel momentarily by catching one of its spikes. The wheel then bounces back enough to throw off the first hook and turns a bit before the second catch hook descends to stop the wheel from the other side. The sounds made by one and then the other of the hooks stopping the wheel is the origin of *tick-tock*.

The escapement is a small thing, but consider what it has made possible in commerce, travel, factories, science, and worrying where your children are at this hour.

Similarly, many innovations in computing have had an effect far out of proportion to their physical size. Cut a hair from your head. Thousands of transistors could fit on the cross-section of that hair. Nothing we know today in computing would be possible without those minuscule components. Even more complex components—smartphone displays, speakers, and the little thingy that vibrates our phones—are just small enough to fit, along with scores of other parts, inside a device thinner than an Oreo. Smartphones—which are the defining technology of the early 21st century, just as computers were for the end of the 20th century—could never have made it this big without things being little.

How USB Really Is Universal

THE PATH OF EVOLUTION, whether organic or digital, is not always smooth. Evolution often creates a feature that sticks to a creature or a machine long after it's needed. Today, on some rare PCs you can find funny little ports designed specifically for keyboards and mice. The Scroll Lock key lives on long after the program it was designed for, Lotus 1-2-3, quietly went extinct. Other evolutionary anachronisms are with us deliberately because of something called backward compatibility.

Universal Serial Bus 3 (USB3) lives up to its name not only because it can connect to any PC peripheral you can name. It's also a universal system that replaces the kludgy serial and parallel ports I talked about in Chapter 9, "The Origins of Computer DNA," along with a variety of others not mentioned. And it remains universally usable by older computers and peripherals that can use only USB1 or USB2. This is evolution at its best and an example of how much difference a couple of small wires can make.

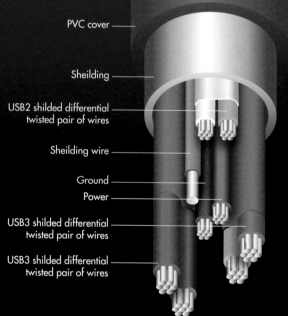

PVC cover

Sheilding

USB2 shilded differential
twisted pair of wires

Sheilding wire

Ground

Power

USB3 shilded differential
twisted pair of wires

USB3 shilded differential
twisted pair of wires

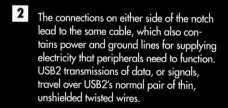 **1** The USB3 connector on a PC looks similar to a USB port but with a notch on one side. USB3 controllers operate using a dual-bus architecture that allows the bus to run USB2 and USB1 on one set of wires while also sending data 10 times faster—5 gigabits per second—through a second set of wires.

2 The connections on either side of the notch lead to the same cable, which also contains power and ground lines for supplying electricity that peripherals need to function. USB2 transmissions of data, or signals, travel over USB2's normal pair of thin, unshielded twisted wires.

3 USB3 signals are carried by shielded, multi-core wires within wires that are configured as two shielded differential pairs (SDP) inside the same cable as the USB2 wiring. The pairs use thicker wires and a layer of braided metal strips as skins surrounding each pair. Each of the USB3 braided pairs can be used for transmission and reception; that means USB3 connections can read and write data simultaneously—**dual simplex**—compared to USB 2.0's **half duplex** scheme

4 Essentially all electrical signals consist of pulses of electricity of a certain time span and voltage. To achieve 5GB bandwidth, USB signals must be shorter so that more of them can be sent in the same length of time. Lower voltages are needed because voltages do not change from one value to another instantaneously. The voltage change requires time, and the smaller the change in voltage, the sooner the voltage change is created.

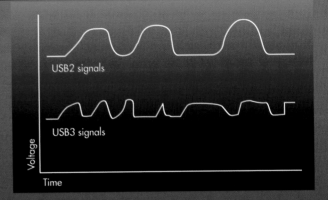

5 Electromagnetic interference that wouldn't affect signals in the longer, larger voltage changes in USB2 transmissions can wreak havoc with USB3 signals. Shielding is needed to cut out the electrical noise that disturbs the integrity of the signal and prevents the bus from achieving that 5GB/s throughput. But USB3 still needs another technology: the "differential" in shielded differential pairs.

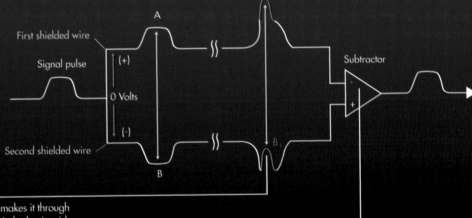

6 Down each of the paired wires, USB3 sends signals that are identical except that their voltages are the opposite of each other.

7 Any electrical interference that makes it through the shielding affects the signals in both wires identically so that the voltage of each is raised or lowered the same amount. The difference in voltage between A and B equals the difference between A1 and B1.

8 When the signals—now distorted if they've hit a pocket of noise—are received, a **substracter** measures the *difference* in the voltages of the two signals. These differences in the values are used to determine the data encoded in the signals.

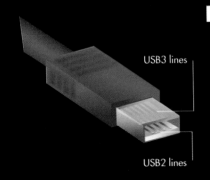

9 The connectors at the receiving end are designed to work with USB3 or USB2 equipment. The common **Standard A** port has pins on *opposite* sides. USB2 and USB3 plugs go into the same port upside-down in respect to each other.

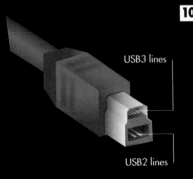

10 For the USB Standard B port, often found on printers, a "penthouse" has been added to the USB2 port to accommodate plugs for USB3. USB2 plugs still connect normally.

How Little Bits Add Up to Big Changes

FOR MANY YEARS we computer users were content with having megabytes of storage at our disposal. Who could want more than 50... okay, 100 megabytes storage? Then, contentment took on a new meaning as we were given *gigabytes* of storage on a single drive. Gigabytes! A thousand times the capacity of megabytes—a billion bytes! Then we started hearing about terabytes? We had to check the dictionary on that one, and sure enough it was 1,000 times the size of a gigabyte. One thousand billion bytes.

And it's not enough. It never will be. Hard drive size has grown faster than the space program and Starbucks combined. And the growth was not due to anything monumental. Instead, the evolution of the hard disk drive has inched in microscopic improvements that yielded miles of new storage. Here are some of the more spectacular improvements.

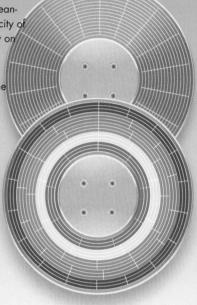

Zoned Bit Recording (1996)

Originally the concentric bands that were the tracks running out from the center of a drive's disk were organized by divisions that looked like pie slices. The surface of a disk defined by the intersection of a track and pie slice was called a sector. The drive needed the sectors to keep track of the location of all the files that had been written to the disk. The innermost sectors were as densely packed with data as the technology back then could manage. The bigger sectors farther out in the pie slice were capable of holding twice as much data. The trouble was that the file-tracking scheme required all the sectors to hold the same amount of data no matter where they were located. Disk space was going to waste.

Then came **zoned bit recording** (ZBR or multiple zone recording or zoned recording). By making some changes in how information was recorded and recognized, ZBR puts tracks into different zones based on the tracks' distances from the disk's center. Each zone is allowed to have a different number of sectors in its tracks. In the simplified diagram of a ZBR disk here, the different zones are represented by different colors, and you can see the greater number of sectors in outlying zones as well as the fact that all sectors are roughly the same length no matter where they are located.

Perpendicular Magnetic Recording (2007)

The earliest drives recorded information to disc a lot like the machine used to paint stripes down the middle of the highway. As the disc spun under the drive's read/write head, an electromagnet would turn on to "paint" the magnetic grains in the disc's surface so their magnetic fields would all line up—north to south—in the direction the disc was turning. Or, to create different bits, the magnet might reverse its polarities to make the north and south poles of the disk fields line up the opposite way—but they were still horizontal.

Linear recording was really a waste of space, which became evident with the advent of **perpendicular magnetic recording (PMR)**. Instead of the magnetic fields being oriented as if they were lying down, PMR pushed the write head's recording field deep into the disc to create fields that are standing up. If you've ever been in a packed elevator, think how fewer people could get in the elevator if they had to lie down, only one person deep. It might make for a more pleasant elevator ride, but it's not the best use of the space.

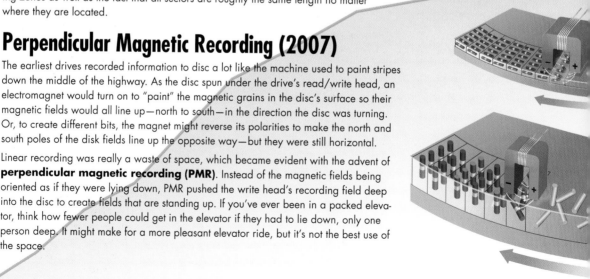

GIGABITS PER SQUARE INCH	
1,000	
100	
10	
1	

1995	1997	1999	2001	2003	2005	20

graph source: storagenewsletter.com

Bit Patterned Media (2013)

Two physical properties of hard disks have limited the recording density of hard discs to 1.20 terabits per square inch. One is that there must be enough magnetized material in each bit so that the read head can distinguish the magnetism of a single bit from the general magnetic noise that exists everywhere. At the same time, the **superparamagnetic limit** sets a minimum size for bits to prevent the magnetized state from becoming thermally unstable and unable to store data.

The hero coming to the rescue this time is **bit patterned media.** It begins with the creation of the disk, when—much like the process in creating musical CDs—a form presses into the disk's surface, creating tiny pillars of hydrogen silsesquioxane on the surface.

In a process called **sputtering,** the disk is put in a vacuum chamber with a **target** of magnetic material. A stream of ions or electrons bombard the target with such force that molecules and electrons from the target explode outward to create a furious cloud of magnetic material. The particles in that cloud settle on the tips of the pillars, turning them into individual magnetic bits, dense enough to accept a strong magnetic recording and separated far enough to escape the superparamagnetic limit. The 35nm gap between pillars shown here gives the disc a recording density of 0.6 terabytes in a square inch. A 12nm gap works out to a density of 3.3TB per square inch.

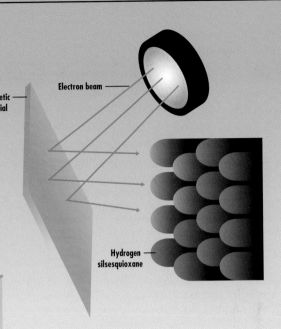

Magnetic material

Electron beam

Hydrogen silsesquioxane

Shingled Memory Recording (2011)

Engineers were able to grow the hard drive by abandoning the commandment that disk tracks must be separate from each other. They lay down tracks like shingles on a roof—one track overlapping the next and overlapped by the track on the opposite side—creating **shingled memory recording (SMR).**

The trick behind SMR is the fact that when a read/write head is writing data it has to churn out a lot more energy to make change in the magnetic orientation of the particles on the surface of a disk. All that energy means the head must write to a wide swath of the track. The resulting magnetic fields making up a pattern that encodes data are weak, but still strong enough to generate electrical currents in the read head when it passes through them.

The write head writes a much wider track than the read head needs. So after SMR writes one track it overlays one edge of the track with the edge of the adjacent track. That leaves enough of the track for the read head to do its job with no errors.

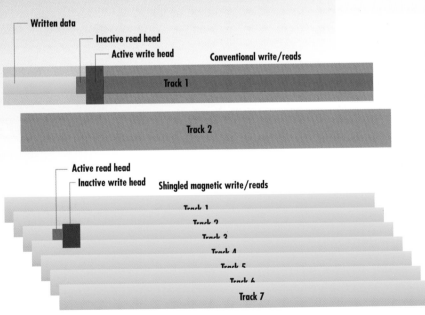

Written data

Inactive read head

Active write head

Conventional write/reads

Track 1

Track 2

Active read head

Inactive write head

Shingled magnetic write/reads

Track 1

Track 2

Track 3

Track 4

Track 5

Track 6

Track 7

2009   2011   2013   2015

How File Compression Makes Files Smaller

1 Files, even those on a compressed disk, can be made still smaller by file compression—a process often called **zipping** a file. This type of compression reduces file size by eliminating the redundancies in the file. This is called **lossless compression**, which means decompression can precisely restore every bit in the file.

2 The compression program uses some variation of a scheme generally called *LZ* (after its creators, Lempel and Ziv) **adaptive dictionary-based algorithm**. As the program reads an uncompressed file, it examines the file for recurring patterns of data. When LZ identifies a pattern, instead of writing the pattern in line with the text, as it does other sections of the file, it writes the pattern to a dictionary. The dictionary is stored as part of the compressed file.

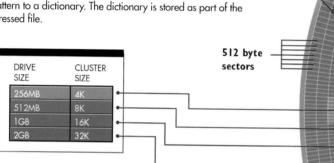

DRIVE SIZE	CLUSTER SIZE
256MB	4K
512MB	8K
1GB	16K
2GB	32K

3 Where the pattern would have been written to disk, LZ instead writes a much shorter pointer that tells where the omitted pattern can be found in the dictionary. **Adaptive** means that, as the algorithm writes more of the file, it constantly looks for more efficient data patterns to use and changes the entries in the dictionary on the fly. In the example here, LZ could have chosen "se" in "sells," "seashells," and "seashore" as one of the patterns for the dictionary, but it's more efficient to use "ells" and "seash."

65,536th file

FAT

Tracks

1st file

512 byte sectors

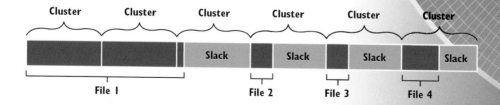

Cluster   Cluster   Cluster   Cluster   Cluster   Cluster

Slack   Slack   Slack   Slack

File 1   File 2   File 3   File 4

4 How much the file shrinks depends on the type of file. Some types of files, such as word-processing documents and databases, are prone to redundancies and are particularly susceptible to compression. Length matters, too; the longer the file, the more likely it is that LZ can find repeated patterns. In the sample on the opposite page, picked because it's unnaturally full of redundancies for so short a phrase, the savings is 18% (40 bytes for the original compared to 33 for the compressed version). Some files can be compressed to as little as 20% of their original size. On the average, however, compression is likely to reduce files to only half their original size.

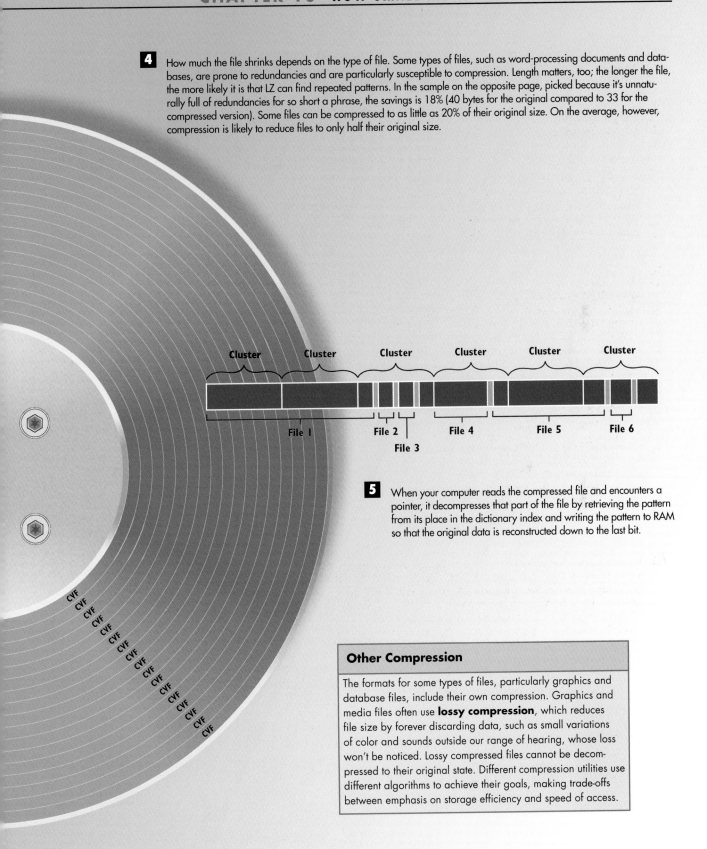

5 When your computer reads the compressed file and encounters a pointer, it decompresses that part of the file by retrieving the pattern from its place in the dictionary index and writing the pattern to RAM so that the original data is reconstructed down to the last bit.

Other Compression

The formats for some types of files, particularly graphics and database files, include their own compression. Graphics and media files often use **lossy compression**, which reduces file size by forever discarding data, such as small variations of color and sounds outside our range of hearing, whose loss won't be noticed. Lossy compressed files cannot be decompressed to their original state. Different compression utilities use different algorithms to achieve their goals, making trade-offs between emphasis on storage efficiency and speed of access.

How Solid State Drives Command the Instant

THE PRIMARY DRAG on a PC's performance is **access latency**, the time it takes for data to move from one of at least six memory levels to the next. Each level is a different trade-off between speed and capacity that balances performance against cost. The biggest gap in both capacity and speed has traditionally been between the hard drive and the rest of a computer. While waiting for data from nearby RAM, the processor might wait twiddling its digits for a few dozen **cycles**—a computer tick that is the shortest time within which a computer can do any work. But if the processor is waiting on data from a hard disk, it may have to wait for *millions* of cycles.

Ordinary hard disk drives have always had this problem: They are mechanical and bound by the laws of common physics. Most of their time is spent, not reading or writing data, but maneuvering the read/write head, floating only thousandths of a millimeter above platters spinning thousands of times a minute, in just the right position only for the drive to send a brief burst of electricity to read or write. It's all awesomely impressive, but also shockingly inelegant compared to the silent, unmoving workings of a **solid state drive (SSD)**.

2 Although a diagram of a floating gate transistor looks a lot like the RAM diagram in Chapter 2, "How Computers Remember," instead of requiring that charges be constantly replenished, NAND transistors include a structure called the **floating gate**. It's called that because, unlike other gates in a transistor, it is not connected to the circuitry.

3 The gate floats on a thin sheet of a substance such as silicon dioxide that makes up the **tunnel barrier** that separates the gate from the **substrate.** The substrate contains the **source**, which is the transistor's storehouse of electrons, and the **drain**, where electrons retire after they've been pulled from the source and through the transistor.

4 Each NAND transistor starts out not containing any charge, which makes it represent a 1. The process of making the transistor stand for a 0 begins when a positive voltage is applied to the drain, stirring up the electrons in the substrate underneath the floating gate.

5 Next, a larger voltage is added to the **control gate** separated from the floating gate by a layer of **dielectric**—an insulator that can be polarized by an electrical field. The voltage pulls the electrons into the floating gate, where they remain trapped even when the computer is off.

1 For marketing reasons, the first wave of solid state drives have the same form factor and connectors as their hard drive predecessors. But peel back an SSD cover and instead of spinning platters and a thrashing arm there are silent rows of **NAND flash memory**. Named after the logic operation "Not And" that's at the heart of flash memory, NAND is close kin to the **DRAM (Dynamic Random Access Memory)** that makes up our computers' workaday memory. Unlike DRAM, flash is non-volatile. It retains all the data stored in it when a computer is turned off. It's the same stuff that throbs inside your smartphones, mp3 players, and little USB thumb drives, and it comes from the same assembly lines.

What makes an SSD so much faster than a thumb drive is a combination of how the NAND chips are **addressed**, and the various caching and computing shortcuts that the SSD's built-in controller uses to read and write the data and to systematically clean out the garbage. (See the next page.)

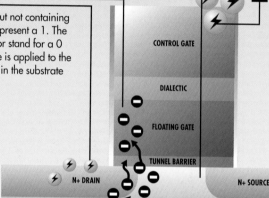

6 To read the transistor, a positive voltage that is lower than the write voltage is applied to the control gate. An additional positive voltage, also lower than the write voltage, is applied to the drain. The strength of the current between the source and the drain reveals whether the floating gate has extra electrons (logical 0) or does not (logical 1).

7 To erase the transistor, a negative voltage is applied to the control gate and a positive voltage is applied to the source. This forces the electrons out of the floating gate and into the source.

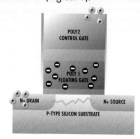
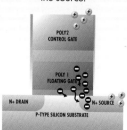

How Solid State Drives Take Out the Trash

THE SECRET TO an SSD's ability to outrace a hard disk drive isn't that it reads data faster than a hard drive. They're both about the same. But the SSD is faster at getting to what needs to be read. The hard drive is bogged down by latency, caused by the fact the read/write head must adjust its position and wait for the right strip of data to sail under it. But an SSD has a handicap of its own. A NAND transistor's grip on a charge is so strong that it is impossible to change the state of a single bit from 1 to 0 as we can with disk drives and ordinary RAM. To change a single NAND bit requires hitting the transistor with a charge so powerful that it affects the state of the tightly packed surrounding transistor. (Think of it as digital collateral damage.) Here's how SSD races around the problem.

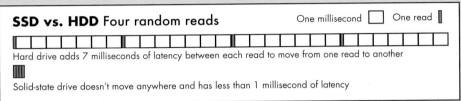

SSD vs. HDD Four random reads   One millisecond ☐   One read ▌

Hard drive adds 7 milliseconds of latency between each read to move from one read to another

Solid-state drive doesn't move anywhere and has less than 1 millisecond of latency

1 Transistors in a solid state drive are organized in rows of 32 to 256. Each row is designated a **page**. Between 4,096 and 65,536 pages are grouped as a **block**. A block, which may contain as many as 2MB, is the smallest unit that the drive can erase. For this reason, **do not** use defraggers or optimizers designed for conventional hard drives.

2 Blocks are grouped together on a circuit board, with typically 1,025 blocks making up a **plane**. Typically a single NAND-flash **die** contains multiple planes. A single flash chip may contain several dies. And one solid-state drive may contain more than one chip.

5 If an SSD is packed with stale, or **garbage**, pages, the drive may spend so much time moving and erasing blocks that writes become noticeably slow. The remedy for this latency is **trim**—also called **taking out the garbage**. The drive uses those times when little drive activity is going on to search for garbage pages and delete them by moving blocks to cache and then back to NAND memory so that free pages are already available for new files when needed.

NAND transistor
Block
Page

Plane

128 pages = 1 block
(typically 512 KB, but designs vary)

1,024 blocks = 1 plane
(typically 512 KB)

3 When it comes to writing data, an SSD encounters a different kind of latency from that of a disk drive, particularly when the SSD has been in use for awhile and has few unused pages. When the computer sends a new file to the SSD, its controller first looks for a block with enough unused pages to hold the file. If the search is successful, the file is written to that block.

4 A disk drive can easily write new data over old data that's marked as deleted. A solid-state drive can't. Even if there is enough room for a new file if the space taken up by **stale**, deleted files is included, the controller must first temporarily write the entire contents of the block to a cache, erase the complete contents of the block, and then return the files to the block, minus any stale pages, and add the new files to the expanded free pages.

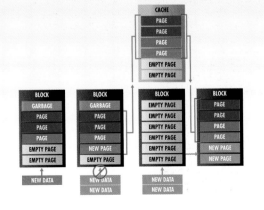

How PCs Use Light to Remember

4 The surface of the reflective layer alternates between lands and pits. **Lands** are flat surface areas; **pits** are tiny depressions in the reflective layer. These two surfaces are a record of the 1s and 0s used to store data.

3 The laser beam penetrates a protective layer of plastic and strikes a reflective layer that looks like aluminum foil on the bottom of the disc.

2 The laser projects a concentrated beam of light that a lens and a **focusing coil** focus even further.

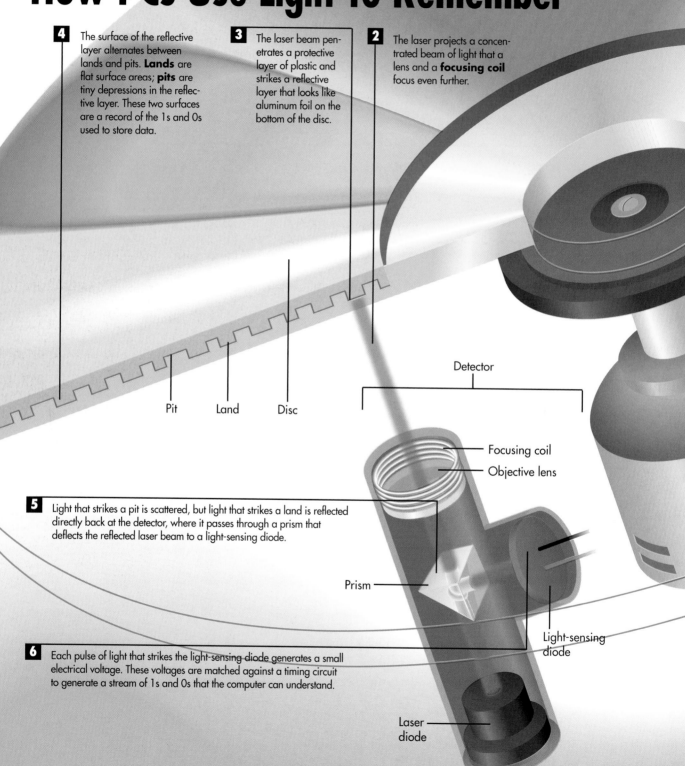

Pit   Land   Disc

Detector

Focusing coil

Objective lens

5 Light that strikes a pit is scattered, but light that strikes a land is reflected directly back at the detector, where it passes through a prism that deflects the reflected laser beam to a light-sensing diode.

Prism

Light-sensing diode

6 Each pulse of light that strikes the light-sensing diode generates a small electrical voltage. These voltages are matched against a timing circuit to generate a stream of 1s and 0s that the computer can understand.

Laser diode

① A motor constantly varies the rate at which the disc (CD, DVD, etc.) spins so that, regardless of where a component, called a **detector**, is located in relation to the radius of the disc, the portion of the disc immediately above the detector is always moving at the same speed.

How We Made the Pits and Lands Smaller

Blu-Ray is the poster product for how little changes yield enormous results. It comes from using a color of laser light narrower than the red laser beam in common DVD. It's a difference of 250 nanometers (nm). If a DVD laser beam were as wide as a football field is long, a blue laser would come to the 70-yard line. But if the number of bits a DVD can store would stretch the length of a football field, the bits on a Blu-Ray would need five football fields. Have a look:

Land

Beam spot

Pit

Compact Disc: A CD uses a red laser that has a wavelength of 790nm. That's a little less than a millionth of a meter; it would take more than 300 dots of red laser light to cover the width of a human hair. The distance between coils of the spiral track carrying data is 1.6 microns (1.6 millionths of a meter). The data is encoded in the form of **pits** (holes) and **lands** (unchanged, level areas).

It's a safe bet that **Blu-Ray** technology foreshadows the end of the Optidigital Age, the far limit of writing and playing data on a small plastic disc. Not that it's at all a shabby limit. But even Blu-Ray has been outdone by hard drives, which we now measure in terabytes and pay for at the cost of a dinner for two at a snazzy restaurant. And every means of storage has been outdone by the clouds. The clouds are, for every practical purpose, infinite.

Still, Blu-Ray will not become a fossil as long as there are movies and marketers to push them to your home theatre.

Beam spot

DVD: The common DVD that's been around for more than 10 years also uses a red laser beam, but it is narrower—650nm. That small difference allows a single-sided, single-layer disc to hold seven times as much as a CD. The coils of the tracks are 0.7 microns apart and the lands and pits are smaller.

Beam spot

Blu-Ray: This high-definition format gives optical storage a leap to much smaller pit and land sizes. The blue ray, actually a blue-purple laser, has a beam that's 405nm wide. The coils of a Blu-Ray disc's tracks are 0.3–0.4 microns apart, about a fourth of the distance that separates common circuit traces in microprocessors. A decade or so ago, if anyone had said the average home would have a device that works, with rarely a hitch, on such a microscopic scale, we would have smiled and ignored them.

25 GB

4.7 GB

0.7 GB

BLU-RAY   DVD   CD

How Optical Disc Drives Write with Light

1 A laser sends a low-energy light beam at a compact disc built on a relatively thick layer of clear polycarbonate plastic. On top of the plastic is a layer of dyed color material that is usually green, a thin layer of gold to reflect the laser beam, a protective layer of lacquer, and often a layer of scratch-resistant polymer material. There might be a paper or silk-screened label on top of all that.

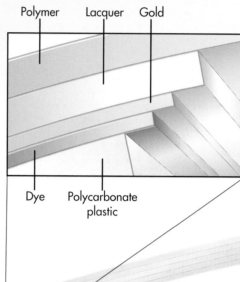

Polymer   Lacquer   Gold

Dye   Polycarbonate plastic

2 The laser's write head follows a tight spiral groove cut into the plastic layer. The groove, called an **atip (absolute timing in pregroove)**, has a continuous wave pattern similar to that on a phonograph record. The frequency of the waves varies continuously from the beginning of the groove to its end. The laser beam reflects off the wave pattern and, by reading the frequency of the waves, the optical drive can calculate where the head is located in relation to the surface of the disc.

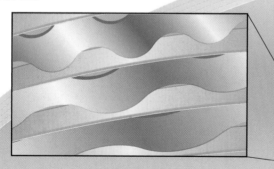

3 As the head follows the atip, it uses the position information that the groove's waves provide to control the speed of the motor turning the disc so that the area of the disc under the head is always moving at the same speed. To do this, the disc must spin faster as the head moves toward the center of the disc and slower as the head approaches the rim.

Laser

Write head

5 The dye layer is designed to absorb light at that specific frequency. Absorbing the energy from the laser beam creates a mark in one of three ways, depending on the design of the disc. The dye might be bleached; the polycarbonate layer might be distorted; or the dye layer might form a bubble. Regardless of how the mark is created, the result is a distortion, called a **stripe**, along the spiral track. When the beam is switched off, no mark appears. The lengths of the stripes vary, as do the unmarked spaces among them. The drive uses the varying lengths to write the information in a special code that compresses the data and checks for errors. The change in the dye is permanent, making the recordable compact disc a write-once, read-many (WORM) medium.

6 To read data, the drive, like an ordinary read-only drive, focuses a lower-powered laser beam onto the disc to read data. Where a mark has not been made on the surface of the disc, the gold layer reflects the beam straight back to the read head. When the beam hits a stripe, the distortion in the groove scatters the beam so that the light is not returned to the read head. The results are the same as if the beam were aimed at the lands and pits in an ordinary disc. Each time the beam is reflected to the head, the head generates a pulse of electricity. From the pattern in the pulses of current, the drive decompresses the data, error-checks it, and passes it along to the PC in the digital form of zeroes and ones.

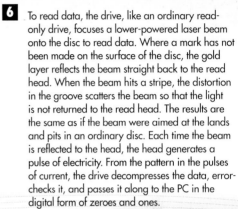

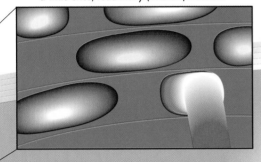

4 The software used to record to a disc sends the data to be stored in a specific format, such as ISO 9096, which automatically corrects errors and creates a table of contents. A recordable CD drive, for example, records the information by sending a higher-powered pulse of the laser beam at a light wavelength of 780 nanometers.

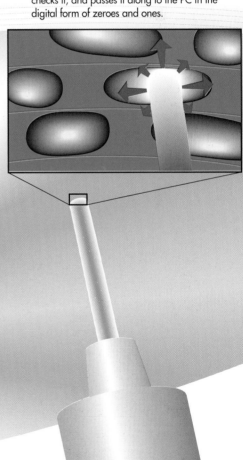

Read head ——————

CHAPTER

11

Honey, I've Shrunk the PC.
And the CD Player and the TV and
the Phone and the Library and the
Newsstand and the Picture Gallery and
the Gameboard and the Earth...

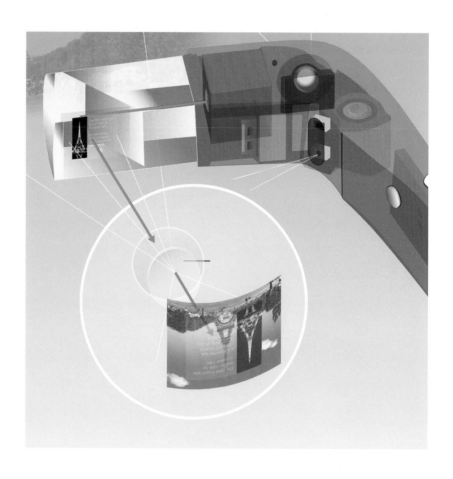

ONE OF MY FIRST computers was a Seequa Chameleon, a knock-off of the first Compaq. The Chameleon, which debuted in 1983 at a price of $2,000, had two 5.25" floppy drives—no hard drive—a 9″ green monochrome screen, and 256 KB of RAM. It was made of strong, heavy metal. *Heavy* metal. I recall a Sisyphean struggle to lug and drag it the length of the St. Louis airport, all the while thinking, "If this is the future of mobile computing, I'm going to buy myself an abacus."

I'm glad I didn't stick to my resolve. There has been a lot of monkeying with the PC along its evolution to become *machina sapiens*. Many of the features that computers began with have been supplanted by faster components that are more capacious—and yet, they've become smaller. The future of computing has turned out to be a device smaller than a paperback, with access to the facts of an encyclopedia and as wearable as jewelry—and just as expensive.

The Seequa Chameleon, Circa 1983 A.D.

Along the path computers took in their evolution, you'll find a lot of fossils. Disk drives that once seemed like mammoth storage were revealed to be mere titmice. Processors whose speeds seemed to challenge the speed of light were, it turns out, only going 55. Keep in mind that there is no finish line in evolution. Every time it seems we've reached the end, someone comes up with a mutation that starts the race all over again.

How Computers Get Smaller...
and Better

PERSONAL COMPUTERS and laptops are proof two species of computing can live in harmony—although for many users laptops aren't just second string computers for traveling. For many, a laptop is the only computer, in the office, at home, and on the road. That's because technology has managed to squeeze laptops to the point that they're not much more trouble to carry than a newspaper. At the same time their abilities have swollen to proportions no one would have imagined just a few years ago. You can get a good look at what's inside a laptop just by gazing into what you'll see in any PC (see Chapter 9, "The Origins of Computer DNA"); after all, they're still computers. Here's a look at some parts and components that make laptops unique.

1. The touch pad. A mouse is almost always the better option, but the venerable touch pad continues as a mainstay of laptop computing.

2. Solid state disk drives, increasingly found in laptops, are fast, resist careless damage, and are thin—just what a mobile computer needs.

3. SD slots are a second home to digital camera memory cards and provide handy offline storage.

4. Keyboards are keyboards. They're the survivors of the computing world—there at the beginning and will be there in the future. Today's ever-more-compact laptops likewise have to get ever more creative in how to cram all those keys into limited space.

5. Just beneath the case exterior are the circuitry and antennas for the new communications heroes: Wi-Fi, Bluetooth, and near-field communication (NFC).

6. Headphone jacks continue to survive, but Bluetooth may eventually make them obsolete.

7. With every new generation of laptop, batteries get lighter, skinnier, and longer lasting.

8. Batteries don't last forever. Power adapters keep it portable by moving the conventional PC power supply into a "brick" outside the chassis. Even the connectors are evolving, as many adapters attach to their laptop using nothing more than the strength of a few magnets.

9. Built-in Ethernet ports, along with Wi-Fi and Bluetooth communications hidden with the slim housing, give you a choice of way to link to networks.

10. Built-in displays are becoming the stars for mobile computing, sometimes with resolutions superior even to your HDTV.

11. A camera and microphone are standard equipment for today's laptops, allowing you to record video of yourself or talk to colleagues or friends with crystal-clear clarity.

12. USB ports aren't as plentiful as they are on a desktop, where they practically come by the dozen, but no laptop is complete without at least a couple of them. If you need more, you can always connect an external USB hub.

13. Built-in HDMI ports let you easily connect your laptop to another screen, be it an HDTV, projector, or desktop monitor. Once hooked up, you can mirror your built-in display on the second screen or expand your display across both.

14. Speakers, sometimes higher-end than you'd expect, are hidden beneath a laptop's chassis.

Under the Hood

Virtually all of the components you'd find under the covers of your average desktop PC you'll also find in your laptop. Processor, RAM, motherboard, video and audio circuitry—it's all there.

Long Gone

There's a bevy of hardware we used to talk about in these pages that no longer come as a standard part of today's laptops. Modems and floppies are right out and, as the cloud becomes the favored place to tuck away music, movies, photos, and everyday files, optical drives are increasingly scarce. If you do need an optical drive, you can hook one up to a USB port. And remember using PCMCIA cards to add memory and other features to your laptop? No? Good. Neither does anyone else.

How iPods Dish Out Media

WHEN IT COMES TO super shrinkage, the iPod is on the short list. It used to be that to hear your favorite song away from home, you had to hope it was one of maybe 100 records inside in a brightly lit device only slightly smaller than a refrigerator called a **jukebox**. And it usually cost you 25 cents a pop. Whether it's an iPod or one of its competitors, its size could be anything from a deck of cards to a matchbook. Only, how many matchbooks can hold thousands of songs?

1 Attaching an iPod to another device through a USB port lets you download and store compressed music (usually MP3 files), videos, and photos. The iPod stores the media on a hard drive, as shown here in an older-style player, or on flash memory. Menus display artists' names, song and album titles, movie titles, and slide shows on an LCD/LED screen.

6 The player's microprocessor moves the media data from RAM to an analog-to-digital converter (ADC) chip for music and to a video codec (coder-decoder) for movies. Either chip converts the data into the signals needed for playback. The ADC sends music through an amplifier for audio output. The codec sends signals to a display adapter that controls the onscreen playback.

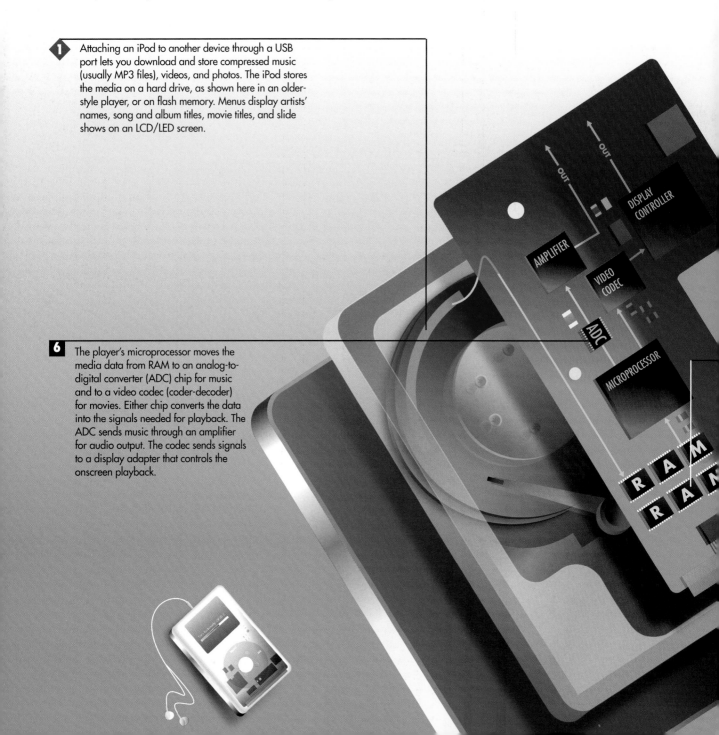

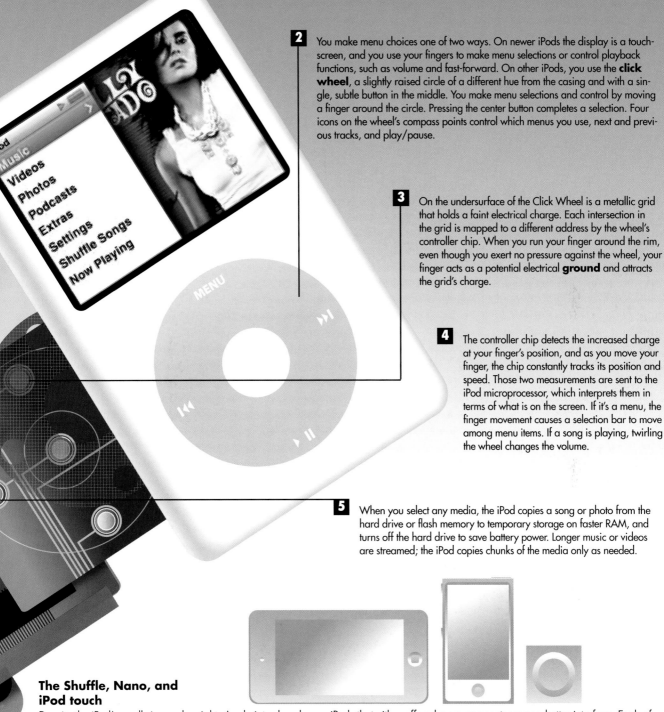

2 You make menu choices one of two ways. On newer iPods the display is a touch-screen, and you use your fingers to make menu selections or control playback functions, such as volume and fast-forward. On other iPods, you use the **click wheel**, a slightly raised circle of a different hue from the casing and with a single, subtle button in the middle. You make menu selections and control by moving a finger around the circle. Pressing the center button completes a selection. Four icons on the wheel's compass points control which menus you use, next and previous tracks, and play/pause.

3 On the undersurface of the Click Wheel is a metallic grid that holds a faint electrical charge. Each intersection in the grid is mapped to a different address by the wheel's controller chip. When you run your finger around the rim, even though you exert no pressure against the wheel, your finger acts as a potential electrical **ground** and attracts the grid's charge.

4 The controller chip detects the increased charge at your finger's position, and as you move your finger, the chip constantly tracks its position and speed. Those two measurements are sent to the iPod microprocessor, which interprets them in terms of what is on the screen. If it's a menu, the finger movement causes a selection bar to move among menu items. If a song is playing, twirling the wheel changes the volume.

5 When you select any media, the iPod copies a song or photo from the hard drive or flash memory to temporary storage on faster RAM, and turns off the hard drive to save battery power. Longer music or videos are streamed; the iPod copies chunks of the media only as needed.

The Shuffle, Nano, and iPod touch

Despite the iPod's small size and weight, Apple introduced more iPods that either offered more compactness or a better interface. Each of them eliminates the hard drive and stores all media in non-volatile memory.

The Shuffle weighs less than an ounce and measures only about 1 × 1.6 inches. It has no LCD screen and stores about 580 songs in 2GB of memory.

The Nano has a color LCD screen and 16GB of memory, and yet it is considerably smaller and lighter than a classic iPod. It stores about 4,500 songs.

The iPod touch has a **multitouch** display, which basically makes it an iPhone without the phone, and it comes with capacities ranging from 16GB to 64GB. See "How Devices Recognize Our Touch" in Chapter 14, "How We Stay in Touch."

How eInk Puts Words on Your eReader

THE MOST SURPRISING thing about a mobile device, such as the Kindle, comes when you turn it off. The screen doesn't go dark. The screen continues to display an image. Sure, the image doesn't move or change, but what keeps it going without running the battery down to zero?

It's called electronic ink. An **electronic paper display (EDP)** looks much like a traditional sheet of paper—thin and flexible. But instead of the mashed wood pulp that goes into ordinary paper, a sheet of electronic paper, about twice the thickness of common paper, is made up of two sheets of thin film that sandwich millions of **microcapsules** containing electronic ink.

1 The forerunner in the industry, E Ink Corp., uses an **electrophoretic frontplane,** a sort of e-paper sandwich filled with a layer of microcapsules that are 100 microns wide, roughly the diameter of a human hair. A square inch of electronic paper contains 100,000 of these microcapsules.

2 Each of the capsules contains a clear liquid polymer. Suspended in the fluid are tiny white and black particles, made of several silicone dioxide-coated layers, beginning with a white or black titanium dioxide pigment. The outer layer is a carbon-based, hair-like surface. The hairs stop the particles from sticking together and hold a positive electrical charge on the white particles and a negative charge on the black ones. These charges allow the particles to be herded through the microcapsules' liquid center.

3 The e-paper's bottom layer uses a **TFT (thin-film transistor)**, **active-matrix** technology also found in the screens of laptops. The organic–carbon-based–transistors are printed directly on the film along with circuits leading to a microprocessor. The processor sends signals to those transistors, causing each to have either a positive or negative charge.

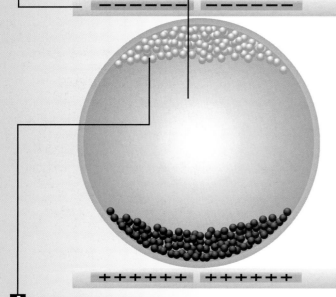
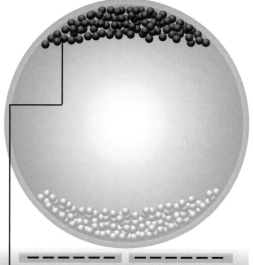

4 On a blank sheet of electronic paper, a processor has sent a positive charge to all of the microcapsules. Because similarly charged materials repel each other, the positively charged white particles move away from the bottom layer to the top surface of the paper, creating a sheet that is completely white.

5 To create dark text or images on the paper, the processor reads the text or images from up to hundreds of books stored in memory chips, and sends signals to the transistors in patterns that correspond to the shape of text or images from the book. These signals give those transistors negative charges that pull the white particles down from the top surface of the paper and push the positively charged black particles up to take the place of the white bits.

E-paper Versus Laptops

Significantly, the signals to the transistors last only microseconds, but the electrical charges remain after the signals have ended. This is why images remain on Kindles and other readers after they are turned off. In fact, like real paper, the Kindle needs a light shining on the front of the paper for anything to be visible to the reader. The brighter the light, the easier it is to read. Laptops, in comparison, are harder to read in bright light. These differences are also why readers' batteries last so long between charges compared to laptop displays.

How Black and White Produce Shades of Gray

1 It would appear that each dot making up electronic ink is either all on or all off. And yet these readers are capable of displaying finely detailed images, such as this one from a first-generation Kindle.

2 Detail and shading are partially a product of the fact that there are more transistors in the bottom film than there are micro pigment capsules. The processor sends opposite signals to transistors placed next to each other so that one transistor forces black particles to the top while the other transistor forces white to the top, with the combination creating gray.

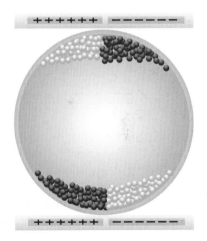

3 The other way e-paper creates shading and detail lies in the fact that each pixel, usually created by two microcapsules, is extremely small. In this photo, shot through a microscope, the red circles identify black dots outside the lettering and the white dots in the black letters. These are defective microcapsules, or capsules stuck in the wrong positions, which give you an idea of the size of the capsules. When you see how many of them go into creating ordinary text, it's easy to imagine how combinations of tiny white, black, and gray microcaps can be mixed to create subtle images. (Also, notice the green circles around gray dots used for anti-aliasing the jaggies.)

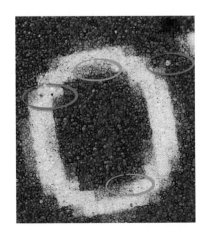

How All Those Smarts Got Packed into a Smartphone

WHEN WE THINK OF "BIG," we usually think of it as being something good. A big bank account. A big mansion. A big stretch limo. A big screen TV. You get the idea. But in computing, ever since Eniac—the 1946 computer that weighted 25 tons and had a footprint of 680 square feet—the path to ultimate computing has been shrinking. It's an evolution that reflects our vastly bigger acceptance and bigger dependence upon computing. These days, you don't leave home without your keys, wallet, and smartphone. And soon the smartphone might make the wallet and keys obsolete.

There was a time when just making a cell phone to also function as a calculator was considered a technological marvel. Now a smartphone is expected to do everything a desktop computer can do—and more. When did your desktop PC tell you your pulse rate, function as a level or a metal detector, take pictures of the puppies in the backyard, or go with you on a walk so you don't get lost? The smartphone has become both jack and master of so many trades, that you have to wonder how all those smarts could be put into a package smaller than a pencil case. You could tear one apart, but there goes your warranty. Or, you could take one to iDoc in Berlin, a company that specializes in tearing apart electronics, so you can learn how to fix them yourself. Ready? The curtain has risen on the latest generation of smartphones in a Samsung Galaxy. Have a look at everything they've packed inside.

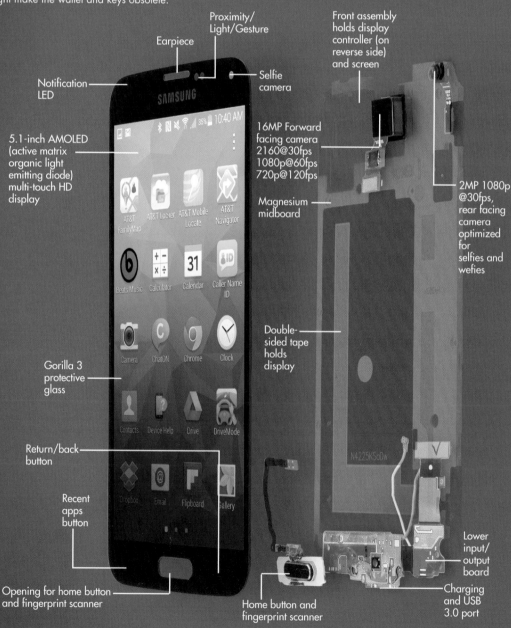

Proximity/Light/Gesture

Earpiece

Front assembly holds display controller (on reverse side) and screen

Notification LED

Selfie camera

5.1-inch AMOLED (active matrix organic light emitting diode) multi-touch HD display

16MP Forward facing camera 2160@30fps 1080p@60fps 720p@120fps

Magnesium midboard

2MP 1080p @30fps, rear facing camera optimized for selfies and wefies

Double-sided tape holds display

Gorilla 3 protective glass

Return/back button

Recent apps button

Opening for home button and fingerprint scanner

Home button and fingerprint scanner

Lower input/output board

Charging and USB 3.0 port

On Reverse Side of Motherboard

SIM slot

Slot for SD memory expansions up to 128MB

HDMI controller

Power management script

RF transmitter

6-axis gyroscope and acclerometer

3-axis electronic compass

GPS receiver

NFC controller

Heart rate biosensor

Audio codec

MIMO (multiple input multiple output) 4G LTE

Wifi 802.11ac

Bluetooth

Pressure sensor

Biosensor control

Snapdragon 801 Quad-core CPU 2.5 GHz 2GB DDR3 SDRAM

16-31MB application memory

Multimode, multiband GSM/CDMA Power amp

Vibrator

Opening for rear camera

Headphone jack coated with water proofing

Buzzer

2,800aMh battery

Rubberized coating

Gasket for IP67 dust and water protection. Toilet bowl safe

How Google Glass Leads to the Borg

THE ULTIMATE user interface for computing is, of course, *Star Trek*'s Borg. But that's in the fictional future. Now, in the real world, the most ambitious and complex implementation of Borgishness is Google Glass. It's a reduction of a computer into a forehead band reminiscent of Lex Luthor. And, indeed, Glass does give the wearer mental and physical powers usually associated only with comic book superheroes and übervillains. Glass is certainly the most extreme example to date of the computer's evolution into smaller and still smaller species.

By projecting text, pictures, and video through a prism so the content lands on your retina, Glass gives you the powers beyond that of lesser humans. Indeed, a journey through a Google Glass is like some science fiction adventure in which we shrink to less than tadpole size and swim through a world where the technologies and hardware we've been used to are so small and jammed together, you'll quickly get lost without a map. Like this one:

Projector   Glass's built-in projector is the "screen" of the forehead computer, allowing the user to see anything from a spreadsheet to the new box office smash. It does this by projecting the screen's contents onto a prism.

The facet of the prism the projection strikes has been coated with an optical film that reflects the projector's image to the eyeball.

At the same time, the film has been applied in a direction so that light from the real-world scene the user is looking at passes straight through the prism to the user's eye.

Inside the eye, both the real-world image and the projector's image hit the retina at the same spot for a heads-up combination image. The projection creates an image that is the equivalent of a high-resolution 25-inch screen seen from eight feet away.

What the eye sees

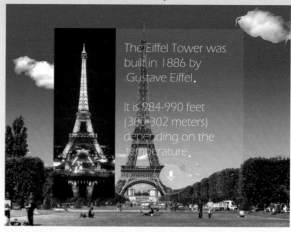

Headband   A narrow, thin titanium headband rests at eyebrow level to serve as scaffolding from which to hang Glass's battery, CPU, sensing components, and audio/visual equipment.

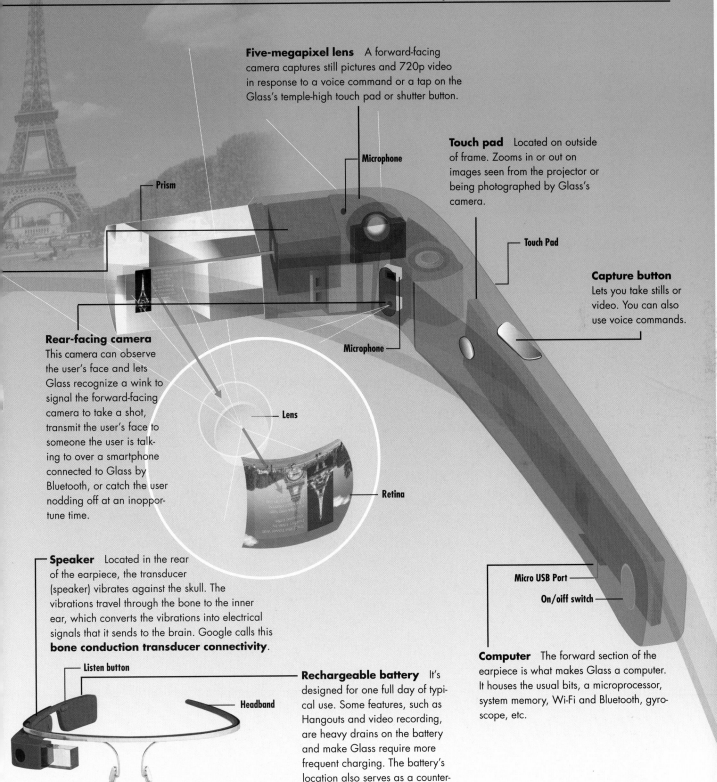

Five-megapixel lens   A forward-facing camera captures still pictures and 720p video in response to a voice command or a tap on the Glass's temple-high touch pad or shutter button.

Microphone

Touch pad   Located on outside of frame. Zooms in or out on images seen from the projector or being photographed by Glass's camera.

Prism

Touch Pad

Capture button
Lets you take stills or video. You can also use voice commands.

Rear-facing camera
This camera can observe the user's face and lets Glass recognize a wink to signal the forward-facing camera to take a shot, transmit the user's face to someone the user is talking to over a smartphone connected to Glass by Bluetooth, or catch the user nodding off at an inopportune time.

Microphone

Lens

Retina

Speaker   Located in the rear of the earpiece, the transducer (speaker) vibrates against the skull. The vibrations travel through the bone to the inner ear, which converts the vibrations into electrical signals that it sends to the brain. Google calls this **bone conduction transducer connectivity**.

Micro USB Port

On/oiff switch

Listen button

Headband

Rechargeable battery   It's designed for one full day of typical use. Some features, such as Hangouts and video recording, are heavy drains on the battery and make Glass require more frequent charging. The battery's location also serves as a counterweight to the components in the forward section.

Computer   The forward section of the earpiece is what makes Glass a computer. It houses the usual bits, a microprocessor, system memory, Wi-Fi and Bluetooth, gyroscope, etc.

CHAPTER

12

The Evolution of the Super Computer

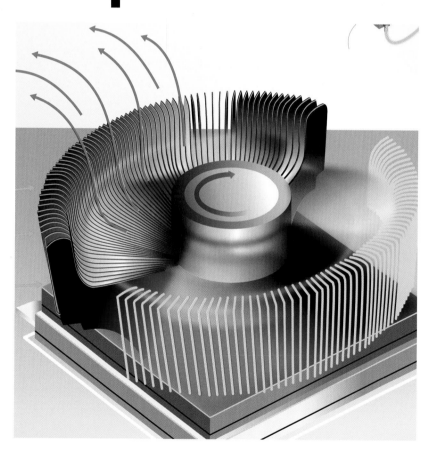

YOU JUST can't please some people. Today we have computers that bring us scenes from a battlefield in another hemisphere while we wait for the bus. Computers give you access to every song you ever listened to or might listen to. They show you on a real-time map where your kids are. They let you design and lay out a magazine in a couple of hours. In a couple of days, you can use a computer to design that new kitchen. They've taken the place of photography darkrooms, musical keyboards, calendars, landline phones, libraries, movie theaters, and having to ask a guy at a gas station how to get to Grandma's house. The iPhone 5, for god's sake, has 1.8 million times the number of transistors of Apollo 11's computer system. What more could you ask?

Some people just want...more.

These people are usually either gamers or computer users who simply aren't satisfied with powerful, terrific, and magnificent. They want the best—the ultimate best, a best that's better than your best. There is no reasoning with these people. Tell them they can get a perfectly adequate computer, tablet, or smartphone with only a half-hour of screen shopping. They don't care. Remind them there is only one game that takes advantage of that dizzying hyperfast video card and that their computers came with a video card built into it. They scoff. Tell them they don't have to build a custom rig from scratch, and even if they do, making it bullet proof is really over the top. They give you a look that says, "You don't have the slightest idea in the world how my mind works. You are mundane." They will buy or build the ultimate in computer—the über computer.

It used to be that this insatiable lust for digital power was found only among desktop PC users. Then, as more and more gamers found themselves traveling to a common site to do their battles, the lust spread to laptops. Now the same epidemic is spreading in tablets and smartphones. You'd think the fact that you can't tinker with the insides of a smartphone would discourage über lust. You'd be wrong. Sometimes that passion takes the polite form of waiting all night outside an electronics store so you can be among the first buying a new phone, game machine, or tablet. But it doesn't stop there. Infected smartphone users are perfectly happy to void their warranties so they can crack through the barriers separating them from the secret software hidden inside the kernels of their digital prizes.

For all these überists the real fun is not in using a great new tablet, phone, or PC. It's in the creation of something still greater—something that proves their alpha status in the digital tribe.

This chapter is dedicated to those people.

How Video Cards Break the Game Barrier

THE MOST SERIOUS CHALLENGE desktop PCs face is not complex spreadsheets or gargantuan databases. It's games. Computer games are voracious users of processing power, and gamers merrily pay top dollar for any hardware that will give them a faster frame rate, which means they can get off a shot before the next guy does. Once upon a time, the need for speed used to be sated by a computer's microprocessor, but today it's the video card (or integrated chipset) that most directly affects game performance.

1 Although one card can do the job for most of us, hardcore gamers often pair two cards, each packing the latest chips and architecture. The two cards split the labor of painting and repainting the screen in a hectic fury. This dedication to displaying battle action can cost upward of $1,000, but it can also make the difference between virtual life and death!

2 The paired cards split the geometrical data that describes the game's three-dimensional world. Each card has a **geometry engine** that translates the mathematical description of a scene or a character into a specific set of points in the 3D arena. Each card's processor performs **rendering** or **rasterization**, which is crunching the intensive math needed to translate the data for a three-dimensional world into polygons that cover a two-dimensional screen. Many GPUs are programmable, meaning that software can teach them new tricks.

3 In early action games, the fights were rigged. If a bazooka shot missed its mark and hit a wall instead, the wall was always unscathed. Hardly realistic. Today's cards employ a **physics engine,** located on one of the board's chips, to calculate real-world reactions for everything from a golf ball's trajectory to the effect a grenade has on a building.

4 Graphics systems use **scissors rendering** to split the work load. One card takes responsibility for the top half of the screen, more or less, and the other card renders the bottom half. If one of the halves is simpler to render, such as a cloudless sky, that card takes on some of the other card's burden to equalize their loads.

5 Some cards provide **supertiling**. This rendering scheme breaks the work into a checkerboard pattern. One card takes the black squares and the other card works on the red squares. A chip on one of the boards shuffles the squares into the proper order before sending the instructions to the display.

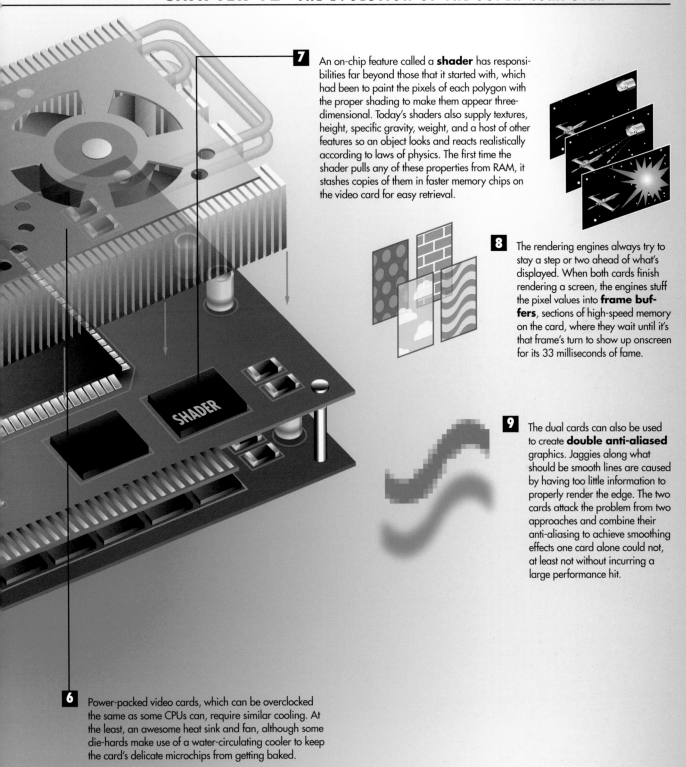

7 An on-chip feature called a **shader** has responsibilities far beyond those that it started with, which had been to paint the pixels of each polygon with the proper shading to make them appear three-dimensional. Today's shaders also supply textures, height, specific gravity, weight, and a host of other features so an object looks and reacts realistically according to laws of physics. The first time the shader pulls any of these properties from RAM, it stashes copies of them in faster memory chips on the video card for easy retrieval.

8 The rendering engines always try to stay a step or two ahead of what's displayed. When both cards finish rendering a screen, the engines stuff the pixel values into **frame buffers**, sections of high-speed memory on the card, where they wait until it's that frame's turn to show up onscreen for its 33 milliseconds of fame.

9 The dual cards can also be used to create **double anti-aliased** graphics. Jaggies along what should be smooth lines are caused by having too little information to properly render the edge. The two cards attack the problem from two approaches and combine their anti-aliasing to achieve smoothing effects one card alone could not, at least not without incurring a large performance hit.

6 Power-packed video cards, which can be overclocked the same as some CPUs can, require similar cooling. At the least, an awesome heat sink and fan, although some die-hards make use of a water-circulating cooler to keep the card's delicate microchips from getting baked.

How Overclocking Multiplies Time

EVERY COMPUTER has an internal clock ticking millions of times a second. That clock is the computer's metronome, conductor, and choreographer. It assures that data and commands pass from one component to another with precise timing. With its clock, a computer is like a troupe of a half-dozen jugglers simultaneously tossing heavy clubs that barely miss colliding with each other on their trajectories from one juggler to the next. Without the clock, a computer is like a troupe of jugglers with concussions and broken bones. But computer **modders**—born experimenters for whom no off-the-shelf PC is fast enough—found ways to raise a PC's heart rate without destroying their PCs. Well, usually.

1 All that a computer does, it does to the beat of its own drummer—a **crystal oscillator** made of quartz that is sandwiched between two plates that conduct electricity. Quartz has a natural **resonance**, a predictable frequency at which quartz crystals of the same size and shape vibrate when electricity passes through them.

CRYSTAL OSCILLATOR

—— AC current

2 During startup, a circuit in the oscillator applies an alternating current (AC) signal to the crystal, and purely by chance, a fraction of the random noise in the current will be at the crystal's resonance frequency. The crystal locks onto its own natural resonance, and the crystal's vibration generates another AC current that switches direction in time to the crystal's vibrating.

3 The oscillator amplifies the signals from the crystal and feeds them back to the crystals. The **loopback** reinforcement increases the strength of the signal while the crystal and circuit filter out unwanted frequencies because they don't contribute to the **feedback**. The signal—measured in hertz, both mega and giga—becomes a steady, dependable rhythm that the computer's components use to coordinate their operations and communications.

4 Few computers today have clock rates based solely on the frequency of the oscillating crystal. It's too slow. Instead, a circuit called a **multiplier** manipulates the clock's **clicks**, or pulses of electricity, by opening and closing switches and slicing the clock's current to create an **overtone frequency** higher than the crystal's **fundamental resonance**.

5 The multiplier's bursts of electricity—clock **ticks**—work as if the electricity for most of the PC were being turned off and on millions of times a second. When the electricity is "off," components are forced to wait—to sleep. When the electricity is "on," the components have a medium by which to send commands and data to one another.

6 Another factor in the speed of a PC is the **frontside bus**—the circuitry that connects the CPU, RAM, and memory controller. The bus has an independent clock that affects the overall speed of the computer. The simple formula for determining the clock speed of a PC is:
Frontside Bus (Hz) × CPU Multiplier × Crystal's Resonance = Operating Frequency (Hz)

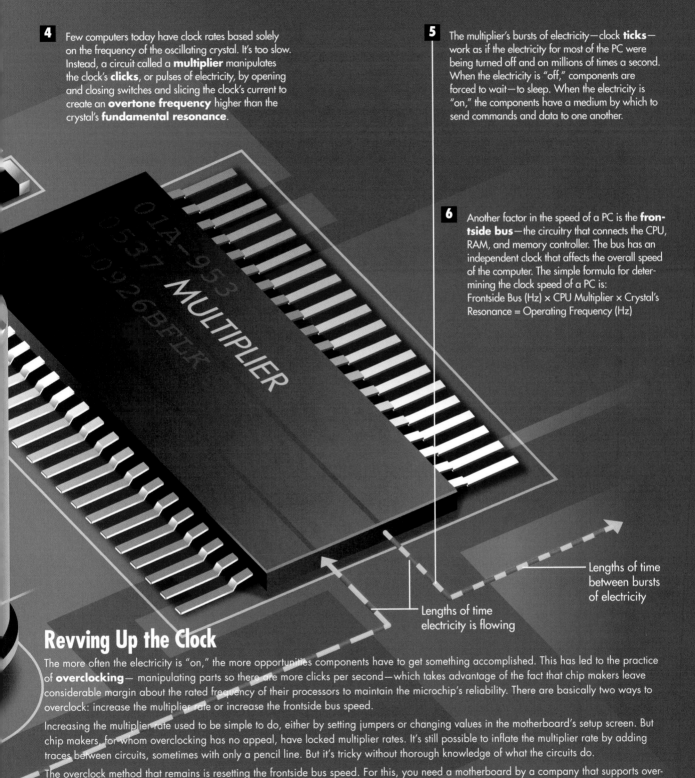

MULTIPLIER

01A-953
0537
D5D926BFLK

Lengths of time between bursts of electricity

Lengths of time electricity is flowing

Revving Up the Clock

The more often the electricity is "on," the more opportunities components have to get something accomplished. This has led to the practice of **overclocking**— manipulating parts so there are more clicks per second—which takes advantage of the fact that chip makers leave considerable margin about the rated frequency of their processors to maintain the microchip's reliability. There are basically two ways to overclock: increase the multiplier rate or increase the frontside bus speed.

Increasing the multiplier rate used to be simple to do, either by setting jumpers or changing values in the motherboard's setup screen. But chip makers, for whom overclocking has no appeal, have locked multiplier rates. It's still possible to inflate the multiplier rate by adding traces between circuits, sometimes with only a pencil line. But it's tricky without thorough knowledge of what the circuits do.

The overclock method that remains is resetting the frontside bus speed. For this, you need a motherboard by a company that supports overclocking. You make changes using controls thoughtfully provided in the set-up screens. You should make changes in small increments and run your PC for a while before going further to avoid *over*-overclocking, which results in overheating, sometime fatal to your PC.

How a PC Keeps It Cool

PCs, OVERCLOCKED OR NOT, are invariably overcooked PCs. The collisions of electrons moving through the traces and wires of microchips and circuit boards generate heat. The heat, in turn, contributes to the electrons' volatility. Like speeding cars, fast-moving electrons can lose the ability to stay on the track, especially as PC companies make circuits— their tracks—narrower. The result is that heat causes errors, as well as faster deterioration of the materials that make up computer components. Overclocking compounds that situation. One study found that every increase of 10° Celsius (C) drops the reliability of PC components by 50 percent. Aggressive computer users and makers have found several ways to cool down their machines.

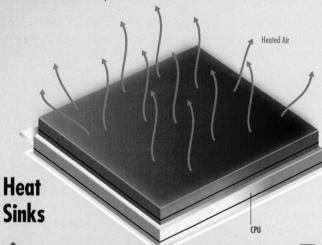

Cool Air

Heated Air

Heat Sinks

CPU

Thermal Paste

Fins

1 With no cooling airs at all, a component such as the CPU transfers its heat by **conduction**. Hot, rapidly vibrating molecules within the chip bump against neighboring atoms and molecules, transferring heat in the process. Eventually the heat reaches the chip's surface, where conduction transfers the heat to the air, allowing the heat to slowly dissipate.

2 The more surface area a chip has, the more heat can be passed on to the air. The added surface is provided by **heat sinks**. The sink is glued to a chip with a highly conductive **thermal paste** that assures there are no gaps filled with the less conductive air. Heat passes into the sinks, usually made of copper or aluminum, which rapidly move the heat to dozens of thin **fins** that multiply the surface area to transfer more heat to the surrounding air.

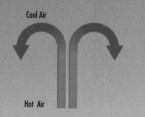

Cool Air

Hot Air

Forced Convection

1 Even with heat sinks and heat pipes, there remains the problem of getting the heat transferred to the air, away from the sinks and pipes, so they can pass more heat into the air. This is performed naturally through **convection**, based on the fact that the more rapidly moving atoms and molecules in hot air are farther apart from each other, making the hot air less dense and, therefore, lighter.

2 The lighter hot air rises, and the denser and heavier cool air falls. Away from the heat source, the hot air cools and sinks; the fallen cool air is heated by the source and rises. The result is a roughly circular convection system. But the cables, drive bays, and expansion boards inside a computer block the circulation, making convection less efficient.

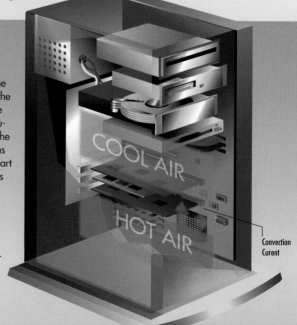

COOL AIR

HOT AIR

Convection Curent

Heat
Pipes

Fins

Pipe

Wick Lining   Vapor

Coolant

2 Heat from the microchip evaporates the coolant, drawing heat from the hot end of the
pipe through a process called **latent heat,**
which occurs whenever a substance changes
its state, such as a liquid becoming a gas.

3 The evaporation increases vapor pressure
inside the pipe at the end touching the chip.
This results in a rush of vapor toward the cool
end of the pipe as the pressure seeks to equalize itself throughout the pipe. At the cool end,
the vapor condenses, releasing the heat it
carried with it from the hot end. The cool end
is typically enveloped by fins that dissipate the
heat to the surrounding air. Evaporation of a
single gram of water uses the energy required
to raise that same gram by 540° C.

1 **Heat pipes** are
supercharged heat
sinks that cool in the same
way air conditioning does—
through **evaporative cooling.**
One end of the pipe is connected to a
microchip in the way a heat sink is; the
other end is in a relatively cool part of
the computer. The pipe is a sealed, hollow tube that contains a small amount of
fluid coolant, usually some combination of
ammonia, alcohol, and water. The rest of
the tube contains a near vacuum with only
a thin vapor of the coolant.

4 The liquid resulting
from condensation
returns to the hot end,
either through a wick
that coats the inside
of the pipe or simply
by running down
the inside of pipes
mounted vertically.

Fluid

5 Not all heat pipes are pipes. **Flat heat pipes** are two thin sheets of metal that create a narrow cavity between them. Some flat pipes are no thicker than 500 microns—about 2-hundredths
of an inch. The space between the metal sheets is divided between hollow areas and sheets of a
thin material with capillaries to act as wicks. The pipes' flat design allows them to fit flush against
the surface of a microchip for maximum transfer of heat, which is carried to a remote heat sink
and fan for dissipation.

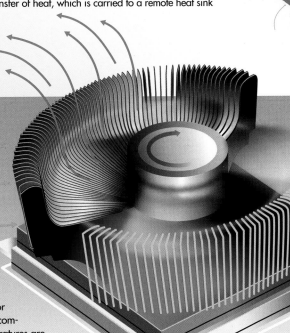

3 One solution is similar to the fan-forced convection found in ovens. A strategically placed fan
blows air across the fins of a heat sink or heat
pipe; some are integral parts of sinks or pipes.
This forces the hot air to circulate without rely-
ing on convection. Other fans, often outfitted
with neon or LED lights, may be fitted in holes
in the computer's case to move the hot air outside the computer.

4 Probes built into the motherboard or added to
the PC by an overclocker read the temperature
of key components, such as the CPU, GPU, and
RAM. The results may be read on an LED display or
may automatically turn fans on as needed to cool components off and to reduce noise levels when temperatures are
not as great.

How Advanced Cooling Refrigerates Your PC

Water Cooled PCs

1 The most popular solution to eliminating the noise of fans while at the same time providing an even lower temperature is the same as that found in cars and the Browning .50-caliber machine gun: water cooling.

2 The same type of thermal paste used with heat sinks holds a **water block** tightly to the CPU. Inside the block is a watertight channel that travels back and forth to create the maximum opportunity for heat from the CPU to transfer to a fluid inside the channel. Similar water blocks may also be attached to the North Bridge and South Bridge chips and the graphics processing unit on the video card—all sources of extreme heat.

3 If more than one microchip is being cooled, they are daisy-chained by tough plastic tubing designed to take turns without kinking. A pump continually moves liquid through the tubing. The liquid might be distilled water, to which additives may be added to improve the water's ability to absorb heat, to discourage corrosion and bacterial growth, to give the fluid a bright color, or to make it glow under ultraviolet light.

4 The pump moves the hot coolant to a metal **radiator** located outside the computer, or at least an area far-removed from the hotter components. The radiator has an undulating channel that gives the metal ample opportunity to absorb heat from the water. The heat moves through the absorbing metal to a system of fins that, as on a heat sink, expands the surface area for the heat to dissipate into the air. There may or may not be a fan cooling the fins, depending on the efficiency of the water system and the owner's desire for a quiet system.

5 The cooled liquid flows through a **reservoir**. The reservoir provides another area where heat can escape. Only part of the reservoir is filled with liquid. Air in the reservoir allows the liquid to expand and contract as its temperature changes without putting undue pressure on the tubing. It also provides a convenient place for adding additional coolant if needed. From the reservoir, the cooled coolant returns to the system of water blocks to continue the cooling process.

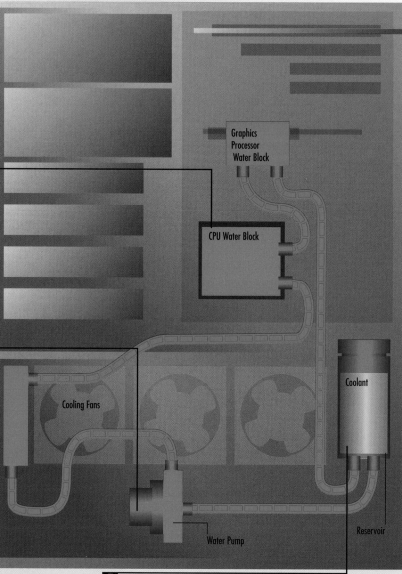

Graphics Processor Water Block

CPU Water Block

Coolant

Cooling Fans

Reservoir

Water Pump

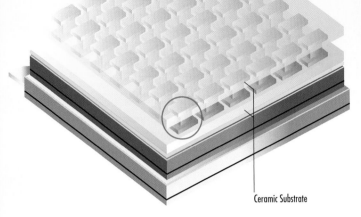

Ceramic Substrate

Peltier Cooling

1 One of the more exotic methods of cooling computers uses the **Peltier effect**, first observed by Jean Peltier in 1834. The effect appears in a device made of two dissimilar metals—metals that react differently to electrical current—that are joined in at least two different places. A Peltier device, also called a **thermoelectric cooler**, can also work with two different types of semiconductors—**n-type**, to which impurities have been added so it has extra electrons, and **p-type**, in which impurities create **holes**, or vacancies where electrons could be. For simplicity, the example just uses semiconductors.

2 When electricity flows through the n-type elements and crosses through a metallic connector to the p-type material, the extra electrons in the n-type semiconductor flow in the opposite direction of the electrical current.

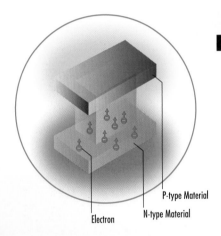

3 After the current continues on and passes through the p-type material, it returns to the n-type through another metallic bridge. This time the hole in the p-type element moves through the metal bridge in the same direction as the current.

P-type Material

N-type Material

Electron

4 In both instances, the electrons and the holes carry heat with them. The junction they are headed for warms, and the junction they are leaving cools off. The cool side of the device is attached to a microchip like a heat sink, and the hot side uses some combination of fins, heat pipes, and fans to dissipate the steady stream of heat originating at the chip. (Despite its high-tech nature, a Peltier device is an electricity hog and only 49% to 60% as effective as a refrigerator compressor.)

Cooling with Crisco

The strangest method overclockers have developed to keep a computer cool is to submerge the motherboard and its expansion boards in cooking oil. Oil has dual strengths—it's an insulator and an excellent conductor of heat, making it a good, if messy, substance for cooling PCs, as well as frying chicken.

Photo courtesy of Tom's Hardware

How Jailbreaking Frees Your Devices

INSIDE THE SVELTE CASES of your smartphone and tablet, there simply is not enough room for a water cooler or a couple of high-powered video cards. But there are ways to hack your mobile devices. In the Apple world, these hacks are called **jailbreaking**. For Android devices, they're **rooting**. With either term, it means going into the most sacrosanct of the devices' code—the ROM—and changing the **firmware** stored there so you can do things such as unlock your phone so it works with different carriers, replace the operating system, or use someone else's soft keyboard with your iPhone or iPad.

You do not have to have the skills of a seasoned hacker to root or jailbreak. Hackers have already dissected the software in both Android and Apple devices' to uncover **exploits**, rips in the software's security. They've created programs that automate the process. (Google them.) Here's how they work…

Jailbreaking

1 When you turn on your iPhone, the boot program examines the **chain of trust**. This is a series of digital signatures that attest to the authenticity of each stage of the phone's **firmware**—the crucial code that joins hardware and software. No stage is allowed to load until its signature is verified.

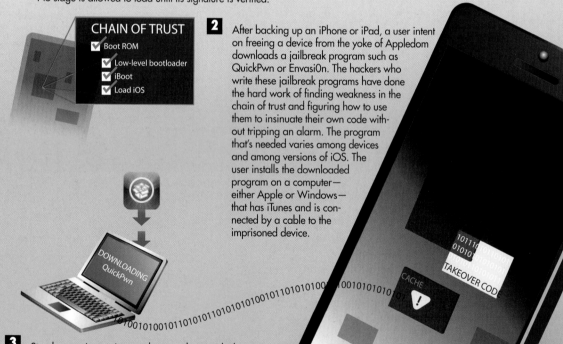

CHAIN OF TRUST
- ☑ Boot ROM
- ☑ Low-level bootloader
- ☑ iBoot
- ☑ Load iOS

DOWNLOADING QuickPwn

2 After backing up an iPhone or iPad, a user intent on freeing a device from the yoke of Appledom downloads a jailbreak program such as QuickPwn or EnvasiOn. The hackers who write these jailbreak programs have done the hard work of finding weakness in the chain of trust and figuring how to use them to insinuate their own code without tripping an alarm. The program that's needed varies among devices and among versions of iOS. The user installs the downloaded program on a computer—either Apple or Windows—that has iTunes and is connected by a cable to the imprisoned device.

TAKEOVER CODE

CACHE

3 Step-by-step instructions and screen shots guide the user through the jailbreak. The user can't see what's going on inside the device—a good thing because it's as complex as it is ingenious. Although the actual machinations vary with program and device, they begin by exploiting a known flaw. One jailbreaker, for example, floods integers into an input/output junction. The flood causes data being held in a cache to overflow, allowing the program to slip its own code into the system undetected. Another approach hides the code in a PDF document or even in the font used to create the document, like a nail file in a cake. When iOS loads the PDF, it swallows the code and executes it without realizing it.

4 The end result is that the jailbreaking program saves its own code into the root, the most sacrosanct of levels, where only Apple's own programs are supposed to exist. The new code lets the device's user download and run unapproved apps from **Cydia**, the underground equivalent of iTunes.

Rooting

1 Rooting is named for its target, the **root**, the innermost code level of an Android operating system, from which comes all authority as to what can be done with the device. On a superficial level, rooting seems similar to jailbreaking, but rooting is more straightforward, owing to Android's less paranoid security. In fact, some Android device makers kindly look the other way. Rooting begins with a backup of the device's files and a desktop computer cabled to an Android smart-phone or tablet.

2 The user downloads and installs on the desktop PC one of several rooting programs, such as Universal Androot or SuperOnceClick. The rooting software may include Android Software Developer Kit. If the kit is not included, the user must download it from http://developer.android.com/sdk/index.html.

3 The user enables the **USB debugging mode** on the Android device, and follows the directions specific to the device. The specifics vary with the software tool used, as well as with time, because Android as an operating system is constantly changing with the changes differing among different device makers. That forces hackers to find new **exploits**—weaknesses and unguarded entries—and devise new ways to exploit the exploits. Generally, rooting operations let the user have his way with parts of the operating system code that are supposed to be off-limits.

The Legality of Jailbreaking

The Library of Congress, which reviews this matter every three years, says that jailbreaking and rooting are legal on phones, but not on tablets—although tablets are pretty much big smartphones without the phone connection. A misstep in either tech liberation can turn your device into a **brick**, a brain-dead collection of electronics. Don't look for sympathy from the manufacturer. However, with the help of other hacker software, you often can resuscitate your device. Sometimes you can't. Think of it as an adventure.

4 After the rooting software gains access to the device's memory area, the user can install a newer version of the Android operating system, or a **ROM manager** such as ClockworkMod. ROM managers allow the use of alternative software to overwrite the device's read-only memory with a new **MOD**. A new program, such as CyanogenMod, includes features that optimize memory, allow hand gestures, enable Bluetooth and Wi-Fi **tethering**, or even bring some of the über to Android in the form of overclocking.

CHAPTER 13

How Cameras Capture Memories

PUT A DIGITAL CAMERA next to a comparably priced camera that still uses film. What's the difference? Certainly it's not anything you can see: They both have a lens, most have some sort of viewfinder to peer through, and they have similar assortments of buttons and knobs.

The important difference between the two cameras is buried inside them. Take off the back of the film camera and you'll see a slot at one end where you insert your cassette of film and an empty spool on the other end to take up the roll of film as each frame is exposed. Between them is the shutter. When the camera back is closed, the film is held firmly against the frame around the shutter by a smooth flat surface called the *pressure plate*.

Take a digital camera and open the back—and you can't! There is no way to open it and see what's inside. This chapter shows you what you ordinarily can't see on your own—that your digital camera is, in fact, a very specialized computer. It has a **microchip** packed with microscopic transistors that process data just like the processor of your desktop PC or even your smartphone (which itself probably has a pretty good digital camera).

This particular type of microchip, as you see in more detail later in the book, is covered with a special type of transistor—millions of transistors, actually—that is sensitive to light and converts that light into electricity. The chip is called an **image sensor**, or an **imager**.

The image sensor's ability to translate different colors and intensities of light into constantly changing electrical currents is what accounts for the other important differences between digital and film cameras. The most obvious is that most digital cameras have an LCD screen on the back of them, like a tiny TV set, where the camera displays the scene to be shot or the photographs already stored in the camera. The LCD has its own array of transistors that do just the opposite of the imager's transistors: They convert electricity into light. (More about that, too, later on.)

If you inspect the two cameras closely enough, you might find some other differences. The digital camera might have, for example, a button or switch for something called **white balance**. It might have controls for onscreen menus, or for displaying information about a shot you've snapped, or a button with an icon of a trash can that's used for deleting files.

But that's about it. Those are all the differences you'll find by visually inspecting your digital camera—even if you tear it apart. With few exceptions, such as the aforementioned white balance, you use a digital camera just as you would a film camera.

But after you click the shutter, letting light fleetingly strike the image sensor, you've created not just one picture, but the possibility for scores of pictures. The future of that picture is limited only by your imagination.

How Digital Cameras Capture the Moment

THE STREET you're driving down doesn't suddenly end here and start again over *there*, with no way to bridge the gap. As far as we know, time doesn't stop for 5 minutes and then pick up again where it left off. We're used to thinking of things as analog—smooth, continuous objects without any quantum gaps between here and there. But in the computer world—and your digital camera is a computer—nothing is smooth and continuous. It's digital. There are gaps between this point and that one, between this moment and the next. Before we can do all the wonderful things available to us now that a computer is packed into our cameras, we and our cameras have to communicate—we with our words; the cameras with a mathematical alphabet of only 0s and 1s.

1 Anything in the universe can be measured in analog or digital terms. **Analog** simply means that the expression of the measurement is analogous to whatever it's measuring. An old-fashioned thermometer with red-dyed alcohol in a tube gives an analog representation of how hot it is because the alcohol rises, literally, as the temperature rises. A **digital** thermometer expresses the temperature in numbers on a small LCD screen. The numbers themselves don't grow larger as the temperature rises.

2 Film is an analog method of recording a photo. Where light strikes the silver halide crystals embedded in film, the crystals clump together. Where the light is stronger, more crystals clump. Where the light is dimmer, fewer crystals clump.

3 The photodiodes that replace film in a digital camera don't look any different after a picture is snapped than they did before. They don't shift about on the surface of the image sensor to clump where the light is stronger. But there is an unseen analog process afoot when a digital photo is taken. Each of the photodiodes collects photons of light as long as the shutter is open. The brighter a part of a photograph is, the more photons hit the pixels that are analogous to that part of the scene. When the shutter closes, all the pixels have electrical charges that are proportional to the amount of light they received. If you picture the photons piling up like little piles of glowing pebbles, you have the idea.

What happens next depends on whether the image sensor is a **CCD (charged coupled device)** or **CMOS (complementary metal oxide semiconductor)**. Don't bother with the full-fledged names. Everyone uses the acronyms, and they won't be on the quiz. You will hear a lot of techno-hype from camera makers citing reasons one technology is better than the other. You can ignore that, too. The type of imager is just one factor that contributes to the photo that eventually will come out of your printer. It's the print that's important. Whether you're happy with it or not doesn't hinge on the type of image sensor. But here, for the sheer joy of knowledge alone, are the differences in how the two types of chips work.

CCD

4 The charges in an **interline CCD** imager, which is what most CCDs are, begin an orderly procession toward their future existence as digital numbers like well-behaved schoolchildren in a fire drill. At one end of the imager, the charges move down and out at the bottom of the column as if someone were continually pulling the bottom can of soda out of a dispenser.

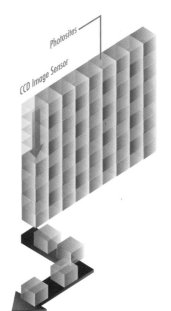

Photosites

CCD Image Sensor

5 When the last charge has rolled out of the bottom of the column, the charges in the second column shift to fill the vacancies left by the newly departed charges. The charges in the third column move to the second column, and the thousands of remaining columns follow their lead like a panoramic Busby Berkeley number.

CCD Image Sensor

Read-out Register

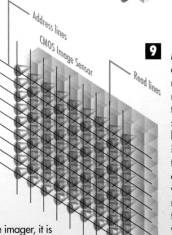

6 When a column of charges falls out of the imager, it is detected by the **read-out register**, which takes them to an amplifier. Until they are amplified, the charges are more like faint static electricity than electrical current. The amplifier pumps energy into the charges giving them a voltage in proportion to the size of each charge, much as a flagging video game character is pumped up with "life force" by jumping on a coin.

CMOS

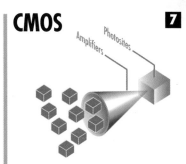

Amplifiers Photosites

7 Unlike the photosites in CCDs—pretty much passive **capacitors** that do little but store an electrical charge until a control somewhere else tells them what to do with it—a CMOS sensor is able on its own to do some of the processing necessary to make something useful out of the charges the photosites have obtained from the light.

Photosites

CMOS Image Sensor

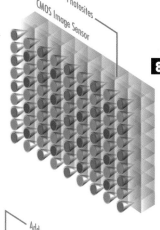

8 The first thing the CMOS image sensor does is use the amplifiers that are part of each photosite. This eliminates the need for the charges to go through an amplifier in single file after they've left the sensor.

Address lines

CMOS Image Sensor

Read lines

9 More importantly, the onsite amplifier eliminates the slow classroom drill CCDs use to leave their nest. As soon as the amplifiers have turned the charges into actual voltages, those voltages are read over a grid of X-Y wires whose intersections correspond to locations of the photosites. It's the voltages' way of saying simultaneously, "Beam us up."

How Autofocus Clears the Picture

PHOTOGRAPHERS can't always rely on automatic focusing because it's subject to the vagaries of any mechanism that cannot see but pretends it can. For the most part, autofocus largely eliminates pictures of relatives with fuzzy faces and blurred birthday bashes. The implementations of autofocus are as diverse as the minds of the ingenious engineers who invent them. Generally there is **active autofocus** and **passive autofocus.** You usually find active autofocus on point-and-shoot cameras. It involves either some form of radar and sonar or triangulation using rangefinders. Passive autofocus, which is common in DSLR cameras, is the subject of this illustration.

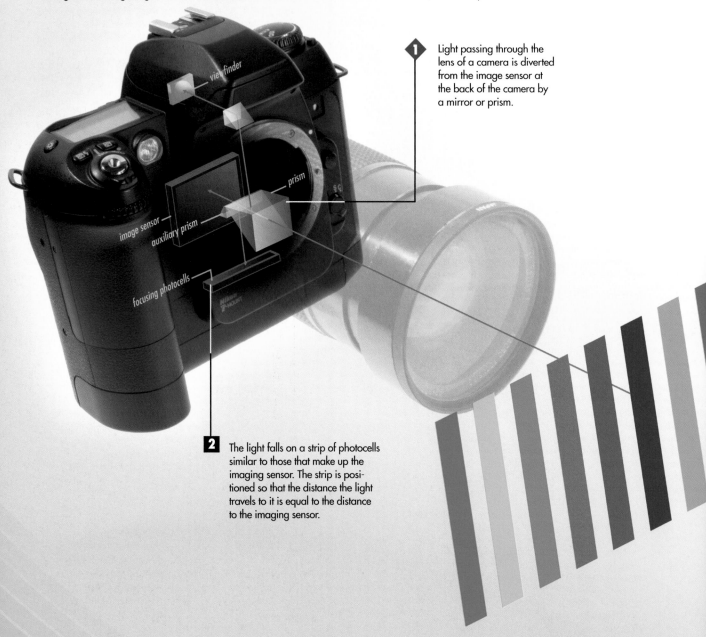

1 Light passing through the lens of a camera is diverted from the image sensor at the back of the camera by a mirror or prism.

2 The light falls on a strip of photocells similar to those that make up the imaging sensor. The strip is positioned so that the distance the light travels to it is equal to the distance to the imaging sensor.

viewfinder

prism

image sensor

auxiliary prism

focusing photocells

3 The camera's processor compares the intensity of the light falling on each photocell to the intensities of the adjacent cells. If the image is out of focus, adjacent pixels have similar intensities; there is little contrast among them.

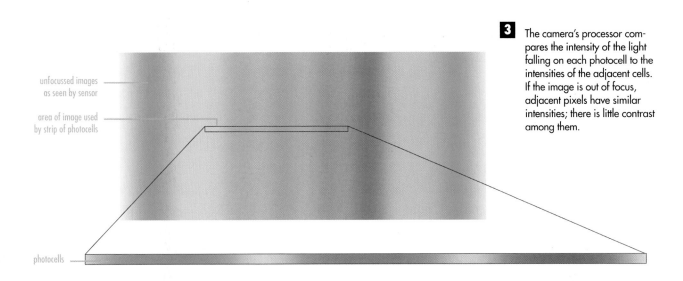

unfocussed images as seen by sensor

area of image used by strip of photocells

photocells

4 The microprocessor moves the lens and again compares the photocell intensities. As the scene comes more into focus, the contrast between adjacent photodiodes increases. When the microprocessor gauges that the difference in intensity is at its maximum, the scene is in focus.

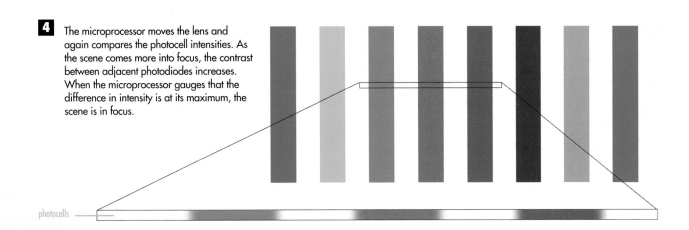

photocells

Autofocus Limitations

Both passive and active autofocus have advantages and disadvantages. Active focusing works at night and in dim lighting, but the infrared light can bounce off glass or mirrors, confusing the camera's processor. Using passive focusing, you aim through windows, and there are no distance limitations beyond which it cannot work. But a blank wall or a scene devoid of straight edges, particularly vertical lines, throws passive autofocus for a loop.

To minimize the effects of shooting through glass, the photographer can put the lens directly on the glass. The infrared light passes through the glass. Any light that bounces back makes the trip too quickly for the camera to use its timing information. With passive autofocus, turning the camera 90° can give the camera the perpendicular lines it needs. In scenes with little contrast, try focusing on an object elsewhere about the same distance away as your subject. Then keep the shutter button pressed down about halfway as you turn to frame your real subject. On some cameras, holding the button locks the focus until you press the button all the way to shoot your photo or until you release it. The camera's processor compares the intensity of the light falling on each photocell to the intensities of the adjacent cells. If the image is out of focus, adjacent pixels have similar intensities; there is little contrast among them.

How Cameras Choose an Exposure

THE MOST COMPLEX part of a digital camera is its exposure system. It's more than a photodiode measuring the light coming through the lens. Among the most versatile cameras, the exposure system has more than one way to measure light and mixes those measurements into a brew made of settings for the type of lighting; the sensitivity of the image sensor; and special settings for action shots, fireworks, black-and-white, or even special effects such as sepia toning. That brew is siphoned to set into action the diaphragm and shutter, all in the blink of an eye.

1 Less-expensive digital cameras—called **point-and-shoot (POS)** models—often have only one of the many ways of measuring light that more-expensive cameras boast. It's called **full-frame,** and it typically uses one photodiode device mounted next to the lens. On better cameras, full-frame metering uses several photodiodes mounted in the path of the light on its way from the lens to the shutter hiding the image sensor. Either type of full-frame averages the intensities of light reflected off a subject to determine a shutter speed and aperture that will produce an exposure that is expected to render everything in the photo. But unless a scene is evenly lit and contains only subjects with the same color value, full-frame exposures are usually less accurate.

Photodiode arrays

Photodiode

2 In the photo here, for example, the bright sunlight falling on the bricks behind the boy riding in his car has made the camera's auto-exposure feature overcompensate and shut down the diaphragm too much. The result is muddy shadows revealing little detail in the most important part of the photo.

3 This occurs because exposure systems think that no matter how bright or how dim something is, it is 18% gray (which is considered a medium gray). In these photographs, you can see white, gray, and black sheets of paper in their true colors when they are all in the same photo. But when each is photographed so that it is the only object measured by the exposure meter, the camera's exposure automatically is set to render the three sheets of paper as the same medium gray.

4 To overcome the perils of using an average of an entire scene's illumination, better digital cameras have alternative ways of measuring light that can be chosen from a menu displayed in the camera's LCD screen or by one of the camera's control knobs or buttons. The first alternative is **center-weighted** measurement. It meters the light in an area that amounts to about a tenth of the total photo area. As the name implies, that tenth is located in the center of the screen on the theory that that's where the most important part of the scene is.

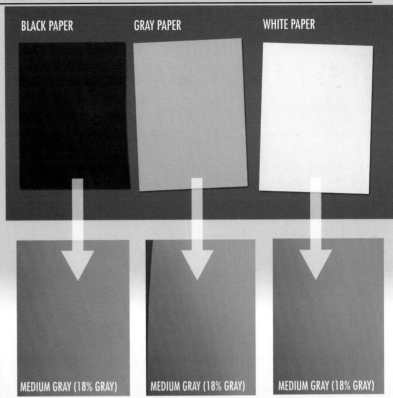

BLACK PAPER   GRAY PAPER   WHITE PAPER

MEDIUM GRAY (18% GRAY)   MEDIUM GRAY (18% GRAY)   MEDIUM GRAY (18% GRAY)

Area covered by center-weighted metering

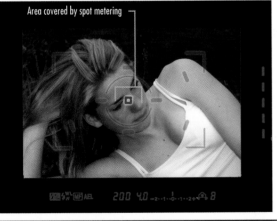

Area covered by spot metering

5 The other common alternative is **spot metering**, which gives the photographer greater ability to expose the part of the scene that is most crucial. Illumination is read from only a small circle in the center of the screen, allowing the photographer to expose for the lighting on a cheek that might be surrounded by dark hair and a beard that would otherwise overwhelm the light readings. When the crucial subject matter is off-center, some cameras have the capability to make small areas on different parts of the image the spot for purposes of metering. For those without such cameras, you can use the **shutter lock** described in the sidebar box.

The Half-Push

When the most important element of a photo is not in the center of the frame, most cameras have a shutter lock feature that lets them focus and get an exposure reading for their picture by aiming the center at that important element. Then, by pushing the shutter button only halfway, the autofocus and auto-exposure settings are locked. The photographer then reframes the picture with that key element away from the center and presses the shutter button the rest of the way.

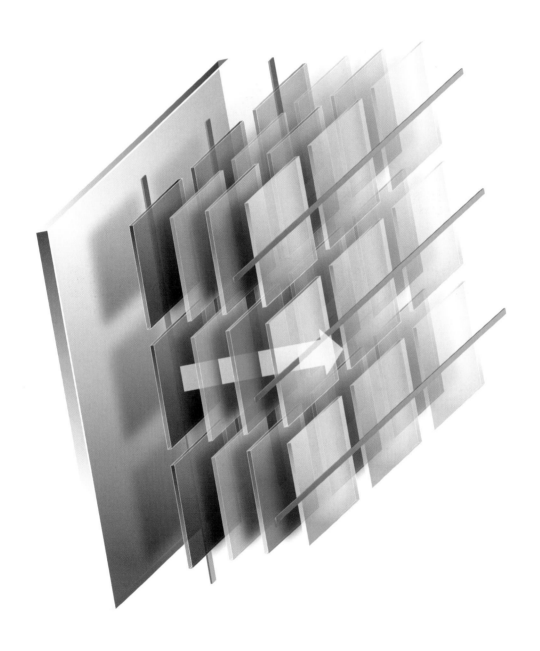

P A R T

4

How Computers Expand Our Senses

C H A P T E R S

Gargoyles... wear their computers on their bodies, broken up into separate modules that hang on the waist, on the back, on the headset. They serve as human surveillance devices, recording everything that happens around them. Nothing looks stupider; these getups are the modern-day equivalent of the slide-rule scabbard or the calculator pouch on the belt, marking the user as belonging to a class that is at once above and far below human society.

—Neal Stephenson, *Snow Crash*

There's not a kid in the last 50 years who didn't, at some time or other, dream of being Iron Man. Think of it: Slipping on some sheets of gaudy colored metal brimming with state-of-the-art electronics that transform your pathetic preteen body into a half-human, half-robot who is unstoppable (except when required for purposes of plot conflict). And, of course, there's also the flying.

All we would-be super humans knew that was just a fantasy. Then along came computers. Things sure changed in a hurry, didn't they? Oh, sure. The first desktops only made you a hero if you were the office geek who knew how to get them running after a crash, but then PCs shrank and evolved into tablets and smartphones and watches and glasses. Computer makers and users realized these mobile gadgets were more than office appliances or at-home game machines. They could give us the power to be interconnected, all the time. And we're not just staying connected, we're interacting with our devices—seeing and touching and hearing—in ways that were pure sci-fi escapism a mere 15 years ago.

With an anytime, all-the-time link to the Internet, these devices give us the power to gather and send voices and images across oceans. We can see, as never before, through a built-in camera's high definition resolution, one that perfectly balances all the strengths of light in a scene into a photo in which nothing is lost in shadows or washed out in highlights. Computing allows us to create and listen to music made with sounds we—the world—had never heard before, and our favorite apps know what music we'd like before we know. Capturing electromagnetic waves millions of years old, from galaxies millions of light years away, gives us fantastic images in glowing colors with a cast of billions of stars, the existence of which we could only guess at before computing came along. (Strictly speaking, that last item is not a function of anyone's smartphone, but with a smartphone you can call up those images in a minute.)

Not all these new abilities have come as conveniently as Tony Stark slipping on an iron exoskeleton. But we're getting there. Google's Glass is a milestone in the evolution of computing from something we use to something we wear to something that's an integral part of our selves. Glass is one of those short branches in the family tree, a creature out testing the evolutionary waters to see if they will support him or perhaps its offspring.

Those waters are telling Google that its descendants need to look a lot less goofy. They are also saying that in the future, although we may not be a part of the Borg, the Borg will be a part of us. Consider all the prosthetics options, from 3D-printed dentures and casts to set broken bones, to Bluetooth hearing implants, to Google's contact lens that continuously measures the glucose level in the tears of diabetics, flashing a yellow light if levels are too high.

We're on the cusp of being able to register colors, touch, movement, and other new sensations from digital components and feed that information to our most personal of personal computers—a brain learning to understand those sensations and act on them. The ultimate evolution of computing will be when we don't distinguish what we do with computing from what we do with our bodies. We're not there yet, but in the meantime, this part looks at all those ways we're bridging our present on into our future.

CHAPTER

14

How We Stay in Touch

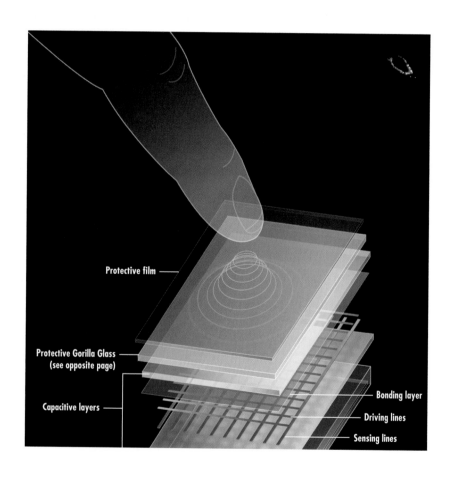

Protective film

Protective Gorilla Glass
(see opposite page)

Capacitive layers

Bonding layer

Driving lines

Sensing lines

PALEONTOLOGISTS are fond of pointing out that an important distinction between the apes, including humans, and the rest of the animal kingdom is the opposable thumb. It enables us apes to grip with a strength and manipulate with a grace that fingers cannot manage on their own. Why, without thumbs, we would be a pitiful sight as we tried to use tablets and smartphones. We'd be lucky to get them out of our pockets and not drop them as we wrote messages with the tips of our noses.

Luckily, that's not our fate. It's fitting that touch—the most intimate way we have of expressing ourselves—is our preferred way of communicating with these little electronic devices we hold so dear. Many of us spend hours with our smartphones, tablets, and game controllers, touching, tickling, pounding, and sometimes even shouting at them. As in the rest of life, there are limits to touching. At least we older users, who were brought up on typewriters and keyboards, find it difficult to deftly tap our fingers on virtual keys the size of couscous.

But things are getting better. VR keyboards are getting better at distinguishing what we meant to touch as opposed to what we did touch. It's getting easier to talk to our devices to find out what song is playing or what's in the latest weather report. We're still working to get our devices to hear correctly what we say. Despite the inroads described in the previous chapter, and the neat tricks and jokes coming out of Siri, our devices are about as good as our pets at understanding the meaning of what they hear.

Happily, we don't have to put all our words in one basket. Computers are getting better at recognizing what they see, including our faces, expressions, and gestures. And they bring to the communications party a wealth of new ways of seeing things. Computers are expanding our vision by making global maps from the reaches of space, and the sensing of such previously invisible things as radio waves, bar codes, gravity, and infrared images. Of course, live images of happenings on the other side of the world have become such commonplace experiences that we are no longer amazed by it all. We're coming to take these experiences for granted—just like we undervalue our thumbs.

How Your Smartphone Knows Where You Are

TODAY, OUR ELECTRONIC gadgets have a skill most of our mothers would have killed for—the ability to know where we are day or night. What gives this gift to our cell phones, tablets, computers, cars, watches, and even running shoes is GPS—the Global Positioning System—24 beacons in the sky that constantly broadcast the information our devices need to tell us just where we are—and how to get to the nearest Starbucks.

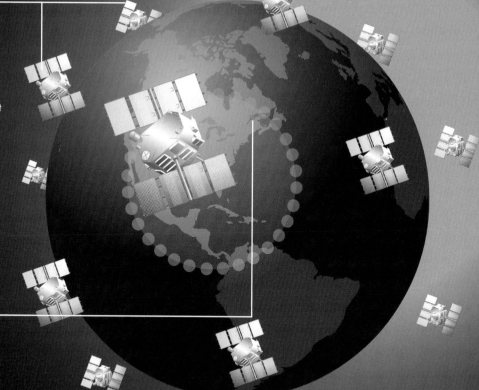

3 On earth, a GPS radio receiver, part of a phone, electronic compass, car mapping system, or a dozen or so other devices, listens to the signals broadcast by at least four satellites. Programmed into the receiver's data is the exact location of each satellite. The GPS device includes a microprocessor that measures how long it took the signals to reach it from each satellite.

1 The satellites, put into space by the U.S. Department of Defense and a number of other outfits, are locked into geo-synchronous orbits that blanket the earth like the nexus of a giant geodesic dome. Relative to the earth and to each other, the satellites maintain the same steady positions at all times.

2 From any point on earth, between five and eight satellites are visible—or would be if your eyesight were good enough or if you used a telescope. Every thousandth of a second, the satellites broadcast information that identifies each one and the time the signal is sent. A ground station constantly updates and corrects the time signals.

- Satellite
- Possible location of GPS receiver
- Actual location of GPS receiver

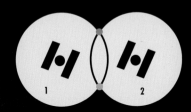

4 Based on a signal from only one satellite, the receiver could be at any point that matches the distance between that one satellite and the receiver. That distance is equal to the radius of a circle that has the overhead position of the satellite at its center and whose circumference represents all the possible locations of the receiver.

5 Now include the information contained in the signals from a second satellite, and the GPS calculations construct a second circle that intersects the first circle at two points. Because both those points are equidistant from the centers of both circles, one of them must be the location of the receiver.

6 A third signal pinpoints the GPS receiver's location—the point at which a circle with the third satellite at its center coincides with one of the two intersections of the first two circles. Because GPS receivers are accurate to within only about few yards, a fourth satellite or more improves the accuracy of the calculations.

7 The longitude and latitude determined by the processor is mapped and turned into a point of light on a phone, tablet, or car's mapping display. If the device with the GPS unit is moving, the dot on the display moves with it. If the display is coordinated by landmark data in the device or with a mapping service database, the map might include symbols for common locations, such as restaurants, service stations, hospitals, malls, and, of course, Starbucks.

How Devices Recognize Our Touch

OUR HANDS are a natural part of communication. Think of how people gesture when they're talking. They jab at the air to make a point, turn their palms upward to show they don't have an answer, and, of course, point at something to say, "This. *This* is what I want." That's especially true when people are communicating with a tablet or smartphone.

1 You can see the electromagnetic field that connects our fingers to mobile devices as an **aura** or **corona** captured by **Kirlean photography,** a photo captured with a sheet of photographic film placed on a metal plate. The object to be photographed is placed on the film. When a voltage is applied to the plate, the charge draws the hand's field down through the film, creating an exposure that reveals the field. You can also feel the effect of the field when your body collects extra electrons from scuffling on a carpet or brushing your hair.

2 The electromagnetic field is put to work in a **capacitive touchscreen**. When you touch the screen of a smartphone or tablet, your finger's electromagnetic field extends through the screen's surface protective layers and warps the field created between two layers of electrical lines that lie at right angles to each other. The lines never touch each other, but their capacitance—the ability of the lines to hold a static charge—increases more where the lines are closer to the center of an area the finger touches.

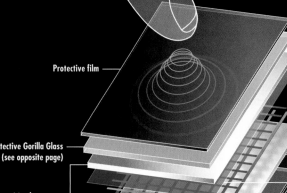

Protective film

3 First, the device captures raw data from your touch.

Protective Gorilla Glass (see opposite page)

Capacitive layers

Bonding layer

Driving lines

Sensing lines

LED or OLEM display

4 This data isn't clean, so it then must filter and remove any background noise.

9 There are a dozen or so touchscreen technologies, but makers settled on capacitive touchscreen because it is the only type of screen that can collect and transmit information for as many as 10 spots at the same time. This **multitouch** capability permits intricate interactions with the device's display by using, for example, fingers moving apart or together to zoom in or out of an image.

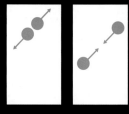

5 The device measures field distortion to find the shape and size of touch area based on how the capacitance over different pixels changes.

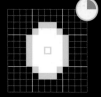

6 The device uses the filtered capacitance information to determine the exact center of the touch.

7 It also detects movement along the surface and how long the touch lasts to distinguish between swipes as well as short and long touches, which can trigger different operations.

8 It relays information to software, which determines how to change the display. The same touch or gesture may be used to obtain different results depending upon the gesture rules established by the software producing the display.

How Glass Becomes Strong and Supple

LEGEND HAS IT that Steve Jobs went around for weeks with a prototype of a new iPhone in his pants pocket. As the scars, scratches, and dents from car keys, coins, and what-not accumulated on the phone's screen, so did Jobs' frustration. "People want a phone they can carry in their pocket!" he told Apple's engineers, who didn't know what to do about the problem. Happily, Corning did. A few years earlier Corning had demoed a glass that was just *this far* from being scratch-proof and unbreakable. But then it was left sitting on the shelf until Jobs, with his god mode at full throttle, explained things to Corning execs. Six months later, Gorilla Glass was born. If you tap, swipe, or otherwise handle a smartphone, you've made contact with the Gorilla.

The GORILLA

1 Gorilla Glass begins as a mixture of glass oxides melted at 1,832°F in a large, V-shaped vat called an **iso-pipe**. In the **fusion draw** process, the molten glass flows evenly over two sides of the isopipe, running down the sides until the two flows meet at the bottom and fuse into a continuous **mother sheet** of glass 0.4 to 2mm thick.

2 Large sections are cut from the mother sheet and placed in a 752°F bath of molten salt and potassium. The bath forces larger potassium ions into the glass, squeezing out the glass's smaller sodium ions. When the glass cools, its contraction squeezes the potassium ions farther into the glass and closer to each other to give the glass a density to withstand everyday punishment.

3 If a scratch does inflict Gorilla Glass, its dense iron compression area acts as a dam to the spread of further damage. But Gorilla Glass is not indestructible. Repeated, forceful abuse takes its toll as new stresses expand the microscopic damage caused by earlier accidents.

4 Beginning with Gorilla Glass 3, silver ions, which are antimicrobial agents, are embedded in the glass. These ions leach to the glass surface—where fingers deposit bacteria—and eliminate nearly all of the germs.

The Willow

1 Willow Glass starts out much like Gorilla Glass, by melting limestone, sand, sodium borate, and other materials that give Willow Glass the ability to bend into shapes that would snap ordinary glass. The molten glass is extruded in sheets only as thick as 0.05mm, compared to 0.2mm or 0.5mm for ordinary glass.

2 Instead of finishing as sheets of glass, Willow Glass is fed into rollers where tabs prevent the surface of the glass from touching anything, including itself, as it is coiled into giant rolls.

3 Willow Glass is not simply molded into curved surfaces, such as on some TVs. It remains flexible even after it cools.

Birth of the Wearable Computer

There are other types of glass too. Sapphire crystal, used with Apple Watch, is more brittle but is second only to diamond in hardness, making it extremely difficult to crack. As a new generation of wrist wearables emerges, you'll see different models sporting sapphire, Gorilla, Willow, and still others. The really interesting stuff will combine Willow with organic light emitting diodes (OLED – see Chapter 15). Willow Glass and OLED, were made for each other. Like Willow, OLED displays can bend. The possibilities are not lost on the mad scientists of the computer industry. Smartwatches that flex to fit the wearer have been proposed by Apple, Samsung, and others.

This display combo has also led to other wild concepts. Imagine a display coiled inside a tube the diameter of a pencil. Grab a handy tab, and you'll be able to pull out the OLED/Willow screen to have a display the size of a 7-inch tablet. Still larger displays will be Time Square's billboard of the future, able to wrap about building corners and curved facades while withstanding the inevitable assault by miscreants. But the ultimate use may be clothing. Imagine being able to change the color and design on a jacket or skirt. You could even display Blade Runner on your pants and sell advertising on your back, putting sandwich boards out of business.

How Game Controllers Let You Play

FOR MANY YEARS, even the most elaborate joysticks required only a trigger, and a button or two. But as games grew more versatile, players needed more versatile tools to control the action. From that need came today's most prevalent controller—a device studded with buttons and pads, and held with two hands. The Playstation's Dual Shock is typical of most gamepads. Despite their almost universal use, little is intuitive about using them, a fact that inspired Nintendo's return to simplicity, the Wiimote—an entirely different kind of controller.

The Gamepad

Four **trigger buttons** are located on the front of the controller. They may be used for shooting actions or in combination with other keys for more complex actions.

The **D-pad**, or directional pad, can activate two **potentiometers** at the same time. Potentiometers consist of two current-conducting strips separated by a material that resists current. The harder the D-pad presses against the potentiometer, the closer the two conducting strips get to each other, allowing more current to pass through them. A microchip combines the strength of the two signals to calculate the intended direction.

Trigger Buttons

Switch Pressed (Open)
Switch Unpressed (Closed)

Action Buttons

OPEN CIRCUIT

LEFT, DOWN

ENCODER

Potentiometers

D-pad

Select Button

Analog Stick

Start Button

Motor

The Dual Shock has 14 switches, two motors, four analog controls, and a light. An **encoder** chip translates all analog signals to digital, compresses the data, adds tags that identify the control generating it, and sends the signals serially to the console, where the software interprets the signals in the context of the game being played.

Two **analog sticks** register the direction in which pressure is applied, much like a conventional arcade joystick, often to control player movement within the game. One of the sticks is commonly used to take over the functions of the D-pad, and the other may control the camera view shown in the game.

Two motors in the handles of the gamepad provide **force feedback**, in the form of vibration, to accompany explosions, gun recoils, blows, and other events. Each of the motors connects to off-center weights. When the motors spin, the unevenness of the weights generates unbalanced force feedback sensations.

Of the more than a dozen buttons on most gamepads, the four **action buttons** on the right side of the Dual Shock are the most used. Unlike most switches, which allow current through when they're pressed, gamepad switches are normally closed, allowing a small current to pass through until they are pressed, cutting off the electricity. The constant current tells the microchip overseeing the signals that the gamepad and switches are working.

The Wiimote

With most games, actions are accomplished entirely by pressing buttons and moving sticks. It's like talking in Morse code. Nintendo altered the formula with their Wii game system. It had no analog sticks and only a few buttons. It looked more like a TV remote control than a game controller, hence the name. Its versatility is in its simplicity. Swing it, and it's a bat, a golf club, or a tennis racket. Point it and push a button and it's a gun. Hold it in two hands and it's a steering wheel. It brought a whole new way of thinking to controller design.

The game's software combines the information sent to it through the Bluetooth signals and translates that into onscreen action that imitates the way the player moved the Wiimote.

A **sensor bar** placed above or below the television connected to the Wii actually doesn't sense anything. Instead, five lights on either end of the bar emit infrared light. The Wiimote detects the lights and uses them to triangulate its position, usually in conjunction with aiming and firing at something on the TV screen.

To control action in a video game using the Wii's controller, the player moves the Wiimote through the same actions a game requires in real life—swinging, prodding, aiming, and twisting.

Infrared Receiver

POWER

A

HOME

1

2

Bluetooth Transmitter/Receiver

The measurements of the three accelerometers, along with any signals generated by the player pressing the Wiimote's button, are sent to the game console through a **Bluetooth device** that also receives instructions from the console to activate the force feedback motor or to play a sound over the remote's speaker.

Rorce Feedback Motor

A small chip in the Wiimote contains three **accelerometers** that measure movement in six directions. Each accelerometer includes several fixed, metal plates, like the teeth of a comb. Between the teeth are silicon plates. Together the silicon and metal plates

generate an electrical charge between them. When a player moves the remote, the silicon plates move in one direction or the other. As the two types of plates get closer to each other, their electrical charge increases, a microchip measures the change and translates that into a specific onscreen movement.

Speaker

Accelerometers

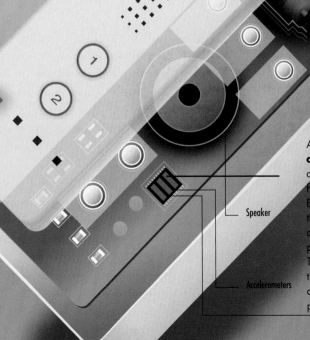

How Game Controllers Let You Feel the Force

1 A **force-feedback joystick** responds to events in a game by moving the joystick on its own. The instructions to make a joystick move are created in software as waveforms, varying degrees of force graphed over periods of time. Here are examples of waveforms of different feedback forces.

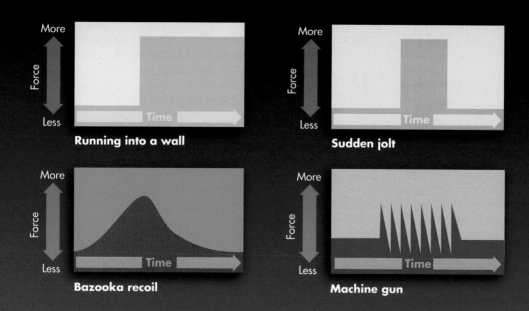

Running into a wall

Sudden jolt

Bazooka recoil

Machine gun

2 The game software doesn't have to send the complete instructions for movements to the joystick. Instead, the software sends a **token**, a much shorter burst of data that identifies the complete waveform the joystick should execute.

3 In the old Microsoft joystick shown here, a 16-bit, 25MHz microprocessor receives the token and looks up the waveform among 32 movement effects permanently stored on a ROM chip. The software can also download its own original waveforms to a 2KB RAM chip for the processor to use.

4 The processor follows the instruction of the waveform that the token indicates and sends electronic signals to two motors—one each for the joystick's X-axis and Y-axis.

5 The motors convey their precise movements to a gear train that transmits the forces to the joystick's two axes, causing the joystick itself to exert pressure.

6 In the joystick shown here, two infrared light-emitting diodes attached to the joystick handle project beams of light that a stationary camera in the base of the joystick detects. Signals from the camera not only tell the software which way you're moving the joystick, but they tell the processor how the motors are moving the joystick, information the processor uses in a local control loop to constantly correct the joystick's motion.

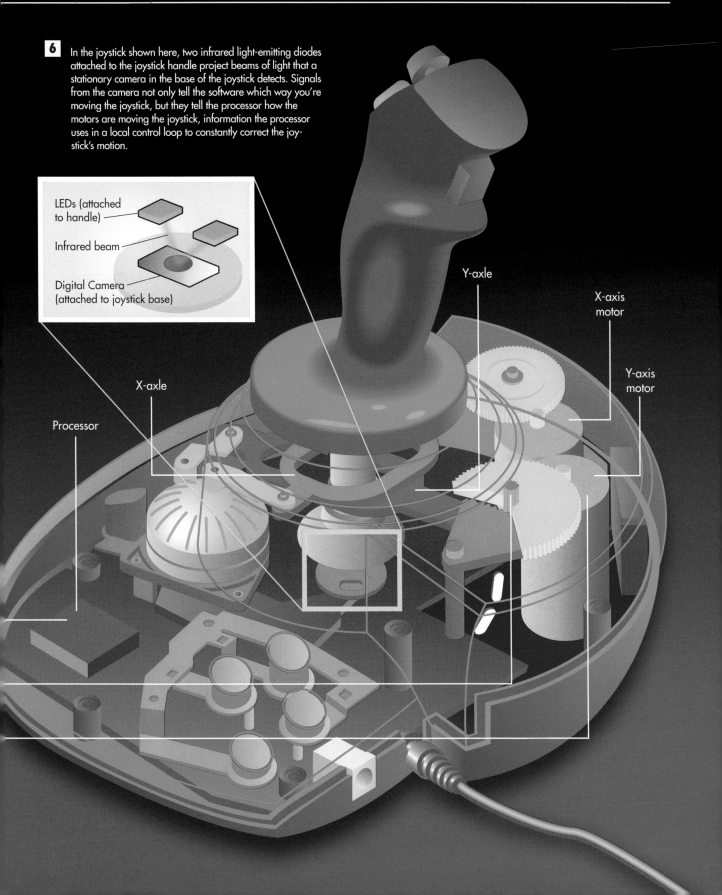

LEDs (attached to handle)

Infrared beam

Digital Camera (attached to joystick base)

Y-axle

X-axis motor

Y-axis motor

X-axle

Processor

How Smartphones Get Good Vibrations

WE'RE ALL FAMILIAR with a smartphone's vibration, whether it's alerting us to a phone call on the QT or setting off vibrations on some table where the phone has been placed. What causes all the racket is a surprisingly small component, like the one in the picture.

In the evolution of computing technology, **haptics**, as such vibrations are called, have barely crawled out of the ocean. Whenever they learn how to run, the little vibrations could really go places, such as providing the sensation of an on-screen button actually moving when you tap it. Haptics, already used in surgical training and long-distance surgery, could make for a changeable Braille display, feeling the plunk of a guitar string or the turning of a virtual page.

There are two types of motors to set off those vibrations: the **eccentric rotating mass motor (ERM)** and the **linear resonant actuator (LRA)**. Whether it's simple or sophisticated, the process begins with a touch, a signal from software, such as a grenade exploding, or a signal from the hardware, such as a call from Uncle Al.

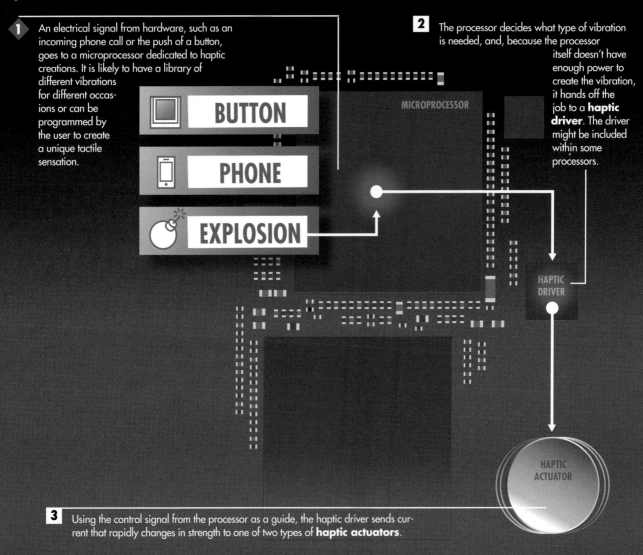

1 An electrical signal from hardware, such as an incoming phone call or the push of a button, goes to a microprocessor dedicated to haptic creations. It is likely to have a library of different vibrations for different occasions or can be programmed by the user to create a unique tactile sensation.

BUTTON

PHONE

EXPLOSION

MICROPROCESSOR

2 The processor decides what type of vibration is needed, and, because the processor itself doesn't have enough power to create the vibration, it hands off the job to a **haptic driver**. The driver might be included within some processors.

HAPTIC DRIVER

HAPTIC ACTUATOR

3 Using the control signal from the processor as a guide, the haptic driver sends current that rapidly changes in strength to one of two types of **haptic actuators**.

A **linear resonate actuator** (LRA) creates a vibration by passing the varying current from the haptic driver through a **voice coil**—the same device used in most audio speakers. Located inside a magnet, the coil creates a magnetic field that pushes a heavy slice of metal against a spring. As the current tapers off, the spring pushes the metal toward the magnet. This dance is repeated as often and as long as needed for the specific vibration effect.

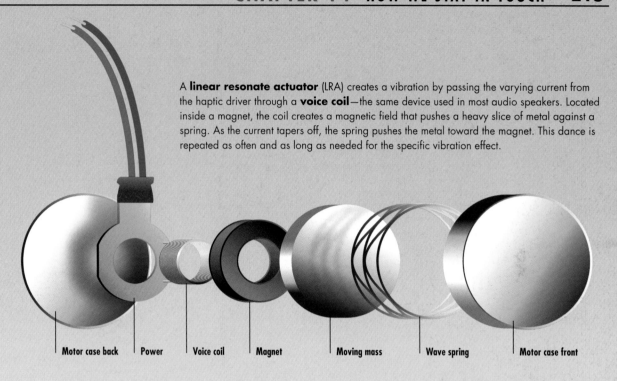

| Motor case back | Power | Voice coil | Magnet | Moving mass | Wave spring | Motor case front |

An **eccentric rotating mass actuator** (ERM) also uses a voice coil and magnet to translate the incoming current into vibrations. But in this device the coil and magnet are positioned to spin a heavy, metal disk around a shaft. A slice along one side of the disk makes it asymmetrical, or *eccentric*. The heaver side of the disk exerts more centrifugal force than the sliced side, causing the center of force in the actuator to continually turn in a vibrating circle.

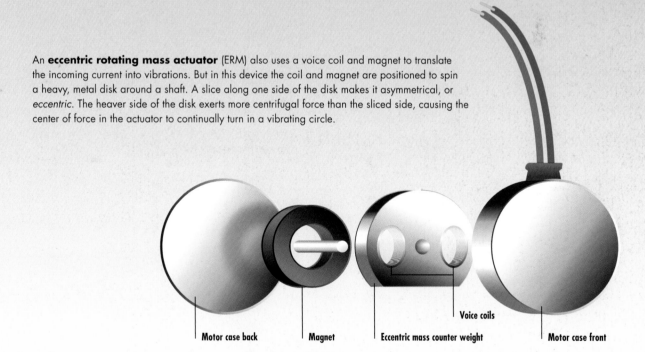

| Motor case back | Magnet | Eccentric mass counter weight | Voice coils | Motor case front |

How Devices Capture Light

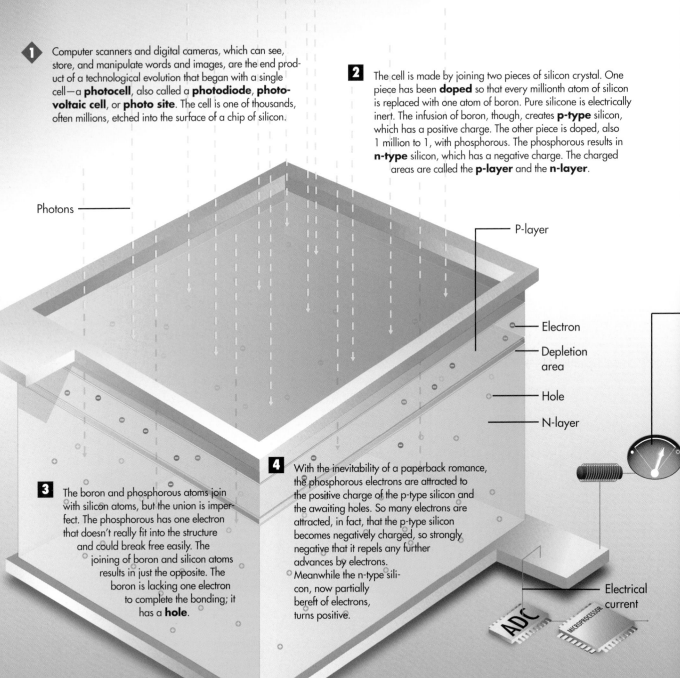

1 Computer scanners and digital cameras, which can see, store, and manipulate words and images, are the end product of a technological evolution that began with a single cell—a **photocell**, also called a **photodiode**, **photovoltaic cell**, or **photo site**. The cell is one of thousands, often millions, etched into the surface of a chip of silicon.

2 The cell is made by joining two pieces of silicon crystal. One piece has been **doped** so that every millionth atom of silicon is replaced with one atom of boron. Pure silicone is electrically inert. The infusion of boron, though, creates **p-type** silicon, which has a positive charge. The other piece is doped, also 1 million to 1, with phosphorous. The phosphorous results in **n-type** silicon, which has a negative charge. The charged areas are called the **p-layer** and the **n-layer**.

Photons

P-layer

Electron

Depletion area

Hole

N-layer

3 The boron and phosphorous atoms join with silicon atoms, but the union is imperfect. The phosphorous has one electron that doesn't really fit into the structure and could break free easily. The joining of boron and silicon atoms results in just the opposite. The boron is lacking one electron to complete the bonding; it has a **hole**.

4 With the inevitability of a paperback romance, the phosphorous electrons are attracted to the positive charge of the p-type silicon and the awaiting holes. So many electrons are attracted, in fact, that the p-type silicon becomes negatively charged, so strongly negative that it repels any further advances by electrons. Meanwhile the n-type silicon, now partially bereft of electrons, turns positive.

Electrical current

ADC

MICROPROCESSOR

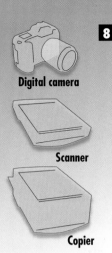

Digital camera

Scanner

Copier

**Biometric
(thumbprint or iris)
scanner**

8 Light-detecting chips built on the CCD and CMOS model turn up in a variety of computer peripherals—from digital cameras to scanners, copiers, and fax machines to biometric identification devices that can visually identify people through their fingerprints, retina scans, and facial characteristics.

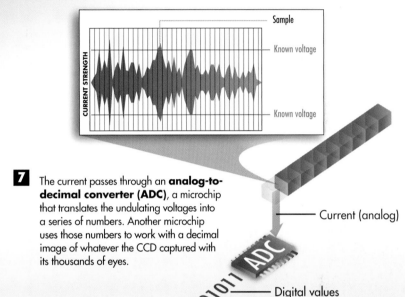

Sample

Known voltage

CURRENT STRENGTH

Known voltage

Current (analog)

Digital values

7 The current passes through an **analog-to-decimal converter (ADC)**, a microchip that translates the undulating voltages into a series of numbers. Another microchip uses those numbers to work with a decimal image of whatever the CCD captured with its thousands of eyes.

5 This static stand-off ends when **photons** (the particle form of light—the other form is energy) strike a photodiode. The photon's energy is transferred to electrons, creating a negative charge. The negative charge and the positive charge of the n-layer create a magnetic field in which electrons from the p-layer are drawn by the positive force into the diode's depletion area, a narrow strip separating the negative and positive layers. The stronger the light that hits a pixel, the more electrons travel to the depletion layer, creating an electrical charge whose strength is proportional to the strength of the light that struck that particular photodiode.

6 Only rarely is a single photodiode used by itself. More often the diode is one of many in a component called a **coupled-charge device (CCD)**. The electrical charges built up by the light striking the photodiodes are passed from one diode to the other, like a bucket brigade. The charges move from the CCD through an amplifier that converts the charges into an electrical current of varying voltages that are an analog representation of the various intensities of the light collected by the diodes. (A **CMOS photodiode array** differs from a CCD in that the CMOS chip provides a small amplifier for each diode.)

How a Flatbed Simplifies Scanning

1 A light source illuminates a piece of paper placed face down against a glass window above the scanning mechanism. Blank or white spaces reflect more light than do inked or colored letters or images.

6 The digital information is sent to software in the PC, where the data is stored in a format with which a graphics program or an optical character recognition program can work.

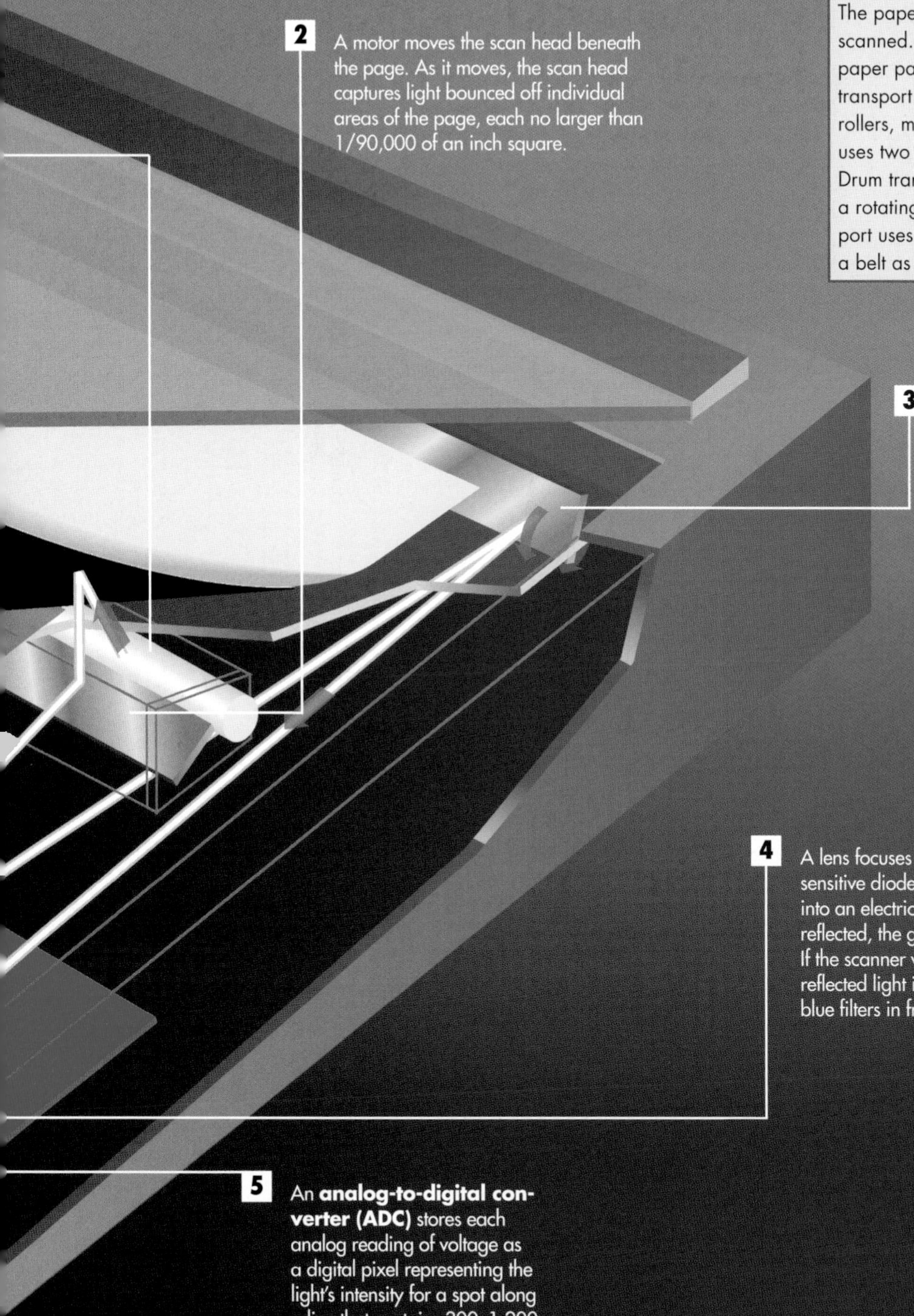

2 A motor moves the scan head beneath the page. As it moves, the scan head captures light bounced off individual areas of the page, each no larger than 1/90,000 of an inch square.

Paper Movers

The paper isn't always stationary when it's being scanned. Higher-end scanners feed sheets of paper past a scan head that stays still. A roller transport feeds a document between two rubber rollers, much like a fax machine. A belt transport uses two opposing belts to do the same thing. Drum transports pass the paper through against a rotating drum. A vacuum straight-through transport uses vacuum tubes to hold the paper against a belt as the belt rolls past the scan head.

3 The light from the page is reflected through a system of mirrors that must continually pivot to keep the light beams aligned with a lens.

4 A lens focuses the beams of light onto light-sensitive diodes that translate the amount of light into an electrical current. The more light that's reflected, the greater the voltage of the current. If the scanner works with colored images, the reflected light is directed through red, green, or blue filters in front of separate diodes.

5 An **analog-to-digital converter (ADC)** stores each analog reading of voltage as a digital pixel representing the light's intensity for a spot along a line that contains 300–1,200 pixels to the inch.

How Codes Keep Track of Everything (Everything!)

BARCODES DON'T GET enough respect. Since 1974, when a grocery clerk was the first to scan what would come to be known as a **universal product code (UPC)**—it was on a pack of gum—12 numbers and lines making up the code have changed not only the way that retail sales work but also how we keep track of everything from museum collections to hospital patients with an ease and accuracy that could not be achieved with only words and conventional numbers. And, in a more complex world, we of course need a more complex code. Enter, the QR code.

Bar Codes

1 The first six numbers encoded in a bar code identify one company that has paid a fee to acquire rights to a unique **manufacturer identification number**. The manufacturer uses the number as the first part of a different 12-digit **UPC** for each product it makes.

2 The manufacturer's six-digit code stays the same for all of a company's products, but it is only the first half of a bar code. The next five digits are the **item number,** or **product code**. The company's UPC coordinator assigns an item number, not just to every product, but to every model or variation of that product. A regular box of detergent powder has a different number from a giant box; each scent has its own number; and powdered versions have numbers that differ from the liquid versions.

3 The last number in the code is a **check digit**. Its value must match a number obtained by running the other numbers through an algorithm.

4 In a retail store, when a UPC passes under a laser connected to a register, it doesn't matter if the right or left side is read first. The bars on the left side are black with white separating them. On the right side it's reversed, white bars separated by black. This lets the register know where the code begins.

Left Numerical digits

0 1 2 3 4 5 6 7 8 9

Right Numerical digits

0 1 2 3 4 5 6 7 8 9

5 If the register's computer determines the check digit doesn't match the algorithm, the scanner beeps to tell the person at the register to rescan the UPC. If the check fails several times, the cashier manually enters the number, which is repeated in a human-readable form under the UPC.

Quiet zones

Start   Middle   End

Manufacturer code   Product code

1 23456 78999 9

6 When a scan is successful, the register sends the number to a computer server. The server checks on the store's current price for that item and sends that price back to the checkout, where it's added to the customer's receipt. For inventory the server may also update how many of that product have been sold.

Matrix Codes

The UPC is good enough if all you need to do is record and read 12 digits. For a more verbose code, you need the capacity of a **2-D bar code**, also called a **matrix code** or **QR code** (for **"quick response"**). The codes are generally about an inch square, but they can represent 7,000 digits or 4,000 characters of text—on the average, a little less than 700 words. Using free apps, the codes are read by most smartphones and onscreen by desktops or laptops not equipped with scanners. Not all varieties of 2-D codes work in exactly the same way, but we'll look at a typical example.

1 Every QR Code contains a **finder pattern**, an arrangement of squares that help the scanner determine the dimensions of the code, which side is the top, and the angle at which the code is being scanned.

2 A pattern of squares forms an **alignment pattern** that tells the scanner if the code is distorted—if, for example, it was printed on a curved can.

3 Along two sides of the code, the scanner that's reading the code superimposes rows of **timing squares**, which you don't see. The scanner uses the timing squares to judge how quickly the code is passing through its reading beam.

4 By calculating the ratio between the light and dark areas in the code, the scanner learns what areas serve to keep everything lined up and which actually contain data. With this information, the scanner determines what data is encoded in the pattern of squares. Part of the ability of a 2-D code to hold so much more information than a bar code is the fact that the code can be read in two directions, just as an M read in one direction becomes an E when it is rotated 90 degrees and a W when rotated 180 degrees.

5 Even if part of the QR code is obscured by another tag or a smudge, the scanner usually can extrapolate what data was contained in the damaged portion of the tag. When not all of the area is needed for data, the leftover space can be used for decoration, like these here, for logos or marketing messages.

You can make your own, free QR code at sites such as visualead.com, where, in a couple of minutes, I created the code on the right. This one points to the *How Computers Work* webpage. (The code may expire by the time you read this.)

How Optical Character Recognition Works

1 When a scanner reads the image of a document, the scanner converts the dark elements—text and graphics—on the page to a **bitmap**, which is a matrix of square pixels that are either on (black) or off (white). Because the pixels are larger than the details of most text, this process degenerates the sharp edges of characters, much as a fax machine blurs the sharpness of characters. This degradation creates most of the problems for optical character recognition (OCR) systems.

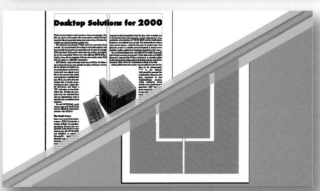

2 The OCR software reads the bitmap that the scanner created and averages out the zones of on and off pixels on the page, in effect mapping the whitespace on the page. This enables the software to block off paragraphs, columns, headlines, and random graphics. The whitespace between lines of text within a block defines each line's baseline, an essential detail for recognizing the characters in the text.

3 In its first pass at converting images to text, the software tries to match each character through a pixel-by-pixel comparison to character templates that the program holds in memory. Templates include complete fonts—numbers, punctuation, and extended characters—of such common faces as 12-point Courier and the IBM Selectric typewriter set. Because this technique demands a very close match, the character attributes, such as bold and italic, must be identical to qualify as a match. Poor-quality scans can easily trip up matrix matching.

4 The characters that remain unrecognized go through a more intensive and time-consuming process called **feature extraction**. The software calculates the text's **x-height**—the height of a font's lowercase x—and analyzes each character's combination of straight lines, curves, and **bowls** (hollow areas within loops, as in o or b). The OCR programs know, for example, that a character with a curved descender below the baseline and a bowl above it is most likely a lowercase g. As the software builds a working alphabet of each new character it encounters, recognition speed accelerates.

5 Because these two processes don't decipher every character, OCR programs take two approaches to the remaining hieroglyphics. Some OCR programs tag unrecognized characters with a distinctive character—such as ~, #, or @—and quit. You must use the search capability of a word processor to find where the distinctive character has been inserted and correct the word manually. Some OCR programs also display a magnified bitmap onscreen and ask you to press the key of the character needed to substitute for the placeholder character.

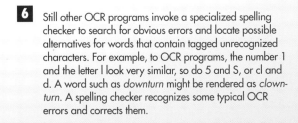

6 Still other OCR programs invoke a specialized spelling checker to search for obvious errors and locate possible alternatives for words that contain tagged unrecognized characters. For example, to OCR programs, the number 1 and the letter l look very similar, so do 5 and S, or cl and d. A word such as *downturn* might be rendered as *clownturn*. A spelling checker recognizes some typical OCR errors and corrects them.

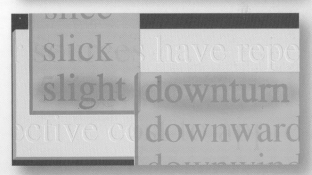

7 Most OCR programs give you the option of saving the converted document to an ASCII file or in a file format that popular word processors or spreadsheets can recognize.

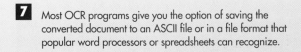
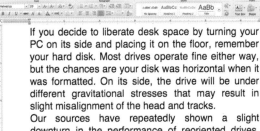

CHAPTER

15

How a Computer Creates Visions

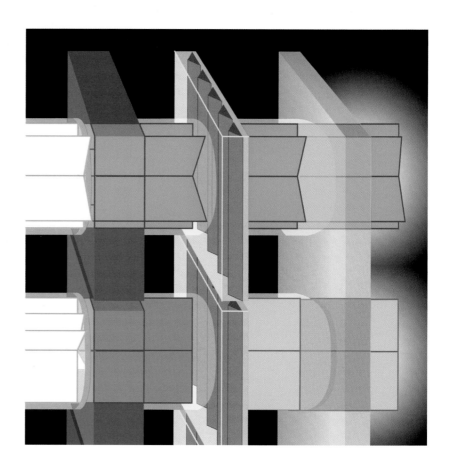

THIS IS how desperate early computer users were to have PCs that could show a picture. They were so determined to have a screen of objects that moved around and changed shape, kind of like the moving images on TV screens, that they created what you see in the small screenshot next to these words.

It's a Pac-Man game created entirely with ASCII characters—for the most part the everyday, mundane letters and punctuation you use for text. Although it's certainly not a treat for the eyes, games like this were amazingly playable—just as capable of providing hours of procrastination as full-blown graphic games of the 21st century.

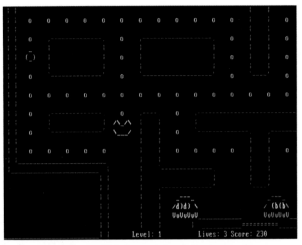

Pac-Man, almost on its own, birthed a generation of video games and gamers.

Yet, for a generation for whom computer output meant data printed to paper, even basic visuals such as this were mind-blowing beyond compare. It's a natural instinct to want to use our eyes, not simply to read, but to see the things we read about. And it's not enough to see them. We have to seem them move. People, wars, sunsets, rush-hour traffic, walking on the moon—these things have more impact when seen than they do when we simply read about them, or even when we see them only as still images.

It took several years for computing to become graphic, mainly because of a prejudice born of the idea that computers were business tools and that graphics, colors, animation, and video were somehow frivolous. The crack in the text-only screen came with the popularity of Lotus 1-2-3, an electronic spreadsheet that could crunch numbers visually, displaying graphs that summarized a vast array of information more easily understood than pages of numbers.

After that, all manner of stuff spewed through that crack, led primarily by video games that used every creative trick in the toolbox to create engaging visuals. And as games endeavored to become more advanced, so too did the displays they were dependent on. As the displays got better, soon everything began to look better as computing became a full partner in the image world with video, games, photography, biometric security, GPS, and, yes, business programs.

Graphics and computing have turned out to be such a natural that I can hardly wait for the second feature.

How an LCD Creates Glowing Colors

2 A **polarizing filter** in front of the light panel lets through only the light waves that are vibrating more or less horizontally. The fact that the polarizing filter is not entirely precise enables the display to create different hues.

3 In a layer of liquid-crystal cells—one for each of the three colors that make up a pixel—the graphics adapter applies a varying electrical charge to some of the cells and no charge at all to other cells. In cells to which current is applied, the long, rod-shaped molecules that make up the liquid-crystal material react to the charge by forming a spiral. The greater the charge, the more the molecules twist. With the strongest charge, the molecules at one end of the cell wind up at an angle 90° from the orientation of the molecules at the other end of the cell.

1 Light emanating from a fluorescent panel behind a portable computer's display panel spreads out in waves that vibrate in all directions.

When LCD Meets LED

Instead of using light from a single panel, some LCD displays use an array of white LEDs. The light-emitting diodes help eliminate a problem caused by the single panel. Light from the panel backlights all the LCDs equally. When LCDs are supposed to produce a solid black, some of the light from the panel still manages to traverse those LCDs, producing a black that's not really black. The result is weak contrast.

The array of LEDs enables the display to turn on backlight only where it is needed—which is any part of the image that's not black. For black areas, the LEDs are turned off, eliminating slip-thr

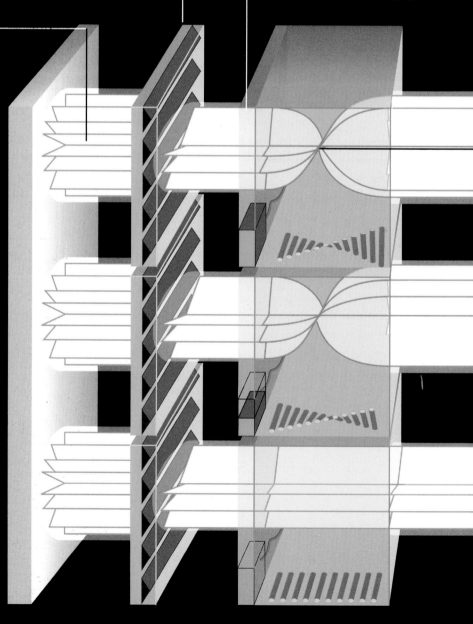

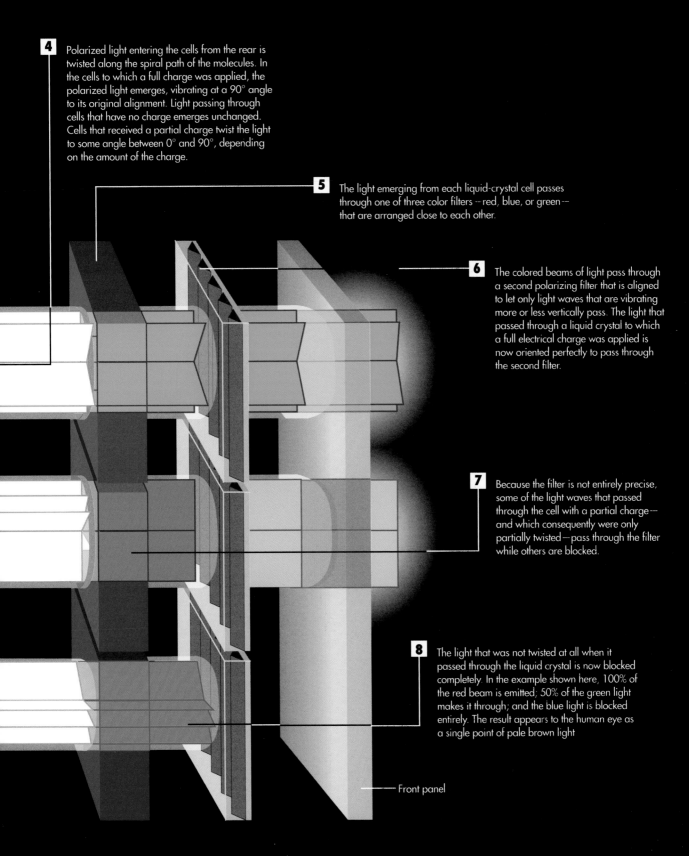

4 Polarized light entering the cells from the rear is twisted along the spiral path of the molecules. In the cells to which a full charge was applied, the polarized light emerges, vibrating at a 90° angle to its original alignment. Light passing through cells that have no charge emerges unchanged. Cells that received a partial charge twist the light to some angle between 0° and 90°, depending on the amount of the charge.

5 The light emerging from each liquid-crystal cell passes through one of three color filters – red, blue, or green – that are arranged close to each other.

6 The colored beams of light pass through a second polarizing filter that is aligned to let only light waves that are vibrating more or less vertically pass. The light that passed through a liquid crystal to which a full electrical charge was applied is now oriented perfectly to pass through the second filter.

7 Because the filter is not entirely precise, some of the light waves that passed through the cell with a partial charge— and which consequently were only partially twisted—pass through the filter while others are blocked.

8 The light that was not twisted at all when it passed through the liquid crystal is now blocked completely. In the example shown here, 100% of the red beam is emitted; 50% of the green light makes it through; and the blue light is blocked entirely. The result appears to the human eye as a single point of pale brown light

Front panel

How Plasma Displays Glow

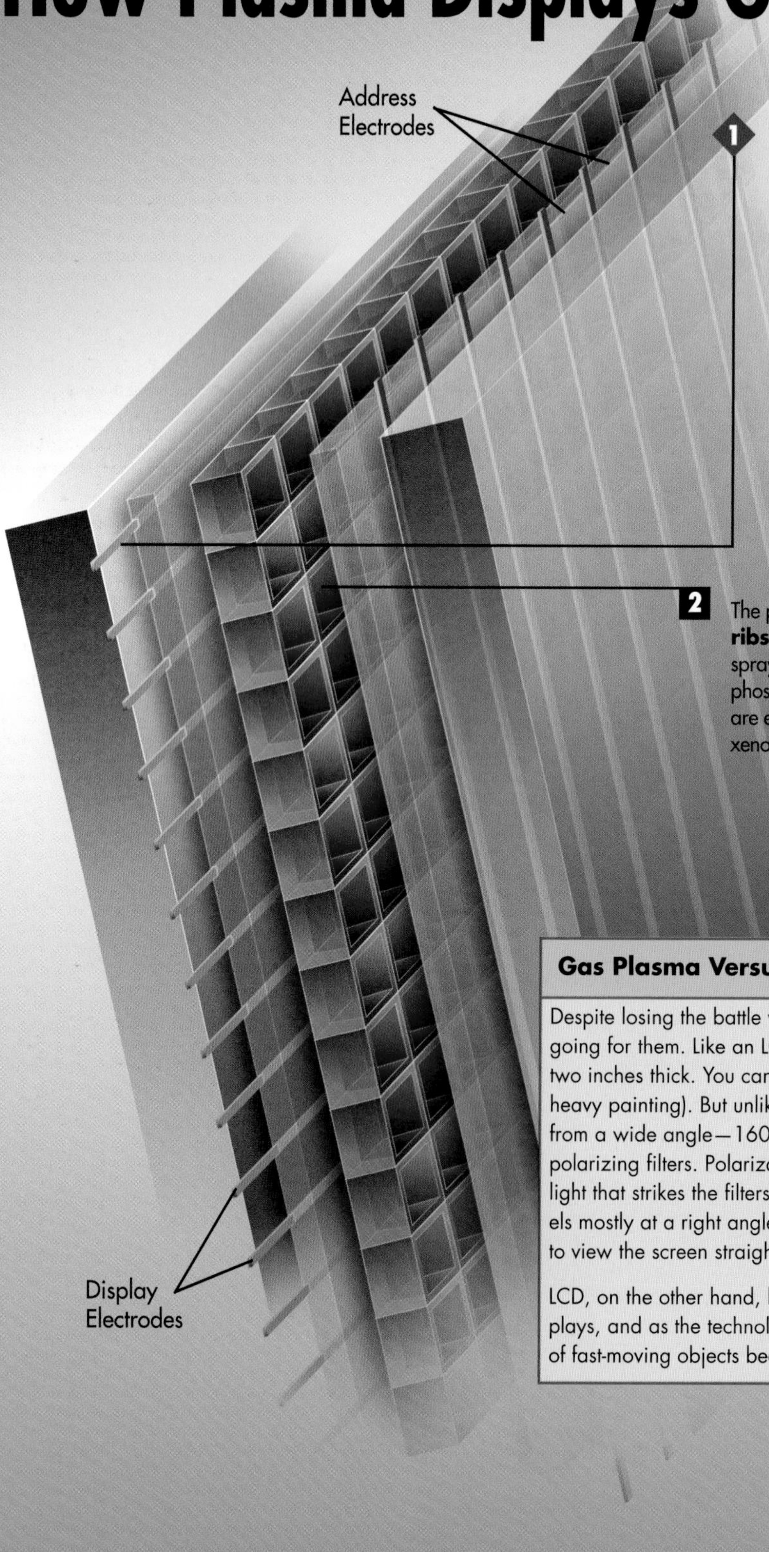

Address
Electrodes

1 A television receiver or a video card controlling a gas plasma display sends electrical currents to two sets of electrodes. The address electrodes running vertically in the rear of the gas plasma display identify which of the display's pixels are affected when electricity passes through another set of transparent display electrodes, mounted horizontally in the front of the pixels. Running through layers of glass and magnesium oxide, which protect and insulate the electrodes from each other, the electrodes extend the length and width of the rows and columns of pixels that make up the display. The electrodes form intersections that sandwich each of the more than three-quarters of a million pixels.

2 The pixels are cells, depressions in ridges called **ribs** that separate the cells. The walls of the cells are spray-painted on the inside with one of three types of phosphors that glow red, blue, or green when they are energized. Trapped inside each cell is a mixture of xenon and neon gases.

Gas Plasma Versus LCD Versus...

Despite losing the battle with LCDs, gas plasma displays have a lot going for them. Like an LCD screen, a plasma display is less than two inches thick. You can hang it on the wall like a painting (a very heavy painting). But unlike LCD, plasma is brighter and can be seen from a wide angle—160°—because light does not pass through polarizing filters. Polarization, by its nature, absorbs most of the light that strikes the filters, and the light that does pass through travels mostly at a right angle to the surface of the screen, requiring you to view the screen straight-on for best brightness and contrast.

LCD, on the other hand, has price advantages, creates lighter displays, and as the technology matures, viewing angles and blurring of fast-moving objects becomes less of a problem.

Display
Electrodes

3 When the display controller wants a particular pixel to glow, it **opens** the **address line** that leads to that pixel's cell. (Opening is accomplished by **closing** a circuit so electricity can flow through it.) At the same time, the controller sends a stream of electricity down the **display line** leading to the same pixel. The electricity, attracted by the charge on the open address line, jumps through the cell to complete a circuit with it. The energy from the electrical current excites the atoms in the gas mixture, turning the gases into a **plasma**, the fourth state of matter high-school science classes don't tell you about when studying solids, liquids, and gases.

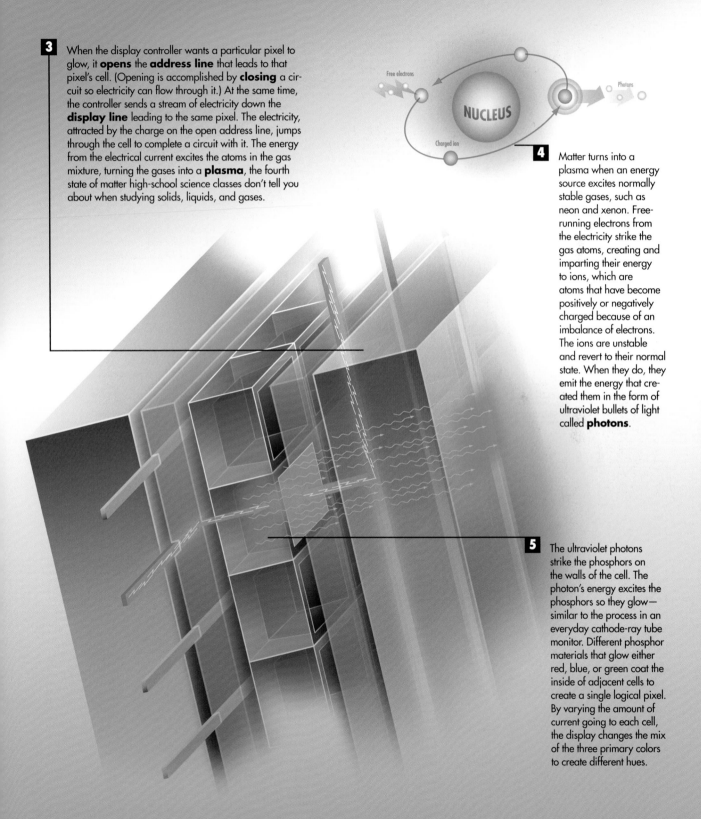

Free electrons

NUCLEUS

Charged ion

Photons

4 Matter turns into a plasma when an energy source excites normally stable gases, such as neon and xenon. Free-running electrons from the electricity strike the gas atoms, creating and imparting their energy to ions, which are atoms that have become positively or negatively charged because of an imbalance of electrons. The ions are unstable and revert to their normal state. When they do, they emit the energy that created them in the form of ultraviolet bullets of light called **photons**.

5 The ultraviolet photons strike the phosphors on the walls of the cell. The photon's energy excites the phosphors so they glow—similar to the process in an everyday cathode-ray tube monitor. Different phosphor materials that glow either red, blue, or green coat the inside of adjacent cells to create a single logical pixel. By varying the amount of current going to each cell, the display changes the mix of the three primary colors to create different hues.

How DLP Spins Colors

1 As an image projection technology, **digital light processing (DLP)** is a revelation. DLP projects brighter, sharper images and have all but replaced film projectors in movie theaters. It works by shining a light through a spinning wheel divided into red, blue, and green filters. The wheel spins fast enough so that each color is produced 60 times a second.

Light source

2 The light strikes a panel of up to 1.3 million microscopic mirrors on the surface of a DLP chip.

3 The mirrors reflect the light through a lens to an ordinary projection screen.

Lens

4 If that were all the mirrors did, the projected image would be a large white rectangle. But each mirror is attached to a flexible hinge that holds the mirror above a pair of electrodes and a circuit called the **bias/reset bus**. The electrodes are connected directly to an array of video memory bits so that each electrode can represent a 1 or a 0.

Screen

LCD Projectors

Another way of casting a computer display image is with a liquid-crystal display projector. Colors and images are created the same way for an LCD projector as they are for a mobile device's LCD panel. The essential differences are that the projector's light source is much stronger, and the image is focused through a lens. But the nature of an LCD means much of the light is absorbed so that an LCD image is dimmer than a DLP projection. In addition, the gaps between the mirrors in a DLP display are smaller than those between the cells that form the LCD, making the DLP image sharper.

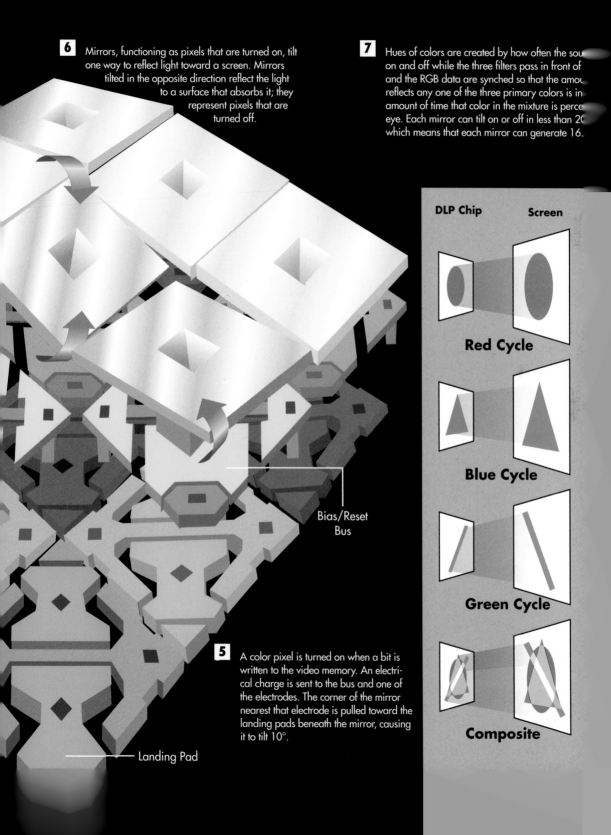

6 Mirrors, functioning as pixels that are turned on, tilt one way to reflect light toward a screen. Mirrors tilted in the opposite direction reflect the light to a surface that absorbs it; they represent pixels that are turned off.

7 Hues of colors are created by how often the sou on and off while the three filters pass in front of and the RGB data are synched so that the amou reflects any one of the three primary colors is in amount of time that color in the mixture is perce eye. Each mirror can tilt on or off in less than 2(which means that each mirror can generate 16.

DLP Chip   Screen

Red Cycle

Blue Cycle

Green Cycle

Composite

Bias/Reset Bus

5 A color pixel is turned on when a bit is written to the video memory. An electrical charge is sent to the bus and one of the electrodes. The corner of the mirror nearest that electrode is pulled toward the landing pads beneath the mirror, causing it to tilt 10°.

Landing Pad

How OLED Lights Up a New Generation of Displays

AN ORGANIC light-emitting diode display (OLED) is more akin to a **plasma display** than everyday LED monitors. Ordinary LEDs produce different colors at various intensities by manipulating light from a separate source as the light passes *through* the LEDs. But each OLED pixel, like those in a plasma display, produces its own light in proportion to the amount of electricity flowing through it.

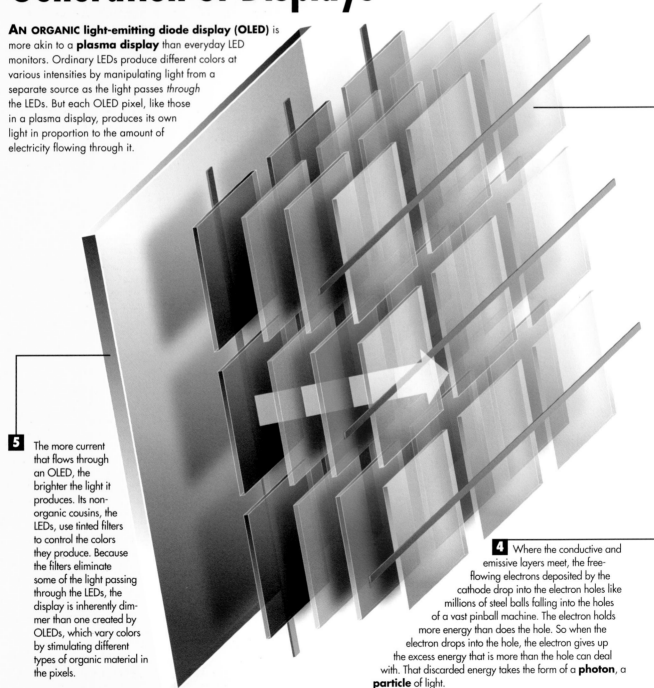

5 The more current that flows through an OLED, the brighter the light it produces. Its non-organic cousins, the LEDs, use tinted filters to control the colors they produce. Because the filters eliminate some of the light passing through the LEDs, the display is inherently dimmer than one created by OLEDs, which vary colors by stimulating different types of organic material in the pixels.

4 Where the conductive and emissive layers meet, the free-flowing electrons deposited by the cathode drop into the electron holes like millions of steel balls falling into the holes of a vast pinball machine. The electron holds more energy than does the hole. So when the electron drops into the hole, the electron gives up the excess energy that is more than the hole can deal with. That discarded energy takes the form of a **photon**, a **particle** of light.

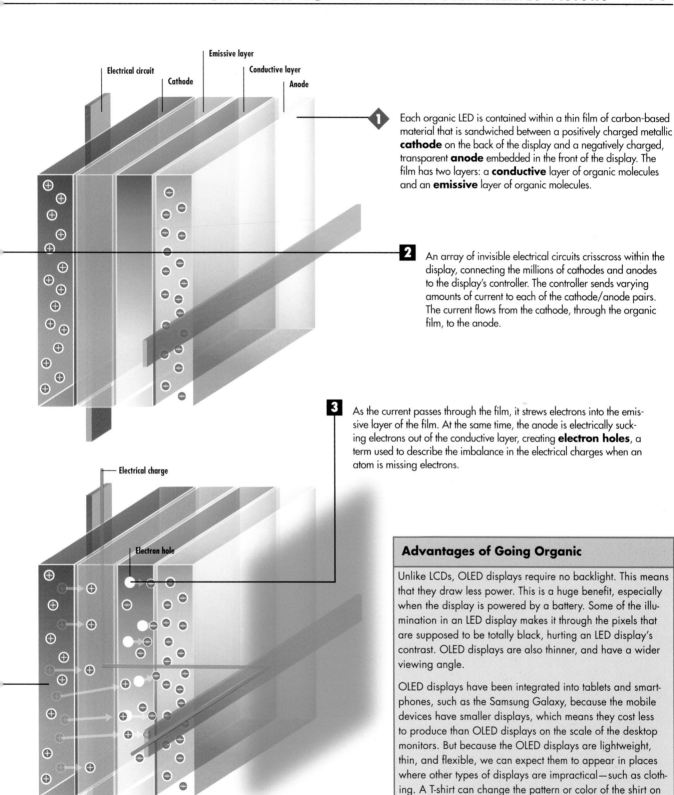

Electrical circuit   Cathode   Emissive layer   Conductive layer   Anode

1 Each organic LED is contained within a thin film of carbon-based material that is sandwiched between a positively charged metallic **cathode** on the back of the display and a negatively charged, transparent **anode** embedded in the front of the display. The film has two layers: a **conductive** layer of organic molecules and an **emissive** layer of organic molecules.

2 An array of invisible electrical circuits crisscross within the display, connecting the millions of cathodes and anodes to the display's controller. The controller sends varying amounts of current to each of the cathode/anode pairs. The current flows from the cathode, through the organic film, to the anode.

3 As the current passes through the film, it strews electrons into the emissive layer of the film. At the same time, the anode is electrically sucking electrons out of the conductive layer, creating **electron holes**, a term used to describe the imbalance in the electrical charges when an atom is missing electrons.

Electrical charge

Electron hole

Advantages of Going Organic

Unlike LCDs, OLED displays require no backlight. This means that they draw less power. This is a huge benefit, especially when the display is powered by a battery. Some of the illumination in an LED display makes it through the pixels that are supposed to be totally black, hurting an LED display's contrast. OLED displays are also thinner, and have a wider viewing angle.

OLED displays have been integrated into tablets and smartphones, such as the Samsung Galaxy, because the mobile devices have smaller displays, which means they cost less to produce than OLED displays on the scale of the desktop monitors. But because the OLED displays are lightweight, thin, and flexible, we can expect them to appear in places where other types of displays are impractical—such as clothing. A T-shirt can change the pattern or color of the shirt on a whim, and it wouldn't be much more trouble to have it display a movie or even, alas, commercials.

How 3D Makes You Duck

THE 3D VISION we take for granted doesn't come to us automatically. Babies are born, as William James describes it, into one great blooming, buzzing confusion. For several months it's the job of the baby's brain to find shape, consistency, and order in the confusion swirling around him. Then the brain convinces the other organs and itself that the constructs it has made out of confusion and that exist only in the mind are, in fact, exactly how the world looks. One tad bit of confusion the brain must reconcile is that its two baby eyes aren't seeing the same things.

Human eyes are about 50–77mm apart, far enough so that a scene shows more of one side to your left eye and more of its other side to your right eye. Through experience, the brain establishes a rule: Objects that reveal more of the opposite sides are nearer than objects that appear flat. The brain finds a name for the rule–perspective—and doesn't think about it the rest of its life unless the topic of 3D displays comes up while you're chatting with your fellow former infants. Then the thing to remember is that there are several ways to produce the illusion of 3D depth on a depthless 2D screen; none of them are perfect, but a few are acceptable.

Anaglyph Stereoscopy

1 Older readers may recall anaglyphs from some of the early 3D movies and comic books. (It actually dates back to the 1920s.) Each frame or page is made from two images, one filtered with red, the other with blue (or green), and projected on a screen or printed.

2 Each image shows the identical scene but from slightly different viewpoints so that if the two images are superimposed, they do not match exactly. The distance separating them from creating an accurate registration is called the parallax. The parallax is greater for objects closer to the front of the image.

3 A person views the anaglyph with anagram glasses, which have a blue (or green) gel filter in front of one eye and a red filter over the other eye.

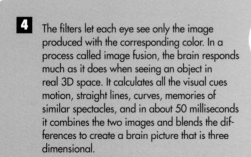

4 The filters let each eye see only the image produced with the corresponding color. In a process called image fusion, the brain responds much as it does when seeing an object in real 3D space. It calculates all the visual cues motion, straight lines, curves, memories of similar spectacles, and in about 50 milliseconds it combines the two images and blends the differences to create a brain picture that is three dimensional.

5 Anyone who's experienced anaglyph stereoscopy will recall the 3D images usually had red and blue fringes caused by parts of each image spilling over to the wrong lens, an effect called ghosting or crosstalk.

THE 3D EXPERIENCE which most people today are familiar with involves wearing dorky glasses, but not the red and green anagram specs; the lenses are colorless (with some having a neutral, gray tint). They're still dorky, though. The glasses, used with movies and 3D televisions, perform the same function as the red and green glasses, but with better color fidelity and fewer visual distractions. These same advantages are to be found in the two families of 3D glasses that take widely different paths to the same destination: active shutter and film pattern retarder (FPR) passive glasses. If you've watched a lot of 3D movies and TV, you've probably already used each of them. Here's how they worked their trickery on your brain.

Active Shutter

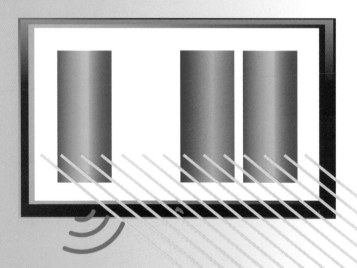

1 Active shutter glasses are used with television displays capable of refreshing the image 120 times a second, twice the rate of standard 2D TVs. Every other scan of the display presents alternative views of a scene separated by the parallax that makes 3D vision possible.

2 A pair of electronic glasses, linked to the TV by a Bluetooth signal, have lenses with a layer of liquid crystals, the same technology that makes LCD displays possible. Circuitry contained in the glasses' temples sends a signal to the left lens that causes the liquid crystals to turn off all light passing through them. This happens at the same time that the TV displays the image that the right eye is meant to see.

3 For an instant, both lenses are blacked out. This is because of the difficulty of timing the switch between left and right lenses precisely enough to eliminate any of the ghost images caused by crosstalk that would occur if both lenses were open at the same time.

4 The circuitry opens up the crystals over the left eye as the TV displays an image of the same scene but from a different viewpoint. Because the TV is displaying a different version every 120th of a second, the combined image going to both eyes is refreshed every 60th of a second, the same rate as a standard TV.

Film Pattern Retarder

1 Unlike a 3D TV that works using active shutter glasses, a film pattern retarder TV displays both left-eye and right-eye images at the same time. The retarder TV instead creates 3D by juggling raster lines. These are the horizontal rows of pixels that fill the screen to create a single frame. Using every other raster, the TV displays the image intended for one eye. At the same time, the TV uses the remaining rasters to paint the image for the other eye.

Left eye image   Right eye image

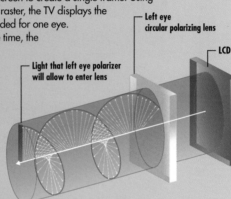

Left eye circular polarizing lens

LCD

Light that left eye polarizer will allow to enter lens

2 The light from each raster passes through a micro-polarizer. This is a filter made up of rows of tiny circular polarizers, or fresnel lenses.

The circular polarizer takes advantage of the fact that different portions of a light wave are refracted, or bent, differently by the material through which they pass.

The fresnel lenses use a similar property created by reflections of a light beam off surfaces at different angles.

3 Either way, the result is that the rays of light from the display are given a rotation. The micropolarizers are designed so that light coming from alternate rasters spins in opposite directions, called right-hand and left-hand.

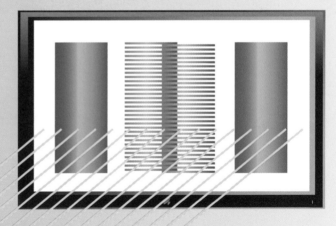

4 When the spinning light arrives at a pair of passive polarization glasses worn by a viewer, micropolarizers in one lens block light spinning in one direction from passing through the left lens. In the right lens, light spinning the opposite direction is blocked. The result is that one eye sees only light coming from one set of alternate rasters while the other eye sees only the light from the remaining lines in the display.

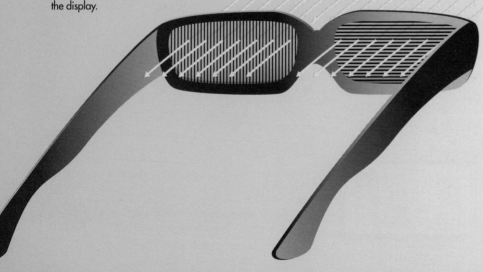

Autostereoscopic Display

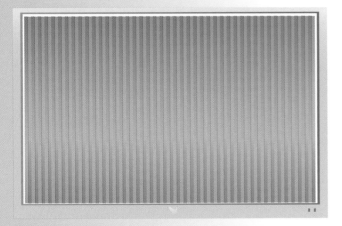

1 Autostereoscopic display is the only one of the 3D technologies presented here that does not require glasses. A display, such as the one in the Nintendo 3DS portable game player, paints the image for both eyes simultaneously, similar to the film pattern retarder technology.

2 The light from each raster passes through a layer on the front of the display called a parallax barrier.

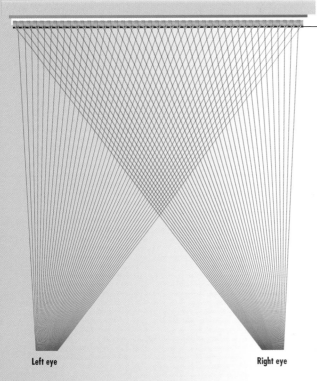

Parallax barrier

Left eye   Right eye

3 The barrier includes a series of slits that are positioned precisely to allow light from every other line of pixels to go to the right or the left.

4 The result is that the right eye sees only every other row, and the left eye sees the remaining rows. The method requires that the viewer's head be positioned squarely facing the center of the display, which is the primary reason that it has not been attempted on larger displays, such as movie or TV screens, that must reach multiple simultaneous viewers seated at various positions.

CHAPTER

16

How Computers Tickle Your Ears

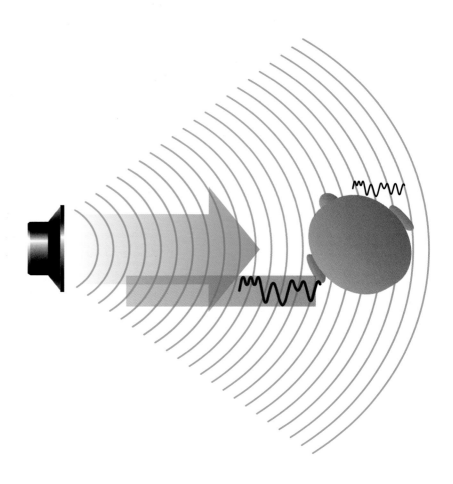

THE CLOSEST evolutional analogy to the beginnings of computer audio is the protozoan. Like some one-celled organism limited to doing the ultimate minimum to exist at all, early PC sound was a one-note beep. It could not be any less of a sound and still be a sound at all.

When you turned on your computer, if it made only one beep, all was well. If it beeped anywhere from two to five times in various patterns of long and short beeps, it was a warning something was wrong. You started rummaging through your stuff looking for a user's manual that could decipher the beep codes. It didn't matter much if you found it or not. Most combinations of beeps meant the same thing: Something's wrong with either your motherboard or your power supply. The exact problem was up to you to figure out. And good luck.

Beeping remained the state of the art in PC audio for several years, even after adapter cards brought graphics to what had been text-only systems. Graphics meant games, and games are a lot more fun with rousing music, the sounds of gun fire and explosions, and characters who actually speak. And yet, the first graphic-endowed computers had not a whisper of any of these. One software maker released a screen saver featuring flying toasters shooting at each other. The best sound effect they could come up with for the gunfire was to make the floppy drive's read/write arm swing back and forth wildly, producing a sound vaguely like that of a machine gun.

Third-party card makers eventually started offering audio cards that filtered and amplified sounds to be sent to cheap speakers. Game makers studied the cards to figure out how to add sounds to their programs. Although it was better than nothing, it still wasn't as good as something.

What finally brought decent sound to computers was the iPod and MP3 recordings. Suddenly just about any tune you'd want to listen to could be ripped from a CD, swapped from a friend, or downloaded from the Internet. As handy as the early iPods were, the 5GB drive on the first iPod held only 1,000 songs, which might sound like a lot until you try to cram the complete discography of Dave Matthews or The Grateful Dead on it. The vast world of music on MP3s demanded vastly larger drives to hold it all. And that meant a desktop PC.

Since then, computer audio has become the audio of choice, partly because of the magnificently improved audio quality, storage capacity, and—for dedicated collectors—the ability to catalog everything from variations of the same song to artist covers to lyrics.

How Your Device Listens

IT USED TO BE if you went around talking to your computer, you might be in for some heavy rehab. Now, with tablets and smartphones, talking to your device is commonplace, more natural than hitting keys arranged in an incomprehensible pattern. Microphones—the ears of tablets and phones—are also participating in the digital evolution. The older microphones—the type we associated with singers and radio announcers—are still in use with desktop computers, but they have jumped the species into mics so small that a spy could hide one in a dimple. Here's how they all work.

Condenser Microphone

1 In a **condenser microphone,** sound waves run into an electrical **capacitor**. ("Condenser" is an outmoded term for capacitor.) The condenser is made of two metal plates. Between the plates is an electrical charge fed by a battery in the mic and held stable by a resistor.

Resistor

Battery

Back plate

Diaphragm

Sound waves

Output audio signal

2 Sound waves push against the outer plate, the **diaphragm**. The plate is thin enough that the **crest** of the sound waves bends it in, which changes the space between the two plates.

3 Just as the pressure inside a sealed water bottle increases if you squeeze the sides of the bottle, the capacitor's **voltage**—a measurement of the strength of the electrical charge that functions as electrical pressure—increases when the plates are closer to each other.

Sound waves

Capacitor charge

4 When the sound wave's **trough** arrives at the outer plate, the wave exerts less pressure and the plate moves back, expanding the volume, which decreases the **capacitance**, the capacitor's ability to hold a charge.

5 The charge that exceeds the capacitance is discharged, creating a pulse of an electrical current. The resulting signal is stronger than that from a dynamic mic, and more responsive to subtle differences in sound.

Dynamic Microphone

1 Sound waves entering a **dynamic mic** encounter a metal diaphragm that is attached to a coil of wire surrounding a powerful cylindrical rare-earth magnet made of the element **neodymium**. The sound waves push and pull the diaphragm, making it vibrate at the same frequencies as the sounds.

2 The diaphragm push/pulls the wire coil back and forth. As the coil passes through the magnet's force field, the magnetism generates an electrical current in the coil.

3 As the coil changes direction, so does the strength and direction of the electrical current, mimicking in electricity the sound waves in the air. The current passes through an amplifier. Without changing the sound pattern carried in the current, the amplifier increases the strength of the current so it can move the sound-producing **cones** in a speaker.

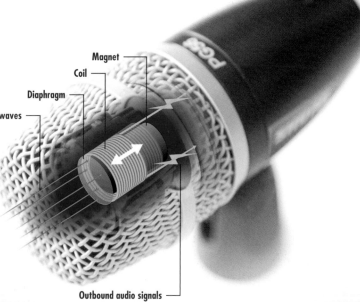

Magnet

Coil

Diaphragm

Sound waves

Outbound audio signals

Electret Microphone

1 The **electret microphone**, a close cousin to the condenser mic, is small, light, and inexpensive. It's also highly sensitive over a wide frequency range and it's omnidirectional—characteristics that lead to it being used in many portable devices. It works through an electrical capacitance between two plates. One of the plates, the diaphragm, is made of a **polarized**, or charged, insulator called an **electret**. Because the plate already has a charge, it does not require a source of electricity as the condenser microphone does.

2 Sound pressure against the diaphragm changes the size of the gap between the two plates, which alters the capacitance and the charge carried by the **back plate**.

3 The changing charge passes to a **junction gate field-effect transistor (JFET)**. Current running out of the microphone from the **source** first passes through a long semiconductor that includes a **depletion area.** It's called that because it has an abundance of positive charge holes (spaces without electrons); the holes attract electrons in the current thereby depleting the current.

4 When the positive charge hits the JFET, the number of charge holes increases and decreases with a lowering of positive charge holes that comes with a negative charge.

5 The rising and falling voltages flow out of the microphone on a circuit leading to cell phone transmissions, recorders, or for interpretation by the smartphone's voice recognition circuits.

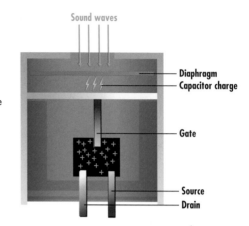

Sound waves
Diaphragm
Capacitor charge
Gate
Source
Drain

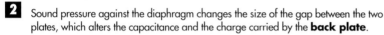

Sound waves
Housing
Diaphragm
Back plate
Semiconductor substrate

MEMS Microphone

Micro Electro Mechanical Systems (MEMS) are semiconductor chips with built-in minuscule mechanical devices. In a MEMS microphone, a condenser mechanism is an integral part of a CMOS (complementary metal-oxide semiconductor).

1 The chip/condenser is housed in an acoustic metal housing with gaps to receive sound waves. As in other condenser mics, the waves vibrate a diaphragm, changing the electrical potential held between the diaphragm and its fixed backplate.

2 Signals generated by the changing capacitance pass to the semiconductor portion of the MEMS, where it is processed by both an analog-to-digital converter and an amplifier.

High-Def Phone Audio

A cell phone with only a single microphone used in the wilds of downtown traffic can hardly compete with the onslaught of surrounding noise. It cries out for evolution. And evolve it did, first to two microphones: one for cell call use and another that faces forward to record a video's audio. Now three mics with **high-definition audio technology,** located in different spots on a smartphone case, enable a phone to pick up sounds from all directions. A specialized processor in the phone balances the sound from each mic with the sound coming from the other two microphones in different positions and runs all the sounds through an algorithm to muffle extraneous and conflicting noise.

To more accurately reflect the human speech range, each of the mics is devoted to different frequencies in the speech spectrum, doubling the range of frequencies it picks up. The system also doubles the bit rate, resulting in voice transmissions that actually sound like voices. The increased amount of data is still able to be transferred over cell phone connections through **wideband adaptive multi-rate coding**, which transmits voice in the 50—7,000Hz frequency range, compared to standard voice transferred in a narrower range between 300 and 3,400Hz. Not all smartphones support this technology.

Location of microphones on Apple iPhone 5
[on back]
[on bottom]

How Speakers Sound Off

MOST SOUND SYSTEMS rely on a mix of equipment to reproduce the range of frequencies the ear can distinguish. The most important are the cone-shaped drivers, which most of us inaccurately call speakers. (Technically, the speakers are the boxes that contain the drivers.)

1 An amplifier sends audio signals over speaker wire or Bluetooth radio waves. The signals don't go directly to the drivers. A crossover filter splits the signals into identical currents—one for each driver—and sends each through a different circuit. Each signal passes through different resistors, which partially block current, and different capacitors and inductors, both of which store energy. Each of the signals emerge from the different circuits stripped of all but high-frequency sounds, low sounds, or both, while preserving the midrange.

2 The signals that now carry mostly high-pitched sound go to the smallest driver—usually either dome-shaped or shaped like a horn with squared-off sides—the tweeter. It produces sounds vibrating from 40 times a second to 26,000 times—or 40Hz to 26kHz. The top range of most human hearing is 20,000Hz. Hertz is a measurement of the number of vibrations—or oscillations—in a second.

3 A small cone-shaped mid-range driver covers the middle range of the sound spectrum. (For reference, middle C on a piano creates a sound wave at 256Hz.) If a speaker has only one driver, it's the midrange. This driver doesn't handle the extremes well, but it reproduces everything else.

4 The biggest driver is a woofer. Its design and size give oomph to percussion and bass notes, any sounds from 40Hz down to 20Hz, or 20 vibrations each second.

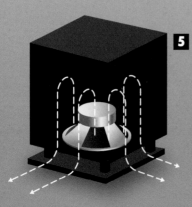

5 Some sound systems include a large driver called a subwoofer, usually in its own housing and often with a separate power supply. The subwoofer handles sounds beneath the lowest pitches that the normal human ear can hear—20Hz. But when the low-pitched sounds are strong—"loud"—enough, we can often feel them, in the form of pressure, when the compacted portion of a wave—the crest—strikes our bodies.

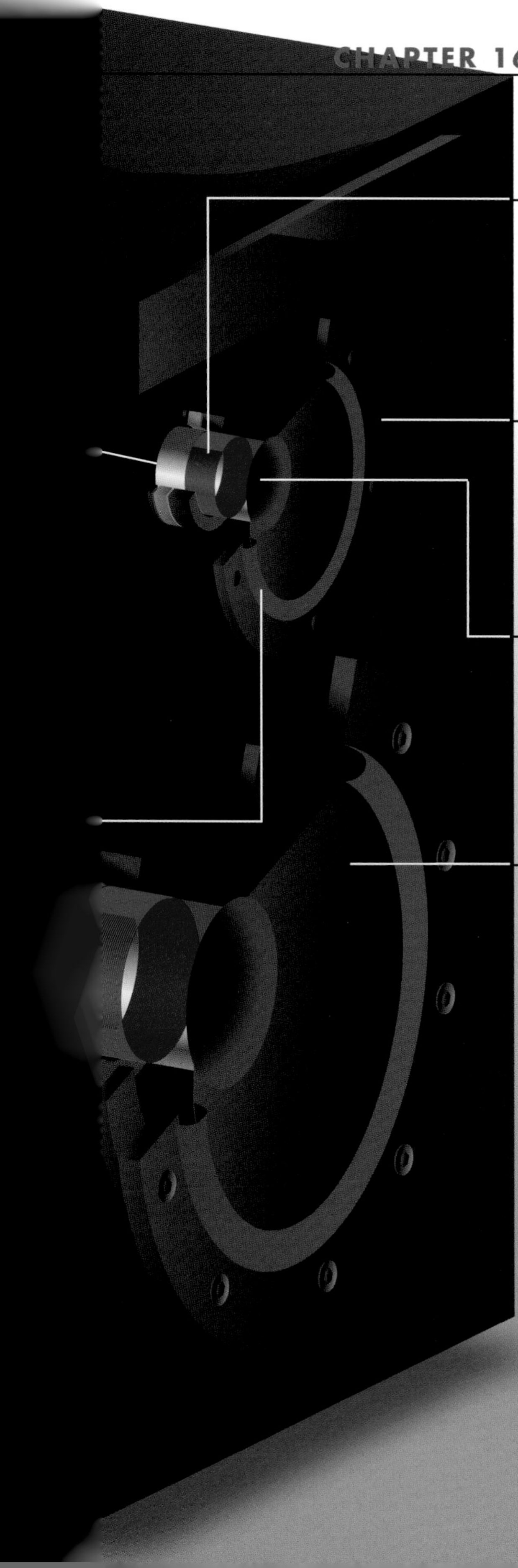

6 After the audio signals leave the crossover circuits, the drivers each go through the identical procedures with the filtered audio signals. Each current passes through a coil built into the driver. The coil wraps around, but doesn't touch, a metallic core.

7 As the current flows through the coil, it creates a magnetic field that moves the core to match the changing frequency of the current passing through the coil.

8 The core is attached to a diaphragm at the center of a driver's cone.

9 The movements of the coil cause the core to move, which vibrates the cone. (On some woofers that do not have grills in front of the drivers, you can actually see the woofer's cone move.) The cone is the most important component in creating realistic sound. It's made of a variety of materials, from paper to rare-earth minerals. The ideal cone is rigid to prevent vibrations getting out of control and has a low mass so that it doesn't take much force to start it vibrating. Finally, it is well damped, so that a sound can stop and the cone won't keep vibrating. To date, acoustic engineers have failed to create a cone with all three characteristics.

Can a Microphone Be a Speaker?

The mechanics and electronics of a speaker driver and the dynamic microphone are mirror images of each other. In the case of a dynamic mic, sound waves move a diaphragm, which in turn moves a magnet back and forth, creating an electrical current in a coil of wire. In a driver, audio signals in the form of electrical current go through a coil, creating a magnetic field. The field pushes and pulls the magnet, which is attached to a speaker cone the magnet vibrates to create sound.

Which raises the question: Could you send audio signals in reverse through a dynamic mic and use it as a loudspeaker?

Yes, you can, but not a very loud loudspeaker.

How Digital Sound Tricks Your Ear
Dolby Noise Reduction

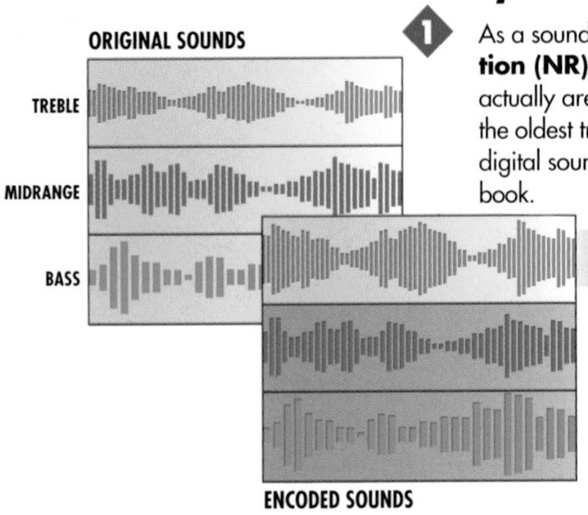

ORIGINAL SOUNDS

TREBLE

MIDRANGE

BASS

ENCODED SOUNDS

1 As a soundtrack is recorded, just before it is embedded on tape, **Dolby noise reduction (NR)** encodes only the soft, treble sounds so they will be recorded louder than they actually are. It's one of the oldest tricks in the digital sound-processing book.

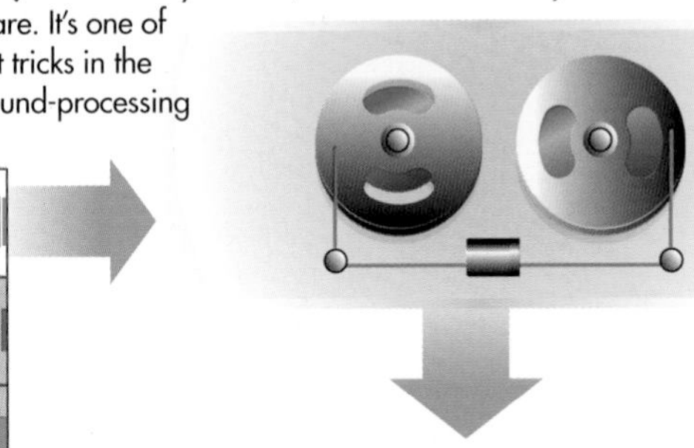

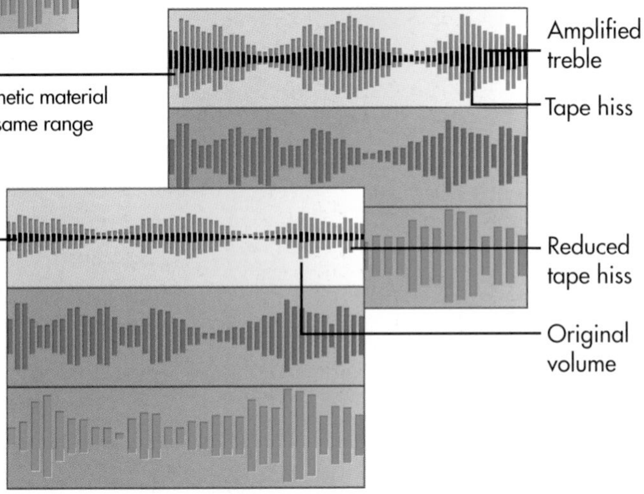

Amplified treble

Tape hiss

2 When the track is actually recorded to tape, the magnetic material embedded in the tape adds an unwanted hiss in the same range that the Dolby encoding amplified.

Reduced tape hiss

Original volume

3 When the track is replayed, the Dolby player decodes the treble sounds to return them to their original volume. However, the process leaves the hiss portion alone so it isn't audible.

Multichannel Sound

1 Full **Dolby Digital 5.1**, also called **AC3**, records sounds in six channels. Five channels record the same range of sounds, from 3Hz to 20,000Hz.

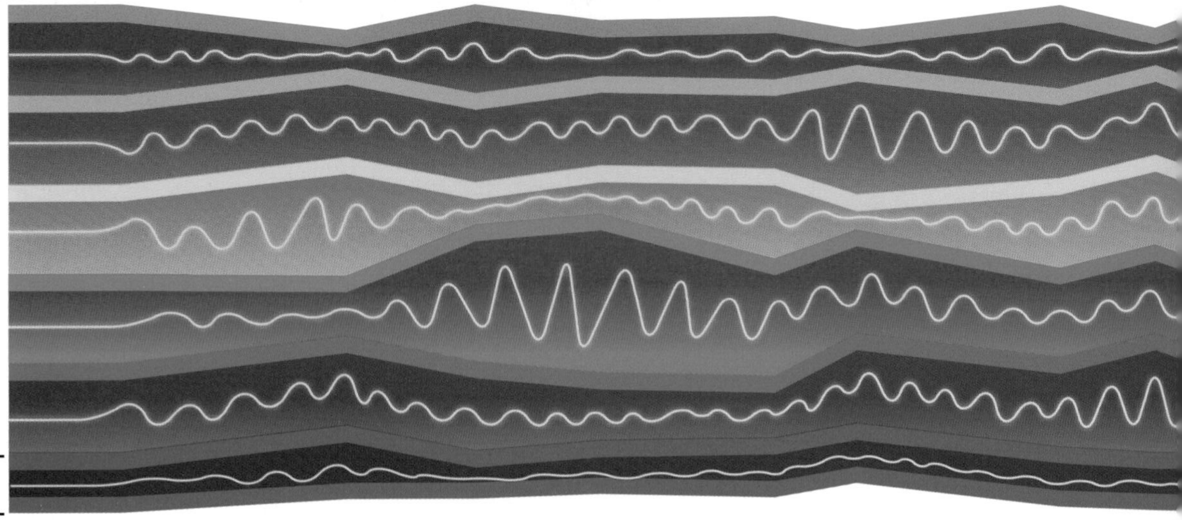

2 The sixth channel, the .1, is narrower. It's the **low frequency effect (LFE)** channel. It carries bass sounds from 3–120Hz, used for explosions, crashes, and similar loud sounds.

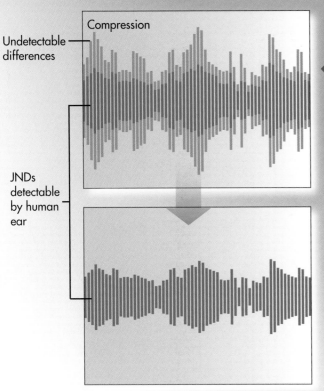

Compression

Undetectable differences

JNDs detectable by human ear

MP3 and Digital Audio Compression

1 A stream of sounds—music, effects, or speech—contains changes in volume, pitch, and overtones that the human ear cannot distinguish because they do not exceed the **JND**—the **just noticeable difference**. If the intensity of a sound doubles, for example, the ear hears only a 25% increase; the extra increase is wasted on human ears. The JND is not a constant. The JND between any two sounds varies with the frequency, volume, and rate of change (which explains why you can listen to a car radio comfortably, but when you start the car the next time, the radio seems ridiculously loud).

2 MP3, Windows Media Audio, Dolby NR, and other forms of audio compression squeeze a sound file to as small as 10% of the original size by recording only the JNDs. It ignores differences the human ear can't distinguish. It also doesn't waste recording bandwidth by capturing sounds such as faint, high-pitched tinkles, which will be drowned out by the pounding of a bass drum.

3 Among the five main channels, Dolby bandwidth is based on each channel's needs. The center channel typically carries more data, and Dolby allots it a wider band of the bandwidth. But as the channels' relative requirements for bandwidth change, Dolby **dynamically**—on the fly—reallocates the sizes of all the channels to be sure the most data, and the most important data, gets through.

4 When replayed on a Dolby Digital 5.1 system, the sounds are separated along the six channels to individual speakers, typically three front speakers and two surround speakers to the sides. The sixth channel, with its explosive bass, goes to a nondirectional subwoofer that can be positioned anywhere. AC3 recordings can be played on systems that have only one, two, or four speakers. In that case, Dolby mixes the signals from the six channels as needed to create the most realistic sound it can for that system.

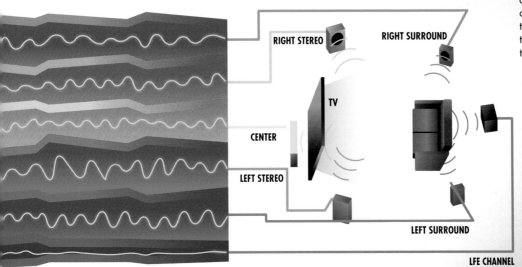

RIGHT STEREO

RIGHT SURROUND

TV

CENTER

LEFT STEREO

LEFT SURROUND

LFE CHANNEL

How 3D Audio Surrounds You

 One of the clues the brain uses to determine the source of a sound is the difference in how each ear hears the sound. An **interaural intensity difference** is detected because the sound is louder to the ear nearer to the source. An **interaural time difference** occurs because the sound reaches one ear sooner than the other ear.

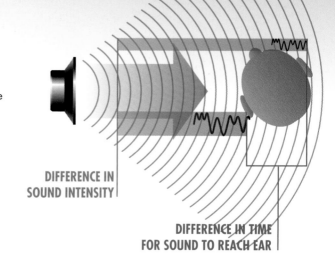

DIFFERENCE IN SOUND INTENSITY

DIFFERENCE IN TIME FOR SOUND TO REACH EAR

SOURCE SPECTRUM

PINNAE SPECTRUM

dB

Hz

dB

Hz

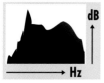

SUPERIMPOSED SPECTRUMS

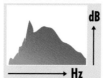

DIFFERENCES IN SOUND AND PERCEPTION

2 Positional clues are also found in how the **pinnae**—the exterior ear flaps—deform the sound waves as they enter the ear. The contours of the pinnae echo, muffle, and accentuate differently the various components of a complex sound, depending on the angle with which the sounds strike the flaps.

3 An important environmental factor is surrounding surfaces. They both reflect and absorb sound. The reflections called **reverberation**, or reverb, give clues to the direction a sound is coming from and contribute to the realism of sound, because in the real world sounds are almost always reverberating off a variety of surfaces.

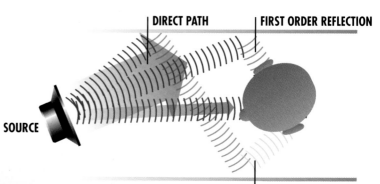

DIRECT PATH

FIRST ORDER REFLECTION

SOURCE

SECOND ORDER REFLECTION

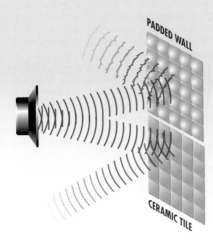

PADDED WALL

CERAMIC TILE

4 The composition of the objects that sound bounces off of also influences its character. An echo in a padded cell sounds different than in a large tiled room.

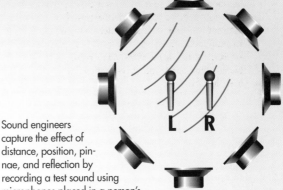

L R

5 Sound engineers capture the effect of distance, position, pinnae, and reflection by recording a test sound using microphones placed in a person's ear canals. As the sound source moves in a circle that has the person at its center, a record is made of the differences between the source sound and the perceived sound as recorded with the mics. Similar comparisons are made between a source sound and the sound after it has bounced off an array of surfaces—from hard to soft, and smooth to rough.

6 The values for the perceived sound are subtracted from the values of the original sound, creating a mathematical filter. The filters are used to create algorithms that software uses with **digital signal processors (DSP)** to create environmental sound that can be applied to any sound to re-create the illusion of a sound coming from a specific direction and reflecting off different surroundings.

SOURCE SPECTRUM

dB

Hz

MINUS

PERCEIVED SOUND

dB

Hz

EQUALS

DIFFERENCE (FILTER)

dB

Hz

7 In an immersive game, for example, the algorithm creates two spheres spreading out from each sound source that mathematically maps to a location in the game's virtual world. The sound cannot be heard until a virtual player enters the outer sphere. Inside the first sphere, the sound changes in volume and character as the player's position changes in relation to the source and to surrounding surfaces. The inner sphere represents a space where the sound gets no louder no matter how close the player gets to the source. The inner sphere is necessary so that the volume doesn't increase infinitely when the player is right on top of the source.

LIMIT TO LOUDNESS INSIDE HERE

SOUND SOURCE

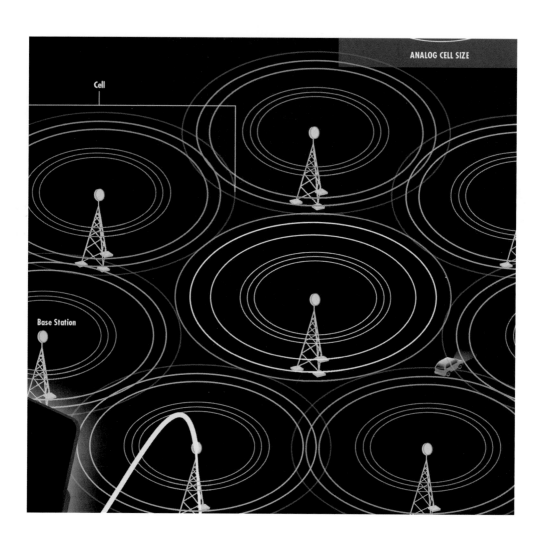

ANALOG CELL SIZE

Cell

Base Station

5

The Little Net That Grew

It was 1957 and the Cold War was sub-zero. The Soviet Union launched the first satellite, Sputnik, shaking the confidence of the United States in its scientific and technology leadership. In response, President Eisenhower created the Advanced Research Projects Agency (ARPA) within the Department of Defense (DoD) to get the U.S. into space (and to boost military missile development). That role was replaced by NASA, and ARPA redefined itself as a sponsor of advanced research projects at various universities and contractors.

In late 1960, Paul Baran of the RAND Corporation wrote a series of technical papers for the Pentagon analyzing the vulnerability of communications in case of a Soviet nuclear attack. A part of the papers were two ideas that would have far greater impact than anyone imagined. Baran said that military command messages and control signals shold be carried over a distributed network that would have redundant connections in case a missile took out part of the system. The best way to do this would be to break each message into blocks and send each block separately over that network, avoiding any parts that aren't working.

Only a year before the foreplay leading to the birth of the Internet, this was considered a monumental achievement in world communications. It's a sample of the cable laid in 1956 by the C. S. Monarch, connecting the United Kingdom and Newfoundland. The vacuum tube was part of several repeaters strung along the cable that periodically boosted the signal on its transatlantic trip.
Courtesy of Lucent Laboratories

A specific distributed military network was never built, but a few years later ARPA began looking for a way its members could distribute messages and data among themselves so they could take advantage of each other's research. They came up with the idea of a distributed network called ARPAnet, built around something called interface message processor (IMP), which connected computers at university research centers. IMP also incorporated a technology called TCP/IP, developed at the National Science Foundation. Standing for transmission control protocol/Internet protocol, TCP/IP calls for breaking up messages and data into packets to which addressing information, error correction code, and identification are added. The packets can all travel to their destinations over the distributed network, and a computer on the other end checks for mistakes and pieces them together in the right order. In 1969, computers at universities all over the country were linked to ARPAnet. The first letter sent over the new network was an "L" sent from UCLA to the Stanford Research Institute.

The ARPAnet continued to expand until, in 1972, it connected 23 host sites. By 1975, one new installation was being added each month. Meanwhile, other types of networks, such as the Computer Science Network (CSNET), designed to be a less-expensive version of ARPAnet, sprang up across the country. In 1974, researcher Bob Kahn and Vint Cerf came up with the idea of a "network of networks" that would let dissimilar networks communicate with one another. By 1982, different networks were adopting TCP/IP as their communications standard, and the term "Internet" was used for the first time. A year later, a gateway was set up between CSNET and ARPAnet using TCP/IP as a common standard so people on the two networks could communicate with each other.

A high-speed (56Kbps) backbone was built by the NSF to connect five supercomputing centers. Because all the transmission time wasn't used, the NSF agreed to let local networks connect to each other through the backbone. The Internet was born, even if people didn't realize it yet. For years, the Internet was the territory of colleges and defense contractors. As the Internet grew, many of the people who nursed it through its infancy were dismayed when, in 1991, the NSF lifted restrictions on the commercial use of the Net.

The first time someone sent out advertising over the Internet—a practice destined to earn the name spam—elicited reactions among Internet purists that were angry and vocal. And equally futile. The Internet and the World Wide Web, a section of the Internet developed to lift it out of its text-only origins and into the world of graphics, sound, and video, had lives of their own. The imp was out of the bottle, and today what started as a modest experiment in communicating is growing at a rate of 100% to 200% a year.

29 OCT 69	21 00	LOADED oP. PROGRAM	1SK
		For BEN BARKER	
		BBN	
	22:30	Talked to SRI	CS/c
		Host to Host	
		Left op. imp. program	CS/c
		running after sending	
		a host dead message	
		to imp.	

The first Internet message, although probably no one at the time realized it, was duly noted in a handwritten log at UCLA on Oct. 29, 1969.

Looking back over the last half century, you find that in no other part of computerdom, is it easier to see evolution in technology than in the Internet. The evolution of other parts of computing are hidden in distant origins, in the microscopic scale at which some mutations take place, and in the mind of engineers better at creating technology than explaining it. But the Internet is something we've experienced directly, even when it was still a gleam in the eye of the technocrats who created it.

In 1964, the Internet was still gestating, but we already had networks linking computers at a single location. A year later, networks spread to connect different locations. For several years, the infant Internet was the province of scientists and universities. In 1969, the first commercial online service, CompuServe, started up, but it wouldn't be until 1981, when the first modem was marketed, that the concept of communicating with anyone anywhere through computers became a phenomenon. That first 300 BAUD modem was so painfully slow that you could speak out loud each of the letters of a message as it popped onscreen and never fall behind. But that didn't matter. You could converse, download programs, play games, and send email—all in real time. We had seen the Internet, and there was no holding it back. The world has shrunk several times since then.

Now the Internet is part of our everyday life. It's how we stay in touch, entertain and educate ourselves, get instant information, shop, and solve problems no one person could solve alone. We've seen it grow, but that's been a lot like seeing one of those animations that illustrate millions of years of evolution by showing an amoeba morphing from a one-celled organism through fish and amphibians, through dinosaurs and birds, through mammals and apes to produce humans.

Radio-Newspaper Receiver for Home Use

DESIGNED to fit the top of a commercial table receiver which it matches in cabinet style, a complete radio-newspaper receiver for home use has just been placed on the market. All necessary apparatus for receiving and printing news bulletins and pictures transmitted over the air are contained in the unit. The news is automatically printed on a continuous sheet of paper that unwinds from a roll as it is received. The instrument can be used in conjunction with any radio receiver, the manufacturer declares, provided it has an output of at least five watts.

Anyone can now own one of these home-model, radio-newspaper receivers

The Internet's missing link. A story from the buried history of the Internet describes a device that, when connected to a radio, prints news bulletin and pictures.

We can see how survival's constant battle has vanquished earlier dinosaurs of the Internet and how some species have swallowed whole smaller Web denizens. AOL has vanished as one of the first major Internet players to become AOL Time-Warner, an 800-pound gorilla in a new, entertainment arm of the Internet. Few know the name of the first browser, Netscape, other than veterans of the Net. What once was a text-only Internet is now dominated by photos, graphic design, audio, and video. A program originally created by a college student so he could remember things about other students in his dorm is now Facebook, the colossus of the Net.

Despite all we've seen the Internet do and our daily use of it, the Net still holds its mysteries created by sheer vastness and by complex technology. It would be a lot easier to explain how the Internet works if you could hold it in your hand. Hardware—real, tangible, with a weight and size— is always easier to understand because you can see it and you can point with confidence to say this gizmo leads to that gadget, every time. The Internet is not just a single thing; it is an abstract system. It's like your body.

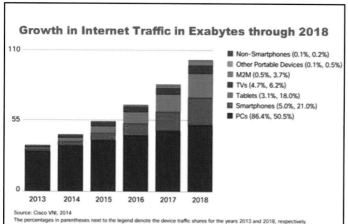

Growth in Internet Traffic in Exabytes through 2018

- Non-Smartphones (0.1%, 0.2%)
- Other Portable Devices (0.1%, 0.5%)
- M2M (0.5%, 3.7%)
- TVs (4.7%, 6.2%)
- Tablets (3.1%, 18.0%)
- Smartphones (5.0%, 21.0%)
- PCs (86.4%, 50.5%)

Source: Cisco VNI, 2014
The percentages in parentheses next to the legend denote the device traffic shares for the years 2013 and 2018, respectively.

Traffic on the Internet by 2018 is estimated by Cisco to grow to 131.9 exabytes a month. An exabyte is 1,000,000,000,000,000,000 bytes. Or you can look at it this way. By 2018 the gigabyte equivalent of all movies ever made will cross the global Internet every three minutes. In 1992 the Internet carried about 100GB of traffic each day.

As a system, the Internet is similar to a living organism. It grows, taking in new "molecules" in the form of PCs and networks that attach themselves to the Net and abandon it without warning. The Net is ephemeral. Some pieces— the supercomputers that form the backbone of the Internet—are always there. Businesses' local area networks (LANs) , home networks, individual computers, and smartphones connected through cell phone airwaves all qualify as individual organs in the Body Internet. But nothing is really fixed in place—hard-wired. Each time you use your computer or smartphone to check email messages, leave a quip on Twitter, bid on a Rolex knock-off, or play World of Warcraft, the information you send and receive may travel via phone land lines, T3 networks, Wi-Fi, satellites, and cell phone signals. The first Tweet you send today might be routed through Chicago and Phoenix before it arrives at its destination in San Diego. Your next message might run though San Antonio, Copenhagen, and a satellite. Without realizing it, you can bounce back and forth among several networks from one end of the country to the other, across an ocean and back again, until you reach your destination in cyberspace.

It's a lot easier to say what you *can* get from the Internet—information of all kinds. Being a system without physical limitations, it's theoretically possible for the Net to include all information on all computers everywhere, which in this age means essentially everything the human race knows (or thinks it knows). But because the Net is such an ad-hoc system, exploring it can be a challenge. And you don't always find exactly what you want. There are still multiple "standards" that browser, Web designer, and hardware developers quarrel over, and some who strike out on their own convinced they have the one, true design for the Internet to follow. The result is that when you jump into the Internet, you're pretty much on your own. With experience, you learn the tricks and secrets buried in browsers, websites, and the Web's bottom feeders—spam, viruses, and scams. The Internet can be frustrating and even dangerous, but the rewards are so great that all the drawbacks are worth it.

CHAPTER

17

How Networks Tie Computers Together

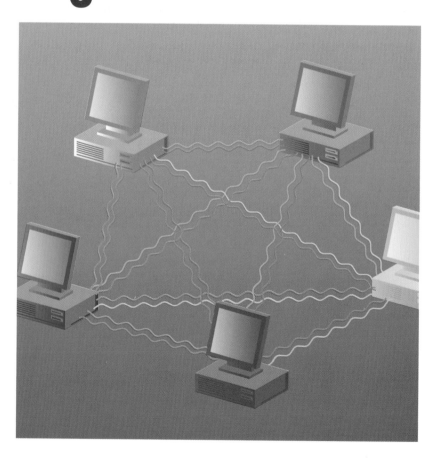

A LOCAL AREA NETWORK (LAN) is, for many people, the entry point to the

Internet. A LAN physically links several PCs to each other and often to a server that hosts shared data or provides access to the Internet. This is accomplished with a variety of materials—twisted-wire cables, fiber optics, copper phone lines, and even infrared light and radio signals.

Whatever the technology, the goal is the same—to send data from one place to another. Usually, the data is in the form of a message from one computer to another. The message might be a query for data, the reply to another PC's data request, an instruction to run a program that's stored on the network, or a message to be forwarded to the Internet.

If the data or program for which the message asks isn't on the Internet, it might be stored on a PC used by a co-worker on the network, or on a **file server**, which is a specialized computer with multiple large hard drives that are not used exclusively by any individual on the network. Instead, it exists only to serve all the other PCs using the network—called **clients**—by providing a common place to store data that can be retrieved as rapidly as possible by the clients. Similarly, a network might include an Internet server that links the LAN to the World Wide Web, or **print servers** that everyone on the LAN can use for printing.

If a network does not have a dedicated server, it is a **peer-to-peer network**. In a peer-to-peer network, each individual's PC (or device) acts as a server to other devices—its peers—on the network and also is a client to all its peers acting as servers. This is the kind of network you probably have at home, and it includes everything from that desktop PC in your office, to your laptop, tablet, smartphone, DVR, and Wi-Fi thermostat.

The network must receive requests for access to it from individual computers, or **nodes**, linked to the network, and the network must have a way of handling simultaneous requests for its services. When a computer has the services of the network, the network needs a way of sending a message from one node to another so that only the node for which it's intended recognizes it, and it doesn't pop up on some other unsuspecting PC or device. And the network must do all this as quickly as possible while spreading its services as evenly as possible among all the nodes on the LAN. LANs are a microcosm of the Internet, even as the LANs are a part of the Internet.

This chapter looks at the most common types of networks.

How Computers Connect to Each Other

TO BECOME PART of a network, a computer or device uses a **network interface** to communicate with the local network's **backbone**, the part of the network that carries the most traffic. Over time, the backbone and connections leading to and from it have used **coaxial** cable, **fiber-optic** cable, **twisted-pair** cable, **radio waves**, and phone and power wiring to link nodes, although twisted-pair cables and radio waves are by far the most common. The combination of connector, circuitry, wiring, wave, and other hardware determines the network's bandwidth.

RJ-45 connector

Coaxial connector

Coaxial Cable

From the connector, data can be sent along **BNC coaxial cable**, like that used for cable television. (*BNC* stands for *Bayonet Neill-Concelman*, a fact you will not be quizzed on.) Coaxial consists of a single copper wire, which is sheathed by plastic and braided copper that shields the center wire from electrical disturbances. Each end of a segment of cable has a **bayonet connector**, which requires only a quarter of a turn to attach the cable. Most broadband connections enter your home (and your modem) via a coaxial cable.

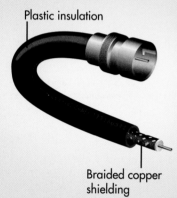

Plastic insulation

Braided copper shielding

Twisted-Pair Wiring

Twisted-pair wiring, the type most commonly used to physically connect a computer to a modem or router, has a plastic outer jacket that encloses four pairs of insulated wire that are twisted with a different number of turns per inch. The twists cancel out electrical **noise** from adjacent pairs of wires and from motors and other electrical devices in the same building.

Each end of the cable terminates in a plastic **RJ-45** connector, which resembles the common RJ-11 phone plug. (*RJ* stands for *registered jack*.)

Each (wired) node on the network has a separate twisted-pair cable that connects the node to a central **router** or **switch**, which is the center of what we call a **star configuration**. All of these devices let the signals from any one computer travel to any other node on the network. Any of the connections can be broken without affecting other nodes.

RJ-45 connector

Color-coded insulation

Copper wires

Fiber-Optic

On networks connecting directly to the Internet or in LANs for which speed is crucial, **fiber-optic** cable carries 1 billion bits a second, enough to carry tens of thousands of telephone calls. Hair-thin fibers consist of two layers of pure silica glass covered with a reflective **cladding**, like a tunnel lined with mirrors. Varying pulses of light from a laser or LED carry the data along the twists and turns of the cable by bouncing off the cladding. The wires cable and phone companies use to reach from their data centers to your neighborhood typically travel along fiber-optic cable.

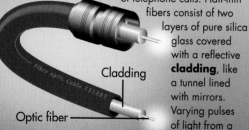

Cladding

Optic fiber

Wireless

Instead of using cable connections, most nodes on modern networks connect to the switch or router via **Wi-Fi** radio signals. This is usually how you connect your laptop, tablet, DVR, and so on.

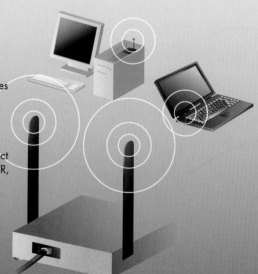

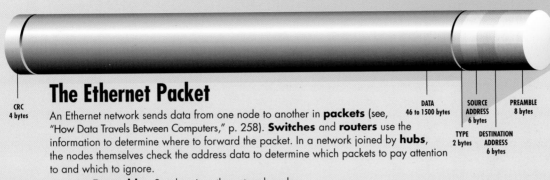

The Ethernet Packet

CRC
4 bytes

DATA
46 to 1500 bytes

SOURCE
ADDRESS
6 bytes

PREAMBLE
8 bytes

TYPE
2 bytes

DESTINATION
ADDRESS
6 bytes

An Ethernet network sends data from one node to another in **packets** (see, "How Data Travels Between Computers," p. 258). **Switches** and **routers** use the information to determine where to forward the packet. In a network joined by **hubs**, the nodes themselves check the address data to determine which packets to pay attention to and which to ignore.

- **Preamble**—Synchronizes the network nodes
- **Destination Address**—A single PC or all PCs on a network
- **Source Address**—The address of the computer from which the packet originated
- **Type**—Defines the format used for the data
- **Data**—The actual information
- **CRC**—Cyclical Redundancy Check, which is used to spot transmission errors

Hubs, Routers, and Switches

In a star configuration, a network uses hubs, switches, and/or routers as traffic cops to move data to the right destination and to ward off intruders from the Internet. Each of these devices is a simple box with several plugs to accept RJ-45 or fiber-optic cables.

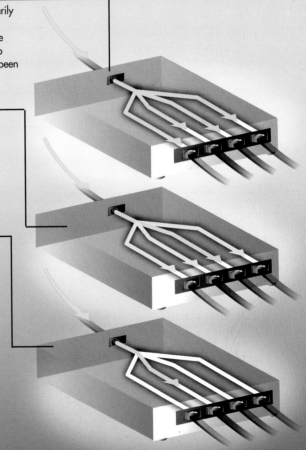

Hubs

1 A hub receives incoming data packets from different nodes and temporarily places them in a memory buffer if the hub is busy with another packet.

2 Each packet the hub receives is sent to every other node regardless of the packet's addressing. Nodes ignore any packets that are not addressed to them. Hubs are increasingly scarce in modern networks, having largely been displaced by switches.

Switches

1 A switch functions similarly to a hub, but a switch knows which of its connections lead to specific nodes. The switch reads a packet's addressing information and transmits the packet out only on the line that leads to the node it's addressed to.

2 Some packets—for example, one announcing that another computer has come online—arrive addressed for broadcast. This means the sending node wants all other nodes to see the packet. The switch sends copies of the packet.

Routers

1 A true router is similar to a switch, except that a router provides connections to the Internet and does not accept or transmit broadcast packets from the network. A router requires a specific delivery address for a node located on the LAN. Most of the router and switch functions are built into the same device.

2 Routers also enforce rules for data packets that might, for example, require the router to block any LAN packet that has a destination address outside the LAN and somewhere in the Internet.

3 If the packet comes from the Internet and is headed toward a node on the LAN, the router can send the signal to a log-in routine or reject it entirely.

4 If the destination address is valid—say, for a tablet logged onto the LAN—the router lets the packet into the network. Before sending the data to its destination, some routers check the packet's CRC segment for errors that have occurred en route. If a packet has an error, the router discards it and sends a message to the origination address, requesting a fresh packet of the same data.

How Data Travels Between Computers

SENDING INFORMATION digitally isn't all that new. Samuel Morse sent the first telegraphed message in the U.S.—"A patient waiter is no loser."—in 1838. He used a binary system—dots and dashes—to represent letters in the alphabet. Before Morse, smoke signals did much the same thing, using small and large puffs of smoke from fires. But for a good chunk of the 20th century, analog signals in telephones, radio, recordings, and TV became the standard ways to send data over great distances. With networking and the Internet, however, digital communications are once more in vogue, even replacing analog signals used in television, radio, and telephone. What makes this all possible is something called a **packet**.

How Analog Data Works

1 Analog communication works with two types of waves:

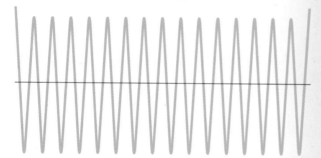

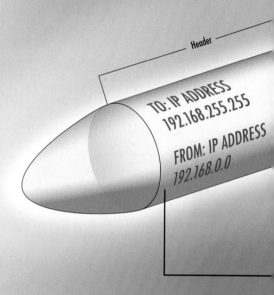

■ A **carrier wave**, or **carrier signal**, is a steady, strong wave that carries no information of its own. It is usually sinusoid, which means it has a constant waveform, both for **amplitude** (its loudness) and **frequency** (how many times it cycles from its high point to low point and back again in a second). An FM radio station broadcasting at 104.5 "on the dial!" is broadcasting a carrier that cycles 104.5 million times a second.

■ An **information wave** is produced by a microphone and a recording on tape, CD, or DVD. It lacks the carrier wave's strength to cover long distances. And unlike the carrier signal, it is irregular, changing form constantly due to the processes that produce it.

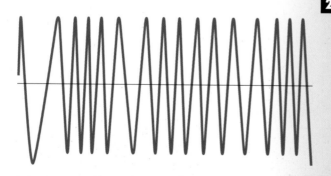

2 When the information wave is superimposed on the carrier, the information wave modulates the carrier (*modulate* simply means to change something). The informational signal could vary the amplitude or the frequency of the carrier. Speech is an example of a modulation. Vowels are the carrier that let you project your words far enough and clearly enough for others to hear you. Consonants are the information signals that transform the "ee" vowel into "me," "we," "see," and other variations on the basic "ee" sound. When the modulate signal is received (by a radio, TV, amplifier, or human ear), the receiver strips away the known values of the carrier signal. What is left is the original information signal.

How Digital Data Move in Packets

1 For digital data transfers, it's convenient to think of the **packet** as the equivalent of a carrier signal. A packet itself has no information, but it encloses, metaphorically at least, the real information traveling to another computer or to a component within the same computer. There are more advantages in packets than simple bundling. Packets permit addressing, error correction, and the use of multiple pathways to get the information from one spot to another. The organization of data packets varies to match the type of data they contain, and they may be called **frames**, **segments**, or **blocks**. We'll look at the most common packet you'd encounter—the Internet packet.

2 The computer sending data creates a packet following a specific organization that the device receiving the data will understand. The stream of data is first broken in a particular number of bytes— the packets.

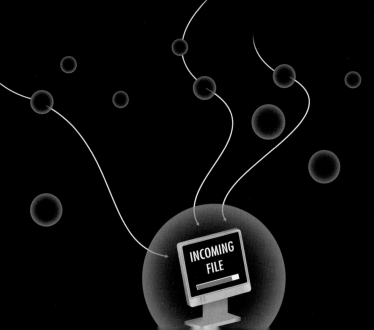

THIS IS NUMBER 28 OF 486

Payload

Footer

+1
+1
+1
+1

4 The computer includes two numbers. The first is the number of packets the information is divided into. The second is the sequence number of this particular packet.

5 The computer follows the form for bundling the actual data—the **payload**—set out by the **Transmission Control Protocol/ Internet Protocol (TCP/IP).** Each packet holds 1,000–1,500 bytes.

6 In the packet's **trailer** or **footer**, there are a few bits that tell the receiving computer this is the end of the packet. It might also include the results of a **Cyclic Redundancy Check (CRC)**. The CRC contains the sum of all the 1s in the packet. The receiving computer does the same calculation, and if the results don't match, the receiver asks the sender to retransmit the packet.

3 To each packet's **header**, the computer adds the **IP address** that the packet is supposed to go to and the sender's IP address.

7 The computer sends each packet into the Internet separately, and each packet takes the best route available at the time it shoves off. This method allows the network to spread the traffic out more evenly, and in the event of serious traffic jam, not all the packets are stuck in the same place. As the packets arrive, they may not be in the correct order. The receiving computer puts them into a buffer and, using their sequence numbers, builds the entire message as the packets arrive.

INCOMING FILE

How Wi-Fi Makes the Internet Portable

TO THE INTERNET

1 All Wi-Fi networks begin with an **access point**, or **AP**, a network node connected directly to a wired local area network or to the Internet. An AP also includes a radio transmitter and receiver operating in either the 2.4GHz radio band or the 5GHz range, or both. (See the box for the distinguishing characteristics of the most popular Wi-Fi flavors.) Access point functions are often built into a switch that also provides ordinary RJ-45 Ethernet jacks for connecting nearby nodes via cables.

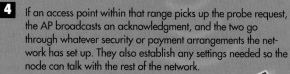

2 Wireless nodes, called **stations**, each have a transmitter/receiver working in a matching bandwidth. Desktop PCs sometimes have a wireless antenna built into the motherboard, but most use an antenna-equipped expansion card or a USB antenna attachment. Notebooks typically have an antenna built-in, but it can always be supplanted with a USB attachment that supports a more advanced Wi-Fi standard. Other devices, like tablets and smartphones, have built-in antennas that can't be replaced in this way.

4 If an access point within that range picks up the probe request, the AP broadcasts an acknowledgment, and the two go through whatever security or payment arrangements the network has set up. They also establish any settings needed so the node can talk with the rest of the network.

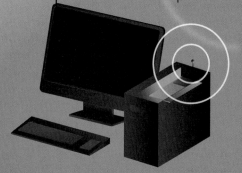

PROBE REQUEST

Differing Standards

There are several forms of Wi-Fi on the market, which are distinguished by their IEEE (Institute of Electrical and Electronics Engineers) designation, 802.11. Originally there was 802.11b and 802.11a, but these days you'll mostly see 802.11g, 802.11n, or 802.11ac. The differences between them are defined here.

Standard	802.11g	802.11n	802.11ac
Range	38'–460'	70'–820'	70'–820'
Speed	6–54Mbps	7–150Mbps	87–866Mbps
Frequency	2.4GHz	2.4 and 5GHz	2.4 and 5GHz

Newer Wi-Fi standards are almost always compatible with the older ones, so 802.11ac devices work with 802.11n or 802.11g access points. The inverse, however, is not true.

3 When a notebook, for example, connects to the network, it broadcasts a **probe request** identifying itself and asking if any other Wi-Fi devices are within **range**. That range covers a 25-foot to 820-foot radius, depending on the standard used and the surrounding environment.

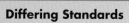

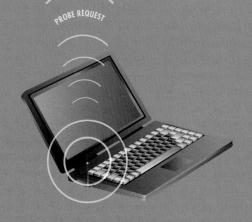

5 Many access points are also routers and switches, dividing Internet access among several stations, both wired and wireless. The Internet sees the entire LAN as a single Internet address, such as 207.8.157.204. It's called an **IP (Internet protocol)** address, and it's how computers see the Internet addresses that we see as words, such as www.howcomputerswork.net.

TO ADDRESS
207.8.157.204

FROM THE INTERNET

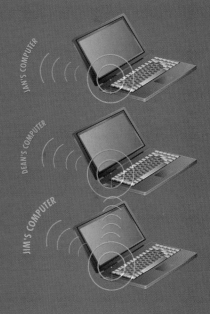

7 Stations are not limited to communicating only through the access point. Stations can exchange information with one another, unaided, on a **point-to-point** basis. The network as a whole can extend beyond the range of the routers, provided there are occasional **extension points** that pick up fading communications to and from access points and rebroadcast the signals with renewed strength.

JIM'S COMPUTER

DEAN'S COMPUTER

JIM'S COMPUTER

6 When the router receives a packet from the Internet, it strips off an encrypted and addressed outer shell. Inside is the name of the real recipient of the packet, one of the stations on the LAN. The router checks the address against a list of rules set up by the network administrator. Unless the rules forbid it, the router passes the packet to the destination within the network. For outgoing messages, the router shrouds each packet in a shell that hides the packet's true origin and gives only the router's ID as a return address.

TO JIM's COMPUTER

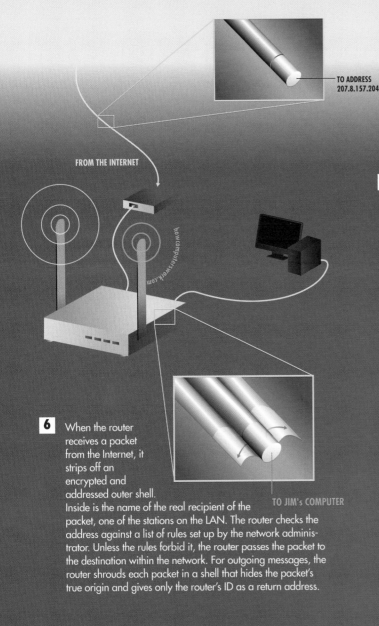

Logging in ...

8 Hot spots are areas where Wi-Fi networks are open to the public. These days you can find an accessible hot spot just about anywhere, from coffee shops and restaurants to college and work campuses, to airports and hotels. Some hot spots charge for Internet access; others are free.

How Bluetooth Keeps Devices Connected

1 **Bluetooth**, named for the Danish King Harald Bluetooth, who unified Scandinavia, is a standard protocol for unifying wireless voice and data communications among mobile telephones, entertainment systems, printers, portable computers, a local area network, and other electronics. It connects all the equipment through one universal short-range radio link.

2 The standard is incorporated in a **radio module**, a microchip that can send both voice and data signals for about 30 feet, or 10 meters (100 meters with a power amplifier). Its signals operate in the free 2.45GHz ISM **(Industry, Science and Medicine)** band that non-Bluetooth devices also use.

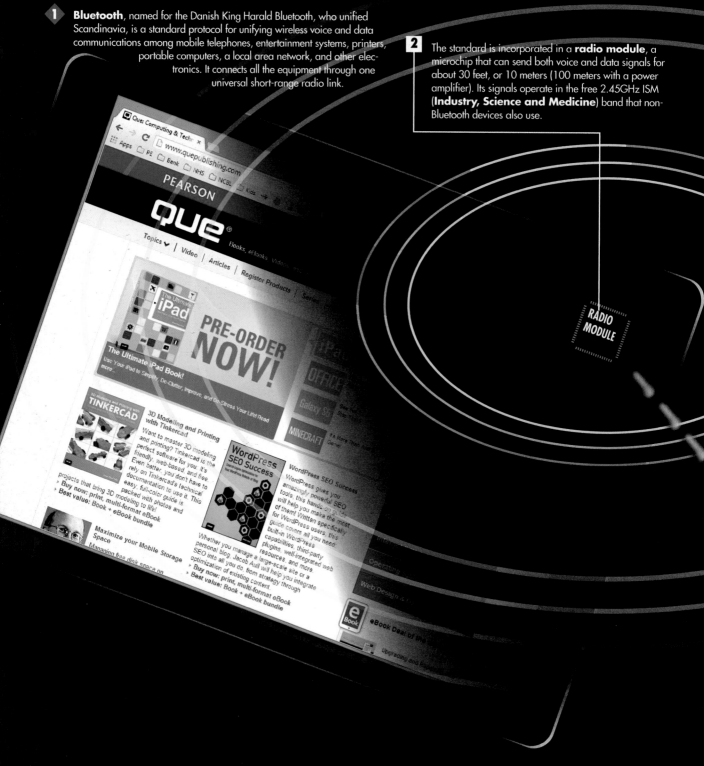

RADIO MODULE

3 In command of the Bluetooth protocol is each device's **link manager (LM)**. This software identifies other Bluetooth devices, creates links with them for voice or data, and sends and receives data at a theoretical 1Mbps (725Kbps, real world). The link manager also determines the mode in which Bluetooth operates:

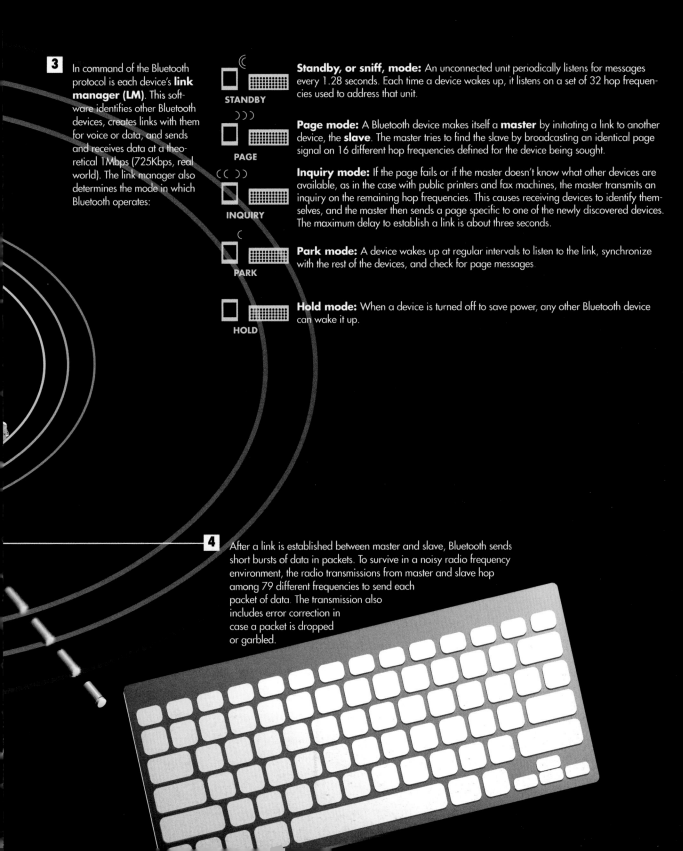

STANDBY

PAGE

INQUIRY

PARK

HOLD

Standby, or sniff, mode: An unconnected unit periodically listens for messages every 1.28 seconds. Each time a device wakes up, it listens on a set of 32 hop frequencies used to address that unit.

Page mode: A Bluetooth device makes itself a **master** by initiating a link to another device, the **slave**. The master tries to find the slave by broadcasting an identical page signal on 16 different hop frequencies defined for the device being sought.

Inquiry mode: If the page fails or if the master doesn't know what other devices are available, as in the case with public printers and fax machines, the master transmits an inquiry on the remaining hop frequencies. This causes receiving devices to identify themselves, and the master then sends a page specific to one of the newly discovered devices. The maximum delay to establish a link is about three seconds.

Park mode: A device wakes up at regular intervals to listen to the link, synchronize with the rest of the devices, and check for page messages.

Hold mode: When a device is turned off to save power, any other Bluetooth device can wake it up.

4 After a link is established between master and slave, Bluetooth sends short bursts of data in packets. To survive in a noisy radio frequency environment, the radio transmissions from master and slave hop among 79 different frequencies to send each packet of data. The transmission also includes error correction in case a packet is dropped or garbled.

How NFC Lets Smart Devices Make Close Calls

WHAT WITH RADIO signals, over-the-air high-def TV, G3, G4 LTE, Wi-Fi, and Bluetooth, you'd think we couldn't possibly use still another form of wireless communication. But this just in from your smartphone news: You're wrong. **NFC (near field communications)** is the latest way to communicate without wires. The twist is that the communications are good for only a few inches and it's more a tête-à-tête of electronic devices than human conversation.

1 Most wireless communications use radio signals—the electronic part of the electromagnetic spectrum—to send and receive information. NFC uses magnetic fields to communicate. Although magnetic fields are powerful enough to overcome the gravitational field of the entire Earth in a battle for possession of an iron nail, magnetic fields don't have much reach. Hence, "near field."

Tim Downs
Employee

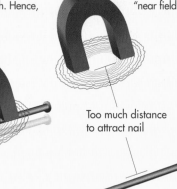

Too much distance to attract nail

2 NFC devices can be **passive** or **active**. A passive NFC device is like a sign on a wall. It contains information that other devices can read, but it's a one-way street. It can't receive any information other devices may have to offer. Think of the nametags that unlock doors, authorize elevators to stop on a particular floor, or keep tabs on your whereabouts.

SHARE PLAYLIST "KILLER JAMS"

RECEIVE PLAYLIST "KILLER JAMS"

3 Not surprisingly, active near field devices can both send and receive information. They can also decide if another device has the right to read whatever information they have, and they might have the ability to grant or refuse another device the ability to change the information they have. Think of using smartphones to exchange business cards or playlists, to make a purchase in place of a credit card, or pay a bus fare.

4 Whether producing a single, short, one-way message or drumming up a regular gab fest, NFC devices use **magnetic induction**. An NFC device sends a tiny electrical current through a tiny coil, creating a tiny magnetic field that reaches a tiny distance—think tapping smartphones together—to a second device.

5 The magnetic field passes through a coil in the receiving device, generating electrical pulses in the device's circuitry. The pulses are decoded into the information the first device sent. Passive devices use the energy generated by the first device to decode or encode data. Active devices have their own power source and generate their own magnetic fields.

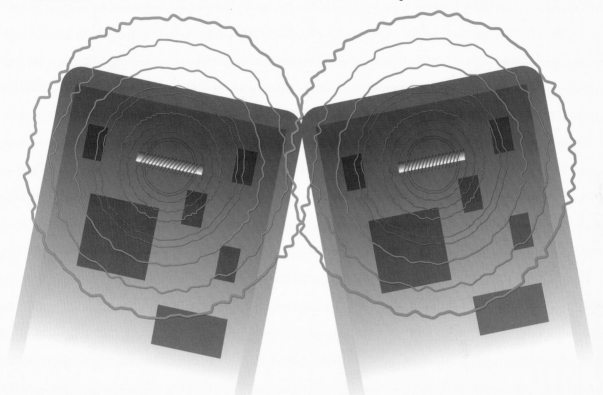

6 Near field works in the 13.56MHz radio frequencies and uses less than 15 milliamps of power. That's enough to send data as far as about 8 inches. Transfer speeds range from 106 kilobits per second (Kb/s) to 848 Kb/s, fast enough when the need is urgent to quickly transmit the data needed to unlock the company's restroom door. Passing along your 500-song MP3 library will take a mite longer.

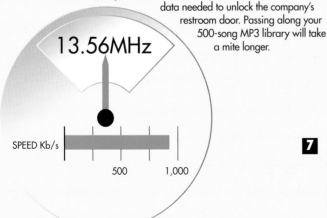

13.56MHz

SPEED Kb/s

500   1,000

7 Although data in a near field session does not go far, it could still be intercepted by other devices. For that reason NFC communications that involve such info as a credit card or bank account number are sent along secure channels and encrypted. Users can add antivirus software to smartphones and store sensitive data behind a password.

CHAPTER

18

How the Internet Brings Us the World

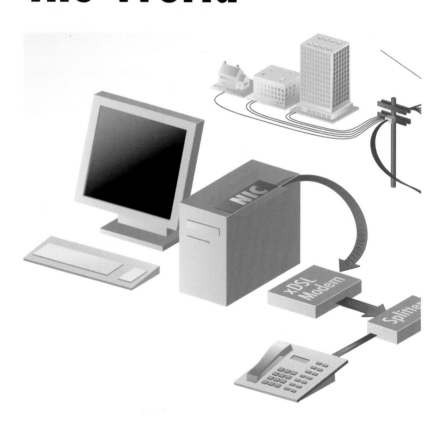

IT DOESN'T make a lot of difference if the Internet represents the accumulated knowledge humans have acquired since they came down from the trees. No matter that virtually any book, movie, or song can be found, somewhere, on the Net. And it doesn't mean a thing that every one of your friends, from the first person you met in kindergarten on up, can be reached through the Internet.

Everything about your Internet experience derives from how you get all that data down that last mile to your computer. And not all last miles are the same. The technologies of DSL and cable, the two most common Internet connections, tout themselves sending data at various maximum speeds. Whatever those speeds are, they are the dreams of the engineers and marketers. It's like me saying I can run four miles a minute—and I can, but only for about 10 feet. The reason I don't live up to my specs is that I've been out of shape since the sixth grade. Internet providers have their own reasons why real broadband doesn't match advertised broadband.

REASON 1: Latency. Latency is idling time. Your car may be able to go 200 mph on a straightaway, but that doesn't mean you'll drive the 200 miles from Houston to San Antonio in an hour. You'll have to sit still, engine idling, at stop signs, yields, train crossings, red lights, and school crossings. At best, legally, you'll be able to drive 70 mph because of a roadway latency called a speed limit. If you make the trip in less than two hours then somewhere along the way, you broke the law.

The Internet has its own set of laws, the most fundamental of which is the speed of light. Nothing moves faster than that, although satellite Internet transmissions come close—until they transfer to earthbound channels. Light in empty space requires roughly 5 ms to travel 1,000 miles. Most ground long-distance Internet traffic also uses light in fiber optic cable, but it doesn't move as quickly as in outer space. **Refraction**—the bending of light waves—lengthens the time it takes data to travel 1,000 miles in fiber optic to 7.5ms. Generally satellite lag time is 50–100ms for every packet of data.

REASON 2: Use of wireless. Wi-Fi has more latency and is more susceptible to radio interference than a wired Ethernet connection.

REASON 3: Malware. A network worm or virus that interferes with a computer's network interface steals performance time, if nothing else.

REASON 4: Application overload. Running other applications while you're surfing slows transmission times by competing with your browser for the CPU's attention.

REASON 5: Overloaded router or modem. If you're not the only one in your household connected to the Internet, your communications may take twice as long—or longer—as you wait others' requests to be processed.

REASON 6: Weather and wireless interference. After your signals leave your location, they still have to fight their way through corruption caused by weather and electrical noise, forcing computers on either end of a connection to ask that damaged packets be re-sent.

REASON 7: Traffic load: During parts of the day when more people are on the Internet, they create a usage spike that feeds a data traffic jam. If you are connected to heavily used sites, such as a multiplayer online game or popular websites, expect some lag.

For all the reasons that you won't see peak delivery speeds, 100% of the time, modern broadband is still a marvel that brings you the world with ever-increasing efficiency. In this chapter you get a look at how it all happens.

How Broadband Crams in the Data

1 Information—data—moves from one place to another riding on the crests and valleys of waves called **carriers**. Carriers are simple, pure waves of sound or electromagnetism, which includes light, heat, radio and TV transmissions, X-rays, and every other type of radiation.

2 Machines generate more complex, but weaker, waves that represent words, images, music, and electronic data. These **modulator waves** superimpose their wave patterns on the simpler carrier waves. The result is an entirely new **waveform**, similar to when two ripples on a pond collide, creating an entirely new set of ripples.

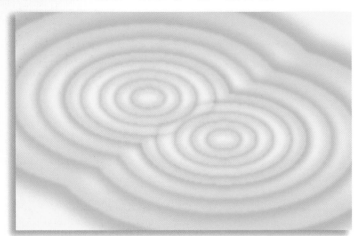

3 How much data a carrier moves from *here* to *there* in one second is that waveform's **bandwidth**. Although we talk of one bandwidth being faster than another, what we're really measuring is **capacity**. For example, imagine two ships traveling from San Francisco to Japan:

- Ship A carries 3,000 tons traveling at a steady 40 knots.
- Ship B is half as fast, traveling at 20 knots.
  However, Ship B carries 15,000 tons, so it has the greater bandwidth. If each of the ships had to transport 100,000 tons, it would take Ship A 366 days to move all the material. Ship B would finish the job sooner, in 150 days, not because Ship B is faster—it's not—but because it has a broader bandwidth (it carries more).

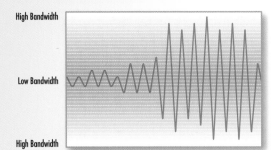

- **Increase the frequency.** Each cycle of the carrier wave is a new opportunity for data to merge with the carrier. The higher the frequency of the waves, the greater its capacity to carry data. We measure frequencies in **hertz**, which is one oscillation a second.

4 Each part of a PC—its processor, disk drives, system bus, video card—has a bandwidth. Any one of these **channels** can become a system bottleneck if its bandwidth doesn't keep pace with the bandwidths of other components. There are several ways to boost bandwidth:

- **Compress the data.** Zipped files and MP3 songs allow an Internet connection to send more information in the same time it would take to send a much smaller amount of uncompressed data.

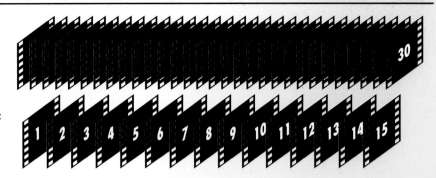

■ **Send less data.** If you don't have the bandwidth to send high-resolution color images, save them as black-and-white at a lower resolution, which requires fewer bits to record the image. If you can't send 30 frames a second of video, send 15 frames.

■ **Cache data.** The device saves copies of frequently repeated data in a special pool of memory called a **cache**. The next time the same data is needed, it can be fetched quickly from the cache.

■ **Reduce latency.** The theoretical bandwidth, or **through-put**, is rarely realized in reality. As much as 60% of a transmission's potential bandwidth is lost when many of the bits being transmitted don't represent data. Instead, they are used for addressing, identification, error-checking, and other necessary chores that are collectively called **latency**. Using improved materials and more sensitive signal detectors can reduce latency.

■ **Multiplex.** Chop a transmission into several pieces and send them all at the same time on different channels, such as different radio frequencies. It's like a grocery store with two check-out counters or 20.

■ **Prefetch data.** A device makes an educated guess as to what data it will have to handle next and **prefetches** that data so it's already waiting to be processed when its time comes. Doctors are prefetching patients when they keep their waiting rooms stocked with more patients than they can treat at one time.

5 We most often hear of bandwidth in connection with Internet connections, particularly **broadband**, which is a high-capacity line, such as DSL and cable. But anything that moves some sort of data has a bandwidth. The charts shown here give you an idea of the relative bandwidths of different means of transmitting data. The band capacities here don't take into consideration latency or methods of overcoming latency, such as compression.

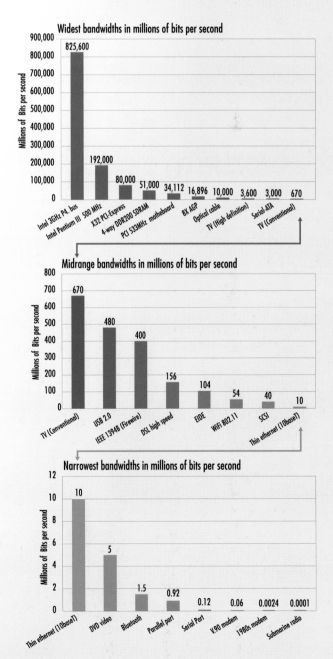

Widest bandwidths in millions of bits per second

825,600	Intel 3GHz P4. bus
192,000	Intel Pentium III 500 MHz
80,000	X32 PCI-Express
51,000	4-way DDR200 SDRAM
34,112	PCI 533MHz motherboard
16,896	8X AGP
10,000	Optical cable
3,600	TV (High definition)
3,000	Serial-ATA
670	TV (Conventional)

Midrange bandwidths in millions of bits per second

670	TV (Conventional)
480	USB 2.0
400	IEEE 1394B (Firewire)
156	DSL high speed
104	EIDE
54	WiFi 802.11
40	SCSI
10	Thin ethernet (10baseT)

Narrowest bandwidths in millions of bits per second

10	Thin ethernet (10baseT)
5	DVD video
1.5	Bluetooth
0.92	Parallel port
0.12	Serial Port
0.06	V.90 modem
0.0024	1980s modem
0.0001	Submarine radio

How DSL Turbocharges a Phone Line

1 There are several forms of **digital subscriber lines**, or **xDSL**, with the *x* depending on the particular variety of DSL. All xDSL connections use the same ordinary pair of twisted copper wires that already carry phone calls among homes and businesses. Unlike cable modem connections, which broadcast everyone's cable signals to everyone on a cable hub, xDSL is a point-to-point connection, unshared with others using the service.

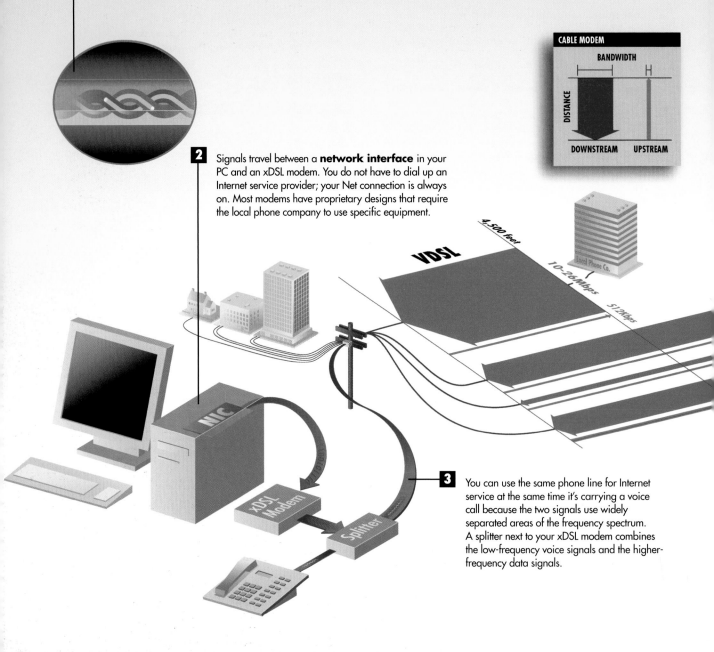

CABLE MODEM

BANDWIDTH

DISTANCE

DOWNSTREAM   UPSTREAM

2 Signals travel between a **network interface** in your PC and an xDSL modem. You do not have to dial up an Internet service provider; your Net connection is always on. Most modems have proprietary designs that require the local phone company to use specific equipment.

3 You can use the same phone line for Internet service at the same time it's carrying a voice call because the two signals use widely separated areas of the frequency spectrum. A splitter next to your xDSL modem combines the low-frequency voice signals and the higher-frequency data signals.

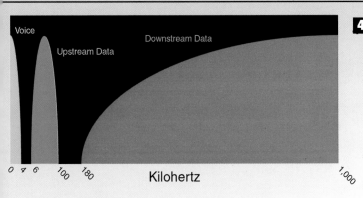

Voice

Upstream Data

Downstream Data

0 4 6   100   180   Kilohertz   1,000

4 The most common form of xDSL is **ADSL**. The *A* stands for **asynchronous**, meaning that more bandwidth, or data-carrying capacity, is devoted to data traveling downstream—from the Internet to your PC—than to upstream data traveling from your PC to the Internet. The reason for the imbalance is that upstream traffic tends to be limited to a few words at a time—a URL, for example—and downstream traffic carrying graphics, multimedia, and shareware program downloads needs the extra capacity.

5 Transmission rates depend on the quality of the phone line, the type of equipment it uses, the distance from the PC to a phone company switching office, and the type of xDSL being used.

6 A splitter on the other end of the line breaks the voice and data signals apart again, sending voice calls into the **plain old telephone system (POTS)** and computer data through high-speed lines to the Internet.

18,000 feet
512Kbps   512Kbps
6-8Mbps   1.5Mbps

21,000 feet
600Kbps-   128Kbps-
7Mbps   1Mbps

ADSL

G-LITE

RADSL

Local Phone Co.

Local Phone Co.

Downstream data moves at about 8Mbps for the most common forms of DSL. That's fast enough to transmit *Moby Dick* in just under six minutes compared to the 14 hours a V.90 modem would take.

Upstream data moves at about 640Kbps.

VDSL (very high-speed DSL) reaches data transmission speeds as high as 10–26Mbps downstream, but only within about 4,500 feet of a phone switch.

ADSL is limited to 18,000 feet from the phone office with downstream speeds of 6–8Mbps, upstream 512Kbps.

G-Lite, or **Universal DSL**, at the same 18,000 feet, allows only 1.5Mbps downstream and 512Kbps upstream. G-Lite eliminates the need for a splitter and is the industry's proposal for a standard modem that can work with any phone lines.

RADSL (rate adaptive DSL) reaches as far as 21,000 feet but is limited to 600Kbps–7Mbps downstream rates and 128Kbps–1Mbps upstream.

THE INTERNET

How Cable Brings the Internet to Your Neighborhood

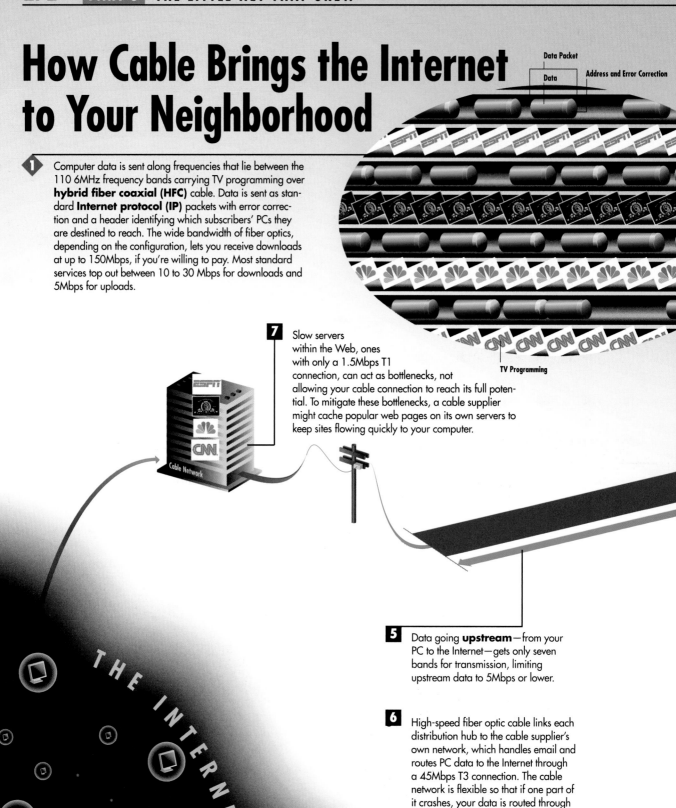

Data Packet

Data

Address and Error Correction

1 Computer data is sent along frequencies that lie between the 110 6MHz frequency bands carrying TV programming over **hybrid fiber coaxial (HFC)** cable. Data is sent as standard **Internet protocol (IP)** packets with error correction and a header identifying which subscribers' PCs they are destined to reach. The wide bandwidth of fiber optics, depending on the configuration, lets you receive downloads at up to 150Mbps, if you're willing to pay. Most standard services top out between 10 to 30 Mbps for downloads and 5Mbps for uploads.

TV Programming

7 Slow servers within the Web, ones with only a 1.5Mbps T1 connection, can act as bottlenecks, not allowing your cable connection to reach its full potential. To mitigate these bottlenecks, a cable supplier might cache popular web pages on its own servers to keep sites flowing quickly to your computer.

Cable Network

5 Data going **upstream**—from your PC to the Internet—gets only seven bands for transmission, limiting upstream data to 5Mbps or lower.

6 High-speed fiber optic cable links each distribution hub to the cable supplier's own network, which handles email and routes PC data to the Internet through a 45Mbps T3 connection. The cable network is flexible so that if one part of it crashes, your data is routed through working sections of the network.

THE INTERNET

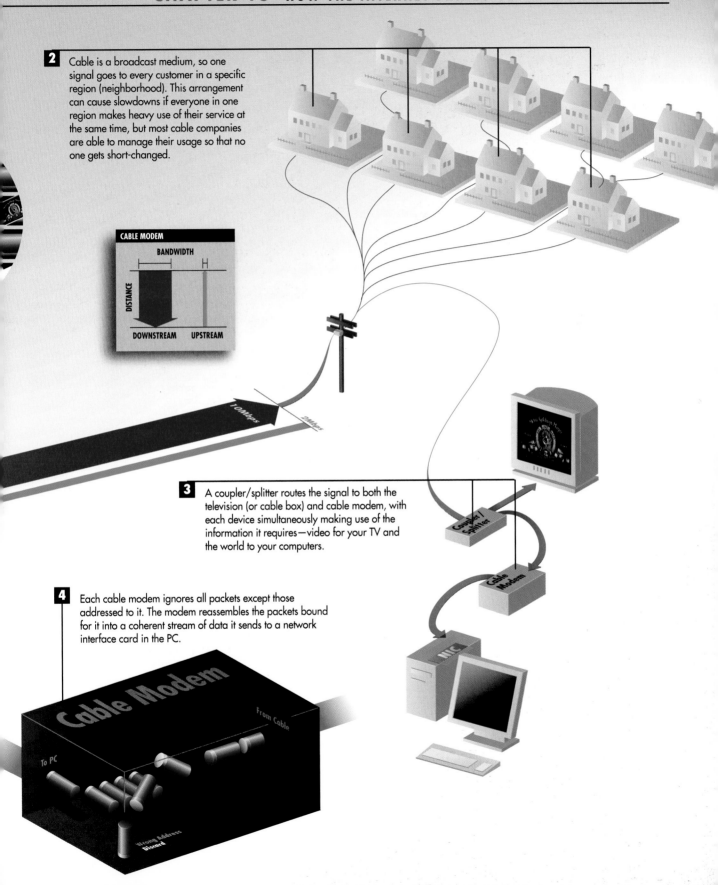

2 Cable is a broadcast medium, so one signal goes to every customer in a specific region (neighborhood). This arrangement can cause slowdowns if everyone in one region makes heavy use of their service at the same time, but most cable companies are able to manage their usage so that no one gets short-changed.

CABLE MODEM

BANDWIDTH

DISTANCE

DOWNSTREAM   UPSTREAM

10Mbps

2Mbps

3 A coupler/splitter routes the signal to both the television (or cable box) and cable modem, with each device simultaneously making use of the information it requires—video for your TV and the world to your computers.

Coupler/Splitter

Cable Modem

4 Each cable modem ignores all packets except those addressed to it. The modem reassembles the packets bound for it into a coherent stream of data it sends to a network interface card in the PC.

NIC

Cable Modem

From Cable

To PC

Wrong Address Discard

How Fiber Optics Lights Up the Future

FIBER OPTICS have been around since 1930, but it's just now that they are massing for a frontal blitz on the old networks, TV services, and the Internet itself for a change that is more revolution than evolution. Fiber optic networks can already bring download speeds of 1 gigabit a second to a few selected cities. That's 33 times the bandwidth of the fastest cable connection. In the lab, fiber optics have moved 26 terabits a second, or 26,000 gigabits. And that's just on one strand of optical fiber. Imagine a 12-strand bundle. It could move 5,000 two-hour HD movies in one second. Amazing.

1 Digital information—video, music, text, or other data— goes through an **encoder/modulator**, which converts the data into pulses of light, a smaller and extraordinarily faster version of the way ships in World War II used to send each other Morse code messages by opening and closing shutters in front of a spotlight.

2 A **transmitter** pushes those light pulses into the optical fiber, which consists of a core made of a flexible, exceptionally pure strand of glass surrounded by **cladding glass** and an outside protective coating. The cladding has a different **index of refraction** from that of the core glass. This turns the junction of the two layers into a long, cylindrical mirror that guides the light pulses by bouncing them along the length of the fiber. This process is named **total internal refraction**.

6 Contrary to what you might imagine, single mode has a larger bandwidth than multimode. The multiple light pulses in multi-strand grow wider in what's known as **dispersion.** Eventually the different frequencies of light create interference for each other and become indistinguishable. Single mode fiber carries a transmission with fewer errors and the ability to cover greater distances.

Repeater

01101011100010011

Encoder/Modulator

Transmitter

7 The light signal, even in a single mode fiber, eventually deteriorates from dispersion and from absorption by the impurities in the glass. This is called **attenuation**. It is corrected by **repeaters** placed at intervals along the length of the fiber. The repeater fires lasers into the light pulses. The light absorbs energy from the lasers, propelling the pulses farther down the length of fiber.

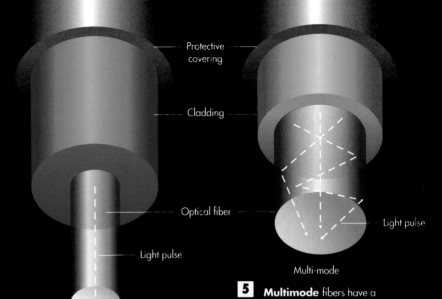

Protective covering

Cladding

Optical fiber

Light pulse

Light pulse

Single mode

Multi-mode

4 **Single mode** fibers have a much smaller core—typically 10 micrometers that permits only one light signal at a time to bounce through the fiber

5 **Multimode** fibers have a larger core, allowing several pulses of light of different frequencies to travel the fiber at the same time.

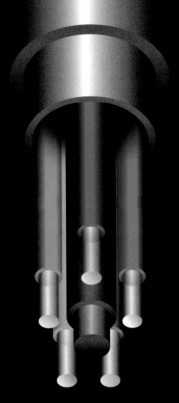

Multistrand

3 Optical fibers come in two configurations: **single strand** and **multi-strand**, which is a collection of single strands bound to a central core to form a cable. Individual fibers in the cable can branch out to serve different destinations. Single strand fibers are subdivided into multimode and single mode.

DEVICES

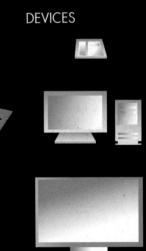

SIGNAL

demodulator

Detector

8 When the light reaches its destination, a **detector** captures the pulses and, in a multimode fiber, sorts them according to their frequencies and angles of travel.

9 A **demodulator** receives the light signals from the detector and converts them into electrical impulses to send the data to computers, TVs, and other electronic equipment.

How Computers Make Phone Calls

PHONES THESE DAYS are so smart it's easy to forget we can call home on them. It's also easy to forget about the digitally challenged siblings that birthed them: **cell phones**. Smartphones and cell phones share basic technologies that make them wireless telephones.

1 Smart/cell phones use one of several schemes for handling multiple radio signals simultaneously, including LTE, 4G, 3G, and CEMA. (Don't sweat the acronyms. We'll get to them on the next page.) All of the schemes use a system of **cells**, each of which is the area covered by a single receiver and antenna at a **base station**. Cells may be as wide as six miles or as small as a single floor of a building. The base antennae are usually on rooftops or share space on antenna towers.

2 The range of the cells overlap with that of other cells to ensure that a cell phone can move from one to another without losing connection, or at least that's the theory. There are a limited number of radio frequencies a system can use. Some cells inevitably use the same frequency, but not cells that are adjacent to each other. That would cause garbled, echoed communications. If any one cell is surrounded by, say, seven other cells, none of the cells can operate on the same frequency as the center cell.

Cell

Base Station

3 When a person turns on a cell phone or smartphone, the first thing the phone does is listen for a **system identification code (SID)** on the **control channel**. That is a special frequency the base station and phone use to set up the frequencies that are used for voice and agree on how to handle a shift from one cell to another.

Mobile Switching Station

Land Lines

4 At the same time, the phone sends a **registration request**, which is passed from the base station receiving its signals to a **mobile telephone switch office (MTSO)**. The office is the connection between all the base stations and conventional wired **land lines**. The MTSO stores a record of the phone's location, determined by the base station with which it's communicating, so that if the MTSO receives an incoming call for that phone, it knows which base station to route it to.

5 As a phone moves toward the edge of the cell it's using, the signal to that cell's base station grows weaker. Meanwhile, the surrounding base stations have been monitoring the strength on all frequencies—not just the frequency ranges assigned to them. When the phone signal to an adjacent cell becomes stronger than the signal picked up by the current cell, the two base stations coordinate their operations through the MTSO and switch the frequency the phone is using to the frequency range of the adjacent cell. This is called the **handoff**.

How Cellular Evolved

MOTOROLA came out with the first cell phones in 1983. Since then cell technology has been evolution gone wild. In 30 years, cell phones have gone through four generations and branched off into so many variations that it's a wonder wireless communication hasn't become a tower of Babel. Generation 1 was the original system, cell phones carrying voice signals using analog signals. Generation 2 (G2) took. cells digital in 1990, using voice over internet protocols (VoIP). Cell service was divided between two incompatible systems, GSM (Global System for Mobiles), used by AT&T and T-Mobile, and CDMA (code division multiple access), adopted by Verizon and Sprint.

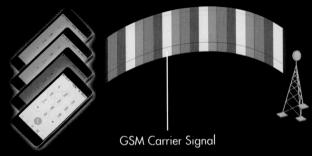

GSM, also called **TDMA (time division multiple access)**, divides the carrier signals into many small slices of time. Different conversations take turns using time slices on the same radio frequency. Because the time slices rotate use of the frequency so rapidly, it appears to each cell user as if it were one unbroken signal.

GSM Carrier Signal

CDMA, also called **spread spectrum**, assigns a code to each packet of digital data being sent as part of a single conversation. The packets are spread among the available frequencies, all of which are monitored constantly by the phone and base station. Receivers on both ends of a single conversation pick up packets from all conversations going on at the same time. The receivers use the packet codes to identify packets that are part of the same conversation and reassemble the individual packets into separate, unbroken signals.

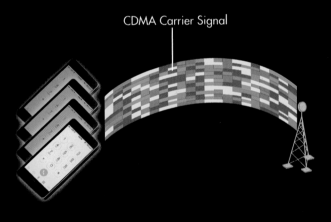

CDMA Carrier Signal

Generation 3 (3G) and **Generation 4 (4G)** have turned out to be more marketing tools than technological developments. Neither is a specific technology, but rather refinements and improvements on previous generations. The 3rd Generation Partnership Project, the group responsible for standardizing GSM, set an Internet bandwidth of 144Kbps for 3G, but 3G system speeds range wildly. The standard did not apply to CDMA systems, but that did not stop Verizon and Sprint from bragging about their 3G networks. The International Telecommunications Union, a standards body, issued standards for a network to be called 4G, but the carriers ignored the requirements, and 4G is primarily a market tool used by CDMA and GSM carriers.

Long Term Evolution (LTE), often used as a modifier term to 4G, has a specific and meaningful technology change. LTE can support up to 200 active clients—smartphones, tablets, mobile hotspots—at full speed for every 5MHz of bandwidth in a cell. LTE uses one radio signal for downlink from the base station to devices and a separate signal for uplink from devices to the station's antenna. LTE uses a scheme called **orthogonal frequency division multiple access (OFDMA)** that allows a system called **MIMO (multiple in, multiple out)**. Strip off the jargon, and what it means is that devices can have multiple connections to a single cell. Signal speeds are the sum of the speeds of the individual connections, and overall connections are more stable because they do not depend on a single signal. LTE, however, only transmits data packets, which means it will be working with G2 and G3 technology to handle voice calls until at least 2020.

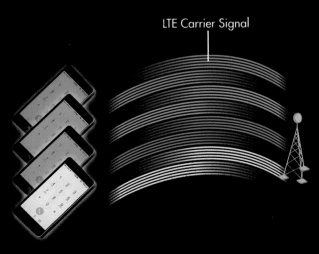

LTE Carrier Signal

How Networks Talk with Each Other

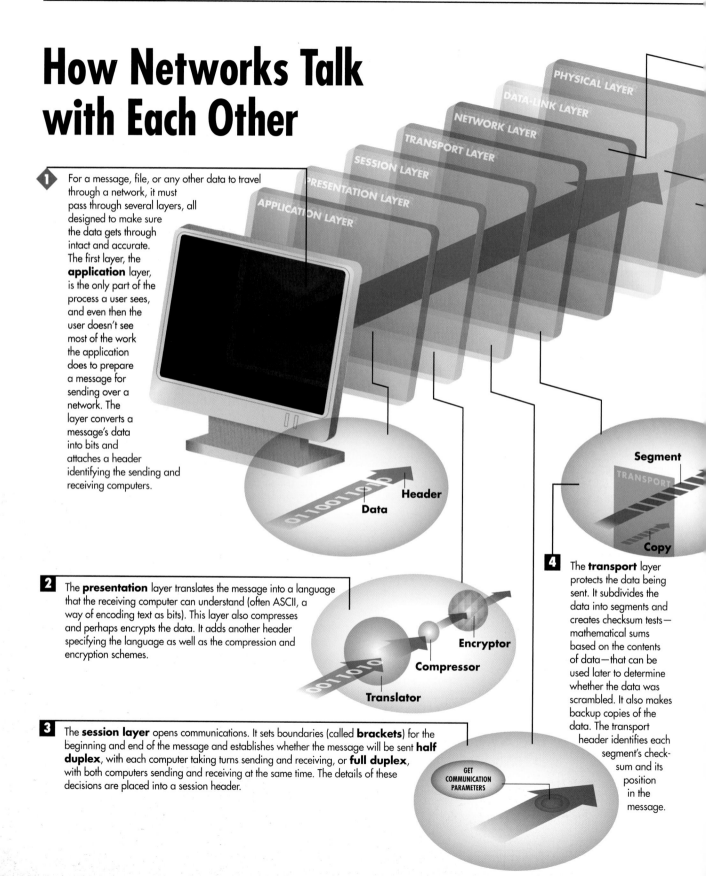

1 For a message, file, or any other data to travel through a network, it must pass through several layers, all designed to make sure the data gets through intact and accurate. The first layer, the **application** layer, is the only part of the process a user sees, and even then the user doesn't see most of the work the application does to prepare a message for sending over a network. The layer converts a message's data into bits and attaches a header identifying the sending and receiving computers.

Header
Data

2 The **presentation** layer translates the message into a language that the receiving computer can understand (often ASCII, a way of encoding text as bits). This layer also compresses and perhaps encrypts the data. It adds another header specifying the language as well as the compression and encryption schemes.

Encryptor
Compressor
Translator

3 The **session layer** opens communications. It sets boundaries (called **brackets**) for the beginning and end of the message and establishes whether the message will be sent **half duplex**, with each computer taking turns sending and receiving, or **full duplex**, with both computers sending and receiving at the same time. The details of these decisions are placed into a session header.

GET COMMUNICATION PARAMETERS

PHYSICAL LAYER
DATA-LINK LAYER
NETWORK LAYER
TRANSPORT LAYER
SESSION LAYER
PRESENTATION LAYER
APPLICATION LAYER

Segment
TRANSPORT
Copy

4 The **transport** layer protects the data being sent. It subdivides the data into segments and creates checksum tests— mathematical sums based on the contents of data—that can be used later to determine whether the data was scrambled. It also makes backup copies of the data. The transport header identifies each segment's check- sum and its position in the message.

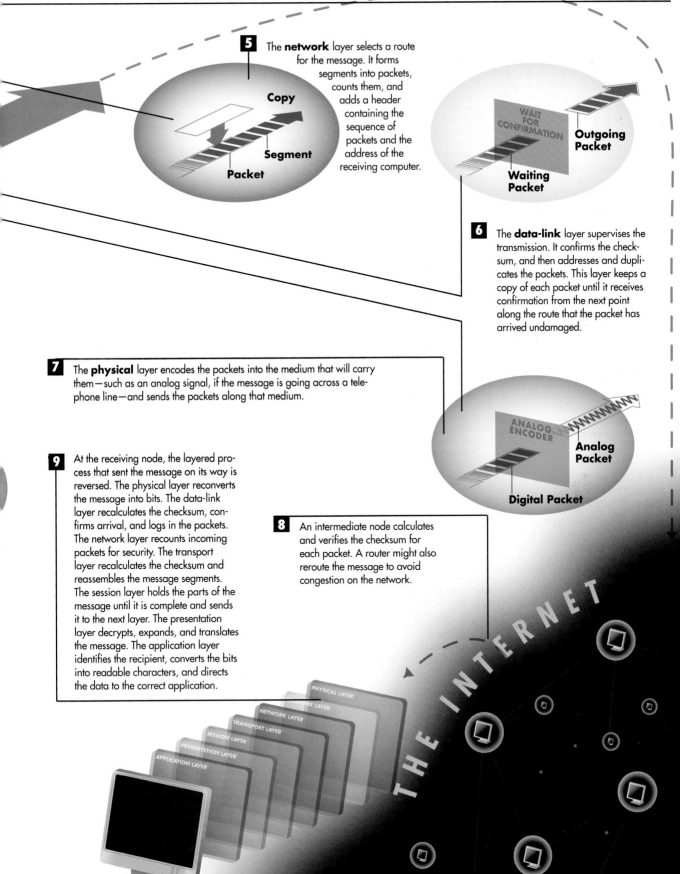

5 The **network** layer selects a route for the message. It forms segments into packets, counts them, and adds a header containing the sequence of packets and the address of the receiving computer.

Copy

Segment

Packet

WAIT FOR CONFIRMATION

Outgoing Packet

Waiting Packet

6 The **data-link** layer supervises the transmission. It confirms the checksum, and then addresses and duplicates the packets. This layer keeps a copy of each packet until it receives confirmation from the next point along the route that the packet has arrived undamaged.

7 The **physical** layer encodes the packets into the medium that will carry them—such as an analog signal, if the message is going across a telephone line—and sends the packets along that medium.

ANALOG ENCODER

Analog Packet

Digital Packet

9 At the receiving node, the layered process that sent the message on its way is reversed. The physical layer reconverts the message into bits. The data-link layer recalculates the checksum, confirms arrival, and logs in the packets. The network layer recounts incoming packets for security. The transport layer recalculates the checksum and reassembles the message segments. The session layer holds the parts of the message until it is complete and sends it to the next layer. The presentation layer decrypts, expands, and translates the message. The application layer identifies the recipient, converts the bits into readable characters, and directs the data to the correct application.

8 An intermediate node calculates and verifies the checksum for each packet. A router might also reroute the message to avoid congestion on the network.

PHYSICAL LAYER
DATA-LINK LAYER
NETWORK LAYER
TRANSPORT LAYER
SESSION LAYER
PRESENTATION LAYER
APPLICATION LAYER

THE INTERNET

How Information Travels the Internet

4 Several networks in the same region might be grouped into a mid level network. If your request is destined for another system within the same mid-level network, the router sends it directly to its destination. This is sometimes accomplished through high-speed phone lines, fiber-optic connections, and microwave links. A variation, called a **wide-area network (WAN)**, covers a larger geographical area and can incorporate connections through orbiting satellites.

5 As the request passes from network to network, a set of **protocols**, or rules, creates packets. Packets contain the data itself as well as the addresses, error checking, and other information needed to make sure the request arrives intact at the destination.

3 A **router** is a device that connects networks. It inspects your request to determine what other part of the Internet it's addressed to. Then, based on available connections and the traffic on different parts of the Net, the router determines the best path to set the request back on its track to the proper destination.

2 Your local host network makes a connection on another line to another network. If the second network is some distance away, your host LAN might have to go through a router.

1 PCs and other devices typically jack in to the Internet by being part of a **local area network (LAN)** that is part of the greater Internet. The network, in turn, wires directly to the Internet through a port called a T-connection. Usually they do this through a cable or DSL modem. Either way, through your browser you ask to see a page of information, and maybe multimedia, located on another computer somewhere else on the Internet.

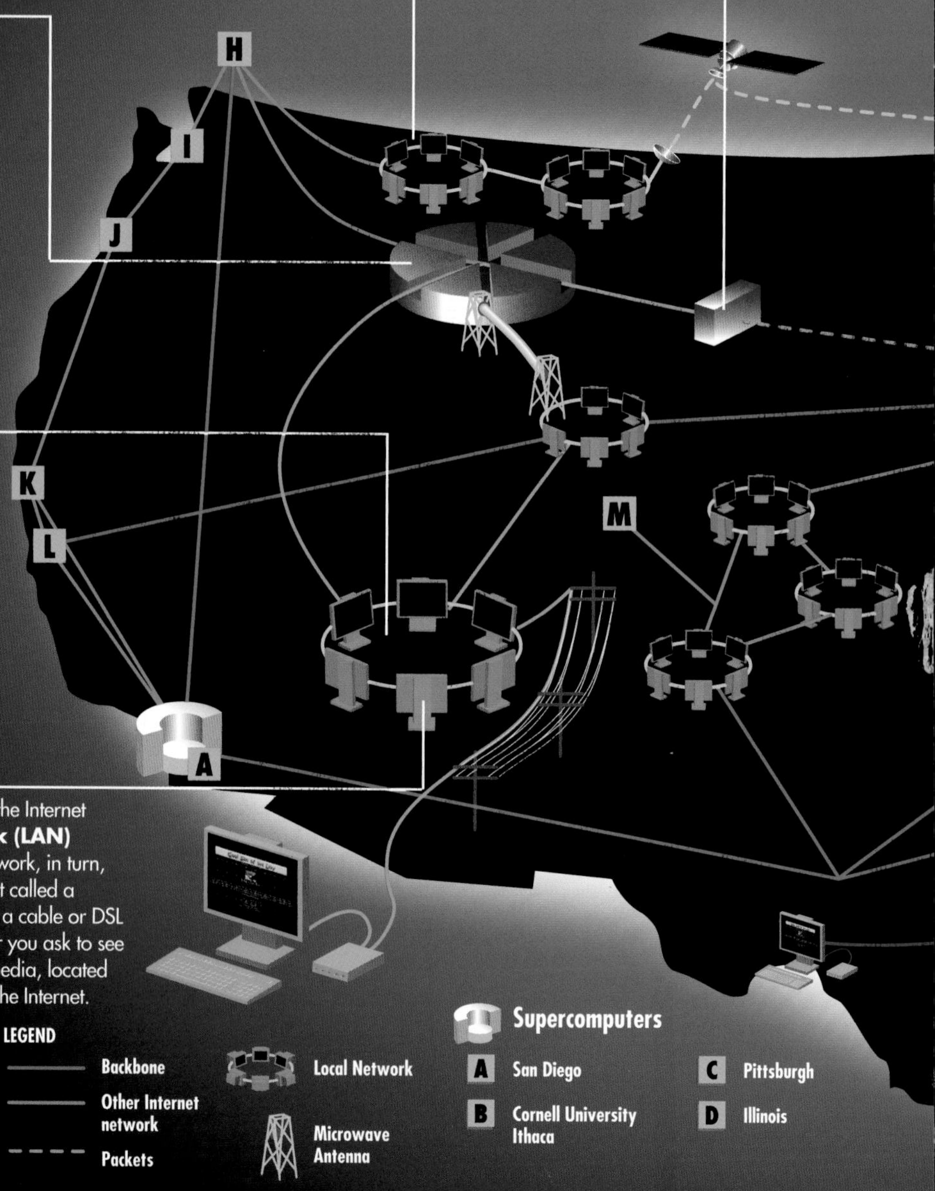

LEGEND

- —————— Backbone
- —————— Other Internet network
- – – – – – Packets
- Local Network
- Microwave Antenna

Supercomputers

A San Diego
B Cornell University Ithaca
C Pittsburgh
D Illinois

6 If the destination for your request isn't on the same mid-level network or WAN as your host network, the router sends the request to a **network access point (NAP)**. The pathway can take any of several routes along the Internet's **backbone**, a collection of networks that link extremely powerful supercomputers associated with the National Science Foundation. The Internet, however, isn't limited to the United States. You can connect to computers on the Net in virtually any part of the world. Along the way, your request might pass through repeaters, hubs, bridges, and gateways.

Repeaters amplify or refresh the stream of data, which deteriorates the farther it travels from your PC. Repeaters let the data signals reach more remote PCs.

Hubs link groups of networks so that the personal computers and terminals attached to each of those networks can talk to any of the other networks.

Bridges link LANs so that data from one network can pass through another network on its way to still a third LAN.

Gateways are similar to bridges. They also translate data between one type of network and another.

7 When the request reaches its destination, the packets of data, addresses, and error-correction are read. The remote computer then takes the appropriate action, such as running a program, sending data back to your PC, or posting a message on the Internet.

Other important stops on the Internet

E SUNY at Buffalo

F OCEANIC: University of Delaware

G Minnesota Computer Center

H University of British Columbia

I University of Washington Information Navigator

J PORTALS: Portland Area Library Services

K Stanford Linear Accelerator

L NASA Ames Research Center

M Weather Underground, University of Colorado

How Online Services Serenade You

1 When you click Play on a song in Spotify, iHeartRadio, or most any other music service, you're actually clicking a link that tells your browser to contact the web server hosting the song.

2 The server sends your browser a small file called a **metafile**. The metafile tells where your browser can find the sound file, which doesn't have to be located on the first server. Your PC also gets instructions on how to play that type of audio.

3 The metafile tells the web browser to launch the appropriate **codec (coder-decoder)**. The codecs are mini-programs that specialize in converting and compressing digital music or video into the raw electrical signals needed to reproduce media on a device's speakers or headphones. Each of the scores of available audio codecs are specialized to work with particular audio file formats, such as .mp3, .wav, .flac, .ogg, etc.

7 As the buffer fills up, the codec processes the file through a digital-to-analog converter, turning file data into voices, music, and sounds while the server continues to send the rest of the file. This process can continue indefinitely. If the buffer empties, the audio replay pauses for a few seconds until your PC accumulates enough data to resume playing. If the sound source is live, the player may instead skip portions of the audio program.

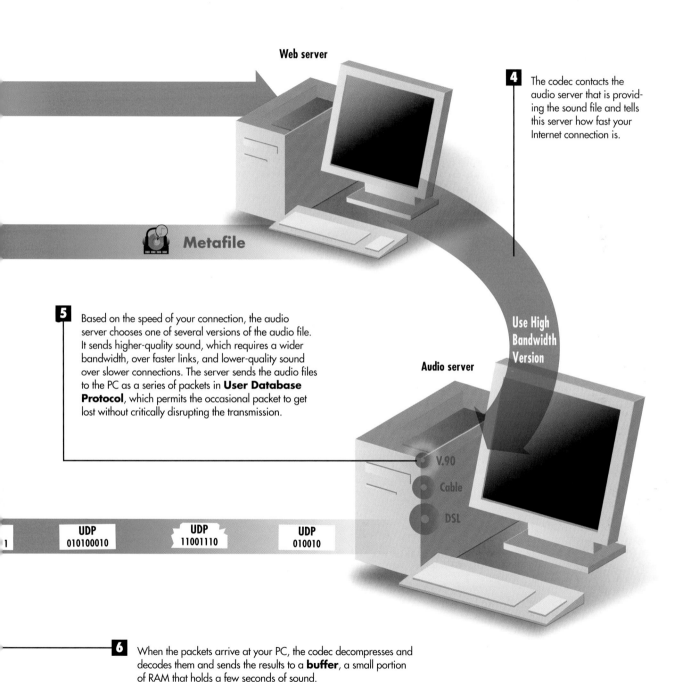

Web server

Metafile

4 The codec contacts the audio server that is providing the sound file and tells this server how fast your Internet connection is.

Use High Bandwidth Version

Audio server

5 Based on the speed of your connection, the audio server chooses one of several versions of the audio file. It sends higher-quality sound, which requires a wider bandwidth, over faster links, and lower-quality sound over slower connections. The server sends the audio files to the PC as a series of packets in **User Database Protocol**, which permits the occasional packet to get lost without critically disrupting the transmission.

V.90

Cable

DSL

| UDP 010100010 | UDP 11001110 | UDP 010010 |

6 When the packets arrive at your PC, the codec decompresses and decodes them and sends the results to a **buffer**, a small portion of RAM that holds a few seconds of sound.

How Movies Flow into Your Home

YOU THINK you sit around watching a lot of TV now? Wait until 2017 when television over the Internet is expected to rise from 1.4 exabytes a month to 8.5 exabytes. ("Exa" refers to quadrillion, the mega-number that follows trillion.) With all those couch potatoes hogging the Internet, how is anyone else going to find the bandwidth to update Facebook, spend hours following one aimless link after another, or learn who's had plastic surgery? By 2017 optic fiber to the home should be out of the gate, but **streaming video** will still take a few technical tricks. Like these.

1 Except for local broadcasts, all video begins its journey to your TV as a deluge from one of many giant satellites. Down on earth, dishes at the **headend**, or **hub site**, of the cable system catch that deluge and separate it into the hundreds of TV programs it contains.

2 Whether live or recorded, the programs pass through a **codec (coder-decoder)**, software that takes advantage of the ways video and human perception work to cut down on the amount of data the videos must use to create an acceptable image. The most frequently used codec is **H.264**.

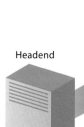

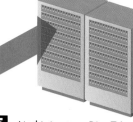

CMTS

Headend

3 **Interframe compression** compares adjacent frames and transmits only those pixels that change from one from to the next. When the camera is still, the background is not transmitted after a **key frame**, or **I-frame**, has established what the background looks like. When the scene changes or the camera pans, causing the background to change, the entire frame is transmitted, creating another key frame.

5 (At this juncture, DirecTV, which transmits video from satellites directly to home antennas, steps out of the picture.) Landline programming is transmitted via fiber optic cable or satellite to local headends. There, the video programs pass through a dozen or more **CMTS—cable modem termination systems**—that duplicate through multiple fiber optic connections to hundreds or more **streaming nodes**. (New York City has about 6,000 of them for Time-Warner Cable alone.)

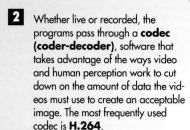

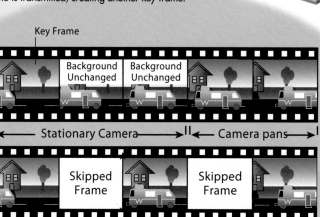

Key Frame

| Background Unchanged | Background Unchanged |

|← Stationary Camera →|← Camera pans →|

| Skipped Frame | Skipped Frame |

4 Codecs also skip frames for slower Internet links. The faster your connection, the more frames you receive and the smoother the video is.

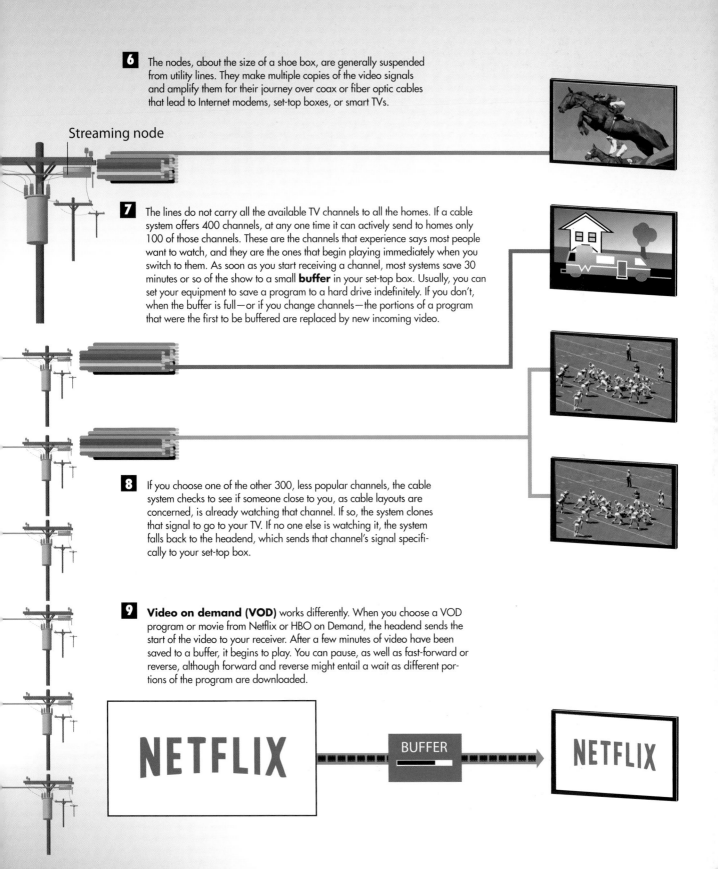

6 The nodes, about the size of a shoe box, are generally suspended from utility lines. They make multiple copies of the video signals and amplify them for their journey over coax or fiber optic cables that lead to Internet modems, set-top boxes, or smart TVs.

Streaming node

7 The lines do not carry all the available TV channels to all the homes. If a cable system offers 400 channels, at any one time it can actively send to homes only 100 of those channels. These are the channels that experience says most people want to watch, and they are the ones that begin playing immediately when you switch to them. As soon as you start receiving a channel, most systems save 30 minutes or so of the show to a small **buffer** in your set-top box. Usually, you can set your equipment to save a program to a hard drive indefinitely. If you don't, when the buffer is full—or if you change channels—the portions of a program that were the first to be buffered are replaced by new incoming video.

8 If you choose one of the other 300, less popular channels, the cable system checks to see if someone close to you, as cable layouts are concerned, is already watching that channel. If so, the system clones that signal to go to your TV. If no one else is watching it, the system falls back to the headend, which sends that channel's signal specifically to your set-top box.

9 **Video on demand (VOD)** works differently. When you choose a VOD program or movie from Netflix or HBO on Demand, the headend sends the start of the video to your receiver. After a few minutes of video have been saved to a buffer, it begins to play. You can pause, as well as fast-forward or reverse, although forward and reverse might entail a wait as different portions of the program are downloaded.

NETFLIX · · · · · · · · · · BUFFER · · · · · · · · · · ➡ NETFLIX

CHAPTER
19

How the Web Puts It All at Your Fingertips

JUST A FEW EDITIONS AGO when I got to this part of the book, I used to compare the World Wide Web to a Model A Ford. It got us where we wanted to go in cyberspace, but it was cantankerous and slow—slated for better things, to be sure, but at some time in the far, far future. And no one today could imagine what an enormous, pervasive effect the Internet is going...blah, blah, blah.

The far future's not as far off as it used to be. In just a few years, the Web has lost most symptoms of terminal crankiness. It's turned out to be a bomb for tasks that would have seemed a natural. (Ordered any groceries online lately?) And it's fulfilled other promises, but not in the way we expected. Previously, I wrote about the Web fulfilling the promise of Gutenberg, with everyone becoming a publisher. But I didn't expect those "publications" to be called blogs or tumblrs or snapchats, nor that they would be as popular as they've become. Not long ago web designers were cautioned not to use graphics, music, animation—anything that would make the Internet cool—because they choked pokey Internet connections. Now we consume high-resolution photos, Flash animations, and even 4K streaming video as if it's old hat. A decade or so ago, a couple of lawyers became nationally scorned by the pioneers of the Internet because they used the Web to advertise their practice—an obvious sacrilege. Today we don't make purchases larger than a pack of gum without consulting the Internet's consumer advice, sales, discount codes, and reviews by thousands of fellow consumers.

The Web is changing how we do everything and creating new standards for commerce, education, and communication. Want to know how much something is worth? Go to eBay. It's the ultimate free market, where the value of anything is quickly determined by a few bids that tell you—in real terms, not some economic gobbledygook—the most that anyone in the world would pay for a pair of Hulk hands signed by Mark Ruffalo.

And then there is Google. Someone joked that Google is a god because it is omniscient and omnipresent. Religious issues aside, it has changed research, scholarship, and the settlement of bar bets around the world. Okay, it might not be a god, but certainly it's an oracle.

How a Browser Opens Pages

1 A website is a collection of files, text, and media that someone has made generally available to others through the Internet. One way to begin a jump through the cyber-space of the World Wide Web is to click a **hyperlink**. A hyperlink is a text phrase or graphic that conceals the address of a site on the Web. When the hyperlink is text, it is usually underlined and in a different color than the surrounding text. The text doesn't have to be the actual address. These three words could hide a link to my page to supplement this book: www.howcomputerswork.net.

2 Another way to direct the browser to a site is to type its **universal resource locator (URL)** into the address space on your browser's toolbar. For example, typing http://www.quepublishing.com aims your browser at this book's publisher homepage. Each part of the URL means something.

Address | http://www.quepublishing.com

http identifies the site as one on the World Wide Web using HTML, or **hypertext markup language**. If the part before the slashes is **ftp**, that means the site is one that uses **file transfer protocol**; ftp exists primarily for making specific files available for downloading.

:// alerts your browser that the next words will be the actual URL, which is broken up by periods. Each period usually is referred to as **dot**.

www identifies the site as part of the World Wide Web. The Web is a subset of the Internet that uses text, animation, graphics, sound, and video (and you don't really have to type www).

quepublishing is the **domain name**. This is a unique name that must be registered with a domain registrar, which has authority to register domain names under the supervision of the Internet Corporation for Assigned Names and Numbers (ICANN).

com is the top-level domain name, which indicates the purpose of the sponsors of the site. A com domain indicates the site is commercial in nature, but anyone can register a com domain for any purpose. Other top-level names include **edu** for schools, **gov** for government offices, and the all-purpose **org,** which is primarily used by non-profit organizations. Outside the United States, the top-level name might refer to a country, such as **uk** for United Kingdom.

index.html is a specific **page file** at the site, and the html tells the browser that the page uses the hypertext markup language—simple codes that determine the page's onscreen look.

http://www.quepublishing.com/index.html

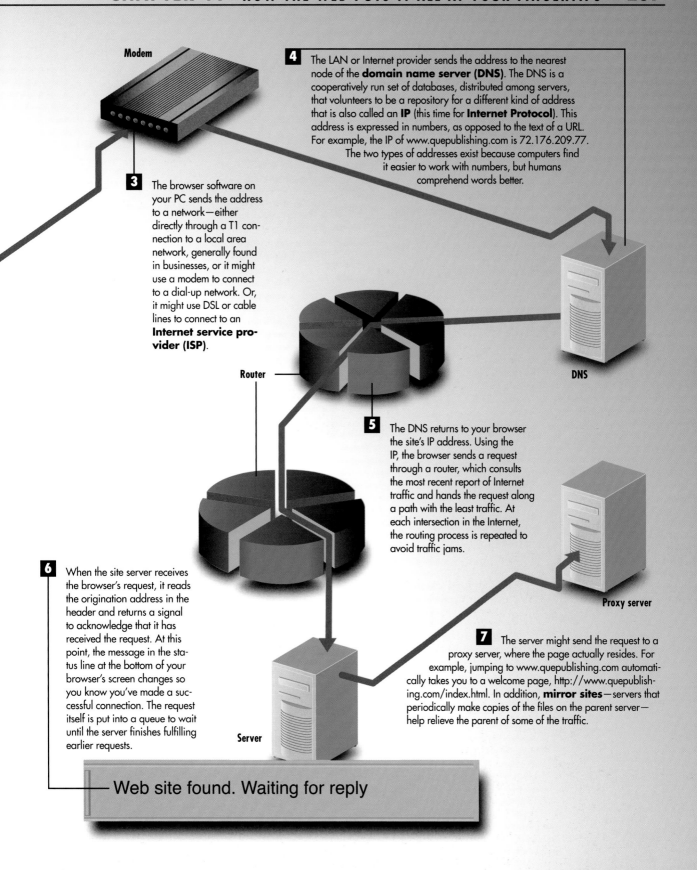

Modem

4 The LAN or Internet provider sends the address to the nearest node of the **domain name server (DNS)**. The DNS is a cooperatively run set of databases, distributed among servers, that volunteers to be a repository for a different kind of address that is also called an **IP** (this time for **Internet Protocol**). This address is expressed in numbers, as opposed to the text of a URL. For example, the IP of www.quepublishing.com is 72.176.209.77. The two types of addresses exist because computers find it easier to work with numbers, but humans comprehend words better.

3 The browser software on your PC sends the address to a network—either directly through a T1 connection to a local area network, generally found in businesses, or it might use a modem to connect to a dial-up network. Or, it might use DSL or cable lines to connect to an **Internet service provider (ISP)**.

Router

DNS

5 The DNS returns to your browser the site's IP address. Using the IP, the browser sends a request through a router, which consults the most recent report of Internet traffic and hands the request along a path with the least traffic. At each intersection in the Internet, the routing process is repeated to avoid traffic jams.

Proxy server

6 When the site server receives the browser's request, it reads the origination address in the header and returns a signal to acknowledge that it has received the request. At this point, the message in the status line at the bottom of your browser's screen changes so you know you've made a successful connection. The request itself is put into a queue to wait until the server finishes fulfilling earlier requests.

7 The server might send the request to a proxy server, where the page actually resides. For example, jumping to www.quepublishing.com automatically takes you to a welcome page, http://www.quepublishing.com/index.html. In addition, **mirror sites**—servers that periodically make copies of the files on the parent server—help relieve the parent of some of the traffic.

Server

Web site found. Waiting for reply

How a Browser Displays Web Pages

1 Stored on the server, the web page itself consists of an HTML text file. HTML is a collection of codes enclosed in angle brackets—<>— that control the formatting of text in the file.

2 The codes also can include the URLs of graphics, videos, and sound files that exist elsewhere on the server or on a different site entirely.

3 When the server is free to respond to the browser request, it sends the HTML document back over the Internet to your browser's Internet provider address. The route it uses to get to your PC can differ vastly from the route your request followed to reach the server.

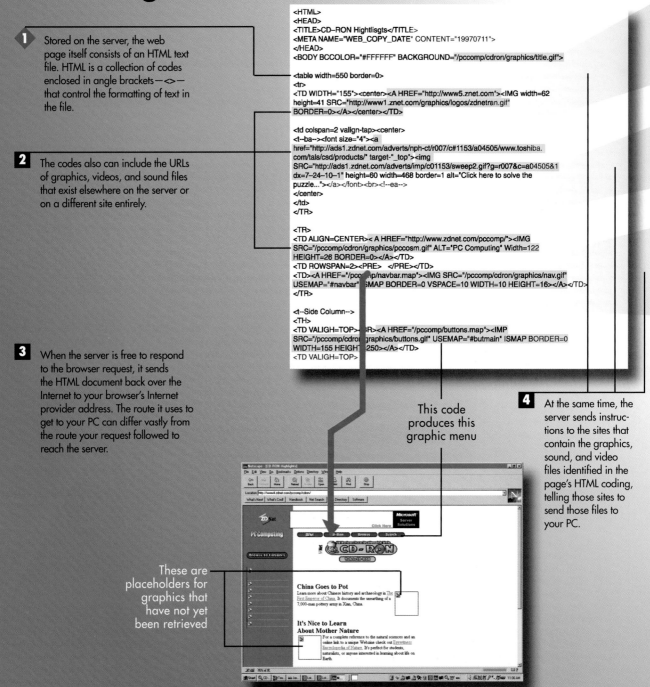

```
<HTML>
<HEAD>
<TITLE>CD–RON Hightlisgts</TITLE>
<META NAME="WEB_COPY_DATE" CONTENT="19970711">
</HEAD>
<BODY BCCOLOR="#FFFFFF" BACKGROUND="/pccomp/cdron/graphics/title.gif">

<table width=550 border=0>
<tr>
<TD WIDTH="155"><center><A HREF="http://www5.znet.com"><IMG width=62
height=41 SRC="http://www1.znet.com/graphics/logos/zdnetran.gif"
BORDER=0></A></center></TD>

<td colspan=2 valign-tap><center>
<!--ba--><font size="4"><a
href="http://ads1.zdnet.com/adverts/nph-ct/r007/c#1153/a04505/www.toshiba.
com/tals/csd/products/" target-"_top"><img
SRC="http://ads1.zdnet.com/adverts/imp/c01153/sweep2.gif?g=r007&c=a04505&1
dx=7–24–10–1" height=60 width=468 border=1 alt="Click here to solve the
puzzle..."></a></font><br><!--ea-->
</center>
</td>
</TR>

<TR>
<TD ALIGN=CENTER>< A HREF="http://www.zdnet.com/pccomp/"><IMG
SRC="/pccomp/cdron/graphics/pccosm.gif" ALT="PC Computing" Width=122
HEIGHT=26 BORDER=0></A></TD>
<TD ROWSPAN=2><PRE>   </PRE></TD>
<TD><A HREF="/pccomp/navbar.map"><IMG SRC="/pccomp/cdron/graphics/nav.gif"
USEMAP="#navbar" ISMAP BORDER=0 VSPACE=10 WIDTH=10 HEIGHT=16></A></TD>
</TR>

<!--Side Column-->
<TH>
<TD VALIGH=TOP>  BR><A HREF="/pccomp/buttons.map"><IMP
SRC="/pccomp/cdron/graphics/buttons.gif" USEMAP="#butmain" ISMAP BORDER=0
WIDTH=155 HEIGHT 250></A></TD>
<TD VALIGH=TOP>
```

This code produces this graphic menu

4 At the same time, the server sends instructions to the sites that contain the graphics, sound, and video files identified in the page's HTML coding, telling those sites to send those files to your PC.

These are placeholders for graphics that have not yet been retrieved

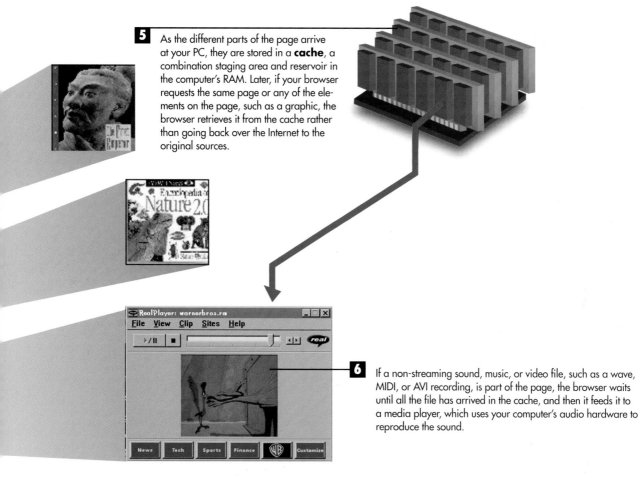

5 As the different parts of the page arrive at your PC, they are stored in a **cache**, a combination staging area and reservoir in the computer's RAM. Later, if your browser requests the same page or any of the elements on the page, such as a graphic, the browser retrieves it from the cache rather than going back over the Internet to the original sources.

6 If a non-streaming sound, music, or video file, such as a wave, MIDI, or AVI recording, is part of the page, the browser waits until all the file has arrived in the cache, and then it feeds it to a media player, which uses your computer's audio hardware to reproduce the sound.

7 Meanwhile, the browser begins using the elements in the cache to reassemble the web page onscreen, following the hidden HTML codes in the main document to determine where to place text, graphics, or videos onscreen. Because not all portions of the web page arrive at your PC at the same time, different parts of it appear onscreen before others. Text, which is the simplest element to send, usually appears first, followed by still and animated graphics, sounds and music, and videos.

8 Older versions of browsers from Microsoft and Netscape featured animated icons in the upper-right corner to indicate when parts of the page are still being received. Modern browsers usually use smaller icons on individual tabs that rotate or otherwise indicate when the browser is processing content. Regardless, animations that have gone static indicate that the browser has successfully retrieved the entire web page.

How Cookies Trade Crumbs of Data

1 When you type in a website's URL, your browser looks in a folder—the location depends on what operating system you're using—to see whether there is a **cookie** there associated with that URL's home page. A cookie is a small, simple text file that you can read with most any word processor.

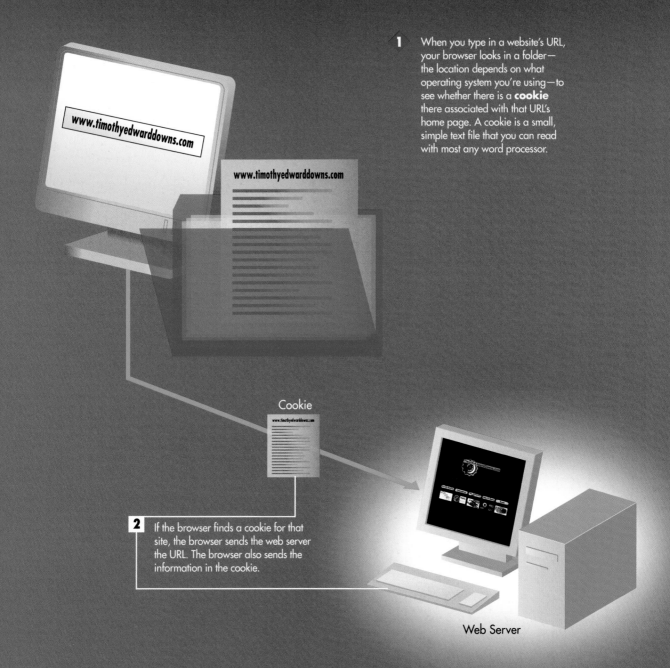

www.timothyedwarddowns.com

www.timothyedwarddowns.com

Cookie

www.timothyedwarddowns.com

2 If the browser finds a cookie for that site, the browser sends the web server the URL. The browser also sends the information in the cookie.

Web Server

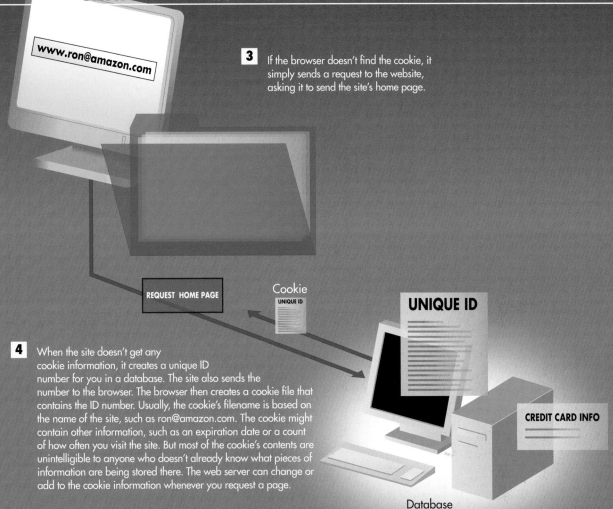

www.ron@amazon.com

3 If the browser doesn't find the cookie, it simply sends a request to the website, asking it to send the site's home page.

REQUEST HOME PAGE

Cookie
UNIQUE ID

UNIQUE ID

CREDIT CARD INFO

4 When the site doesn't get any cookie information, it creates a unique ID number for you in a database. The site also sends the number to the browser. The browser then creates a cookie file that contains the ID number. Usually, the cookie's filename is based on the name of the site, such as ron@amazon.com. The cookie might contain other information, such as an expiration date or a count of how often you visit the site. But most of the cookie's contents are unintelligible to anyone who doesn't already know what pieces of information are being stored there. The web server can change or add to the cookie information whenever you request a page.

Database

5 Not all information is stored in the cookie. You often allow sites to store other information, such as your credit card number, but that type of information is encrypted and saved in the site's own database. Each time you visit the web site, it recognizes you by the ID number in the cookie and uses the information in its database to automate such operations as filling in forms and one-click shopping.

www.ron@amazon.com

What a Cookie Is Not

A cookie is only a text file—it is not a program. It cannot ferret out personal information or documents stored elsewhere on your computer. Basically, all a cookie can contain is information given to it by the web server that placed it there. If you're still concerned about privacy, you can delete any cookies on your system, but be aware that you're giving up the convenience of automatic logins, easier online shopping, and pages customized to display your local weather and news.

How Google Knows Everything

1 Google is constantly **crawling** the Internet, indexing the information on the millions of pages found on the Web. Google uses another software program, called **Googlebot**, that, like a robot, works independently of its controller, Google itself. Googlebot asks a web server for a page, much as you might ask the server at Amazon.com to send you a page about a book you're thinking of buying.

Indexable text

Googlebot

Web page

2 When Googlebot has downloaded the page, the robot extracts the full text it finds there and sends it to Google's **indexing** program.

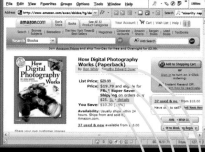

3 The Googlebot then finds all the links on the page and adds them to a **queue**, a list of pages it will crawl (or clone). The Googlebot is not simply a single program visiting one page at a time. You get a better idea of how it works if you think of it as an army of Googlebots swarming throughout the Web. (Googlebot makes thousands of requests per second. It could crawl faster but it doesn't because if it operated full-throttle, it would overwhelm many web servers, and the servers would not be able to deliver pages quickly enough to users.) When a Googlebot crawls these new pages, it repeats its actions at the first page—sending words to the indexer and gathering links.

LINK QUEUE

Web server

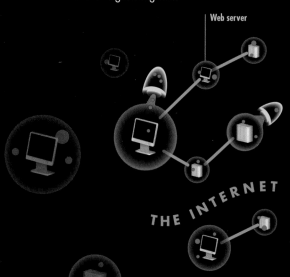

THE INTERNET

4 To make sure Google's index is as up-to-date as possible, Googlebot crawls the same pages continually. It performs calculations on pages to determine how often they change and, based on the results, decides how often to crawl that site. Sites that frequently change, such as news sites, need to be crawled constantly throughout the day, and are called **fresh crawls**. The robot may crawl sites that rarely change, such as just once a month.

CRAWL SCHEDULE

PAGE	FREQUENCY
Amazon Home	10 min.
CNN	5 min
History of Aardvarks	Monthly
New York Time Page 1	Daily

INDEXER

5 The **indexer** receives the text and stores it in its database. The index is sorted alphabetically by search term. Each index entry contains the list of pages on which the term appears. The indexer doesn't index commonly used words, called *stop words*, such as *the, on, is, or, of*, and *why*, and doesn't store single digits, single letters, and some punctuation marks.

6 When you enter your search, it's sent to Google's web server. The web server forwards it to Google's index servers.

7 Google's index servers match your search term to the most relevant documents that contain the term. The method Google uses to match queries to documents is Google's secret sauce, the key to its ability to return the most relevant results.

RESULTS

8 Google uses hundreds of ever-evolving factors to decide which documents are most relevant, but the best known is Google **PageRank**, a rating based on how often others visit a page. Google also considers your own personal browsing history, where it found the search terms on the page and, if you use multiple search terms, how close those terms are to one another. If popular pages link to a page, that page will have a higher rank than if it is linked to from only unpopular pages.

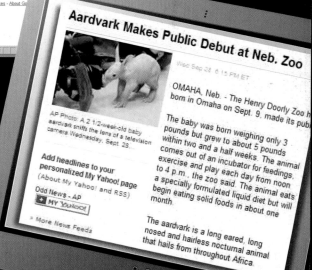

9 When the index server determines the results of the search, it sends a query to Google's **doc servers**. They retrieve the stored documents, which include site names, links, and snippets that summarize each page. The doc servers send the results to the web server, which sends the results to you.

How eBay Sells Everything

DENVER, CO

1 When you go to the eBay site, you are automatically routed to one of eBay's data centers, which are located all over the United States. Companies like eBay maintain data centers in different locations as a way of ensuring they will always be up and running to serve millions of users.

SACRAMENTO, CA **SANTA CLARA 1, CA** **SANTA CLARA 2, CA**

2 The data centers mirror one another; no matter which data center you connect to, you get the same information, auctions, and functions. The centers are connected to one another via a high-speed SONET (Synchronous Optical Network) fiber-optic network.

5 The search servers send the search request to a cluster of database servers running an Oracle database on top of Sun SPARC hardware. This database is in essence what eBay really is—it contains all the details of every single auction on eBay. With millions of items for sale every day, the database requires organization in the form of tens of thousands of unique categories. Eight of those categories sell more than a billion items annually, including toys, clothing, accessories, collectibles, sports, books, movies, and music. Consumer electronics is a $2 billion category, and computers sell $2.1 billion.

8 When the transactions are complete, the buyer and seller are tasked with the all-important duty of rating the transaction experience. These ratings are crucial to eBay because they help to assure its users that they are not dealing with swindlers or deadbeats.

HDTV PLASMA DISPLAYS

...er logs on to eBay
...gain, the system
...to one of the web
... data center.

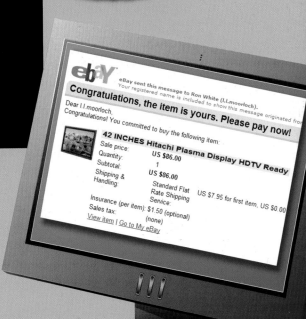

4 If the buyer types **HDTV plasma displays** in the eBay search box, the request is shunted to separate search servers. These computers run an application written using J2EE (Java) and running on top of Sun Microsystems hardware.

...esults show all the plasma displays on auction. If the buyer
...of them, eBay's auction software compares his bid to any oth-
...r more than the minimum needed to top the previous winning
...e partially hidden, with only the amount needed to win being
...f that bid is topped later, the hidden portion may be used to
...idder's lead.

7 The time a bid is placed is also recorded in the database in case of ties. Flags in the database signal when the auction ends. The database sends all the information about the winning bid to the application server. The application server sends the information to the web server so it can be posted for all to see, and it also automatically creates emails to the winning and losing bidders and the seller. The sale costs the seller about $2 plus 1.5% of the sale price.

CHAPTER

20

How We Keep in Touch the Internet Way

EVOLUTION is a trickster. You may spend a lifetime studying the evolution of living organisms, but would you ever have predicted a platypus—part mole, part duck, and part kangaroo? Who would have expected the mighty dinosaurs would develop into tiny sparrows?

Technological evolution is just as sneaky. When the Internet was toddling among a few exclusive spots, it looked as if it were going to develop into an important way for academics to confer and for the military to maintain communications after someone dropped The Big One. After the same early Internet escaped from the profs and generals, it still looked as if it would grow up to be a sober part of the community—a way to research topics in minutes, to store new information for the ages, to get a diploma from your kitchen, and have instant access to financial information and tools.

Only the most whacky student of the Internet in the 1980s would have predicted that the primary job of the Net would be as a venue for sharing gossip, jokes, funny pictures, political diatribes; trading recipes; and finding out if that new cute boy will be at the party Friday night. But take a look at the image on this page.

This is how people use the Internet every day. Texting 92%. Emailing 76%. Social networking 59%. Tweeting 15%. That means 242% of the Internet is used for the sort of communications that used to take place under hair dryers or over a beer.

This is natural selection. The folks who came up with Facebook, Twitter, and chat rooms devoted to vegans, vampire fanatics, and sports obsessives never dreamed their little online program would become part of the world's largest way of saying, "Wassup?" No marketing campaign could have made a run-away success out of swapping messages limited to only 140 characters. These things became the major use of the Internet because it is the natural selection of the human race. It's solitary computer users just wanting to touch and be touched by other solitary computer users, which is to say, all of us.

AVERAGE SMARTPHONE USAGE
How is the average person using their mobile device on a daily basis

TEXT MESSAGING	92%
TAKING PHOTOS	92%
INTERNET BROWSING	84%
EMAILING	76%
APP DOWNLOADS	69%
GAMING	64%
SOCIAL NETWORKING	59%
NAVIGATION	55%
WATCHING VIDEO	54%
TWEETING	15%

Average smartphone usage. Image courtesy of Pew Research Centers Internet & American Life Project / Anchor Mobile SMS Marketing.

How Email Outraces Snail Mail

1 Using an email client, Jane creates a message to go to Bob. She also attaches a photo of herself for the company website, which is encoded using a standard algorithm, such as MIME, uuencode, or BINHEX. Just as easily, Jane could enclose a word processing document, spreadsheet, or program.

2 The encoding turns the data making up the photograph into ASCII text, which computers commonly use for unformatted, simple text. The email software might also compress the enclosure before attaching it to the message so it takes less time to send.

4 The client sends the message to the SMTP server and asks for confirmation. The server confirms that it has received the message.

Internet

3 The client software contacts the Internet service provider's computer server over a modem or network connection. The client software connects to a piece of software called an **SMTP** server, short for **Simple Mail Transfer Protocol**. The server acknowledges that it has been contacted, and the client tells the server it has a message to be sent to a certain address. The SMTP replies with a message saying either, "Send it now," or "Too busy; send later."

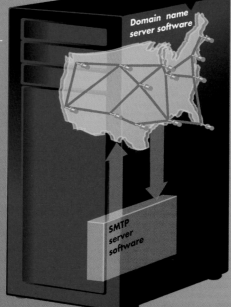

Domain name server software

SMTP server software

Internet service provider's email server

Internet router

5 The SMTP server asks another piece of software, a **domain name server**, how to route the message through the Internet. The domain name server looks up the domain name—the part of the address after the @ character—to locate the recipient's email server. The domain name server tells the SMTP the best path for the message.

6 After the SMTP sends the message, the email travels through various Internet routers. Routers decide which electronic pathway to send the email along based on how busy the routes are. The message might also pass through one or more **gateways**, which translate the data from one type of computer system—such as Windows, Unix, and Macintosh—to the type of computer system that's the next pass-through point on the route.

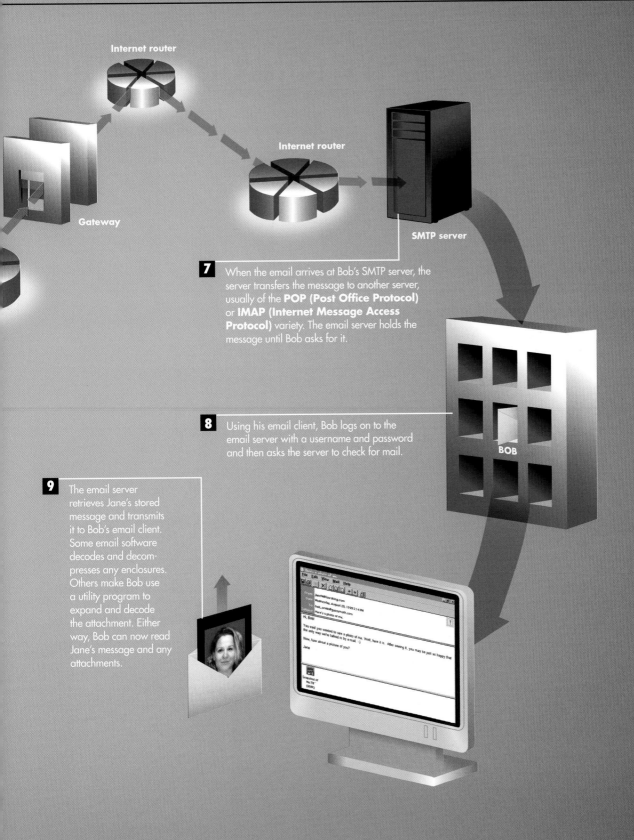

Internet router

Internet router

Gateway

SMTP server

7 When the email arrives at Bob's SMTP server, the server transfers the message to another server, usually of the **POP (Post Office Protocol)** or **IMAP (Internet Message Access Protocol)** variety. The email server holds the message until Bob asks for it.

8 Using his email client, Bob logs on to the email server with a username and password and then asks the server to check for mail.

BOB

9 The email server retrieves Jane's stored message and transmits it to Bob's email client. Some email software decodes and decompresses any enclosures. Others make Bob use a utility program to expand and decode the attachment. Either way, Bob can now read Jane's message and any attachments.

How Facebook Lets Your Cat Go Viral

YOU KNOW FACEBOOK. This tool for telling friends, or anyone who cares, what you've been doing lately started in 2004 as a way for dormies at Harvard to stay in touch with each other. Since then it has been a time-lapse example of technical evolution. Now, more than 1.3 billion users access Facebook each month, more than any other Internet app. It scans in 105 terabytes of data every 30 minutes. Facebook's role as host of the World-wide Party and Gathering of Like Minds uses a single, monolithic program of 62 million lines of code that constantly shuffles and reconnects names, jobs, addresses, employers, friends, brand names, clients, colleagues, schools, likes, links, and, yes, lost loves to create the world's largest database of how everyone relates to everyone else.

Although no one has made a definite count, the consensus is that Facebook is dominated by cute pictures of cats. Here's how your photo of Tabby can be seen by millions.

1 When you signed up with Facebook, it gave you the opportunity to share parts of your life with its database—where you went to school, where you worked, who you married, who's in your address books, what your favorite movies and music are. Even if you didn't give up the particulars, Facebook had your name and most likely where you were when you signed up. The first thing you did was to put friends' names in a search bar to see if they had Facebook accounts. Facebook remembered their names, too.

2 When the search returned the name of a roommate from college, you sent a Facebook request to be **friends**.

3 Regardless of the roommate's answer, Facebook sent you a list of the roommate's Facebook friends, suggesting that you may want to add some of them as your friends. Using facts about you to find people you could make friends—from being Willie Nelson fans to having a mutual fondness for lemon pie—is a process that never ends. Every new friend opens the field to not only that new friend's friends, but that person's friends' friends. You will soon find yourself friends with people you've never met.

4 To launch a picture of the cutest cat anyone's even seen, you use the **Timeline**. There the picture, along with anything you have to say about it, joins your previous posts for transmission to your friends, or any smaller group you may choose. Facebook may also put some limits on who sees the kitty. Facebook uses a program code called **Cassandra** to create a **social graph**—a global mapping of everybody on 50 million web pages and how they're related. Cassandra looks at your friends' records to see who has also posted cat pictures, has connections to companies selling pet supplies, has clicked icons on other pictures of cats to indicate a **Like** or to make public **comments**, or whose timeline shows they have attended more than one performance of the musical *Cats*.

5 The kitty's photo is one of 3 billion photos uploaded each month to be processed by Haystack, another part of the Facebook system. It keeps track of more than 240 billion uploaded photos, each in four resolutions. From this storehouse, Haystack serves about 1.2 million photos every second.

6 The picture is also one of 25 billion pieces of information, including 4.5 billion likes a day, and 4.75 billion other shared items, such as comments and status updates. A process called the **Hive** uses an algorithm called **map-reduction** to break that data into pieces, manipulated in parallel by separate computers, to generate an organized database of the information. The technique sorts a petabyte of data in only a few hours. Duplicate copies of the database go to an estimated 60,000-plus servers on both coasts of the U.S. and in Sweden.

7 When your friends log onto Facebook, a web page serving system called **Big Pipe** uses that organized information to create **pagelets**, sections of each page. The **cover image**, likes, **chat window**, and dozens of other page sections are retrieved in parallel and provide a complete page even if something is broken.

8 Included in your selected friends' News Feed is your posting of a cute kitty. Some number of your friends click the post's Share button, which starts the whole process over again, sending the photo to their friends, who share it with their friends, all in a chain reaction until, if the kitten really is all that cute, the picture goes **viral** and has life of its own.

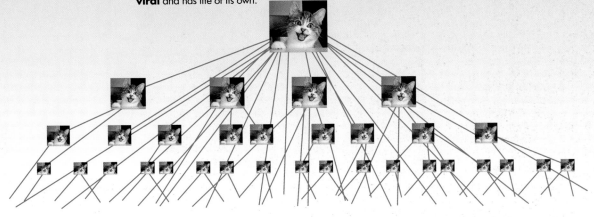

How Twitter Changes Communication

WHEN DETRACTORS want to trivialize the Internet, they pick on Twitter. It's an easy target. Messages on Twitter are limited to 140 characters, leading to a sort of digital haiku. But, come on, what can you say of importance in 140 characters?

Ask Egyptians who rose up against president Hosni Mubarak, brandishing not guns but smartphones. Twitter and Facebook allowed the revolutionaries to communicate with each other in real-time and to get information to other countries that helped bring pressure on Mubarak to resign.

Or ask the thousands who read the steady stream of tweets from a man in Watertown who had a box seat from his bedroom to the action as Boston police closed in on one of the suspects in the bombings at the finish line of the city's annual marathon. The TV networks could report only that they had nothing to report.

Here's how the number-one tool of the ad hoc revolutionary and the citizen journalist works.

 Although it works from a computer keyboard just as well as from any phone, Twitter began its life by piggybacking on cell phones. Even if you're not talking on your cell phone, the phone is still jabbering away. It's communicating to a **cell phone tower** using a stream of data called the **control channel**. The channel's purpose is to keep track of the phone's location in relation to the myriad cell antennas that connect phones to the network. When someone calls you, the tower uses the channel to tell your phone to play its ringtone and to assign a pair of voice channel frequencies for the call.

Antenna

Control Channel

SMS

Multiport fiber terminal

Base transceiver station

Meet us at at the restaurant by the place near that thing.

Timothy

FTTT (fiber to the terminal)

2 The control channel also handles **SMS** messages, which preceded the smartphone and provided fodder for the creation of Twitter. SMS stands for **small message system**. Because the system was devised as a way to take advantage of short, otherwise unused snatches of bandwidth, "small" means 160 characters in the Latin alphabet. In Chinese the maximum is 70 characters. (There is actually a bit more space left, but it's used for digital housekeeping—a time stamp, the destination phone number, the originating number, and so on.)

3 The creators of Twitter deliberately designed it to piggyback on SMS. They ignored protocols that could work with longer messages because those systems were not widely supported by cell phone companies. SMS was intrinsically supported by all cell providers.

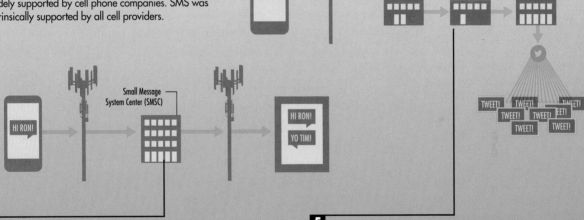

4 When someone sends you a text message, it travels from your friend's phone to a tower; from there it goes to a **small message system center (SMSC)**, which determines the cell that has the best connection with your phone and sends the message to that cell's tower, which sends it to your phone. Your reply takes the same pathway in reverse.

5 When you send a text message from your phone to Twitter, the message follows much the same path, with some side excursions to a **mobile switching center**, which transmits the tweet to a **signal transfer point (STP)**. From there, the message goes to an SMSC, which then sends the text to Twitter's website. Twitter sends the message back out to the people in your network using the same process in reverse—10,000 to 15,000 tweets each minute.

How Internet File Sharing Works

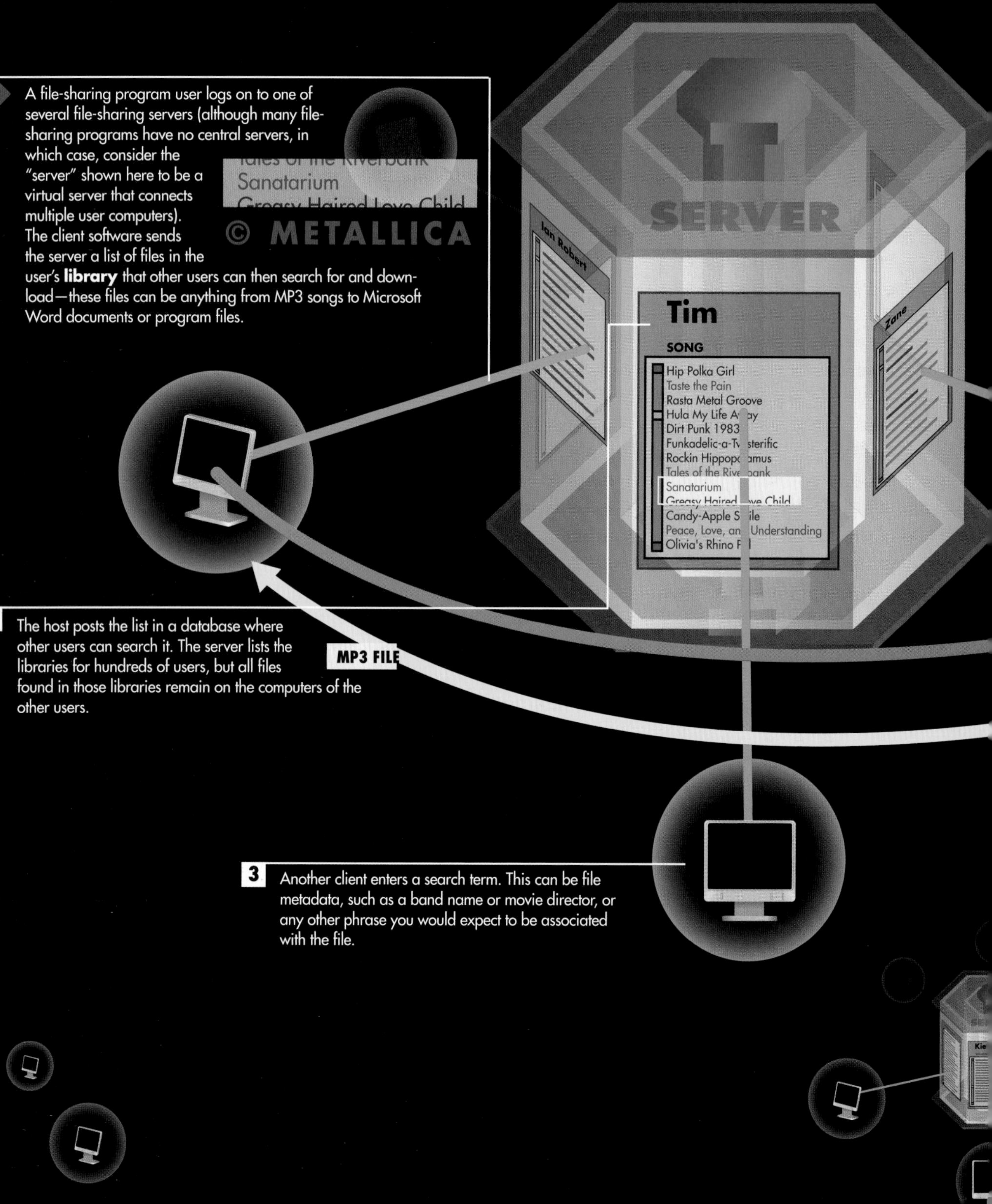

1 A file-sharing program user logs on to one of several file-sharing servers (although many file-sharing programs have no central servers, in which case, consider the "server" shown here to be a virtual server that connects multiple user computers). The client software sends the server a list of files in the user's **library** that other users can then search for and download—these files can be anything from MP3 songs to Microsoft Word documents or program files.

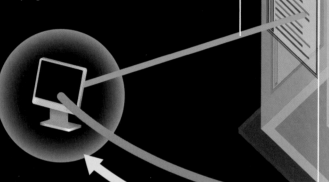

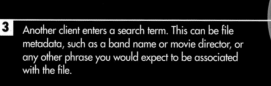

2 The host posts the list in a database where other users can search it. The server lists the libraries for hundreds of users, but all files found in those libraries remain on the computers of the other users.

MP3 FILE

3 Another client enters a search term. This can be file metadata, such as a band name or movie director, or any other phrase you would expect to be associated with the file.

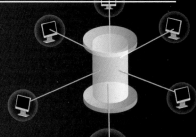

4 The client looks at all the library records on the server and displays any titles that match at least some of the search criteria. The results include the names of the files, the type of Internet connection, **Internet protocol (IP)** addresses of other clients making those files available, and other assorted trivia.

The traditional structure of the Internet has been **server-concentric**. Data and programs are stored at relatively few centrally located servers, or **hosts**. All data requests from PCs (**clients**) go to one of the servers. The host also handles all replies back to the clients.

5 The user selects one or more of the files for transfer. His client software sends a message to the other client using its IP address. The message asks permission to download the song, and the remote client obliges by becoming a server and sending the file to the computer that asked for it.

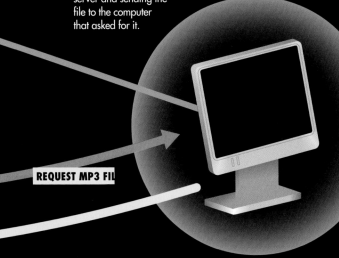

REQUEST MP3 FIL

Distributed structure is, rather redundantly distributed. Except for consulting servers to get digital driving directions, each computer using the host software's protocol communicates directly with other clients. A PC can be a host and a client at the same time.

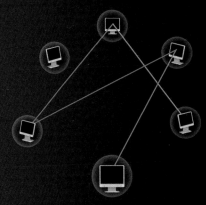

6 At the same time someone is downloading a file, other users are finding songs on that person's hard drive and are downloading them. Several uploads/downloads can run simultaneously by taking turns sharing the Internet connections.

True peer-to-peer structure: No central host servers provide files for client PCs. Instead, the software is both host and client at the same time. Searches are more random, slower, and might turn up fewer hits. However, this structure makes it difficult, although not impossible, to police.

How BitTorrents Spread the Wealth

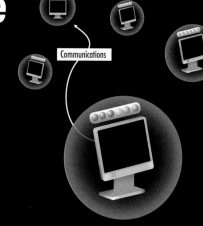

Tracker

Communications

Initial Seeder

IT OFTEN SEEMS as if the purpose of computers in the Grand Design of Things must be to provide free movies, songs, and software to the world's college students. The file-sharing scheme that started it all, Napster, had a fatal flaw: The media companies could easily track down the computers on which everything from *Aida* to *Deep Throat* was laid out like a smorgasbord before ravenous downloaders. This forced file traders into the new territory of **peer-to-peer** computing, which distributes data among millions of computer users, making it harder (though not impossible) to assign culpability to those sharing copyrighted content. The most popular **P2P** dodge, the BitTorrent protocol, is estimated to account for about 11% of all Internet traffic. And it all starts with a seed.

1 A file, whether a video, song, book, or software, is placed on the Internet by the **initial seeder** using BitTorrent **client software**. Through a system of open **ports** shared by computers, the seeder's client sends a small text file called a **.torrent** to a PC acting as a **tracker.** The torrent announces a new file is now available for downloading. The .torrent contains the URL of the file's location, the name of the file, its length, and the length of the file's individual **bits,** which will be scattered throughout the Internet like clips of film strewn on the projection room floor. In **trackerless** versions of BitTorrent, seeder PCs may also be trackers.

2 Here, a file is represented by the row of colored circles. Unlike Napster-era file swapping, an entire file is not downloaded from a single source. Instead, a downloader receives the file in chunks—the circles. The locations of these chunks, called **seeds**, are sent to the other trackers, which maintain records of where the pieces of a file are squirreled away.

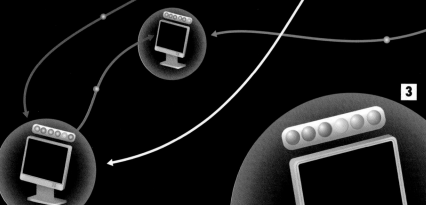

Communications

3 The client software in another computer, Peer 3, checks with the tracker, looking for the very file that Peer 5 has. Peer 3 downloads a BitTorrent from the tracker, and using the information it contains, Peer 3 asks the initial peer to send part of the file. Meanwhile, the tracker looks for other peers that have the same file *in toto*, and for **seeds**, who have only pieces of the file. Unlike ordinary http transfers that send a file from a single source in a continuous sequence from beginning to end, BitTorrents are sent randomly from many sources and in a **rarest-first** scheme that first sends bits of a file that are harder to find before sending readily available bits.

The universe of peers and track-ers exchanging requests and bits of files is called a **swarm**. The chart from the BitTorrent client Azureus shows the ping times among more than a million members of a single swarm, all participating at the same time and all joined in the manner of "six degrees of Kevin Bacon." The trackers police the swarm, looking for **leeches**—persons who download files without contributing seeds of their own files. Trackers—or more precisely, the client soft-ware trackers use—can slow down sending bits to leeches and reward seeders who con-tribute to the swarm with faster download times.

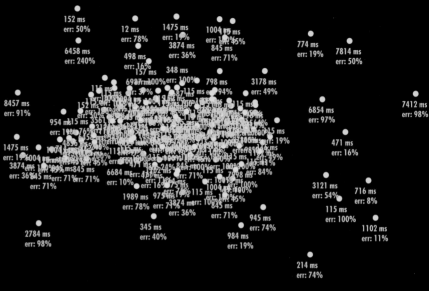

5 Below you can see one BitTorrent user's relationship to others in the swarm, represented by the circles orbiting him, with whom he is exchanging pieces of a file. The yellow lines are his download connec-tions. Data travels along the lines at speeds proportional to the actual upload and download speeds. The dimmed circles in the orbit are computers that have been **snubbed** because their connections are so low, they're a waste of time. In the center is a pie chart that represents how much of the movie that per-son's received, in this case about 75%.

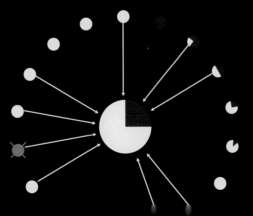

Sure It's Fun, but Is It Legal?

Although file-sharing and BitTorrent can be used for fully legiti-mate purposes, the bottom line is that you're violating the law if you download copyrighted material to which you don't have any rights. BitTorrent transfers tend to be hit-and-run violations, making it harder to determine who's involved than it was in the Napster heyday when servers operated 24/7 with hard drives that brimmed over with content for illegal downloading. With the introduction of trackerless trackers, it becomes even harder to catch someone in the act, but not impossible. BitTorrent sites and users engaged in illegal transactions have been success-fully tracked, sued and, in some cases, jailed. So the question is, are you feeling lucky? Well, are you?

How Clouds Encompass Us All

Look! Up in the sky! It's a bird! It's a plane! It's...." No, it's your data--—the business plan you wrote, those pictures of the family at the beach, your resume, your complete collection of every Dave Matthews concert ever bootlegged. It's all up there thanks to what we call **cloud computing**. Your files are, of course, in reality, not strewn across the sky, but safe and snug within the storage system of dozens of networked computers. The pieces may move from computer to computer, even country to country, to different computers each time you save a file, but they're all there.

Sounds like a good way to lose track of data, doesn't it? But the opposite is true. Cloud storage is the surest way to stash your digital stuff because when your files are saved in a cloud, it doesn't matter if you're in the office, at home, or at the beach. Install the correct app and plug-in the correct usernames and passwords and you have instant access to anything you put up there.

1 Cloud storage has two parts. The first—the **front end**—is you or other computer users, all called **clients,** working at their PCs. Every time a client saves or opens a file, the request is passed to the **back end**—an elaborate system that makes up the electronic clouds. Because the client's files are saved in a cloud, the client does not have to be at an office or personal computer to retrieve them. With correct usernames and passwords, clients may retrieve their files on other computers, tablets, and smartphones to share them with others through a service such as Dropbox, Google Drive, or OneDrive.

2 The client's request first goes to a **central server**, a computer responsible for managing all the traffic coming from hundreds or thousands of clients. To make sure all client requests are handled properly, the central server follows a set of rules, called **protocols**, written to ensure there are no gaps, contradictions, or impossibilities embedded in the client request.

3 After the request passes the central server's inspection, the server uses **middleware** software, so called because its digital turf lies between the clients and the legions of file servers whose purpose is to be repositories of whatever a client creates. With the demand for storage space so large and so immediate, a dedicated server for each client is impractical and, as we'll see, not a good idea. But the middleware lets the storage system act as if the client does have a direct path to a dedicated, single-client server.

4 At the same time the middleware pulls a trick on the numerous high-powered computers that make up the cloud—also called **server farms**—where the stored file resides. Because most of the servers are not running at full capacity, the central server uses empty storage space and otherwise idle processor time to create **virtual computers**. Each virtual computer operates as though it were the only computer on the farm. A neat juggling act of timing lets each virtual computer have its opportunity to send and receive information and get access to the server's hard drives in the times when the other virtual servers are at rest.

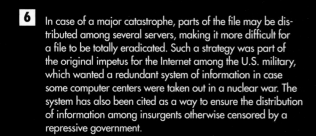

6 In case of a major catastrophe, parts of the file may be distributed among several servers, making it more difficult for a file to be totally eradicated. Such a strategy was part of the original impetus for the Internet among the U.S. military, which wanted a redundant system of information in case some computer centers were taken out in a nuclear war. The system has also been cited as a way to ensure the distribution of information among insurgents otherwise censored by a repressive government.

VIRTUAL COMPUTER

You are here

01101010011
0110101 ******
****
*** **ENCRYPTING** ***
****
****
****
    ****

5 When the central server receives a request from a client to save a file, it may first **encrypt** the file to deter hackers who would break into the server's farm to steal sensitive information. Then the central server consults a record of traffic and storage use among the hundreds of servers at more than one farm location. (Google is estimated to have 1 million servers.) A reputable cloud has twice the number of servers needed to store all of its clients' file. In case of server malfunction, the cloud stores all of its data in more than one place and in more than one physical location. Doubling the number of servers and keeping copies—and sometimes copies of previous versions of a file—is referred to as **redundancy.**

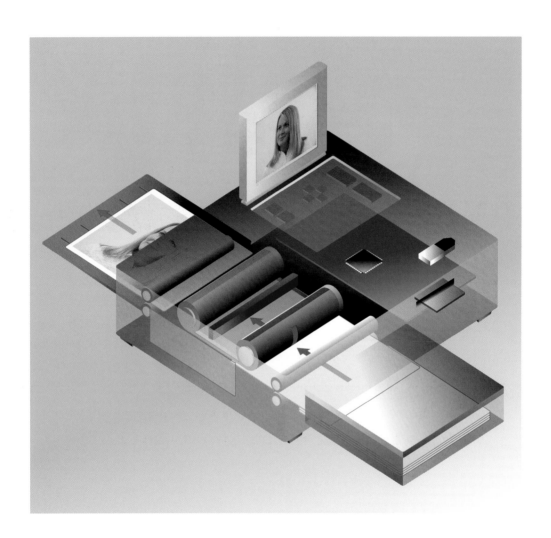

PART

6

How Printers Put Data in Our Hands

CHAPTERS

From the earliest days the hands of printers have wielded a great power, the magical power to reproduce words a thousandfold.

—Helmut Presser

In the early days of personal computers, when people thought it was simply a revolution rather than a fundamental change in our existence, someone came up with the idea that all this computerized data would lead to the "paperless office." We've entered the second century in which we have been using computers, and more trees than ever are giving their lives to produce hard copies of everything from company budgets complete with full-color graphs to homemade greeting cards. Not only are we creating more printouts than ever before, but computer printing has gained a third-dimension, with printers that can print functional three-dimensional objects. These **3D Printers** may now be the domain of high-end labs and enthusiasts with cash to burn, but the day is coming when you'll find one in every home, just like the inkjets and laser printers of today. And they'll change everything.

Whoever made that erroneous prediction about the end of printing missed an important fact. That person was probably thinking about how offices used paper in the age of the typewriter. Back then there wasn't much you could put on paper except black letters and numbers—most often in an efficient but drab typeface called Courier. If all those ugly memos and letters had been replaced by electronic mail, the world would not have suffered a great loss. But what forecasters didn't see is that software and printing technology would make possible fast, easy, graphic, and colorful hard copies of reports, newsletters, graphs, and, yes, company budgets and greeting cards, that even IBM's best Selectric could never come close to producing.

Speed and ease were the first improvements in printing. Whereas a simple typo on a typewriter might just be whited out or hand-corrected with a pen, today—because of the speed of printers—it's easier just to correct a mistake onscreen and print a fresh, flawless copy. Graphics were the next big advance. The day of the all-text document ended with the first software that could print even the crudest line graph on a dot-matrix printer. Now anything that's visual, from line art to a halftone photograph, can be printed on a standard office printer.

That scenario has its evil twin. We often are so trusting of our computers ability to automatically remedy the mistakes in our lives, that a fresh, flawed copy comes out of the printer with such speed and cleanliness that it looks perfect. It's almost unthinkable that in this beautiful, double-justified text in sleek Helvetica with a thin line between the main body of text and a perfectly-centered page number, there lurks an uncaught typo of the word "shiite."

The computer printer has opened the door to vast world of typefaces and typographical effects. Once the only way to give words emphasis was to underline them. Today, we can make words bold, italic, double-underlined, narrow-faced, heavy black faced, small caps, reversed, outlined, and drop-capped. Not only are we capable, sometimes we actually use them—all of them—in the same document. How can we help it? Laborious typing has turned into fun-filled laser printing.

There are literally thousands of free typefaces today, where a 100 years ago there were but dozens at best, and most commercial printers had only a few of the costly molds for for those fonts in hot type. Now at no extra cost, we can give our documents comic book text, blood-dripping letters from posters for Resident Evil XIII, or type that tries to portray you as a person of such elegance that your business cards are printed with a beautiful but illegible script

Soon it was color, which began as an expensive luxury, but as the quality and speed of color printers increased, so too did the cost decrease. A $100 printer can copy a document, scan a photo for you to retouch, and then spit out the fixed version photo on high-quality photo paper, suitable for framing.

Paper hasn't disappeared from the office. Instead, it's taken on a whole new importance. And the lowly printer that used to turn out crude approximations of characters is now one of the most important components of a computer system. Thanks to the birth of 3D printing, the tide isn't going to turn anytime soon. If anything, printers will gain an even more prominent role in our homes and lives.

CHAPTER

21

How Black and White Printing Works

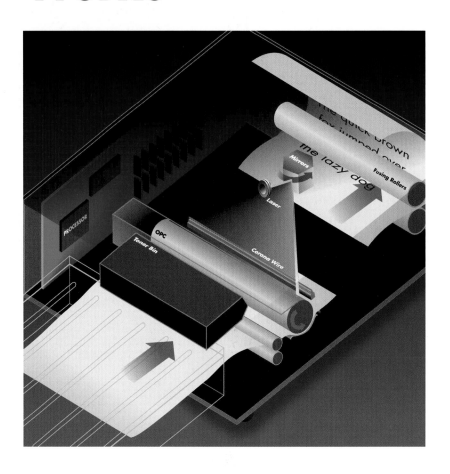

ALL 2D COMPUTER PRINTING these days is based on the dot matrix. Whether it's a laser printer going through an intricate ballet of movement and time or an ink-jet printer spitting dots of color on paper, the printer is limited to producing dots. Thousands of dots on a single page, but still dots.

Regardless of how the dots are created, there must be a common method for determining where to place the dots. The most common schemes are bitmaps and outline fonts. Bitmapped fonts come in predefined sizes and weights. Outline fonts can, on the fly, be scaled and given special attributes, such as boldfacing and underlining. Each method has its advantages and disadvantages, depending on what type of output you want.

Bitmapped images are the computer's equivalent of Gutenberg's type. Bitmaps generally are limited to text and are a fast way to produce a printed page that uses only a few type fonts. If the hard copy should include a graphic image in addition to bitmapped text, then, to create the graphic, your software must be able to send the printer instructions that it will understand.

Outline, or vector fonts, are used with a page description language, such as Adobe Postscript or Microsoft TrueType, that treats everything on a page—even text—as a graphic. The text and graphics used by the software are converted to a series of commands that the printer's page description language uses to determine where each dot is to be placed on a page. Page description languages are no longer so much slower than matrix printers. Outline fonts are more versatile at producing different sizes of type with different attributes or special effects, and they create more attractive results. It is the printing triumph of the bit.

How Printers Make Cookie Cutter Text

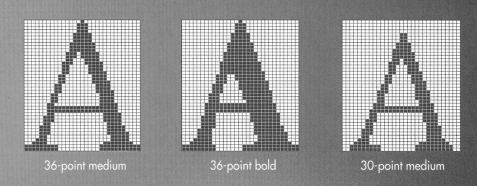

36-point medium   36-point bold   30-point medium

1 Bitmapped fonts are typefaces of a specific size and with specific attributes, or characteristics, such as boldface or italic. The bitmap is a record of the pattern of dots needed to create a specific character in a certain size and with a certain attribute—sort of like a cookie cutter. It can make one and only one kind of type; after all, a Christmas tree cookie cutter can't make a gingerbread boy. The bitmaps for a 36-point Times Roman medium capital A, for a 36-point Times Roman boldface capital A, and for a 30-point Times Roman medium capital A are all different and specific.

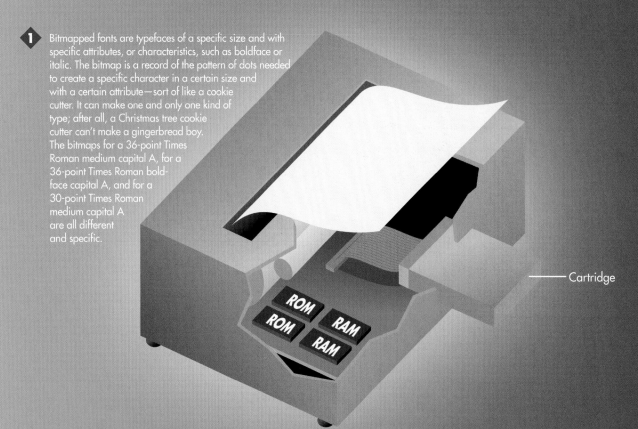

Cartridge

2 Most printers come with a few bitmapped fonts—usually Courier and Line Printer—in both normal and boldface varieties as part of their permanent memory (ROM). In addition, many printers have random access memory (RAM) to which your computer can send bitmaps for other fonts. You also can add more bitmapped fonts in the form of plug-in cartridges that some laser printers use.

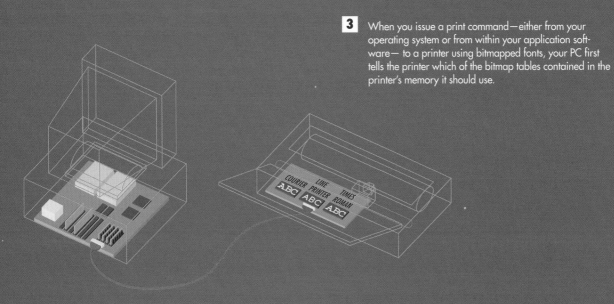

3 When you issue a print command—either from your operating system or from within your application software— to a printer using bitmapped fonts, your PC first tells the printer which of the bitmap tables contained in the printer's memory it should use.

4 Then, for each letter, punctuation mark, or paper movement—such as a tab or carriage return—that the software wants the printer to create, the PC sends an ASCII code. ASCII codes consist of hexadecimal numbers that are matched against the table of bitmaps. (Hexadecimal numbers have a base of 16—1, 2, 3, 4, 5, 6, 7, 8, 9, 0, A, B, C, D, E, F—instead of the base 10 used by decimal numbers.) If, for example, the hexadecimal number 41 (65 decimal) is sent to the printer, the printer's processor looks up 41h in its table and finds that it corresponds to a pattern of dots that creates an uppercase A in whatever typeface, type size, and attribute is in the active table.

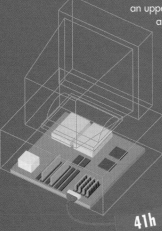

BITMAP TABLE	
3Fh	?
40h	@
41h	A
42h	B
43h	C

41h

5 The printer uses that bitmap to determine which instructions to send to its other components to reproduce the bitmap's pattern on paper. Each character, one after the other, is sent separately to the printer.

How Outline Fonts Set the Imagination Free

36pt

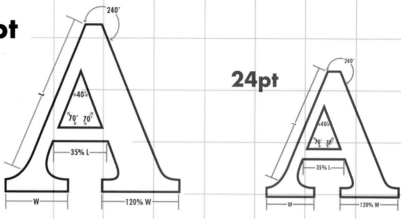

24pt

1   Outline fonts, unlike bitmapped fonts, are not limited to specific sizes and attributes of a typeface. Instead, they consist of mathematical descriptions of each character and punctuation mark in a typeface. They are called outline fonts because the outline of a Times Roman 36-point capital A is proportionally the same as that of a 24-point Times Roman capital A.

2   Some printers come with a page description language, most commonly PostScript or Hewlett-Packard Printer Command Language, in **firmware**—a computer program contained on a microchip. The language can translate outline font commands from your PC's software into the instructions the printer needs to control where it places dots on a sheet of paper. For printers that don't have a built-in page description language, printer drivers translate the printer language commands into the instructions the printer needs.

3   When you issue a print command from your application software using outline fonts, your application sends a series of commands the page description language interprets through a set of algorithms, or mathematical formulas. The algorithms describe the lines and arcs that make up the characters in a typeface. The algorithms for some typefaces include hints, special alterations to the details of the outline if the type is to be either extremely big or extremely small.

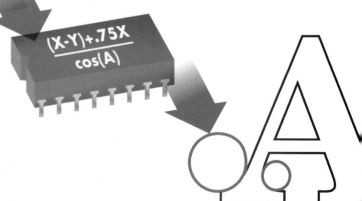

4 The commands insert variable values into the formulas to change the size or attributes of the outline font. The results are commands to the printer that say, in effect, "Create a horizontal line 3 points wide, which begins 60 points from the bottom and 20 points to the right." The page description language turns on all the bits that fall inside the outline of the letter—unless the font includes some special shading effect within the outline.

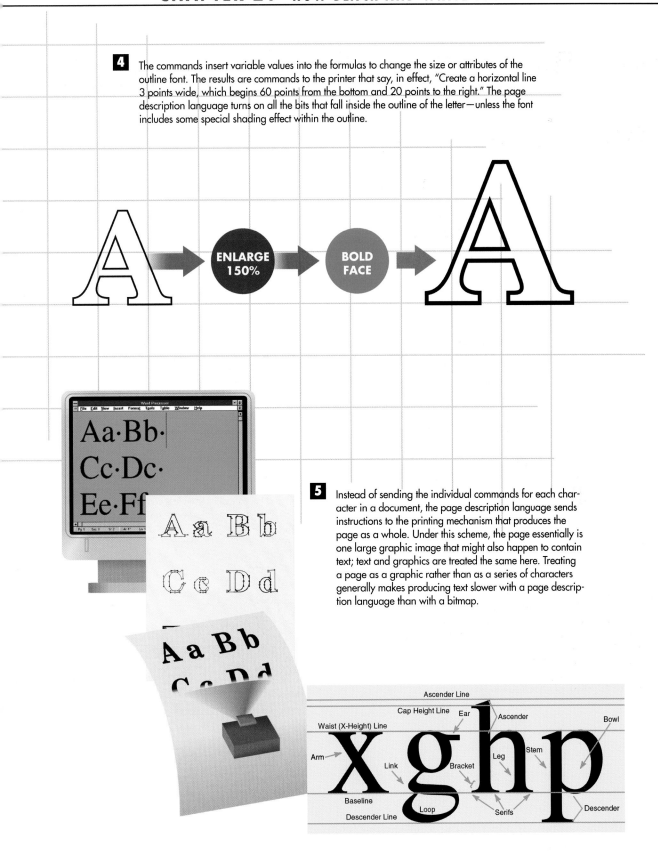

5 Instead of sending the individual commands for each character in a document, the page description language sends instructions to the printing mechanism that produces the page as a whole. Under this scheme, the page essentially is one large graphic image that might also happen to contain text; text and graphics are treated the same here. Treating a page as a graphic rather than as a series of characters generally makes producing text slower with a page description language than with a bitmap.

How a Printer Writes with Light

2 The instructions from the printer's processor rapidly turn on and off a beam of light from a laser.

1 Your PC's operating system and software send signals to the laser printer's processor to determine where each dot of printing toner is to be placed on the paper. The signals are one of two types—either a simple ASCII code or a page description language command.

The Art of Being Negative

In this description, the electrical charges in all instances can be reversed and the result would be much the same. The method described here is true of most printers that use the Canon print engine, such as Hewlett-Packard models, which are the standard among laser printers. This approach is called **write-black** because every dot etched on the printer drum by the laser beam marks a place that will be black on the printout. There is, however, an alternative way that a laser printer can work, and that way produces noticeably different results. The other method, used by Ricoh print engines, is called **write-white** because everywhere the laser beam strikes, it creates a charge the same as that of the toner—the toner is attracted to the areas not affected by the beam of light. Write-white printers generally produce darker black areas, and write-black printers generally produce finer details.

9 The rotation of the drum brings its surface next to a thin wire called the corona wire. It's called that because electricity passing through the wire creates a ring, or corona, around it that has a positive charge. The corona returns the entire surface of the drum to its original negative charge so that the laser beam can draw another page on the drum's surface.

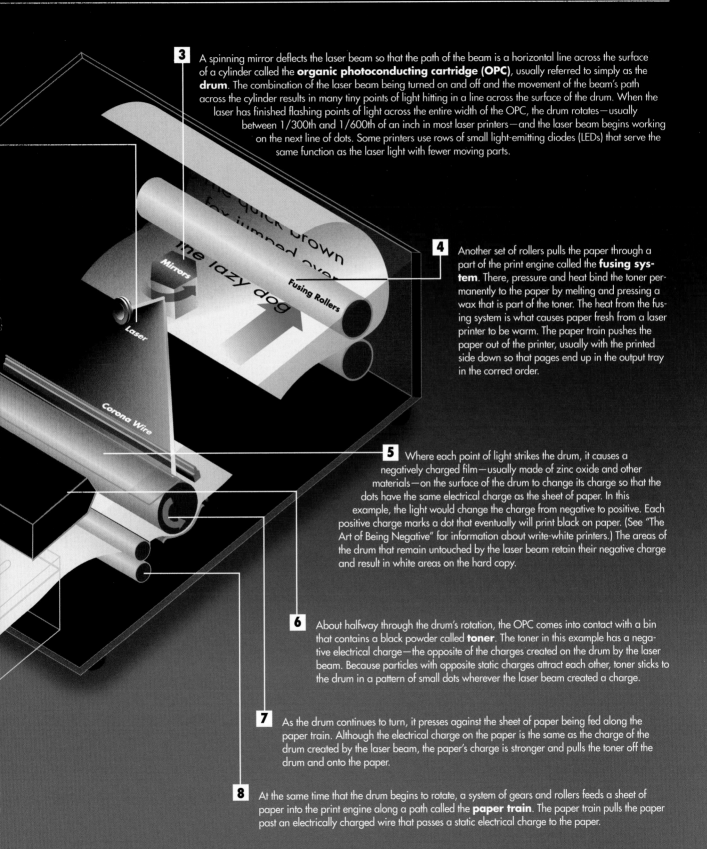

3 A spinning mirror deflects the laser beam so that the path of the beam is a horizontal line across the surface of a cylinder called the **organic photoconducting cartridge (OPC)**, usually referred to simply as the **drum**. The combination of the laser beam being turned on and off and the movement of the beam's path across the cylinder results in many tiny points of light hitting in a line across the surface of the drum. When the laser has finished flashing points of light across the entire width of the OPC, the drum rotates—usually between 1/300th and 1/600th of an inch in most laser printers—and the laser beam begins working on the next line of dots. Some printers use rows of small light-emitting diodes (LEDs) that serve the same function as the laser light with fewer moving parts.

4 Another set of rollers pulls the paper through a part of the print engine called the **fusing system**. There, pressure and heat bind the toner permanently to the paper by melting and pressing a wax that is part of the toner. The heat from the fusing system is what causes paper fresh from a laser printer to be warm. The paper train pushes the paper out of the printer, usually with the printed side down so that pages end up in the output tray in the correct order.

5 Where each point of light strikes the drum, it causes a negatively charged film—usually made of zinc oxide and other materials—on the surface of the drum to change its charge so that the dots have the same electrical charge as the sheet of paper. In this example, the light would change the charge from negative to positive. Each positive charge marks a dot that eventually will print black on paper. (See "The Art of Being Negative" for information about write-white printers.) The areas of the drum that remain untouched by the laser beam retain their negative charge and result in white areas on the hard copy.

6 About halfway through the drum's rotation, the OPC comes into contact with a bin that contains a black powder called **toner**. The toner in this example has a negative electrical charge—the opposite of the charges created on the drum by the laser beam. Because particles with opposite static charges attract each other, toner sticks to the drum in a pattern of small dots wherever the laser beam created a charge.

7 As the drum continues to turn, it presses against the sheet of paper being fed along the paper train. Although the electrical charge on the paper is the same as the charge of the drum created by the laser beam, the paper's charge is stronger and pulls the toner off the drum and onto the paper.

8 At the same time that the drum begins to rotate, a system of gears and rollers feeds a sheet of paper into the print engine along a path called the **paper train**. The paper train pulls the paper past an electrically charged wire that passes a static electrical charge to the paper.

CHAPTER

22

Printing Gutenberg Never Imagined

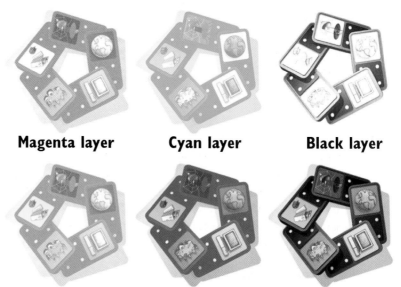

Magenta layer   Cyan layer   Black layer

Yellow and   Yellow, magenta,   Yellow, magenta,
magenta   and cyan   cyan, and black

utenberg's movable type printing press depended on arranging rows of metal letters by hand. Made from an alloy of lead, tin, and antimony, each letter was molded on one end to create a mirror image of the character to be printed. They were placed, molded side out, on a tray, one after the other, until an entire line of mirrored words was created. And then the type setter started on the next line. When a page's worth of type was done, the type was bound into a form, coated with ink, and a press forced parchment or paper against the type to pick up the ink.

It may sound like a slow way to print the Bible, but it was an amazing revolution in the spread of ideas and information throughout Europe. The other amazing thing about Gutenberg's press is that it took 500 years for someone to come up with something better. As late as the 19th century, Mark Twain sank all the money he earned making people laugh into various machines to automate the assembly of type into rows of text. Or that's what they were supposed to do if they worked.

Movable type loaded into a case to take on life as printing.

Why did it take 500 years to come up with something better? Because Gutenberg's press was the evolutionary equivalent of the first fish that sprouted legs and decided to explore dry land on foot. Soon after that, for millions of years, feet were dominant. Every self-respecting creature had at least two. It was only when wings came along that animals had a different way to get places. Even then, walking still hasn't gone out of style for millennia.

You have to have fundamental evolutionary breakthroughs before you see inventions such as laser, inkjet, and 3D printers. The car isn't a breakthrough invention; it's a gradual evolution from the horse-drawn wagon. The interstate highways are currently the highest state of evolution in roadways, but there's been no fundamental breakthrough in them since the earliest footpaths.

Computing is a fundamental, evolutionary breakthrough. The first computer and the first transistor are not important because of what they were able to do at the time of their creation. They are important because they opened up a world of other inventions: streaming video and audio; topological weather forecasts; "big data" that allows us to look at people, nature, and society in a depth we've not had before. No one came up with a better way of printing for 500 years because technology builds for centuries on one tiny improvement after another until, suddenly, there's something no one had imagined. No one created computing with the idea that it would design space ships, teach us languages, track our money, or even calculate how long we will live. If someone in, oh, 1944 had said, "I'm going to create something that will enable us to send pictures from here to China in a matter of seconds, and while it's at it, translate a letter from English to Chinese," that person would have been called crazy. (And he would have been.) There was nothing in 1944 to suggest to any sane person that all the things we take for granted today would ever be possible.

The point of this is that we're all in the same situation Gutenberg was. We're just now seeing powerful, enabling technology emerge and swiftly change how we live as individuals and function as societies. Can you imagine what will be available 500 years from now? No, you can't. In the next 500 years several fundamental evolutionary breakthroughs will surely occur. But we have no more specific idea of what they may be than Gutenberg had of printers that created text with light, printers that created body parts from something called plastic, or all the other previously unimaginable printers in this chapter.

What we can hope is that the coming evolutionary breakthrough is something that, like the computer, has far-ranging effects—effects that, after thousands of years, will enable us to have decent societies built on all the principles that we know, even now, they should be. Peace. Justice. Health. Prosperity. We know the world should have those in abundance. We just don't have the thing—that little piece of movable technology—that will lead to making our best and noblest ideas into physical reality.

How Printers Create Color

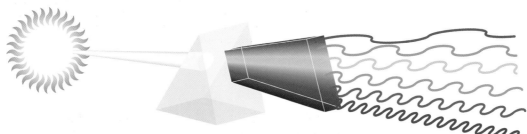

1 All color is made up of different combinations of light. We see all the wavelengths that make white when we pass white light through a prism, which breaks it into the spectrum. Although the spectrum is a continuous blending of colors, using only a few of those hues are necessary to produce color printing. Different mixtures of those primary colors re-create virtually any color from the spectrum by either adding colors or subtracting them.

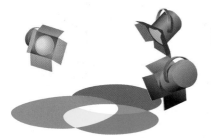

2 **Additive** color is used to create colors on televisions, computer monitors, and in movies. Three colors—red, green, and blue—are emitted to produce all other colors and white by adding various intensities of those primaries. Each time a color is added, it increases the number of colors the eye sees. If red, green, and blue are all added at their most saturated shades, the result is white.

3 **Subtractive** color is the process used when light is reflected from colored pigments—rather than emitted as in additive color. Each added color absorbs (subtracts) more of the shades of the spectrum that makes up white light.

All colors reflected

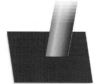

No colors reflected

Red only reflected

Red and blue reflected

4 Color printing uses four pigments: cyan (blue-green), yellow, magenta (purple-red), and black. This system is called **CYMK**. (K stands for black.) Some low-end color inkjet printers save the cost of a black-ink print head by using equal portions of magenta, yellow, and cyan to produce black. But the resulting black lacks density, which is why better personal printers include a print head for black ink.

Yellow layer

Magenta layer

Cyan layer

Black layer

Yellow only

Yellow and magenta

Yellow, magenta, and cyan

Yellow, magenta, cyan, and black

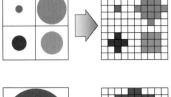
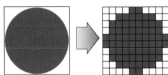

5 All color printers use tiny dots of those four inks to create various shades of color on the page. Lighter shades are created by leaving dots of unprinted white. Some printers, such as dye-sublimation, control the size of the dots and produce continuous-tone images that rival photography. But most printers create dots that are essentially the same size no matter how much of a particular color is needed. The most common color printers create up to 300 dots of color per inch, for a total of 8 million dots per page. Many printers can create about 700 dpi, and a few printers can create up to 1,440 dpi.

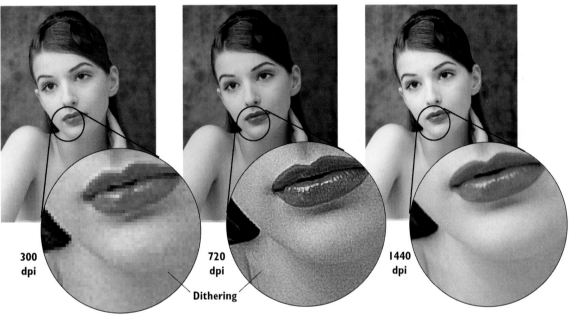

300 dpi

720 dpi

1440 dpi

Dithering

6 For all shades beyond the eight that are produced by overlaying the primaries, the printer generates a varied pattern of differently colored dots. For example, the printer uses a combination of one magenta dot to two of cyan to produce a deep purple. For most shades of color, the dots of ink are not printed on top of each other. Instead, they are offset slightly, a process called **dithering**. The eye accommodatingly blends the dots to form the desired shade as it hides the jagged edges, or **jaggies**, that the dots produce. Dithering can produce nearly 17 million colors.

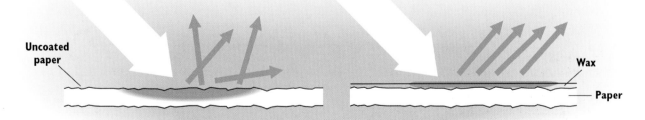

Uncoated paper

Wax

Paper

7 The type of paper used in color printing affects the quality of the hard copy. Uncoated paper, the type used with most black-and-white office machines, has a rough surface that tends to scatter the light, reducing the brightness, and it tends to absorb ink, which slightly blurs the image.

Paper coated with a fine varnish or wax takes applications of ink more evenly so that the ink dries with a smooth surface that reflects more of the light hitting it. The coating also helps prevent the paper from absorbing the ink, producing a sharper image.

How an Ink-Jet Sprays Images

1 An ink-filled print cartridge attached to the inkjet's print head moves sideways across the width of a sheet of paper that is fed through the printer below the print head.

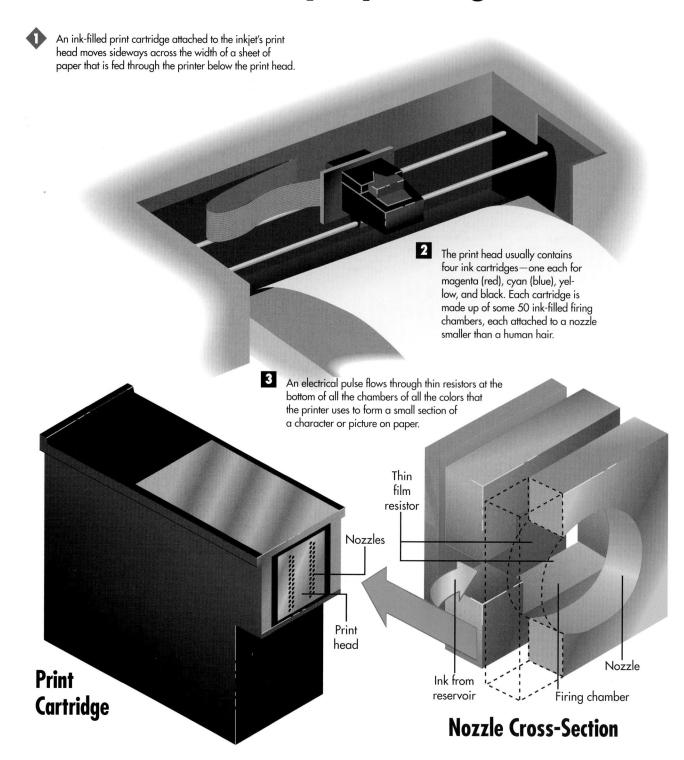

2 The print head usually contains four ink cartridges—one each for magenta (red), cyan (blue), yellow, and black. Each cartridge is made up of some 50 ink-filled firing chambers, each attached to a nozzle smaller than a human hair.

3 An electrical pulse flows through thin resistors at the bottom of all the chambers of all the colors that the printer uses to form a small section of a character or picture on paper.

Thin film resistor

Nozzles

Print head

Ink from reservoir

Nozzle

Firing chamber

Print Cartridge

Nozzle Cross-Section

Ink from reservoir

Nozzle

Firing chamber

Bubble

Resistor

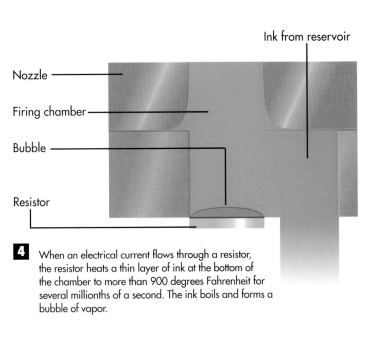

4 When an electrical current flows through a resistor, the resistor heats a thin layer of ink at the bottom of the chamber to more than 900 degrees Fahrenheit for several millionths of a second. The ink boils and forms a bubble of vapor.

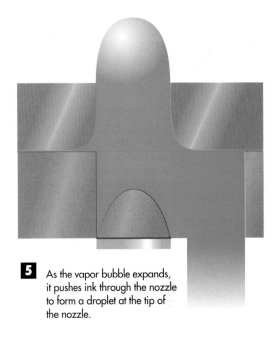

5 As the vapor bubble expands, it pushes ink through the nozzle to form a droplet at the tip of the nozzle.

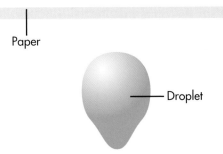

Paper

Ink dot

Droplet

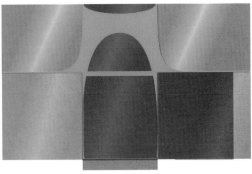

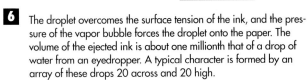

6 The droplet overcomes the surface tension of the ink, and the pressure of the vapor bubble forces the droplet onto the paper. The volume of the ejected ink is about one millionth that of a drop of water from an eyedropper. A typical character is formed by an array of these drops 20 across and 20 high.

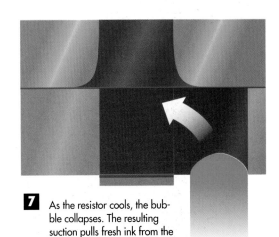

7 As the resistor cools, the bubble collapses. The resulting suction pulls fresh ink from the attached reservoir into the firing chamber.

How a Printer Spits Out Photographs

Pigment Inks

1 Photo-quality printers often use more colors of ink—the usual black, cyan, magenta, and yellow, with the additions of light red, light blue, and gray or green. Photo printers use inks that get their colors from either **dyes** or **pigments**. Dye inks are slow to dry and fade when exposed to light and pollutants, but have a wide **gamut**—the range of color shades they create. Pigment inks are dye-based inks. Pigment inks have dye ink's brilliance, but withstand better the assaults of light and the environment.

2 The use of thousands of **piezo-electric nozzles** gives photo printers greater control over the size of sprayed ink drops compared to ink jet nozzles. The back wall of each nozzle is made of **piezo**, a crystalline substance that bends when electricity passes through it. The wall's bending sucks new ink into the nozzle.

3 Current to the nozzle shuts off. The piezo flexes back into its normal position, forcing a droplet of ink out of the nozzle.

4 Varying the amount of current sent through the piezo changes how much the nozzle wall flexes, which determines the amount of ink pulled into and shot out of the nozzle. The nozzles create drops as small as two picoliters.

Photo Paper

For the highest quality and longest-lasting images, photo printers use special papers made to work with the type of ink the printer uses. **Ceramic-coated porous papers** absorb inks quickly, but their ceramic coating leaves dyes exposed to light and gases. **Plastic-coated swellable papers** protectively encapsulate particles of dye and pigment when the ink seeps into the paper's fibers.

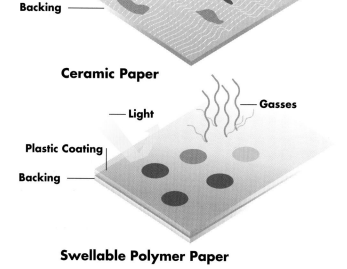

Backing

Ceramic Paper

— Light

Gasses

Plastic Coating

Backing

Swellable Polymer Paper

Dye Sublimation Printer

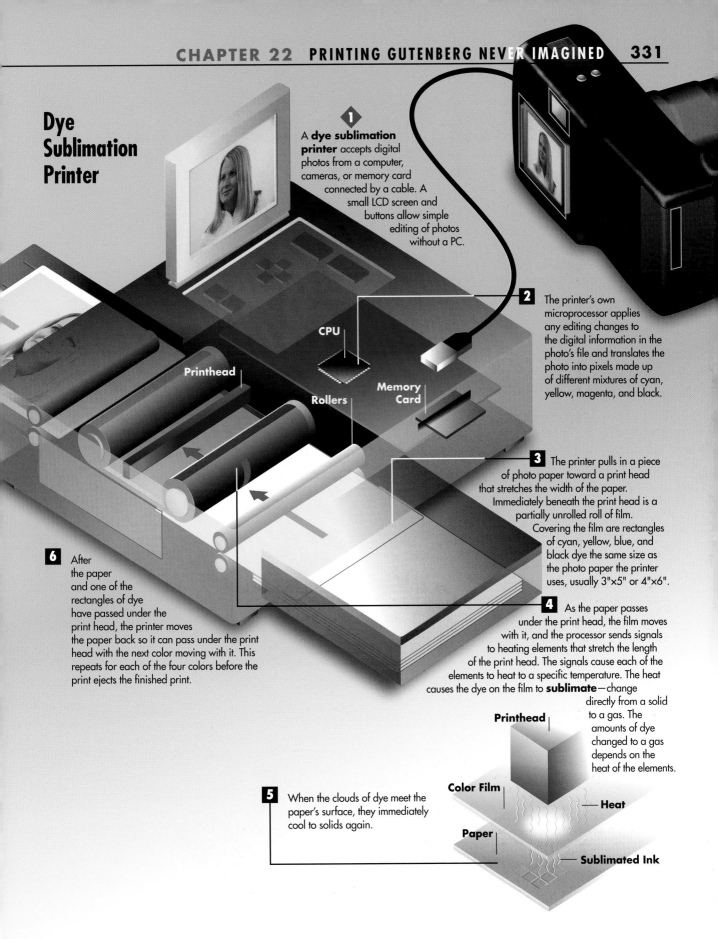

1 A **dye sublimation printer** accepts digital photos from a computer, cameras, or memory card connected by a cable. A small LCD screen and buttons allow simple editing of photos without a PC.

2 The printer's own microprocessor applies any editing changes to the digital information in the photo's file and translates the photo into pixels made up of different mixtures of cyan, yellow, magenta, and black.

CPU

Printhead

Rollers

Memory Card

3 The printer pulls in a piece of photo paper toward a print head that stretches the width of the paper. Immediately beneath the print head is a partially unrolled roll of film. Covering the film are rectangles of cyan, yellow, blue, and black dye the same size as the photo paper the printer uses, usually 3"×5" or 4"×6".

4 As the paper passes under the print head, the film moves with it, and the processor sends signals to heating elements that stretch the length of the print head. The signals cause each of the elements to heat to a specific temperature. The heat causes the dye on the film to **sublimate**—change directly from a solid to a gas. The amounts of dye changed to a gas depends on the heat of the elements.

6 After the paper and one of the rectangles of dye have passed under the print head, the printer moves the paper back so it can pass under the print head with the next color moving with it. This repeats for each of the four colors before the print ejects the finished print.

5 When the clouds of dye meet the paper's surface, they immediately cool to solids again.

Printhead

Color Film

Heat

Paper

Sublimated Ink

How a Laser Printer Creates in Color

1 Like its monochrome ancestor, a color laser printer begins by creating the image of the page to be printed on a revolving photosensitive drum or belt by rapidly turning on and off a laser beam. Wherever the light strikes the drums, it creates an electrostatic charge. The drum makes four complete revolutions, during which the laser paints the dot pattern for each of the four colors used in printing: black, magenta (red), cyan (blue), and yellow.

2 As the drum turns, it comes into contact with a cartridge containing toner powder. The cartridge is divided into four compartments, one each for black, magenta, cyan, and yellow toner. A different configuration used in tandem printers appears in the inset illustration.

3 Every rotation of the laser-charged drum picks up a different color and transfers it to a secondary transfer belt.

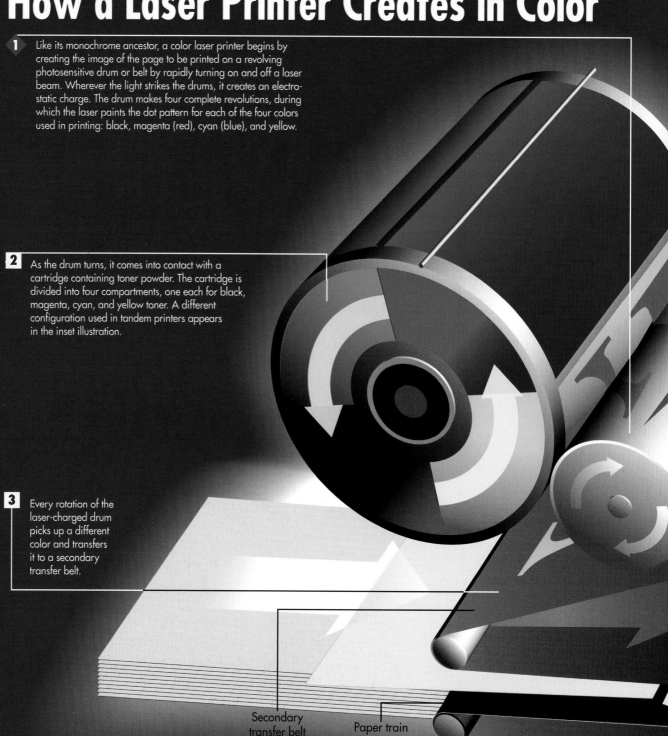

Secondary transfer belt

Paper train

Tandem Color Laser

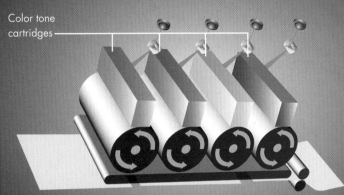

Color tone cartridges

Tandem color laser printers have separate lasers and photostatic drums for each color. The colors are transferred to the secondary belt in one turn of the belt instead of the four that a single-drum color laser printer requires.

Fuser makes toner stick to paper

4 After all the colors are on the belt, the paper train grabs a sheet of paper from a bin and moves it along a path beneath the secondary belt. A roller presses the paper against the belt, transplanting all the color toners to the paper at one time.

How a Solid Ink Color Printer Works

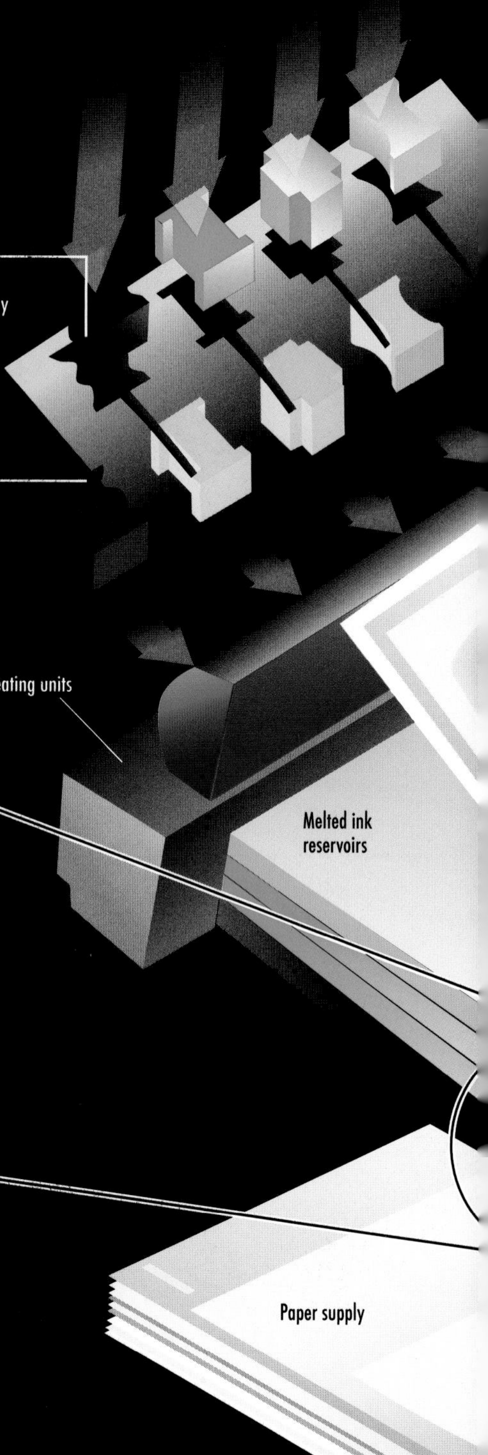

1 A solid-ink color printer such as the Tektronix Phaser 350, which prints six pages a minute on ordinary paper, uses inks that are solid at room temperatures. They are loaded into the printer as wax-like blocks for each of the four colors the printer uses. The holes for loading the blocks are shaped differently for each color to prevent loading a color into the wrong hole.

Ink supply

2 As each color is needed, four heating units melt the inks into liquids that collect in separate reservoirs in the print head.

3 Ink flows to a print head that, in the Phaser 350, consists of 88 vertical columns of four nozzles, one for each color. The print head extends across the entire width of the page, and it produces an entire line of dots in a single pass while moving back and forth horizontally only ½ of one inch.

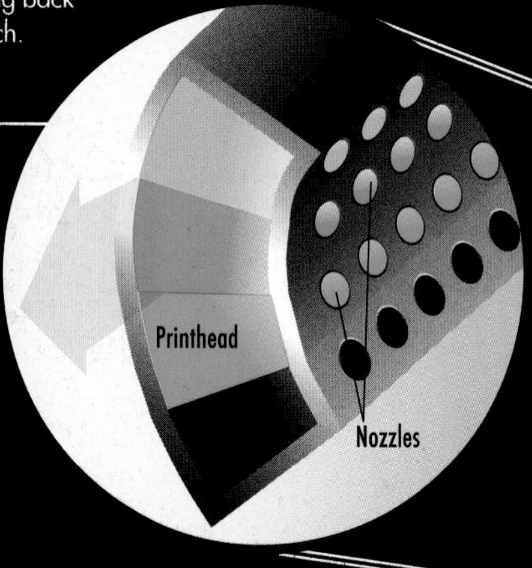

Heating units

Melted ink reservoirs

4 Each nozzle is operated by a **piezo controller**. The controller varies the amount of electricity passing through the rear wall of the individual ink chambers for each nozzle. The wall is made of **piezo**, a crystalline substance that flexes in response to the amount of current passing through it.

Printhead

Nozzles

Piezo

Paper supply

As the wall moves back, it sucks ink in from the reservoir and back from the mouth of the nozzle. The farther the wall flexes, the more ink it pulls in, allowing the controller to change the amount of ink in a

6 When current changes, the wall flexes in, vigorously pushing out a drop of ink onto an offset drum coated with a silicone oil. The drum is slightly warm to keep the ink in a liquid state.

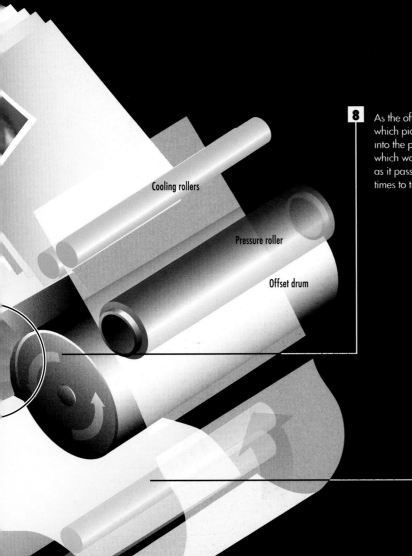

Cooling rollers

Pressure roller

Offset drum

8 As the offset drum turns, the ink comes into contact with the paper, which picks up the dots of color. The pressure roller pushes the ink into the paper to prevent it from spreading on the paper's surface, which would blur the image. The ink dries and refreezes immediately as it passes between two unheated rollers. The drum revolves 28 times to transfer enough ink to cover an entire sheet of paper.

7 The paper supply feeds a sheet of paper into a path that takes it between the offset drum and a roller pressing against the drum.

How Printers Create in 3D

OLD JOKE: A man tells a sculptor of horses, "Your work is so lifelike. How do you do it?" "Simple," the sculptor replies, "I start with a big rock and chip away anything that doesn't look like a horse."

For centuries that's the way we've made most our stuff—from toys to turbines. We started with a piece of metal, stone, or wood and milled, ground, or carved it to become whatever it was we needed. These methods are all **subtractive processes**. Now that is changing with the increased use of **additive manufacturing**—or more commonly, **3D-printing**.

There are many varieties of 3D-printing, but they all are additive. Some material—a liquid, a powder, bits of plastic or metal—are added together until they take on the size and shape of whatever a 3D printer is creating. The result is a real object you can hold in your hand—or use to replace a scarce part, display as sculpture, wear as jewelry, or replace a bone. .

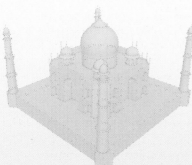
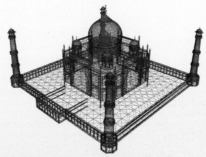
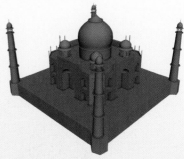

1 All 3D printers have in common that their work starts with a **computer-aided design (CAD)** that describes in mathematical terms the size and shape of an object. It begins with points in a three-dimensional space along the X (width), Y (height), and Z (depth) axes. Located at the intersection of three or more surfaces, the points define the object.

2 CAD adds lines between certain points to create a **wireframe** vision of what the object will look like if it consisted only of corners and intersections. Although the object may appear to have some curved surfaces, they are actually constructed from myriad flat triangles, the simplest and most versatile shape for constructing three-dimensional objects. The smaller the triangles, the more realistic the design appears.

3 The computer can, in effect, paint those surfaces, finally making the object recognizable by humans. We see only the "painted" sides of the object facing us. Other planes are hidden behind those opaque surfaces, although the software lets you tilt, turn, and flip the image so that you can view it from all angles.

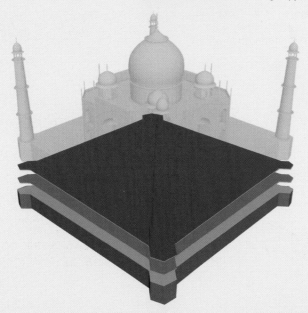

4 For 3D printing, CAD software transforms the design into virtual horizontal cross-sections typically 0.15mm to 0.5mm thin. The design is saved as an **STL formatted file** that a variety of 3D printers read. Free STL files are widely available on the Internet. Some printing enthusiasts use the Kinect game device to scan objects and gather the data a 3D printer would use to re-create the objects. In any case, that's where printing methods diverge.

Inkjet 3D Printing

1 **Inkjet 3D printing** should be familiar to anyone with an inkjet. The principle is the same, except that instead of liquid ink, the 3D printing cartridge contains a powder, such as plaster or resin, that is sprayed through a system of jets that pass over the construction area.

2 An ultraviolet light causes newly sprayed material to immediately harden and bond with the underlying layer. The printer may add wax or a polymer to the layers to strengthen them.

3 By using colored powders in a **multi-tank cartridge**, it's possible to make a full-color object. Multi-cartridges also can deposit a material that serves as a temporary support. Chemicals dissolve it from the finished object to create voids.

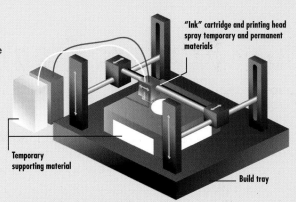

"Ink" cartridge and printing head spray temporary and permanent materials

Temporary supporting material

Build tray

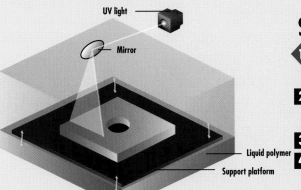

UV light

Mirror

Liquid polymer

Support platform

Stereolithography

1 In a dark room, a **stereolithographic** printer positions a platform in a vat of liquid polymer so that the platform is just below the surface (typically 0.2mm).

2 A **digital light processor** focuses a sharp-edged pattern of bright light on the liquid above the platform. The light pattern matches the shape of the first layer of the object being printed.

3 The light causes the polymer to harden in the shape of the light's pattern.

4 The printer moves the platform down the distance of one layer, and the light again hardens another layer of polymer, which binds to the first layer. The process repeats itself until the liquid can be drained from the vat, leaving the solid model.

Granular Fusing

1 Working with materials as varied as candy and titanium, **granular fusing** uses a beam of heat to **sinter**, or fuse, thin layers from a powdered form of the material being shaped. As with stereolithography, a platform lowers with each new layer to leave free the space needed for the next layer.

2 **Selective sintering** uses a laser to bind the powder, typically ceramic or plastic, without melting it. The laser sinters the powder, heating it only enough to cause the atoms in each granule to break free and intermingle with atoms from adjacent granules.

3 **Electron beam melting** works with metal powder in a vacuum. The electron beam melts the powder layer by layer, one layer into the previous one. The result is an object that is dense, strong, and without voids.

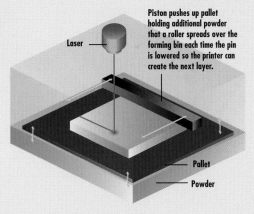

Piston pushes up pallet holding additional powder that a roller spreads over the forming bin each time the pin is lowered so the printer can create the next layer.

Laser

Pallet

Powder

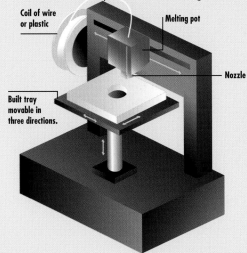

Coil of wire or plastic

Melting pot

Nozzle

Built tray movable in three directions.

Molten Polymer Deposition

1 The printer feeds plastic, ceramic, or filament from a coil to an extrusion nozzle, which heats the filament to about 500°F. to melt it.

2 A computer controls **stepper or servo motors** that can move the nozzle horizontally and vertically with extreme precision. The computer also tells the nozzle when to turn on and off the flow of molten material.

3 The extruded material hardens immediately after leaving the nozzle, forming one of the object's layers as the printer moves the nozzle in the pattern needed to create that layer. The size of the excretion can vary from that delicate enough for jewelry to thick enough to fabricate furniture. When one layer is done, the printer deposits new material on the previous layer to create another section.

PART

7

So, What's Next?

Computers in the future may weigh no more than 1.5 tons.

—Popular Mechanics

IT WAS 1967. IBM invented the floppy disk. The programming language Pascal was used for the first time. The video game Pong was invented. MIT's Marvin Minsky said, "Within a generation… the problem of creating 'artificial intelligence' will substantially be solved." And movie theaters were showing *The Graduate*, starring a young Dustin Hoffman as a recent college graduate who hadn't found his place in the world. At a party of his parents' friends, one of them pulled Hoffman aside to give him a clue for success in one word: "Plastics."

"I just want to say one word to you. Just one word. Plastics."

Plastics did go on to have a pretty good run. Now, 47 years later, what word would wily wonks whisper to those getting started? I have a few ideas, and I'll whisper them to you in a second. But you should know they are based on extrapolating the past evolution in computing into computing's future. And, of course, the future is rarely predictable. The one truth I've always found in predictions is that what finally comes to pass is almost always something no one ever predicted. Expensive, fancy coffee shops on every corner? Brand-new designer jeans sold with holes in the knees? Pomegranate martinis?

Who knew?

So, now that I've given the necessary warning that fate does what it darn well pleases, here are my words for success, starting with….

QUANTUM

You've surely heard of quantum physics, but you don't understand it. No one does. That's what makes it such a hot prospect for the future—that and the fact that its natural stomping grounds are the fundamental building blocks of matter and time. Talk about getting in on the ground floor!

One other aspect of quantum physics that suggests endless possibilities is that even if we don't really understand how quantum physics works, that doesn't stop us from using it in computers and other technology. One of the not understood quantum fundamentals is that on the atomic level you can't be sure of anything. It's so fundamental that there's a name for it: the **uncertainty principle.** It goes something like this: It's impossible to say where an atom's electron is and how fast it's moving at the same time. The act of observing the electron can only be done by bouncing some force off it, usually electromagnetic waves, and seeing what results you get. But when you bounce something off a particle in quantum-land, you're nudging it one way or the other so that it's no longer in the same place or traveling at the same speed.

Quantum math says it could be anywhere—from gallivanting around a nucleus, as it's supposed to do, to being imbedded deep within Saturn's moon Titan. The best we can do is calculate the **probability** of an electron being somewhere. (I'd guess Titan's probability is on the low end, but I'm not a mathematician.) Microchips use the electron's wayward ways to store data. Changing the charge in a transistor raises the probability that some electrons will wind up on the other side of a wall that the odds say they could not ordinarily pass through. No one says how they get there, but it's probable enough that they do get there. When the charge is removed, the probability that they'll pass back through the wall—back to where they started—nosedives. They're trapped even if power is turned off, giving us flash memory.

Even a peek inside D-Wave's quantum computer provides little clue as to how it works.

Another quantum property that could find its way into computers is **entanglement**, or as Einstein called it, "spooky action at a distance." Despite Einstein's skepticism, scientists have verified that when two electrons become entangled—just how that happens varies—they *instantaneously* affect the state of each other even if they are separated by light years. If one electron is spinning clockwise and the other counterclockwise, changing the rotation of the first electron to counterclockwise results in the second electron reversing itself to spin clockwise.

The immediate application of this spookiness is that it eliminates the time used by electricity or light to send information from one point to another. Spooky communications has already been demonstrated in a PC. Entanglement is in the same stage that radio waves were when they were first discovered; it took a while for radio waves to evolve into TV, satellite transmissions, mobile phones, radar, and garage door openers. Get to work, young graduate, on entanglement, before everything gets sorted out by someone else.

Entanglement plays a role in the holy grail of quantum: the **quantum computer.** Quantum computers do not use ordinary bits that have one of two values, 1 or 0. Instead they have **qubits**, which can represent a 1, a 0, or a superposition of 1 and 0 so that the qubit can simultaneously represent 1, 0, and all the values in between. As the number of qubits in a computer increases, the number of superimposed values rises exponentially. This gives them the computing muscle to instantly create unbreakable codes and to solve complex problems. But a problem with qubits is finding out what their values are. Directly observing qubits effectively turns them into bits, and their wealth of potential data is lost.

Researchers see entanglement as the tool to read quantum states. By entangling qubits so that one reflects the state of another, it's possible to observe the state of a remote qubit to learn the value in a qubit back in the computer, without destroying the qubit's special state. If, after reading that, you could use some ibuprofen, you're not alone.

As I'm writing this, there's no word on whether this scenario for quantum computing will work. But a company named D-Wave Systems plans to have an operational quantum computer by 2015.

There's a lot of skepticism about that plan because no one outside DWave has been able to spend the time with the computer needed to test it. At the same time, no one doubts that someone at some time will come up with a quantum machine that works.

QUANTUM DOTS

So called because they're small enough that they operate at the quantum physics stage, **quantum dots** are created by bombarding a semiconductor material, such as silicon or cadmium selenide, with beams of atoms or ions that pound 100 to 1,000 atoms of the material into a single crystal a few nanometers wide.

When a laser, or an ultraviolet or blue light—both of which carry more energy than other shades of the spectrum— strikes a quantum dot, the light's photons energize the dot's material, which expels the extra energy as a second light. The

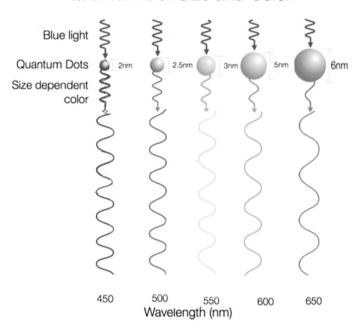

Quantum Dot Size and Color

trick is that the dot doesn't necessarily emit the color of light that it has been absorbing. The dot's size determines now much energy it emits, which determines the color. The biggest quantum dots produce the shortest wavelength, creating red light. The smallest dots create shorter wavelengths, producing blue. In-between sizes put out the other colors in the spectrum.

Even at the early stage in Q-dot development, its achievements and potential come shining through. In video displays, Q-dots increase the size of the color gamut—the range of colors a display can produce—by 40% to 50%. At the same time it uses 15% to 20% less electricity, furthering battery life in smartphones and tablets. Amazon's Kindle Fire HDX 7 is the first tablet to burn bright with quantum dots, putting to shame Apple's Retina displays on similarly sized tablets.

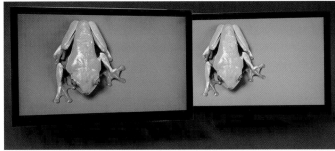

The monitor on the left is juiced up with quantum dots for a greater gamut.

That's just for starters. Early work with quantum dots suggests they could replace transistors. And in quantum computers, which currently envision dealing with particles smaller than an atom, Q-dots could turn out to be a more manageable medium to work with.

Expanding beyond the computing realm, quantum dots may one day save your life. Medical imaging has begun to use **colloidal** (in liquid solution) quantum dots. Because quantum dots can be used in a fluid, they can become dyes. When joined with proteins that target specific cells, such as cancer, they literally light up diseased or malignant tissues. The photo below shows human red blood cells, in which specific membrane proteins are targeted and color-labeled with quantum dots. In this case, the number of purple features, which indicate the nuclei of malaria parasites, increases as malaria development progresses.

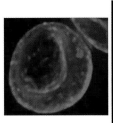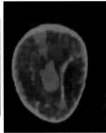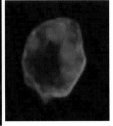

DEEP LEARNING

A few years ago, a list like this one would have included artificial intelligence. Today AI is becoming the new jet-pack, a clever idea in science fiction, but lacking in science fact. Most attempts at AI have involved writing complex rules for a computer to follow independently in complex situations.

Why have none of them succeeded? First, think about how your intelligence was developed. You learned speech, how to walk, throw a ball, dance, and laugh at jokes, which are all intellectual skills involving interaction with the external world. But you didn't learn those skills by anyone else telling you how to do them. (OK, dancing may be the exception, at least if you're a white male in high school.) Most of the things we know and the skills we use came from assimilation. As infants and toddlers we heard our parents making sounds, so we attempted to do the same with our baby gurglings and sounds like "Ba-ba-ba-ba!" Eventually our brains recognized a pattern. Certain words were used around certain people, objects, and actions. It takes about two years for us to understand the fundamentals of speech, but we do it so naturally because the brain can't easily communicate with others until it has learned language.

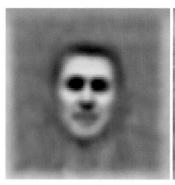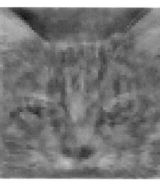

This is what Google's deep learner decided were the proper generalized images for a human and a cat face.

Now some computer scientists are throwing away rule-based programs for a field called **deep learning.** It lets computers learn on their own. Sort of. The computers do get some guidance and correction. But basically what deep learning uses are large numbers of processors and equally huge amounts of data to feed to those processors. Mention that combination and what leaps to mind is Google, which has plenty of both. And, in fact, Google's on the forefront of deep learning.

The fundamental concept is that billions of computer connections can work like the cortex's billions of neurons. Google set up 16,000 processor cores and for three days showed the system 10 million images from randomly selected YouTube videos. If you're familiar with Google and its YouTube service, then you know that many of those random images had to be of cats. The researchers did nothing to label cat images or define the concept of a cat, and yet the artificial neurons developed an ability to recognize not only cats but also flowers and human faces and body shapes with little outside prompting. Linking those images to one of 22,000 categories to choose from—some of which required handling such niceties as the difference between two types of skate fish—the network was accurate 15.8% of the time. That may not sound all that impressive, but it was a 70% improvement over the previous state-of-the-art system. And when the 22,000 categories were reduced to 1,000, accuracy was better than 50%. Google has already used the system to improve the speed recognition of Iris—Google's Betty to Apple's Veronica—Siri.

All right. So you still wouldn't put the system up against a Las Vegas blackjack table. It still has a way to go. But that's the good news. That means there's time for you to wiggle into what is still one of the next big things.

GRAPHENE

Suppose you took the "lead" out of your pencil. (You know it's really graphite, a form of carbon, right?) Then you squashed it and rolled it like pizza dough until it was just *one molecule thick.* You'd have graphene, the product that's the hottest substance since...well...since plastic.

The difference between graphite and graphene—and by the way, don't try smashing your pencil to make graphene; there are much easier ways—the difference is that when carbon atoms are all bunched together in graphite, their electrons are bouncing around, giving themselves a sort of collective mass. But spread the atoms into a thin sheet, and the electrons behave as if they are massless with particles moving through empty space at near the speed of light. And that makes for a different story.

You have something that looks like a shadow you can pick up and hold. Graphene is 35% better at conducting electricity than copper. Electrons move 1,000 times better than in silicon. It conducts heat better than any other substance. It stretches up to 20% of its length, but it's stiffer than diamond. It's totally impermeable; not even helium atoms can squeeze through it.

That all suggests wonderful possibilities, although few of them have, yet, come to fruition despite more than 8,000 patents for its use, mostly in China and the United States. One Polish manufacturer gives samples to anyone who asks, hoping one of them will come up with a marketable use and then buy more graphene. Everyone who looks at graphene agrees that it's a mind-blowing substance…for something. Sounds like a field perfect for a young graduate.

Graphene is said to be 200 times stronger than steel. Some researcher determined that a sheet the thickness of plastic wrap would support an elephant poised atop a pencil, in turn standing on the sheet. (Image courtesy of Extreme Tech)

3D PRINTING

So far most applications for 3D printing have been limited to art, jewelry, and things as far ranging as spare parts for a dish washer to a PEZ dispenser with your own head on it. More impressive uses are on the way in medicine, where 3D printers have been used to fabricate living skin. As 3D printers get bigger, someone's going to find a way to print a bungalow or a Bentley.

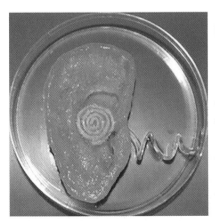

Look at it this way. When Gutenberg invented his printing press, did he imagine such spin-offs as color printing, daily newspapers, education, engraving, rock concert posters, bumper stickers, or laminated kitchen floors? This is a perfect example of how we started this discussion, with the observation that whatever you predict, the odds are the outcome is going to be something no one's imagined. If that sounds good to you, check out Amazon's 3D printer store and get to work.

A 3-D printer created this ear using a gel made of calf cells. The living tissues are coated with silver nanoparticles that pick up sounds beyond the normal human hearing range.

Index

Symbols

0 bit, 22
1 bit, 22
3D, 234
  active shutter glasses, 235
  anaglyph stereoscopy, 234
  autostereoscopic display, 237
  creating with printers, 336-337
  film pattern retarder, 236
  glasses, 235
3D audio, 246-247
3D objects, dressing, 100
3D printers, 314
3D printing, 345
3D worlds, plotting, 98
3G (Generation 3), 277
4G (Generation 4), 277
24-bit graphics, 87
μ-law codec, 145

A

AC (alternating current), PC power
  supplies, 150
AC3, 244
accelerated graphics port (AGP), 50
accelerometers
  iPhones, 153
  Wiimote, 211
access latency, 162
access points (APs), 260
accumulation registers, 33
action buttons, 210
active content, 114
active matrix technology, 174

active shutter glasses, 3D, 235
adaptive dictionary-based
  algorithm, 160
ADC (analog-to-digital converters),
  16, 217-219
  dial-up modems, 145
additive color (color printing), 326
additive manufacturing, 336
address buses, 46
address lines, 22
address lines (pixels), 229
address registers, 33
addresses, 26
ADSL (asynchronous digital
  subscriber lines), 271
adventure games, 97
affinities, 39
AGP (accelerated graphics port), 50
ahead of time compilation (AOT), 71
Airbrush, 93
alerts, 119
algorithms, prime numbers, 124
alpha blending, 100
alternating current, 13-14
ALUs (arithmetic logic units), 32, 37
AM (amplitude modulation), 10
American National Standards
  Institute (ANSI), 75
amperage (amps), 13
amplitude modulation (AM), 10
amps (amperage), 13
anaglyph stereoscopy, 234
analog, 16
analog data communication, 258
analog local loops, dial-up modems,
  144-145
analog sticks, 210

analog-to-decimal converter (ADC),
  16, 217-219
anchor, 155
AND gates, 35
Android, 63
anodes, 15, 233
ANSI (American National Standards
  Institute), 75
antispam software, 122–123
antivirus software, 116–117
AOL Time-Warner, 252
AOT (Ahead of Time
  compilation), 71
AP (Access Points)
  NAP, data transfers, 281
  Wi-Fi networks, 261
Apple, 62
  iPhones, 153
  iPods, 173
application layer (networks), data
  transfers, 278
application overload, 267
applications, 61
apps, 75
  killer apps, 57
  running mobile devices, 94-95
APs (access points), 260
architecture, ARM architecture, 41
arithmetic logic units (ALUs), 32, 37
ARM architecture, 41
ARM processors, 129
ARPA (Advanced Research Projects
  Agency), 250
ARPAnet, 250
art, compressing, 88–89
artifacts, 89
assembly language, 66

atip (Absolute Timing In Pregroove), CD-R drives, 166

attachment viruses, 114

auctions (online), 296

audio
  3D audio, 246-247
  digital audio compression, 245
  Dolby Digital 5.1, 244
  Dolby noise reduction (NR), 244
  JND, 245
  MP3 files, 245
  multichannel sound, 244

audio ports, 133

aura, 208

auto exposure (digital cameras), 198-199

autofocus lenses (digital cameras), 196-197

automatically recalculating spreadsheets, 85

autostereoscopic display, 3D, 237

B

back plates, 241

backchannel, 111

backdoors, 109

banding, 89

bandwidth
  boosting, 268-269
  capacity, 268
  carriers, 268
  channel bonding, 51

banners, 108

Baran, Paul, 250

bar codes, 220

batteries, 170
  Google Glass, 179
  motherboards, 47

Bayesian filters, 123

bayonet connectors, coaxial cable, 256

beeps, 239

Bell Labs, 20

bias/reset buses, DLP projectors, 230

big iron, 56

Big Pipe, 303

bilinear filtering, 102

binary notation, 19

binary trees, 81

BIOS (basic input/output) system, 133
  keyboard scan codes, 136-137
  motherboards, 47

bit addresses, 26

bit patterned media, 159

bit sensors, 26

bitmaps, 100
  bitmap tables, 142
  cookie-cutter text, 318-319
  printing, 317

bitmap tables, printers, 142

bits, 19

BitTorrents, 308-309

BIU (bus interface unit), 37

black-and-white printing, 317
  outline fonts, 317, 320-321
  printing, 317
  vector fonts, 317
  write-black method, 322
  write-white method, 322

blacklists, 122

blocks, 27, 163

Bluetooth, 135
  development of, 262
  hold mode, 263
  inquiry mode, 263
  LM, 263
  page mode, 263
  park mode, 263

radio modules, 262
  sniff mode, 263
  standby mode, 263

Bluetooth devices, Wiimote, 211

Blu-Ray, 165

BNC (Bayonet Neill-Concelman) coaxial cable, 256

Boolean logic, 19, 67

brackets (session layer), 278

branch target buffer (BTB), 37

branches, 67

branching, 37

Bricklen, Dan, 57

bridges, data transfers, 281

broadband, 269

browsers
  displaying web pages, 290–291
  domain names, 288
  ftp, 288
  http, 288
  hyperlinks, 288
  mirror sites, 289
  page files, 288
  URL, 288
  web pages,
    displaying, 290-291
    opening, 288-289

brute force, how hackers get in, 109

BTB (branch target buffer), 37

buffers, 114, 283

buffers (printers), 142

built-in displays, 170

Burn, 92

bus interface unit (BIU), 37

buses
  address buses, 46
  data buses, 46
  expansion buses, 46
  external buses, 46
  frontside buses, overclocking, 185

Z

X-Y